Battling Nelson,
the Durable Dane

Battling Nelson, the Durable Dane

World Lightweight Champion, 1882–1954

MARK ALLEN BAKER

McFarland & Company, Inc., Publishers
Jefferson, North Carolina

LIBRARY OF CONGRESS CATALOGUING-IN-PUBLICATION DATA

Names: Baker, Mark Allen, author.
Title: Battling Nelson, the Durable Dane : World Lightweight Champion, 1882–1954 / Mark Allen Baker.
Description: Jefferson, North Carolina : McFarland & Company, Inc., Publishers, 2017 | Includes bibliographical references and index.
Identifiers: LCCN 2016049660 | ISBN 9781476663722 (softcover : acid free paper) ∞
Subjects: LCSH: Nelson, Oscar, 1882–1954. | Boxers (Sports)—Denmark—Biography. | Boxing—United States—History.
Classification: LCC GV1132.N46 A3 2017 | DDC 796.83092 [B]—dc23
LC record available at https://lccn.loc.gov/2016049660

BRITISH LIBRARY CATALOGUING DATA ARE AVAILABLE

ISBN (print) 978-1-4766-6372-2
ISBN (ebook) 978-1-4766-2625-3

© 2017 Mark Allen Baker. All rights reserved

No part of this book may be reproduced or transmitted in any form or by any means, electronic or mechanical, including photocopying or recording, or by any information storage and retrieval system, without permission in writing from the publisher.

On the cover: Battling Nelson delivering a solid right to the face of the "Passaic Cyclone," Battling (William) Hurley (Library of Congress)

Printed in the United States of America

McFarland & Company, Inc., Publishers
Box 611, Jefferson, North Carolina 28640
www.mcfarlandpub.com

To the family of Adam James and Sarah Ryg Nielsen,
especially Wylie Garrett Nielsen whom the angels
brought to join our families forever

The Sweet Science, like an old rap or the memory of love, follows its victim everywhere.

—A.J. Liebling

Table of Contents

Acknowledgments viii

Preface 1

One—1882–1899: From Copenhagen to Hegewisch 3

Two—1900–1903: Making Headlines 20

Three—1904: Positioning for the Title 40

Four—1905: Five Memorable Lightweights 55

Five—1906: McGovern and the Fight of the Century I 76

Six—1907: Repositioning for the Ascent 102

Seven—July 4, 1908: The Fight of the Century II 117

Eight—September 9, 1908: The Fight of the Century III 128

Nine—1909: Retaining the Title 142

Ten—February 2, 1910: A Disappointing Loss 162

Eleven—1911–1912: Mounting a Comeback 188

Twelve—1913: Fay and a Final Descent 202

Thirteen—1914–1917: At Long Last, Freddie Welsh 213

Fourteen—1918–1954: The Final Rounds 234

Appendix: Records 255

Chapter Notes 262

Bibliography 279

Index 281

Acknowledgments

Having encountered and conversed with those who met Oscar "Battling" Matthew Nelson, I was inspired to write a biography of the former lightweight champion, who, despite his own valiant efforts and even those of institutions such as the International Boxing Hall of Fame, remains relatively little known today.

"Battling" Nelson was not a dazzling pugilist, but he was one of the most rugged and indestructible fighters the sport has ever known. As a boxing historian and, as fate might have it, a major sponsor of the June 7, 1992, annual induction weekend at the International Boxing Hall of Fame in Canastota, New York, at which Nelson was inducted, I am proud to have the honor to produce this work.

Oscar Nelson wrote and self-published his autobiography, *Life, Battles and Career of Battling Nelson, Lightweight Champion of the World*, in 1908, forty-six years before his death. This work was an invaluable resource that has been cited numerous times inside this book. Contemporaneous newspaper accounts of events in Nelson's life both public and private also played an enormous role in this work. Having spent thousands of hours reading the white newspapers of the early twentieth century, I'm not the first historian—see Ward's masterful *Unforgettable Blackness: The Rise and Fall of Jack Johnson*—to be nauseated by the racist derision with which black Americans in general, especially those who came in contact with Oscar Nelson, were routinely portrayed. Some of these views, from Nelson himself and from a variety of newspapers, have been included as a reminder of who we were, where we have been, and how far we still have to go. In the words of Dr. Martin Luther King, Jr., "In the End, we will remember not the words of our enemies, but the silence of our friends."

Those who know me know of my proud association with the International Boxing Hall of Fame in Canastota, New York. My service—as an author, biographer, historian, chairperson, sponsor and volunteer—has been particularly rewarding because of some incredible individuals: Edward Brophy, Jeffrey S. Brophy, Chris Bowers, Rachel Shaw, and Mike Delaney; as well as Angelo Testani, Anthony Testani, Eric Warren, Ruth Tabor, Craig Bailey, Grace Rapasadi, Melody Smith, Mike Burch, John Hunt, Jean Palmer, Alexia Conrad, Carol Burch, Pat Prettyman, Dr. Juan Kassab, Charlene Barres, Pat Orr, Chuck Sgroi, Ada Sgroi, Doug Gustin, Joyce Gustin, Deb Gustin, Nanci Knox, Mike Brophy, Holly Lynch, Diana Colon, Scott Rapasadi, T.J. Tornatore, Kim Myers, Geoff Burch, Joey Fiato, Don Ackerman, Walt Stokes, Randy Smithers, Henry Brown, Scott Flaherty, Mike Rouse, Matt Enigk, Tito Colon, Rich Brophy, Ross Stagnitti, Marie Sgroi, Jim Clark, Jennifer Warner, Tammie Alter, Kyle Cashel and Linda Pease; and also Mike Milmoe, Donald Hamilton, Bob Davidson, Jimmy

Acknowledgments

Prettyman, Billy Backus, and Tony Graziano. I would like to single out in particular the efforts of Jeffrey S. Brophy for his outstanding research and ongoing friendship.

This book would not have been possible without the assistance of the Library of Congress and their Digital Collections and Services staff. The George Grantham Bain photographs came to the Library of Congress with very little description but tremendous potential. I am proud to display many of those images in this work. Also, I owe much to Chronicling America, a website providing access to information about historic newspapers and select digitized newspaper pages, produced by the National Digital Newspaper Program (NDNP). NDNP, a partnership between the National Endowment for the Humanities (NEH) and the Library of Congress, is a long-term effort to develop an Internet-based, searchable database of U.S. newspapers with descriptive information and select digitization of historic pages. I wish to also extend my appreciation to the University of Sussex and Heritage Auctions for their assistance.

Living in the historic state of Connecticut, I am fortunate to have a great support system. My gratitude to all of the independent bookstores, especially Bank Square Books in Mystic, and Byrd's Books in Bethel. Also, my gratitude to Larry Dasilva (Nutmeg TV), Larry Rifkin (WATR), Ray Bendici (*Connecticut* magazine), Nathan Grube (*The Travelers*), and Geeta Schrayter (*Rivereast News Bulletin*). Also, my appreciation to our state's historical sites and institutions, especially Nathan Hale Schoolhouse in New London, Fairfield Museum, Jonathan Trumbull House, the Litchfield Historical Society, and Norwich Historical Society. Also thanks to friends Dana Beck and Brian Brinkman, Kelly and Dennis DiGiovanni, Ann and Mark Lepkowski, Paul Mancuso, Mark and Michelle Brett, and Jim Risley.

For Oscar, I would be remiss not to ask your support for a cause: Alzheimer's Association National Office, 225 N. Michigan Ave., Fl. 17, Chicago, IL 60601. Alzheimer's Association is a not-for-profit 501(c)(3) organization.

To my family, Marilyn Allen Baker, Aaron, Sharon and Elliott Baker, Elizabeth Baker and Mark Taylor, Brad, Rebecca and Elijah Lane, and Cyndie Long, thank you for your love and support. A special note of gratitude to Richard Long, my wonderful father-in-law, whom I shared some memorable moments with in Ireland, and who continues to inspire me to do more. To the memory of Ford William Baker, James Buford Bird, Flavil Q. Van Dyke III and Deborah Jean Long.

"The only man I know who behaves sensibly is my tailor," quipped George Bernard Shaw. "He takes my measurements anew each time he sees me. The rest go on with their old measurements and expect me to fit them." My wife Alison has never relied on the old measurements, and that is why I love her so.

Nobody in life can bear to feel themselves forgotten. To have that one moment, that you were certain was your eternity, snuffed out like a candle is unbearable. Yet it happens. Even tougher to endure, at least to some, is failing to set alight that candle anew, or to watch in disbelief when you can no longer even afford the candle. As both an author and historian, I ask that you light a candle in memory of Oscar "Battling" Matthew Nelson.

Preface

Oscar "Battling" Matthew Nelson was without question one of the toughest and most durable professional boxers ever to enter a ring. Although obscure today, he was selected by the Hall of Fame as part of their third induction class. Often appropriately called the most hardwearing boxer in ring history, he is still overlooked, yet boxing scribe Bert Randolph Sugar ranked him number fifty-one out of one hundred among boxing's greatest fighters—ahead of John L. Sullivan, Carlos Monzon, Carmen Basilio and Bob Fitzsimmons.[1] To have been deceased for over six decades and yet still acknowledged at this level—among the most distinguished individuals ever to participate in your profession—is an awe-inspiring accomplishment.

From the moment he set foot in the ring, he presented himself as a man's man, a Danish immigrant of integrity who never smoked, drank or took a dive, and in both his pugilistic exploits and his often very public behavior established a heroic image of himself as an athlete—a world lightweight champion—and sportsman, reporter, entertainer, real estate mogul, businessman and lady's man. As his fame grew, taking a page out of the John L. Sullivan book of boxing etiquette, his self-dramatizations hardened into myth, if only for a short period of time. As the first champion in his division to ever mount a comeback, he broke new ground, even if it wasn't always pretty, or ultimately successful.

The fascinating underpinnings of his career include a meteoric rise from beating a strongman at the circus to defeating Joe Gans, perhaps the greatest lightweight champion of all time; a tetralogy of unforgettable Bay Area battles with Jimmy Britt; an intense trilogy with elite boxer Ad Wolgast; legendary fight promotions with James W. Coffroth and George "Tex" Rickard; and even a return to the big top.

Fighting in era when his occupation was considered uncivilized and corrupt, he wore his profession on his sleeve, as genuine as they come. However it came at price: his fiancées became as common as sparring partners; his first true love came in the form of a beautiful and wealthy heiress, soon to be a countess, whose family abhorred pugilism and pugilists; his first marriage, to a talented cartoonist, was measured in days; and his final love was not found until the last rounds of his life.

In the years since his death in 1954, there has been little disagreement over the significance of his life: a bona fide ring champion whose endurance was second to none, and whose trilogy with Joe Gans was one of the greatest in sports history. And little disagreement over his death: another genuine ring hero who died penniless and suffered from a chronic or persistent disorder of the mental process caused by brain disease or injury, and marked by memory disorders, personality changes, and impaired reasoning.

Preface

It has been well over a century since Battling Nelson first stepped into a boxing ring, over a century since his self-published autobiography and nearly a quarter century since his induction into the International Boxing Hall of Fame. And it is now time to revisit an extraordinary life, beyond the imagination of the finest Hollywood screenwriters, yet so genuine that you can't help but empathize with this man.

The true story of Oscar "Battling" Matthew Nelson is a "rags, to riches, to rags" tale. And, in a land that prides itself on accounts of the underdog finally reaching new heights in a profession and retiring comfortably, this can be disconcerting. Don't allow it a consideration, as it is every bit as important to the sport of boxing as Oscar was himself.

"Things may not be immediately discernible in what a man does," to modify a line from Ernest Hemingway, a former pugilist turned scribe, "and in this sometimes he is fortunate; but eventually they are quite clear and by those and the degree of alchemy that he possesses he will endure or be forgotten." Battling Nelson shall endure.

ONE

1882–1899

From Copenhagen to Hegewisch

> I wasn't much on muscle or breadth of shoulders then, but I had worked hard and long for two years hauling ice, shoveling coal and doing some butchering also, and, for a kid, had a beaut of a sleep producer [knockout punch] myself.
> —Oscar "Battling" Matthew Nelson[1]

Most of the stories he remembered were from his parents, Nels and Mary Nelson, snippets—principally in Danish, but a few in broken English—of how they, along with their small family, had made the long journey from Copenhagen, Denmark, to New York in 1883. Oscar "Battling" Matthew Nelson, born on June 5, 1882, in the cruise home port, was part of that Nelson contingent.[2]

Remembering the stories, but not the journey, was pleasant for Oscar, as his imagination would fill in the rest. Picturing, often as it would turn out, his family's silhouette pressed against a ship's rail fighting for their first glimpse of a new world was as real to him as it was for anybody. And, as commonplace as that image had become to so many immigrants, it never failed—as it has never failed with so many others even to this very day—to invoke a tremendous sense of pride, not to mention a perpetual respect for all those whose courage blazed a path for those who followed. While he would state emphatically, "though born on foreign soil I herewith proclaim myself as an American in every sense of the word," he would also delight in the moniker "Durable Dane."[3]

Copenhagen, Denmark

The Danish are a proud people, and much of that dignity stems from their rich heritage. And nowhere does it appear to reflect more than in Copenhagen, Denmark. In a city that was founded more than 800 years ago, one might expect that nearly every obstacle to its development had been endured. And one would be correct; the city of Copenhagen has withstood fires, plagues, sieges and wars. And it has done so with an incredible sense of gravitas. As its nerve center, Copenhagen has long been the heartbeat of Denmark—since, in fact, 1167 when Absalon, a Danish archbishop and statesman, built a castle near the site.

Situated in northwestern Europe, Denmark—with Danish as its official language—is the southernmost of the Nordic countries, which also include Finland, Iceland, Norway and

Sweden. And it is Sweden and Norway, along with Denmark, that form the cultural region of Scandinavia.

In the early fifteenth century, the fishing village of Copenhagen would become the Danish capital; eager to educate, engage and evolve, this soon included the University of Copenhagen (inaugurated 1479) and a role for the city as the epicenter of trade for the country. It was a transformation that did not go unnoticed, as the Swedish army, under King Charles X, besieged Copenhagen in 1658—an action eventually repelled.

Having endured the king, Copenhagen would face even greater challenges. In 1711, the city was devastated by a bubonic plague, which killed almost a third of the population. Then, seventeen years later, a series of fires burned through the city, destroying most of its treasured medieval buildings. Traumatized, but not neutralized, by these catastrophic events, a tenacious city rebuilt.

Containment, as all historians recognize, has never come easy to Europe. The War of the Second Coalition (1798–1802) was a part of the French Revolutionary Wars and pitted the conservative European monarchies, Britain, Austria and Russia, including the Ottoman Empire, Portugal and Naples, against France. The alliance, though successful for a time, did not anticipate a number of key factors, most notably a Russian withdrawal and Napoleon's ascension to power in late 1799. This coalition was eventually defeated. Although borders had been redefined and treaties—the Treaty of Lunéville in 1801 and the Treaty of Amiens in March 1802—signed to support an end to the hostilities, nothing could prolong the inevitable. By 1805, a third coalition was formed by Britain and they were again at war with France.

The First Battle of Copenhagen, part of the War of the Second Coalition, was fought between the Danish and the English fleets on April 2, 1801. The British fleet, under the command of Admiral Sir Hyde Parker and Vice Admiral Lord Nelson, along with Rear Admiral Thomas Graves, was up against a huge Danish fleet, anchored just off Copenhagen and led by Commodore Olfert Fischer and Captain Steen Andersen Bille. It would be the irrefutable Vice Admiral Horatio Nelson who would lead the main attack, much to the chagrin and disapproval of his commander—the famous defiance now a noteworthy historical event. The cease-fire on this day, considered to be Nelson's hardest-fought battle, was exemplary of a force to be reckoned with, that of the Danes—it was through their heroic and obstinate effort that Copenhagen stood proud.

The Second Battle of Copenhagen—history seldom devoid of a rematch—was fought from August 16, 1807, until September 5, 1807. In order to keep Denmark from surrendering its fleet to Britain's enemy Napoleon, the British bombarded the city, causing considerable damage. In return for a Danish capitulation, the British agreed to leave Copenhagen within six weeks. The war lasted until 1814, when the Treaty of Kiel ended the hostilities.

During the decades that followed a spirit of nationalism prevailed in Denmark. It was, as many felt, an overdue consolation. Immediately following the adjournment of the European Revolutions of 1848, Denmark turned their attention to a constitutional monarchy—a form where the governing powers of the monarch are restricted by the terms of a constitution. But military conflict again engaged the Danes at the First Schleswig War, or the Three Years' War, which began on March 24, 1848, and lasted until May 8, 1852. It would prove to be only the first round of a military conflict known as the Schleswig-Holstein Question, or who should control the duchies (a territory of a duke or duchess) of Schleswig and Holstein. The antagonism between the Germans and Danes ran deep, and despite a Danish victory in the first war, the conflict could not be defused.

The Second Schleswig War erupted on February 1, 1864, and lasted until October 30, 1864. It concluded when Schleswig-Holstein fell to Germany, being tantamount to a loss of one-fourth of Danish territory—the northern half of Slesvig (Sønderjylland) was Danish, but the rest of Shleswig-Holstein was German. This, as might be anticipated, did not sit well with many Danes. Not only would they have to now serve under Prussian rule, which would require German military service, but they would have to witness the intolerable repression of their culture.[4] For many Slesvig Danes, it was high time to look for a new home.

To cease what many viewed as a pattern of turbulence, Denmark then turned to a policy of neutrality in Europe. Such a position, they understood, could reduce hostilities and enhance investment opportunities. Industrialization, despite the country's lack of natural resources, came to Denmark and thrived by the second half of the nineteenth century. Although the economic shift brought diverse job skills and expanded trade, it also brought new hardships. Various Danish farmers, and there were many in this agrarian society, shifted to dairy and pork production in an attempt to combat low-priced exports. This, however, was not simple, nor was it inexpensive. Growing unemployment—the Danish population was now exceeding labor demand—soon limited opportunities. For many Danes, including the family of Oscar "Battling" Matthew Nelson, the search for a better standard of living became paramount.

Land, as many believed, implied prestige, opportunity and perhaps wealth. Danish families, many of them large, understood—as only one child could take over the family farm thus diminishing the enthusiasm of their siblings—that they were limiting their options by staying in Denmark. Single farmers, many under the age of thirty, also acknowledged this and soon opted for emigration. However, just where was the solution?

The promise of free or inexpensive land, combined with better wages and the possibility of building a better life for themselves or their family, led many Danes to the United States. It was a decision supported by friends and relatives who had made the long journey before them, letters they had read in Danish newspapers, and improved transatlantic transportation. And adding even more incentive, in the United States an immigrant who could claim 160 acres of unoccupied government land and homestead it could earn the title in five years in accordance with the Homestead Act of 1862. Up until 1850 the number of Danes entering the United States had only "averaged about 60 a year, but after the American Civil War that figure would increase dramatically. Seeking a better future, a near 400,000 Danes would reach American shores by 1990."[5] Most of this immigration, which would include the Denmark-born family of Nels and Mary Nelson, happened between 1880 and 1920, when about 10 percent of the entire Danish population departed.[6]

Migration

America was no stranger to Danish immigration, as during the eighteenth century, it had seen resident Danes pick up their rifles during the American Revolution. But larger numbers really weren't recognized until 1840, when the Mormon Danes arrived. This being said, religion was a relatively minor factor compared with the increase in the birth rate and the economic difficulties facing Denmark.[7] Worth noting is the case that unlike countries such as Norway, Denmark's laws were comparatively benign toward dissident sects, and once the

Most of the stories Oscar Nelson remembered were from his parents, Nels and Mary Nelson, snippets—principally in Danish, but a few in broken English—of how they, along with their small family, had made the long journey from Copenhagen, Denmark, pictured here, to New York, in 1883 (Library of Congress, Prints and Photograph Division, LC-DIG-ppmsc-05759).

emigration movement began in the mid-nineteenth century, it included both rural and urban emigrants.[8] A majority of Danish emigrants came from the capital city of Copenhagen, no doubt enhanced by the fact that it was one of the largest port towns in all of Denmark and was actively harvesting the new demand for immigration. And as this need grew, so did the number of available cruise lines and vessels willing to accommodate it. In the beginning emigrant vessels were relatively small; most traveled on brigs and schooners which would accommodate between 75 and 150 passengers. But demand also saw to an increase in the size of the vessels and their frequency of sailing. By the 1870s, these sailing vessels[9] had increased in size over four times those of the smallest vessels used only two decades before.

Cargo ships were the vessels used to initially transport emigrants, later followed by ships better suited to accommodate the task. Their cargo holds, typically the deck immediately below the main deck of a vessel, were converted into temporary quarters. Inexpensive housing was reached via steep and narrow ladders that were erected below a main hatch. This "tween-deck" was often referred to in English as "steerage," or the part of the ship allotted to passengers or a certain type of traveler. The ceiling height between decks—a factor that determined the design of the passenger housing—was often six to eight feet.

To say that the lodging was cramped would certainly be an understatement, as the goal was to accommodate as many passengers as possible. Ceiling height determined the number of rows of bunks (placed for volume not convenience), or the rough boards intended to hold from three to six persons. In essence, these berths, or "family bunks," were viewed as having an unlimited capacity. Later, a sales feature of some immigrant vessels was enough headroom between the bunks that an adult could sit up in bed.

A bunk might include a straw mattress, in one form or another, but any bedding was the obligation of the passenger. Many passengers were also quickly reminded that straw also welcomed fleas and lice, not to mention disease. Sickness was common due to heat, humidity and poor ventilation. The rocking of the vessel, which often contributed to seasickness, was less felt in the middle of the ship, so naturally these became the most popular berths. What little natural light was available was admitted through open hatchways or through skylights in the deck.

These poor conditions, not to mention the influx of "undesirables"—forced Asian laborers, along with women presumed to be immigrating to work as prostitutes, and even the legal immigration of Chinese laborers—forced the United States Congress to pass three significant immigration acts: the Page Act of 1875, the Chinese Exclusion Act of 1882 and the Immigration Act of 1882.[10] The latter legislation attempted to define accommodations, including light and air, provisions, medical care, discipline and sanitary concerns, privacy, dangerous elements, and passenger control. It also included control elements such as inspection and penalties. The goal was to control and regulate what many would view as the most massive of all human migrations in our history, or what amounted to nearly "27 million immigrants settling in the United States between 1880 and 1930."[11]

Steamships, which first came into use during the early 1800s, also significantly altered transatlantic transportation. The British side-wheel paddle steamer SS *Great Western* was the first steamship designed and constructed for regularly scheduled transatlantic crossings. Developed by the great engineer Isambard Kingdom Brunel in 1838, the oak-hulled paddle-wheel steamship inaugurated the era of the transatlantic ocean liner. The White Star Line's RMS *Oceanic* then capitalized on all its predecessors by having its first-class cabins amidships, with the added amenity of large portholes, electricity and running water. New standards for ocean travel—comfort did not mean forsaking profit—seemed to be set with the launch of each new vessel, this as transatlantic crossings began to capitalize on the market potential.

In Denmark, a new shipyard began construction (1870) near Larsen's Plads on the Copenhagen Harbourfront—now Amaliehaven, besides the royal residence Amalienborg—complete with piers and quay. It would be from this site that the Thingvalla Line, founded in Denmark in 1879, hoped to accommodate the need of many Danes for affordable, comfortable and safe transatlantic passage. And in 1879, the main route between Scandinavian ports and America was indeed established by the company. Their westbound route started off at Copenhagen, calling at Kristiania (Oslo) and Kristiansand before crossing the Atlantic seas to New York. This allowed the line to compete effectively against the German lines that had serviced these needs before. Also, since the crew and customs on board were Scandinavian, passengers felt a greater degree of comfort. Records support that at least two dozen such transatlantic journeys were made by the line in 1883. These passages were taken by the SSs *Hekia I, Geiser, Heimdal, Island,* and *Thingvalla,* all part of the Thingvalla line.[12] It would be no exaggeration to say that Oscar, scarcely one year old, was aboard one of these voyages.

The Gilded Age

Oscar's parents had relatives in the West, so their stay in New York City would be brief. This was not an unusual decision, as during the previous decade, almost half of all Danish immigrants to the United States settled in family groups; and besides, their port of call was, let's just say, a bit intimidating.

In 1883, native New Yorkers, not to mention visitors, became captivated with the construction and opening of the Brooklyn Bridge. After thirteen years of assembly, John Augustus Roebling's wonder stood resplendent in its majesty as it linked the boroughs of Manhattan and Brooklyn. The cable-stayed bridge spanned the East River and was the first steel-wire suspension bridge constructed.

When New Yorkers weren't chattering about the bridge they were discussing their friend in Washington, President Chester Alan Arthur—a familiar face who had succeeded James Garfield upon his assassination. Arthur, though born in Fairfield, Vermont, grew up in upstate New York and practiced law in New York City. He was, as many saw it, part of the New York

In 1883, much of the attention in New York City centered on the construction and opening of the Brooklyn Bridge. After thirteen years of assembly, John Augustus Roebling's wonder stood resplendent in its majesty as it linked the boroughs of Manhattan and Brooklyn (Library of Congress, Prints and Photograph Division, LC-USZ62–74616).

City Republican political machine. Although initially distrusted, Arthur would go on to earn the respect of many while garnering the praise of his contemporaries. Of the president, author Mark Twain would later summarize, "It would be hard indeed to better President Arthur's administration."[13] This from the man who coined the period, the Gilded Age.

From the 1870s to about 1900, America, as Twain saw it, was dealing with serious social problems masked by a thin gold gilding. The rapid economic growth had fueled an increase in immigration, and it proved a bit too expeditious for even industrialization to handle. American wages were indeed higher than most countries, especially for skilled workers, but jobs were competitive, and inevitably poverty took a toll on many immigrants. Countless business sectors, such as manufacturing, mining and finance, thrived, while the reliance on railroads, now a major sector, increased. For those who had lived through the panic of 1873—a period that witnessed bank reserves plummet—optimism still prevailed, as many believed it was just a matter of reaching an economic balance.[14]

Oscar was too young to realize the world that existed around him. His entrance into this country would coincide with vaudeville's first theater opening in Boston, Massachusetts—a theatrical genre that would become extremely popular during much of his life, and a form of entertainment he would grow to love.

The American West was known as the Wild West, still a time of unmistakable lawlessness. Gunslingers like Charles Earl Bowles, aka Black Bart, were still robbing stagecoaches, even if the time for gentleman bandits was drawing to a conclusion—it would be eight more years until the frontier was officially declared closed.

As for the popular sport of boxing, all eyes were focused on "The Boston Strong Boy," or John Lawrence Sullivan. Hailing from Roxbury, Massachusetts, Sullivan stood five feet ten inches tall and weighed 190 pounds. Bold and brash, as a teenager he would fight in Boston barrooms, issuing a challenge that he "could lick any man in the house." Having won the Bare Knuckle World Heavyweight Title the previous year by knocking out Paddy Ryan in nine rounds—the fight that lasted just under eleven minutes—Sullivan was the first of a new breed of fighters. His charismatic style, not to mention his unification of the heavyweight crown, did much to advance the sport of boxing in America. In 1883, Sullivan would fight six different antagonists, in six separate battles, sending all six to the canvas before the fourth round— four of the six knocked out only moments into the fight. And when his fists weren't making headlines, his womanizing, drunken hijinks and big mouth, usually did—let's just say he was a godsend to a burgeoning newspaper industry. Boxing, or the paradox of using force to overcome force, has always been a contradiction. Sullivan, as captivating as he was controversial, was well on his way to becoming America's first national sports superstar, and the first athlete to earn more than a million dollars.

A Place to Call Home

Oscar would later recall, "We landed in Oshkosh, Wisconsin, that fall (1883), and settled down on a neat little truck farm (large scale market garden) which father had purchased."[15] Incorporated in 1853, Oshkosh, Wisconsin, was a relatively new city, owing much of its development to the lumber trade. When the Nelson family arrived, the city was experiencing what would be the largest percentage in population growth in its history, increasing from 15,748

A rare view ringside at the Sullivan versus Kilrain fight held in Richburg, Mississippi, on July 8, 1889. With a knockout in the seventy-fifth round, Sullivan (left) retained the Bare Knuckle World Heavyweight Title (Library of Congress, Prints and Photograph Division, LC-USZ62–78647).

in 1880 to 22,836 in 1890.[16] Home to one of the largest groups of Danish Americans in the United States, Wisconsin not only included members of their family but an environment that would make it easier to make friends and assimilate into the community.[17]

As the family's comfort level grew with their resources, they deemed it time to move on. "We remained there (Oshkosh) for one year," Oscar would late remember, "after which we moved to Dalton, Illinois, a place not far from Chicago proper. The following spring we moved to our present home Hegewisch (HEG-wish), Illinois."[18]

Hegewisch was a quaint neighborhood on the southeast side of Chicago. Founded along a rail line in 1883 by Adolph Hegewisch, president of the U.S. Rolling Stock Company, it was also accessible. It was his vision to create the perfect workingman's community, and one that could easily assist his company, which just happened to border the new town. The concept attracted many, including the Nelson family, who felt that they too could grow with their surroundings. Optimism and new construction was everywhere, or so it seemed. St. Columbia Church was new, as was the first public school and by 1888, the year Oscar was sent to the former, the Hegewisch Opera House opened over on 133rd and Erie. Other industries servicing this community included truck gardening, meatpacking and ice cutting, the latter industry enhanced by its proximity to both Wolf Lake, an 804-acre body of water that straddles the Indiana and Illinois border, and Lake Michigan, the second-largest of the five Great Lakes by volume.

In 1889, Hegewisch became part of nearby Chicago. The initial vision Adolph Hegewisch had had for the community—including plans to build two major canals, the first to shorten the Calmut River and the second to connect Wolf Lake to Lake Michigan, as an incentive for other factories to locate near the town—never came to fruition. With few options, the tiny town became part of a growing metropolis that was thriving as a major grain market and food-processing center. While Hegewisch had never reached its projected 10,000 residents by 1885, the 500 names living there in 1889 were content to call it home.

"The winter seasons found nearly every able bodied man, youths, and mere kids like myself employed cutting storing and packing the big cold cakes (of ice) for the Chicago market," Oscar recalled. "Boys were employed to drive the horses used for hauling the ice."[19] (The seasonal harvest of ice, a practice that dates back centuries, was part of the American culture until the advent of cost-effective household refrigeration.) The demand for so many food products that required refrigeration created a thriving business for ice harvesting. Wherever ice could be found—be it on a pond, canal, lake, or reservoir—if it was thick enough, ice companies deployed teams of men, horses, and machines to harvest it for distribution across the United States. For many, including fisherman and farmers, such seasonal employment was the perfect fit—January and February were the primary harvesting months. Employed by John Daline, the Ice Man of Hegwisch, Oscar quickly exhibited a proficiency in the business.

The first step was to remove the snow and examine the ice—harvesters bored holes to measure its thickness. If the ice was thick enough, they then examined the surface—surfaces too rough had to be planed smooth. A marker or groover was used to etch a grid of rectan-

For many, including fisherman and farmers, seasonal employment such as ice cutting was the perfect fit—January and February being the prime harvesting months. Employed by John Daline, the Ice Man of Hegewisch, Nelson quickly showed a proficiency for the business (Library of Congress, Prints and Photograph Division, LC-DIG-ggbain-11584).

gles—soon to be blocks of ice called "cakes"—across a selected ice field. A cutter, often horse drawn, then followed these lines, slicing about two-thirds of the way into the ice. The smaller blocks were then chipped off and loaded into horse-drawn wagons or sleighs for local delivery, while the larger cakes were guided through man-made channels, broken into the appropriate size, then fed up an elevator conveyor into an icehouse or nearby refrigerated rail car. The latter blocks, arranged to minimize melting, were then used in later deliveries. This method, not always cost effective, proved to be as difficult as it was dangerous. For Oscar, the advantages—his initial week's work netted him 90 cents, or 15 cents per day—outweighed the risk. When he finally left Daline's employment to get back to school at his father's insistence, his salary had reached a dollar per day.

The G.H. Hammond Company, a Northwest Indiana meatpacking plant, was Oscar's next employer.[20] The company was established by George Hammond, a Detroit butcher, and Marcus Towle, a pioneer in the concept of refrigerated rail cars (Towle was the first to utilize chipped ice from the Great Lakes to ship frozen processed beef by rail to Boston). Again Oscar's proficiency and hard work paid off, as he was quickly "promoted to cutter, timekeeper, and finally assistant foreman," this while he was also attending night school.[21]

It would be this type of work to which Oscar would attribute his strength and endurance. "Though not very tall I was stockily built for a youngster," he would later confess, "and when I quit the Hammond Company I was really doing a man's work."[22]

The Sweet Science

While employed as a meat cutter at Hammond, during a period of unseasonably warm, dry weather that sometimes occurs in autumn, Oscar, now fourteen years old, had heard the word that the circus was coming to town. Working only three or four days a week, thanks to an early Indian summer, Oscar was not only delighted with the thought of seeing the circus but also hoped that he might take one of the many jobs they typically offered to the locals. Acting quickly, he applied for, and received, the job of carrying a banner in the parade and buckets of water for the elephants. For his efforts he was handed passes for the show.

"The Great Wallace Shows" were created in 1884 by Benjamin Wallace and his business partner John Anderson. Then, in 1890, Wallace bought out his partner to form the B.E. Wallace Circus. And it was *that* version that attracted Oscar's attention.

Even at his young age, Oscar had already garnered the reputation—suffice it to say that the youth in Hegwisch held few secrets among their peers—"as a shifty, hard-hitting sort of a kid."[23] So, upon learning that Wallace shows carried a world-renowned prizefighter who would meet all comers, speculation began as to who, if anyone, might challenge the "man-eater," aka Wallace's Terrible Unknown. Not surprisingly, the Wallace show refused to divulge their fighter's identity or any information regarding his propensity for slaughtering and devouring humans.

Now Oscar wasn't bashful, but neither was he overly aggressive, so it took one of his comrades to present his challenge to the circus manager.

"What would you give if our champ knocks the block off your great slugging unknown?"[24]

A buck was the response, but the challenger must stand up for three rounds in order to

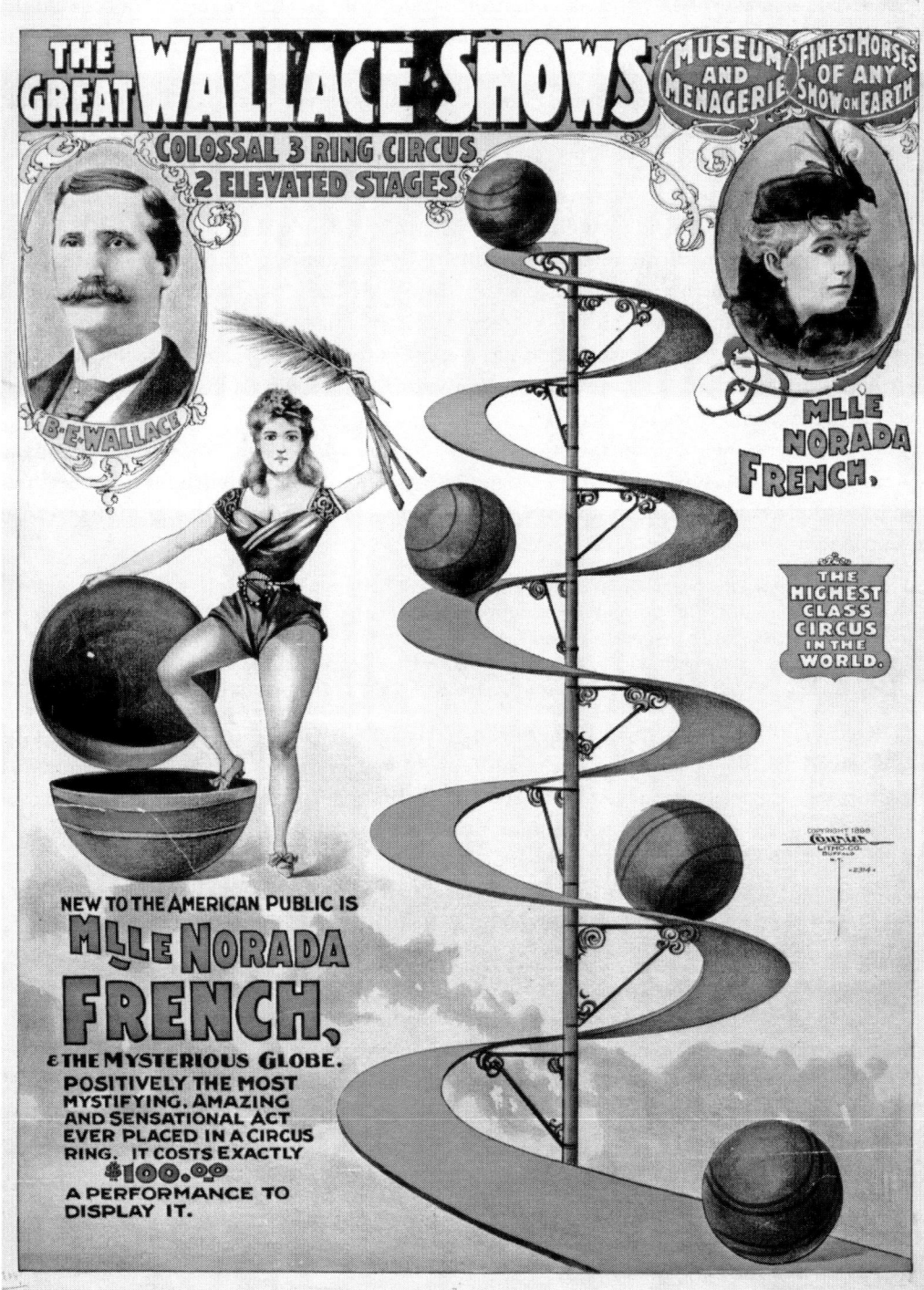

The Great Wallace Shows were created in 1884 by a livery stable owner from Peru, Indiana, named Benjamin Wallace and his business partner John Anderson. Then, in 1890, Wallace bought out his partner to form the B.E. Wallace Circus (Library of Congress, Prints and Photograph Division, LC-USZC4–13573).

earn it. The manager then added an additional caveat: if the challenger was successful, he would be given the opportunity to earn even more money. Oscar later said, "That suited me to a nicety."[25]

So, on September 3, 1896, in Hammond, Indiana, only a few miles from Hegewisch, Oscar "Battling" Matthew Nelson would make his professional ring debut. The big white tent, on the circus grounds, was filled to capacity awaiting the entrance of an unassuming—dressed in a thin, well-worn red sweater and a pair of low rubber shoes—local teenager. The sawdust-covered arena inside would feature what many believed to be nothing short of a human sacrifice, or the dismemberment of one of the community's most naive youths.

When the circus manager hauled Oscar into a side tent and warned him about his inevitable destruction, the youth didn't know exactly what to think, nor what to expect. Regardless of the fact that the surroundings were frightening for Oscar, the feeling of exhilaration felt by every boxer before a fight was intoxicating—it would be as invigorating as it was unnerving, a nonpareil addiction.

Once inside the main tent, Oscar met face to face with Wallace's Terrible Unknown. Pacing the floor nervously like a caged tiger, his opponent, acknowledged to his friends as "Jack," looked every bit as inexorable as Oscar had anticipated. Even years later (1908), Oscar would describe the scene in detail:

> Jack was as tough a looking fellow as I had ever seen or have met since. He stood about five feet six, and, of course, was a few inches taller than I. He possessed broad, compactly built shoulders, had a square, heavy jaw, and, all in all, was a rather likely looking fellow. He would have passed for a twin brother of Kid Broad. I wasn't much on muscle or breadth of shoulders then, but I had worked hard and long for two years hauling ice, shoveling coal and doing some butchering also, and for a kid, had a beaut of a sleep producer myself.[26]

Oscar could still remember him growling, "All right, we'll see him stand it out."[27] As the band played the Francis G. Spencer classic "Down Went McGinty," the audience erupted in laughter, this as it was announced that "one Bat Nelson, the Packing-house Pride, would take the chance of his life and attempt to stand up before the ferocious onslaughts of 'Wallace's Wonderful Unknown.'"[28]

The sight of a few confident and familiar faces in the crowd settled a bit of Oscar's uneasiness, if only for a few moments before the opening bell. The Unknown immediately rushed his opponent—a strategy that would soon prove deadly to nearly every opponent Oscar Nelson would face—and was met by a solid left that seemed to come from the heavens. A crouched Unknown was nearly out on his feet, blood streaming from his nose and mouth. And before he could regain his control, he met with a tremendous right uppercut that landed squarely over his heart. As his trainers screamed frantically to knock the youth's block off, the Unknown somehow managed a punch squarely on Oscar's jaw. Standing his ground, Nelson prepared for his counter. The Unknown, not used to such competition, then made a grave error—he failed to move away from his opponent. Oscar then returned a solid left to the jaw, and down went Wallace's Terrible Unknown, the ferocious man-eater who was destined, or so everyone believed, to devour his opponent. Left standing in the ring was the most promising pugilist in the county.

After the confrontation, the Unknown's manager was so adamant that Oscar join the circus that he followed him home to Hegewisch where he offered him a salary of $50 per week plus expenses. However, Oscar's parents would have nothing to do with such a proposition, emphatically stating that the young man's services were needed at home.

Overjoyed by his victory, Oscar forgot—or perhaps took for granted—that one of his comrades had held safe his articles. He had left behind his coat and vest, the former of which included a week's wage of $5.40 and a Waterbury watch. One can imagine the exuberance felt by everyone, as Oscar had played the role of David who triumphed over the Philistine Goliath, in need of neither sling nor stone. The following day, an attempt to retrieve the missing articles—believed at that time to have been stolen by a circus hand—proved fruitless.

When the dust settled from the event, Oscar and company had a story for the ages. But there was far more to the victory than just a tale to tell. The young man now had, in his own words, "the boxing bee in my bonnet."[29] In retrospect, what would prove even more amazing was Oscar Nelson fighting for the lightweight championship of the world against Joe Gans, exactly ten years later at Goldfield, Nevada, on September 3, 1906.

In a small town the size of Hegewisch, news travels fast, so it didn't take long for it to reach the best scrapper in the vicinity, Ole Olson. When Olson challenged Oscar's claim as the champion of Hegewisch, a match was scheduled for June 5, 1897, at the White House Club—an athletic club organized following Nelson's first victory.

In a town populated primarily by Swedes and Danes, nobody could imagine a more popular yet more polarizing boxing card. As intense as the rivalry would prove, one thing was certain: there would be a Scandinavian champion taking home the $3.00 purse that Sunday afternoon.

His opponent, like the circus behemoth, had an advantage in three key boxing elements: height, weight and reach. Without formal training to compensate for these deficiencies, Nelson would have only instinct in his corner—something that might, or may not, carry him to victory. When the opening round commenced, Ole rushed his opponent, opting for infighting over his obvious advantage in reach. Oscar stalled off the assault—with covers and counters, or blocking punches and counterpunching—to even the first round. The second round was a mirror of the first, with the exception of two things: Oscar's left uppercuts seemed, at least to him, to be having a slowing effect on his opponent, and he had become the aggressor by the end of the round. When the bell sounded for the third and finally round, Oscar rushed his opponent to fire "a series of heavy swings and short-arm jolts at close quarters."[30] The assault sent his opponent to the floor, a process that would repeat itself before Oscar finally delivered a crushing straight left that flattened Ole. "Enough," the Swede bellowed in a cry that preceded by decades that of "no mas," and enough it was.[31]

But there was trouble in Hegewisch. Oscar's victory would not sit well with the Swedes. Calling to mind the event, Oscar would state, "Angered over the defeat of their pride, [the Swedes] started a war of extermination with us Danes. Then and there the trouble began and some fun as well. We lined up in the White House yard and the two factions charged each other, each side willing to 'go the derby,' or Battler's route, or die. It was the dandiest battle royal I ever took part in." The Danes would win the free-for-all. The day would also mark the first time Oscar "was triumphantly carried off the battlefield by his admirers."[32]

A prideful performance indeed, but once again the fisticuffs did not sit well with Oscar's parents. When the youngster arrived home, an argument ensued. Oscar then ran away from home. On the evening of June 15, 1897, on his way out of town, he dropped a note in the mail to his mother that read, "Gong away, ma, to seek my fortune."[33]

Well, if you don't know where you are going, any road will take you there, so Oscar Nelson headed northwest, surviving through odd jobs. Eventually landing in Huron, South

Dakota, over 500 miles "as the crow flies" from Chicago, he took a position at Kimmel & Edler's meat market for $15 per month. Even if it was steady employment that would last until Christmas, Oscar considered his efforts a bargain, so he asked for a raise to $20 a month. When the market denied his request, Oscar quit and moved on.

Having made the acquaintance of a local cowboy, Oscar headed to a nearby ranch to test his skills as a cattleman—ever since his ice-harvesting days he had always been good on a horse, so why not collect cattle instead of cakes? Raised, like so many youths, on stories about the Wild West and the exploits of Buffalo Bill, it sounded exciting.[34] But when winter set in, he had enough of herding cattle, so Oscar hiked over to Miller, South Dakota, and secured a job as a waiter at the Vanderbilt Hotel owned by B.F. Torrey—an early pioneer of South Dakota, Torrey had located to Miller in 1882. His ambition, combined with[35] honesty of character, always impressed Oscar Nelson.

Still carrying the boxing bug, when Oscar heard of a decent boxing club holding weekly fights in Sioux Falls, South Dakota, he couldn't resist the opportunity to test his luck, even if the distance to the club was over 130 miles. Following a personal examination by the manager, Oscar was given a bout against lightweight Freddie Green on May 10, 1898, with the stipulation that if he "managed to make good" he would be matched the following night against Solider Williams.[36]

In 1880, Sioux Falls, a town whose history was rooted in the cascades of the Big Sioux River, had a population of 2,164.[37] But that figure would change dramatically with the arrival of the railroads—the Great Dakota Boom decade of the 1880s saw a 370 percent increase in population.[38] With over 10,000 people soon calling Sioux Falls home, the growth in optimism was quickly reflected by new construction. Nonetheless, this transformation came to a grinding halt by the early 1890s due to a severe plague of grasshoppers and a depressed national economy. It would then be up to state and local government—dominated by those with real estate holdings—to halt any negative publicity with hopes of regaining settlement and land interest. Boxing, as they saw it, was a diversion—a chance for residents to escape their own battles, be it insects or land values.

Just thrilled beyond belief, Oscar went out and bought a pair of green boxing trunks—stating in 1908 that he had worn the lucky color ever since—to go with the regulation fighting shoes he would wear Saturday night. He felt like a real fighter, even though he would later say, "I was an unknown and from a place called Hegewisch, Illinois."[39]

The first to enjoy the guilelessness of the now fashionable fighter was that of the master of ceremonies, who had never heard of Hegewisch, nor had any idea where it was. Despite the chaff, he would, however, remember his name, Battling Nelson. While shaking his head in disbelief, he would retort, "Whew! What a good fighting name! A regular Admiral Nelson, eh?"[40]

Although "The Battler" was confident, he was also filled with humility—the first feeling to last a lifetime, the latter not so much. His mind raced and was full of recollections of his only two ring battles, the sound of the crowd, the smiles on the faces of his comrades and even his hometown. He had promised himself that if he ever became famous he would not turn his back on Hegewisch, and it would, as far as he was concerned, become synonymous with Battling Nelson. Oscar would never forget this promise.

When "The Champion of the Dakotas" entered his familiar confines, he needed no Introduction—everyone knew Freddie Green. Classy and experienced, Green, to use Nelson's

Words, was "a shifty, clever fellow, raw of bone and had a reach like a gorilla."[41] In comparison, Battling Nelson was unknown, inexperienced and didn't even have a trainer.

With a purse of $7.50 on the line, the gong tapped for round one. Green danced like a pro and tossed repeated jabs to Bat's face. The "strike and move" strategy was new to Bat and in stark contrast to his slow and awkward manner. Nevertheless, his confidence grew with each passing round. In the fourth, however, Green drew first blood; the act both angered and humiliated Bat. Let it be said that born on this date was Nelson's trademark anger—once invoked by an opponent, he became an indefatigable warrior. From this point forward he took the fight to Green, working him in clinches like a pro. Despite a few wild punches by his opponent, Green wisely pulled back in the fifth. By the sixth round, Nelson, having never battled this length, was a bit winded. During the round Green came within range and took some damage to the ribs, along with a solid left to the jaw. To Bat's delight, Green tried to exchange blows with him; Green, knowing nothing of Nelson's abilities, figured why not? At the end of the round, Bat believed he had his weary opponent beaten.

As the bell sounded for the seventh, Bat continued his aggression. "I boxed and cuffed him about the ring until he was groggy," he called to mind. "Then I stepped back and handed him a left hook full to the jaw. They carried him out of the ring unconscious."[42] Three battles and three titles: Champion of Wallace's Circus, Champion of Hegewisch and Champion of the Dakotas. Of the purse, collected at ringside by the pass of a hat, half was sent back to his mother.

Soldier Williams was next on the Sioux Falls menu, where Battling Nelson was now the talk of the town. This thrilled Oscar, who was still a bit sore but invigorated by the newfound attention. Delighted with both the attendance and the fight itself, the club's manager increased Sunday night's purse to $10.00. The fight, to be held inside an open ring pitched on the picnic ground of the club, was expected to draw a large crowd.

As for his enigmatic challenger, Nelson would state, "Williams was no spring chicken at the game. He had a string of victories to his credit up to the time he met me."[43] As the bell sounded for round one, both fighters charged from their corners slinging wild punches in hopes of a quick knockout—as the aggressor Williams was clearly no fancy boxer, but a rough-and-tumble type of fighter who was hoping for a short and easy night at the office. The edge stayed with Williams up to the sixth round, when Nelson was beginning to note signs of fatigue. In the seventh, Oscar challenged him with a solid right to the body, an attempt to slow Williams. Instead of countering, as he had done the entire fight, Williams retreated. Sensing a capitulation, the Battler planted a left hook to the jaw, then a right, before smothering him with combinations. Miraculously, a helpless Williams was saved by the bell.

In the eighth and final round, a revived Williams bolted from his corner. A bevy of quick combinations from Oscar, however, quickly halted the assault and sent Williams to the floor. Managing to barely get to his feet, the fighter was met by a powerful Nelson right that sent him down for the count.

Nelson's story gets a bit cloudy following the fight. The Spanish-American War, which took place in the Caribbean and the Philippines from April 25, 1898, until August 12, 1898, and was a confrontation between Spain and the United States, had just broken out. It was prompted by Spanish atrocities in Cuba and the destruction of the warship *Maine* in Santiago harbor on February 15, 1898. The newspaper coverage of the conflict ignited a spirit of nationalism, even as far west as South Dakota. It would later be Oscar Nelson's claim that he served in the army from May until September 1898, and that he had volunteered while in Huron. His claim would become a bone of contention many years later when he would file to obtain a Spanish-American War pension. With the United States having successfully invaded Cuba, Puerto Rico, and the Philippines, an end to the conflict would come with the Treaty of Paris (1898). The treaty allowed the United States temporary control of Cuba and ceded ownership of Puerto Rico, Guam and the Philippine islands. It should be noted that in Nelson's autobiography, *Life, Battles and Career of Battling Nelson, Lightweight Champion of the World*, published in 1908, there is no mention of his service.[44]

"After defeating several Northern champions I decided to return home and secure, if possible, a few good bouts in the neighborhood of Chicago," Oscar would proudly state.[45] From his parents and siblings, to even strangers who had only heard stories about him, everyone welcomed him home to Hegewisch. The Battler soon targeted another hometown product, that of Eddie Herman—his friends had told him the fighter had been "cleaning up every fighter in the vicinity." Oscar also reluctantly resumed his studies, contrasting it with secret training sessions at night. Unlike his parents, the only future he saw for himself was in a ring.

On New Year's Day 1899, Oscar "Battling" Matthew Nelson began what he viewed as a professional career by boxing Eddie Herman to a six-round draw.[46] Even though it wasn't a victory, it generated interest—not to mention a $10 purse—from nearly everyone in Hegewisch.[47] And it also persuaded Oscar to cease his studies and begin a career as a professional boxer. At the age of sixteen, in his mind, he had beaten some quality fighters: a circus champion, two club fighters and now a Hegewisch hopeful. However, circus fighters are seldom taken seriously; club fighters, as he would learn but not readily accept, were typically a dime a dozen—club managers picked fighters like peaches in a basket and the basket was often bottomless; and local pugs, many whose reputation exceeded their abilities, seldom attracted attention beyond county lines. Yes, some professional fighters have been discovered in clubs, but that has been where they were born, seldom made. While victories meant something to Oscar, in the big picture, that of professional boxing, they meant little or nothing.

On April 6, 1899, Nelson accepted a battle with another local favorite, Eddie Penny. Not only was Penny well liked, but the betting odds ran heavily in his favor. The Battler, however, saw things a bit differently and made short change of Penny in the very first round; in this case a Penny was worth $10 (Nelson's purse). The decisive victory garnered him a modicum of attention, particularly with the managers of various Chicago clubs.

Bull Winters, a friend of Penny, was Nelson's next contest scheduled for May 3, 1899. When the opening bell sounded, Bull lived up to his name by charging the Battler like he was waving a red cape. A composed Nelson sidestepped the Bull's wild swings, then backed off his fierce rushes. When it became clear that his opponent was winded, Oscar targeted him in the middle of the ring. With hands to his side, Nelson approached the unassuming Winters, shifted a bit to line up with his target, then let go with a massive right to the jaw, followed by a devastating left hook to the body. Down he went, and as Nelson would later recall, "They carried him out a bellowing." When the club members passed the hat, a mere $2.50 marked the effort.[48]

After this display, it was time for the club managers to come up with a ringer to match against Nelson—a chance, you know, to recover some of the cash they had lost on side bets. But even that proved to be an unwise idea, as the Battler sent an impostor, named Unknown John Smith, to the canvas in the second round of a June 1, 1899, battle. For his efforts, Nelson picked up another $2.50, giving him a total of $25 for the year. Without complaint, he returned to Hegewisch and resumed training at the White House Club.

The Nelson Family

Shared by about 5 percent of the population, Neilsen was the second most common surname in Denmark. As a Danish patronymic surname it means "son of Neils." Furthermore, Neils is the Danish version of the Greek name Nikolaus or Nicholas, meaning "victory of the people." Alternate versions of the surname include: Nelsen, Neilsen, Neilson, Nielson, and also the Swedish form Nilsson and the Irish form of Nelson.

Bearing in mind the difficulty of immigration, especially the language barrier, it was not unusual for immigrants to English-speaking countries, such as the United States, to change the spelling of their surname, or to have their surname misspelled. Therefore Neilsen could become Nelson, Nelsen, or Neilson.[49] It was common for individuals, or families, to refer to more than one surname—using Oscar's family for example, there were times when his brother Charlie used the surname Nielsen. Numerous boxing sources refer to Oscar as Oscar Neilson, Oscar Mathæus Nielsen, or Oscar Mathæus "Battling" Nielsen. Legal documents, such as those filed with the United States Exemption Board, are signed simply "Battling Nelson" (1918) or "Oscar Matthew 'Battling' Nelson" (1951). Oscar "Battling" Matthew Nelson is his full name, the name he loved and the name he will be addressed as.[50]

Nels Nelson, a carpenter by trade, and his wife, Mary, were responsible for eight living children; the couple had two children who were deceased. Albert was the oldest, four years advanced to Oscar; Henry was only two years older; then Oscar, who was followed two years later by Johnny and two years after that by Charlie. The only daughter of the family, Ida, was born two years after Charlie. Arthur was next, three years after Ida, and finally Harry, who was twelve years younger than Oscar. It was a large family by today's standards but common for the time.

Here is how Oscar described his siblings in 1908: "Albert was a machinist, Henry a blacksmith, and Johnny a molder. Charlie was a junior at the University of California and was studying to become an M.D.," but Oscar stated he wouldn't be surprised if he turned out to be a preacher. "Arthur was a motorcycle racer who once rode a mile and a quarter in a minute. My youngest brother Harry, the smartest kid of them all, was then attending the boy's School at Quincy, Illinois. He is inclined to be scrappy, and is already exhibiting signs of following in my footsteps." And "my only sister Ida is living with the folks at home."[51]

Worth noting was that three of Oscar's brothers witnessed his victory over Wallace's Unknown. Albert nearly fell off his chair when he saw Oscar being led into the ring, and Harry, in Oscar's own words, "tossed up both hands and fainted dead away of fright."[52] The identity of a third brother was not given.

At age seventeen, a maturing Oscar Nelson was of medium height and build and had a long Danish face with a squared-off chin. His light brown hair complemented perfectly his captivating blue eyes, and to say he melted many a Hegewisch heart would be an understatement. Having dropped out of his studies, boxing was now his future. Even if his parents disagreed with his choice, they knew he could not be dissuaded. His inexorable determination to make a name for himself would work to both his advantage and disadvantage for many years to come.

Two

1900–1903
Making Headlines

"Gone away, ma, to seek my fortune," was the childish note which I mailed to Ma from Hegewisch on the evening of June 15, 1897. Ma still has the letter, and she is a witness to the fact that "I made good" my childish brag.
—"Battling" Nelson[1]

Still growing by over 20 percent every decade, the population of the United States topped the 75 million mark in 1900. This as a dream for many still seemed only one opportunity away.[2] Of the total population, 66.8 million, or 88 percent, were white, while African Americans—about 90 percent of them finding a home in the South—accounted for 8.8 million. The Hispanic population made up just over 500,000. Expansion, wars and legislation were just some of the factors driving these numbers. A great example was the Foraker Act of April 12, 1900, that established a civilian (albeit limited popular) government on the island of Puerto Rico—a recent possession of the United States as a result of the Spanish-American War. And even with these growth factors, it remained a white man's world.

Oscar's growth should be noted as well. Turning eighteen in June, he was getting bigger, faster and stronger. His first fight of the year, which would ironically take place on Independence Day, July 4, 1900, would be a memorable one. "After I had taken a long rest in which I learned how to shoot big game on a Western hunting trip, I decided to fight a negro," Oscar would state. "His name was Feathers Vernon, and I met him at a picnic which was held in Dalton, Illinois."[3] Just how the match was made, and under what conditions, remains a mystery, but one could assume that there was a substantial side bet. Feathers, aware of Nelson's punching power, would never come close enough to take a fight-ending wallop, which was what Oscar so much desired. The six-round dance ended without a winner, or in boxing what is termed as a no decision. Both fighters would split a $10 purse, or so they thought. Just as the president of the club was handing out payment, a fight broke out and the money was knocked from his hand.[4] In the scramble Oscar lost a bulk of his take but would later brag, "I have fought close to one hundred battles so far, but I had more fun during that scrap than I have ever had since. I licked a dozen negroes during the melee."[5]

Just after that, Oscar was contacted by the manager of the old Star Theatre in Chicago. It was this club that was responsible for his first big break, a chance to step up in competition. In front of a large club, which attracted primarily dedicated boxing fans, he could now hone his skills and hopefully line his pockets. Thrilled at the opportunity, it was hard for Oscar to contain his excitement. On August 30, against Charles Dougherty, a new journey was about to begin. Smart enough to recognize that an initial victory could lead not only to a return engagement but bigger purses, Oscar was more determined than ever to drop his opponent in record time. And that he did. Dougherty was sent to the Promised Land in seventy seconds. A $15 purse—made up in nickels and dimes—was Oscar Nelson's reward for only a minute and ten seconds' worth of work. Not bad for the latest club star. During the remainder of the year, all of Nelson's fights would be held in Chicago.

The First Loss and More

A hurricane, with estimated winds of 145 miles per hour, made landfall in Galveston, Texas, on September 8. An estimated 8,000 people were killed and the city destroyed over the course of several days. The storm continued on and later tracked over the Great Lakes while still sustaining winds of almost 40 mph (as recorded over Milwaukee, Wisconsin) before passing north of Halifax, Nova Scotia, on September 12. The entire country seemed to pause, in thought and prayers, for all those affected by a storm that would become the deadliest hurricane in U.S. history.

Bad weather and boxing, was it an omen? On September 14, 1900, local favorite Joe Hedmark would meet Oscar Nelson. Hedmark, who had not only met some decent competition in the form of Tommy White and Tommy Cleary, had yet to lose a fight and was coming off a twenty-round draw against Tommy Moran in Brooklyn. He would be Oscar's first real opponent. Not only was Hedmark strong and quick on his feet, but he had the advantage in height, weight and experience. And like Nelson, he was equally trying to make a name for himself.

From the opening bell, Hedmark showcased his skills—he stalled to get Nelson to come in on him and then planted a full swing under his chin that sent Oscar sprawling on the floor. Getting up, Nelson, forever the Battler, then went right back at Hedmark. As the second, third and fourth round passed, it was clearly Hedmark's fight. Nelson tried to take him in the fifth, but Hedmark's reach advantage could not be overcome. Following some fierce exchanges in the sixth, the referee gave the fight to Hedmark. Battling Nelson had been given his first loss and a six-round education he wouldn't soon forget. He did however put some credence behind his moniker the Battler, as Nelson was dropped seventeen times during the memorable battle, while Hedmark only five—as if once was not enough.

Lacking proper instruction, Oscar was not seasoned enough as a fighter to understand the obstacles—height, weight and experience—he needed to overcome. Experience speaks on behalf of itself, so let's take a minute and chat about size. A taller boxer not only signifies a reach advantage, but it also implies that his punches are fired downward, which could affect his balance. A taller fighter, especially a novice, also has an inclination to lean forward, which could open him up to uppercuts. To take advantage of these weaknesses required experience and instruction, something Nelson lacked. A shorter fighter does not want his adversary to dictate range, because that is where they can maximize their power. To negate Hedmark's reach advantage, Oscar needed to take the fight inside and to a range that would enhance his power. Solid defensive skills, particularly in the arms and shoulders, will prevent damage, as will good footwork, but Oscar had neither. So he had to depend on his firing power from the inside and his ability to endure Hedmark's punishment. Certainly Oscar could have danced out of Hedmark's range, but that would have been uncharacteristic of the Battler.

Reflecting on the defeat, Nelson would later state, "Hedmark was a combination of Terry McGovern and Dal Hawkins. He was fast as a bullet, strong, shifty, and could hand out a punch like Jeffries. He had it on me in weight, height and experience."[6] Nelson had been licked fair and square. His $15 purse was well earned.

Just a week later the Battler was back at it, this time against Harry Griffin. Later sources revealed that this may have been Young Griffin and not Harry Griffin, so Nelson may have been confused.[7] Despite his previous loss, or because of it, the event drew a larger crowd. Oscar began getting the best of his adversary after the third round and easily picked up the six-round decision. Griffin, much to the chagrin of a partisan audience, did not impress and was even knocked off his feet during the confrontation. For young Oscar Nelson, the $35 purse was his largest yet.

Nelson's only fight during the month of October came on the eighth, at Billy Gain's Logan Square Club, against a crafty fighter named Young Bay. Six rounds later, it was the Battler's hand that the referee chose to raise. Nelson put $10 in his pocket for the event.

On November 2, Oscar Nelson met Clarence Class, a fighter who was determined from the opening bell to never give his opponent a clear target. "Class was fast on his feet, and throughout the fight forced me to chase him around the ring like a six day pedestrian," Oscar would later summarize.[8] The clever footwork of Class enabled him to fight to a draw and split the $7.50 pot.

Two three-round exhibitions, at Eddie Santry's benefit on November 12, were next on Oscar's agenda. Exhibitions often include a reasonable admission charge and give an audience a chance to see a fighter up close and personal. For fighters, it typically means easy money, as they would spar these distances in training anyway, so why not pick up some pocket cash? The Battler would impress and outbox Jack Readle followed by Joe Curtin. If Santry's name sounds familiar, it's because he was a fashionable area featherweight who turned to the political arena; he won the Democratic nomination for the state legislature in September 1916 and was a sponsor of a bill to legalize boxing in Illinois.[9]

One of the colored boxers fighting around Chicago was Black Griffo, his surname a reference in style to Australian Young Griffo. Nelson decided to meet the talented fighter at Silvie Ferreti's place, or Turner Hall, located on the corner of Twelfth and Halsted streets, in Chicago. Griffo would last only three rounds before being dropped by Nelson's "left half scissors hook"—a soon to be trademark punch.

On November 22, Nelson was slated to meet Ed Burley, or as he put it, "Another member of the 'Ham What Am' brand, was selected by the Chicago fight promoters to try his hand and break, if possible, my winning streak."[10] Burley turned out to be a five-round punching bag, Nelson dropping him in the fifth with a solid combination to the jaw. For his efforts, the Battler picked up $10. As for Burley, his name and likeness would surface in 1908 with the publication of Nelson's autobiography. Inside the work, on page 160, was a tasteless cartoon depicting Bat Nelson, "Coon Hunter," standing over the bodies in "Battling Nelson's Colored Morgue." One of the five bodies depicted is that of Ed Burley.[11] As repulsive as this image is today, it is important to point out that racism and bigotry permeated society. It was also a time that saw a black Canadian professional boxer, George Dixon, win the (American) bantamweight championship in 1891 and the vacant world featherweight title in 1892, and again in 1898, to become the first fighter ever, black or white, to win championships in two different weight classes.[12]

Nelson was scheduled for two fights in Chicago on December 1, 1900. The first battle was against Pete Boyle. Having bested Boyle for four rounds, here is how Oscar saw the fifth: "[I] had Boyle hanging on the ropes and all but out, when Mr. [George] Siler sprang forward and stopped the fight."[13] Siler's contention was that Nelson had fouled his opponent, and he gave the fight to Boyle. Nelson was dumfounded, as was the crowd, by the decision. He would later assert, "I had done nothing during the round which warranted me being disqualified. I was paid $25 for my participation in the fiasco."[14]

Siler was not just any referee, but an arbiter who would become one of the finest in the fight game. But he, too, had good days and bad days. He had refereed the James J. Corbett versus Bob Fitzsimmons heavyweight championship fight on March 17, 1897, and was criticized for his slow count over a floored Fitzsimmons in round six.[15] Unforeseen by both Oscar Nelson and George Siler was that they would meet again in a boxing ring.

Nelson was also due to meet Danny McMahon in a four-rounder at the Hibernian Society hall the same day. "I instantly donned my street clothes, grabbed a rattler and in a few moments I was on the spot ready to proceed with my second fight."[16] Both fighters put on an impressive four-round display that ended in a draw. The Battler collected another $5 to add to his daily pot, making it a $30 day. A dubious victory by foul over Jack Percente followed.

In his final ring appearance of the year, Nelson went up against Jack Martin on December 8. From the start it looked likely to be an even match, until Nelson was dropped to the mat for an eight count in the second round. Humiliated, the Battler fought hard from that point forward, dropping his opponent six times during the fight. Later, Oscar was given the six-round victory. For Nelson opponents, it was becoming increasingly apparent that if you intended to embarrass the fighter, you would pay a price.

Having fought twelve fights in 1900, Oscar Nelson added seven victories, two losses, two draws and one no decision to his record. Memorable would certainly be his loss to Joe Hedmark, not to mention his first loss by foul to Peter Boyle, but both were easily forgotten by the enormous exposure he gained from his new venue—as a bona fide member of the Chicago fight scene, confidence, publicity and purses were now a mainstay.

1901

The year begins with a bang as oil is discovered at Spindletop in Beaumont, Texas. The "black gold" creates a mad rush to the southern Midwest. This while America is getting ready to swear in President William McKinley for a second term. The president will get a new vice president during this period of office, Theodore Roosevelt, who replaced Garret Augustus Hobart who died in office on November 21, 1899. Roosevelt, who had always had a passion for the sweet science, served as assistant secretary of the navy under McKinley, resigning after one year. "TR," as his friends would call him, then served brilliantly with the Rough Riders, gaining national fame for courage during the war in Cuba. The flamboyant Roosevelt would become a mentor to many, including Oscar Nelson.

With a third-round knockout of Black Griffo, a repeat of the previous November's performance, Oscar Nelson successfully began his year in Chicago on March 17. He would then

Teddy Roosevelt, Jr., son of the assistant secretary of the Navy and future president of the United States, punching the speed bag inside the gymnasium at the Racquet Club (Library of Congress, Prints and Photograph Division, LC-DIG-hec-43997).

head to Milwaukee to meet Mickey Riley. Oscar, no longer on his home turf, watched Riley dance six rounds to a points victory. The decision did not sit well with the Battler, or with his friends in the crowd, who began shouting various remarks, including the repetitive command of "Speech!" Despite the identical prompting from his own corner, Nelson remained speechless. When he finally gathered the nerve to begin a word, in this case "Gentl-," he was struck squarely in the mouth with a silver dollar. The direct hit induced others in the crowd to withdrawal their ammunition from their pockets and try their luck. Well, it wasn't long before the ring and its periphery were covered with coins. Oscar's seconds—upon Nelson's promise of 10 percent of the take—then scrambled to grab all the coins they could, which amounted to $109.23. Placing a new spin on the old adage "Putting your money where your mouth is," Oscar's take in coin was $98.31, which, combined with his $35 purse, enabled him to send $100.00 home the following morning—a chance, perhaps, to show his parents that the fight game wasn't all that bad.[17]

  The next day found Oscar Nelson in, of all things, Messrs. Sisson and Sewell's, a gentlemen's furnishing store. It was now time, he thought, for a makeover. There he set himself up with a $7 suit, a $1 derby, and a $1.50 pair of shoes. And to cap it all off, a necktie—green, of course. Recalling Thomas Edison's quote, "Opportunity is missed by most people because it is dressed in overalls and looks like work," Oscar saw chance in a pair of trunks, not overalls, and it was work, hard work. While a new suit didn't erase the bitterness of some recent losses, it didn't hurt either.

Photograph showing Theodore Roosevelt on a platform speaking to those gathered in Concord, New Hampshire. Roosevelt replaced vice president Garret Augustus Hobart who died in office on November 21, 1899 (Library of Congress, Prints and Photograph Division, LC-USZ62-7347).

Nelson was back in Milwaukee—a city he would later consider bad luck—to meet Charles Berry on May 3. In this, his first meeting with the fighter, Nelson would battle to a six-round draw. Disappointed by the decision, there was little Oscar could do but pocket the $50 purse and prepare for his next fight a bit further north.

In Omro, Wisconsin, on May 18, Nelson met the scrapper Harry Fails. (I know, it's hard to believe that Harry, as a professional pugilist, didn't alter his surname.) While the six-rounder was bitterly fought, and included some impressive exchanges, it ended in a no decision. Not only did this upset both fighters, but it infuriated a large group of vociferous boxing fans. Sensing the disappointment, management had only one option, a rematch. So another meeting was scheduled for May 24. Well, as often was the case in situations like this, word got to the authorities about the event. "The sheriff of the county came over and told us that if we attempted to fight at Omro he would arrest the whole bunch," Oscar recalled, "and a few might get [tossed] in the pen."[18] Unsure of the severity of the penalty, but convinced that if the sheriff didn't stop the fight he would lose his job, it was high time for most to rethink the battle.

Let's just say that most fighters don't like ultimatums. And why would they? Their conflicts are quickly solved in a ring, man to man. As for boxing promoters, they don't like threats either but consider them part of the business. So an alternate plan was quickly determined and enacted. Everyone, minus those being monitored by authorities, went to work setting up accommodations for just over the county line, which happened to be Rhinelander, Wisconsin. Everything looked promising. That is until Mother Nature had her say and delivered snow—it was the first time that Oscar had ever seen snow in May. Transportation slowed, as most people had trouble seeing 100 yards ahead of them. This left Oscar, sporting his new suit, no choice but to run—his derby collecting as much snow as his shoes—to the new venue.

Once across the county line, it was into a nearby barn where people assumed their positions and began placing their bets. The combatants immediately changed into their fighting togs. The frozen warriors were slowly thawing as they tangled hard for ten punch-filled rounds. In the end, however, it would be the right hands of both fighters that would be held aloft to signal a draw. The referee, whose father just so happened to own the barn, likely figured this was the only way in which the venue wouldn't be torn apart board by board.

"There was no purse to fight for," Oscar would remember, "but the generous sports began showering us with coin." Once divided, which meant[19] in some cases prying up floor planks to grab the money that fell between the cracks, both fighters each had $150. For Oscar's hardship, he treated himself to a new $12.50 suit to replace his $7 iridescent ensemble. He also decided to rest a bit, or as he would state, "I hit the road for a tour of the northern resorts."[20]

In a sign of the times, American anarchist Leon Czolgosz assassinated U.S. president William McKinley at the Pan-American Exposition in Buffalo, New York, on September 6. McKinley would die eight days later. Succeeding him as president of the United States was a young Theodore Roosevelt, a man whose jaunty personality, varied interests, and "cowboy" persona would redefine masculinity.

Nelson's next battle didn't happen until November 10. To get him back into condition, he took a four-round affair with novice Bill Heck in West Pullman, Illinois. While it ended in a no decision, the $5 purse cured any disappointment.

Five days later things were a lot different. Again facing Joe Percente, only this time in Milwaukee, Oscar was determined to beat this pug, even if it was Percente's hometown and it was Milwaukee, a city where he is still to win a fight. Percente, was just coming off a brutal ten-round loss against Adam Ryan, a contest that saw a crowd so incensed against the referee's decision that it stormed the ring in hopes of a human sacrifice. Had it not been for police

The Pullman Industrial Complex, located at 111th Street and Cottage Grove Avenue vicinity in Chicago, took pride in their products, and in their mind there was no competition (Library of Congress, Prints and Photograph Division, il0377).

intervention—it took two hours for them to disperse the crowd—referee Sig Hart, a gentleman whose name will surface again later in association with Jack Johnson, never would have made it out of the venue. This time, six rounds came and went, with Percente given the win. Confounded by his inability to gain a victory in the city, Oscar just shook his head.

In what Nelson would call his first "raw deal," he would do battle against Eddie Santry in Chicago on November 29.[21] Santry was an established and talented featherweight; for Oscar to even be considered for the match spoke volumes for his career at this point—it likely had something to do with Oscar's participation in the fighter's benefit. Although Nelson wanted a ten-round fight, Santry's management insisted on six—Oscar had no choice but to take the fight. The bout, refereed by Jimmy Bardell, would take place in the old Pyramid Athletic Club in Chicago.

From the opening bell Oscar had his way with Santry, battering him side to side while setting the pace for the fight. In the sixth and final round, Nelson sent Santry to the floor with a powerful punch to the jaw. The crowd erupted, as did Oscar, as Santry was all but out. "I noticed Santry saying something as he was falling but I could not make it out," Oscar would later claim. "Imagine my surprise when a minute later Referee Jimmy Bardell grabbed the fallen Santry by the right hand and held it aloft."[22] Santry had won the fight. Everyone, especially Oscar, was dumbfounded by the decision. Dreams of newfound glory were extinguished nearly as quickly as they came. Before the fight Santry had told Bardell the fix was on. Santry would be awarded the decision, but not before allowing Oscar to stay the limit.

"It was a beautiful frame-up indeed—from Santry's end," Oscar would state later. "At the time I was an unsophisticated kid and little suspected that I was being robbed. That's why they put one over me."[23] Incensed, Nelson went to Bardell who confirmed the frame. Following the fight it was back to Milwaukee on December 2 to fight—who else?—Joe Percente, only this time the fight concluded in a six-round draw. After the bout, Oscar made the two-day trip back home to Chicago.

At home, Oscar was playing pool with a friend in a hall on Wabash Avenue. Following a brief exchange—boys will be boys in such an environment—that nearly led to fisticuffs, he coincidentally came into contact with Johnny Hertz, manager of a local fight club. Hertz took a liking to Nelson's style and made him an offer, "Well, I'll tell you, I've gotta fella over here named Mike Walsh, and he was to go on tonight, but the other man failed to show up. If you want to fight you can have the chance. He is a much bigger fellow than you, however. He is a middleweight. If you can make any kind of showing I will give you $75."[24] Delighted, Oscar accepted, dragging the pool hall crowd with him over to the American Athletic Club at Thirty-First Street and Wabash.

Standing six inches taller than Oscar and outweighing him by more than his fair share, Mike Walsh wanted no part in licking a kid, or in this case a nineteen-year-old. But, after some prompting, both fighters slipped into their togs, and into the ring they went. Despite Walsh being tougher and far more experienced, Nelson held his ground. Then, in the sixth and final round, Walsh took a haymaker to the jaw, and out he went. The Wabash poolroom had a different hero, and Oscar had $75 to line his pocket.

The fight year drew to a close on December 17 in Milwaukee, or old "Jonahville" as Oscar called it. Scheduled to battle against the recognizable face of Charles Berry, Nelson reluctantly accepted the fight. Again, Berry stalled, held in clinches and danced out of range. The result, as anticipated, was a decision for Berry. Oscar, with a few more holiday dollars in his pocket, hiked his way back home to Hegewisch to enjoy Christmas.

Seven years later, Nelson would recall 1901 as the "hardest and unluckiest year" of his fighting career.[25] In eleven fights, he would add two wins, four losses, three draws and two no decisions to his record. Memorable indeed was the Santry six-round education and Oscar's first ten-rounder, even if it was in a barn. As for Milwaukee, he wouldn't be back anytime soon, but remember, all fighters are stubborn, and Oscar was resolved to vindicate himself as a boxer to that city.

On Christmas Day, Oscar's father called his son into a tiny parlor for a serious talk—likely this was a conversation Nels reluctantly promised Mary he would have with his son. The Danes in Hegewisch talked; close-knit communities were like that. And although Oscar's skills as a pugilist weren't widely known, they weren't a mystery either. The conversation, as one might anticipate, was an appeal to halt the fight game. Oscar remembered him saying, "Before you leave home you must promise."[26] Well, Oscar couldn't promise, but he did agree to think it over. The family then gathered their things and headed downtown to Dad's Knight Bar, a local Hegewisch hangout. When the Nelsons came through the door, they immediately noticed two fellows arguing. As was typically the case, the quarrel was over who made the better railroad cars, Pullman, home to sleeping cars, or Hegewisch, the worldwide leader in working cars, or flat and freight cars. Well, even during the holidays, such a disagreement doesn't take long to escalate into a "who can lick who" challenge. When the chap from Pullman threw the name Frankie Colifer in the face of the man from Hegewisch, well, the obvious challenger became, you guessed it, Oscar Nelson.

It was then that Oscar witnessed a story he would often recall: "You tink dey got boy over dere vot can beat my boy—vot?" Oscar would recall his father piping up in his broken

English. "My bane a vonder. I bet—I bet—I bet you von tousand dollars," the old Dane said excitedly. "Bat," he said as he turned to Oscar, "you go an' leek dis Pullman boy, and eef you dake a leekin—vell, I leek some myself?"[27] An old man who had just begged his son to quit boxing had a change of heart.

1902

The news traveled fast, throughout both Hegewisch and Pullman. The two boys would meet on January 13, 1902, in an empty barn adjoining Pete Kelley's saloon in West Pullman, for the pride of the region. Scheduled for six rounds, it looked as if the entire two towns—Pullman employees on one side of the barn, and both the Swedes and Danes (Oscar having now made peace with the Swedes) on the other—had turned out. With the battle even into the fifth round, Oscar delivered a shot to the stomach that doubled over Colifer. Then he followed with a cannon to the chin that sent the hope of Pullman flat. But at the count of nine, Colifer somehow managed to get up. It was here that Oscar delivered a sharp right to the jaw that finally put his opponent away for good. The fighting honor of Hegewisch now intact, Oscar took home $50 for the victory, along with a matching share of side bets. Far more important, however, Oscar's corner now included his father.

The injection of family pride and community credence bolstered Oscar's belief in himself. It was back to Wisconsin, this time Fond du Lac, to confront the familiar face of Charles Berry on January 21. Nelson was looking forward to a bit of revenge, having lost to the fighter last December. Convinced that Berry could not beat him in a distance match, Oscar had pleaded for a twelve- or fifteen-round contest. However, in the end, the fight was scheduled for eight rounds and Berry again picked up the decision. Oscar believed it had something to do with him knocking Berry through the ropes and over an eight-foot drop. While Berry wasn't hurt, nor was his manager, Paddy Dorrell, who broke the fighter's fall, the referee, one Tom Ryan of Oshkosh, was none too pleased with the event. For Nelson's display, and defeat, he received $75.

Still a bit under the weather from a severe cold, Nelson finally got Joe Percente to fight him away from Milwaukee on March 13. The eight-round battle, held in Oshkosh, finally saw Oscar at the end of a victory. Four days later, it was back home to Chicago and Kid Ryan, in a six-round feature bout on a lovely St. Patrick's Day evening. As the luck of the Irish had shined last year on this day for Nelson, he hoped it would again, as Ryan was an aggressive fighter. Shutting down Ryan's early rushing tactics with some fierce infighting, Oscar was showing some skill. He then was able to move his challenger back a bit and into range before delivering a masterful series of hooks. The performance enabled him to pick up the lead. The fatal blow came in the fifth, a "left half scissors hook" to the liver of Ryan. The precision blow, inside the American Athletic Club, sent his opponent down for the count. A $75 purse and a sweet side bet made for another memorable Feast of Saint Patrick.

The Nelson trademark blow was a quick hook that lands on the top of an opponent's liver. Unexpected, the blow is so painful that it has a paralyzing effect. As Oscar describes it,

> The left half scissors hook is dealt with the side of the left hand. In coming out of a clinch, fight fans will notice that the left hand of a fighter is withdrawn, as a rule, from under the right arm of the opponent. It is just at this moment that the blow must be delivered. Instead of hitting with the knuckles of the fist I take a

Nelson would credit boxer Joe Choynski for helping him perfect his trademark blow, "the left half scissors hook" (Library of Congress, Prints and Photograph Division, LC-DIG-ggbain-04855).

swing of not more than six inches and plunge the side of my hand with thumb and forefinger on top of my opponent's liver.[28]

Nelson would credit boxer Joe Choynski for helping him perfect the blow.[29]

The following week, on March 21 in Chicago, it was time to greet a cyclone, that of "Cyclone" Johnny Thompson. Scheduled for six rounds in front of the Wabash Athletic Club, while the funnel cloud never set down, he did manage to go the distance—Nelson having given him a sound beating. The Battler picked up the win and the snug sum of $100.

Shortly after the Thompson battle, Oscar received a challenge from William Rosser, the pride of West Pullman. Of course, any Pullman provocation ignited Nelson's interest, so he accepted. To be held in Harvey, Illinois, on April 5, the fight had an added twist. About a week before the bout, while the Battler was training at the White House Club, one Frank Reiger, a heavy gambler who never had much good to say about Nelson, visited him and asked what he thought his chances were. Nelson looked at him and said, "Why, I'll knock him out in one round."[30] Well, that suited Reiger just fine, and he offered the Battler $10 to $1 that he couldn't knock him out that quick. Nelson took the bet and handed an intermediary his $4, while Reiger put in his $40, or 10 to 1. Then Nelson pondered just how in the world he was going to manage to complete such a feat.

The idea was simple, he thought, when both fighters were called to the center of the ring for instructions, instead of going back to his corner, which was customary, he would instead take one step toward his opponent's corner. The trick worked perfectly, as when Rosser stood up, he was in perfect striking distance of a mighty Nelson right to the jaw. Collapsing into the center of the ring, Rosser made two valiant efforts to rise but was unsuccessful. He was counted out then carried to his dressing room by his handlers. Victorious, Nelson would go on to claim that his two-second knockout was the shortest in ring history. Ironically, the same referee, Malachy Hogan, who had worked a record-setting four-second battle in 1897, had also worked this fight.[31]

Following the battle, Nelson was very pleased to be presented with a gold watch by Billy McLatchey, owner of the club where the event took place, for his record kayo, but far more thrilled to collect his $44 from "Noisy" Frank Reiger. Refusing to give ground, Pullman was fast at work trying to find another fighter to take down Nelson. On April 12, 1902, Danny McMahon, a Philadelphia boxer who had met Nelson before (1900), answered their call inside a West Pullman ring. The uneventful six-rounder ended, much to the disappointment of Pullman, in a draw. "It was the closest," Bat would remember, "I came to losing a decision in the town which loves my native Hegewisch like Battling Nelson loves the smallpox."[32]

Only days later, Oscar had an unusual experience. While resting comfortably on the front steps of his home, along came a fellow who stopped and asked if he was "Kid" Nelson. Taken back a bit, Oscar confirmed, "Some call me 'Kid' and some call me 'Battling.'" The fellow then questioned Nelson's ability as a fighter and then proclaimed, "I think I can lick you myself." At which point some fluttering could be heard at the front door as Oscar's father stuck his head out and stated emphatically, "Vot, you dink you kin leek my boy, vot!"[33]

The young gentleman was shown to be Pudden Burns, a citizen of Hegewisch and an auto mechanic. When Oscar instructed him to pick up some money before they talked, the kid reached into his pocket a pulled out a roll of cash. Just like that, Oscar had his next fight.

The neighborhood clash was set for May 17, at the Hegewisch Opera House, a mere block from the Nelson home. The entire town was buzzing with curiosity over the match, Oscar thinking in the back of his mind that the Swedes may have put Burns up for the task. Regardless of who was behind his opponent, a match was a match, and Oscar was hell-bent to win in his own backyard. As it was, Pudden put up a sound defense, despite being outboxed by his neighbor. However, it wasn't enough, and the decision went to the Battler. Burns didn't argue and even confirmed he thought Nelson had won. With $75 for the trick, Oscar Nelson could now stay home for a few more days. More importantly, Oscar had again proven himself to his father, something he so sorely wanted to do. Taking his son aside, and outside the view of others, his father stated, "Go ahead, veen de champeenship!"[34] With that one moment, the name Oscar "Battling" Matthew Nelson took on an entirely different meaning—a son had finally made good.[35]

Revitalized, Oscar Nelson left for nearby Hammond to meet Battling Billy Hurley on June 14. But it didn't take long for his newfound energy to subside, in fact only six rounds, when he was handed a draw for effort. Not only at this event, but on other occasions over the past couple of years, he had concerns about the integrity of the officials. What Oscar saw, felt, and heard during his fights was not being reflected in the decisions he was given. It was now time, he thought, to move on.

The New York Central Railroad inaugurated the Twentieth-Century Limited passenger train between Chicago and New York City, New York, on June 15, 1902. This was just over six months after the country had witnessed a terrible train collision in the New York Central Railroad's Park Avenue Tunnel that killed seventeen and injured thirty-eight. The United States rail system was growing at an incredible pace, no better exemplified than by the Chicago, Milwaukee, St. Paul and Pacific Railroad (often referred to as the Milwaukee Road) that operated in the Midwest and Northwest of the United States.[36] If the heart of the country belonged to its government, then its circulation system was the railroad.

Summer having just begun, Oscar packed up his fighting togs, bundled up his Spalding fighting shoes and bid his family good-bye. He then set out for the freight yards and hopped beneath a rail car on a train heading south. Riding the rods, or the brake beams beneath a railroad car through which the brake shoes operate, was always an adventure and extremely dangerous. Losing his grip, Oscar could fall to the tracks in what would be certain death. But, having heard a few tales about Hot Springs, Arkansas, from its serious interest in sports to the rejuvenating effects of its waters, it seemed like a logical destination. Oscar's concern, however, was the condition he would be in upon arrival. Could his ears take the ringing from

Battling Nelson delivering a solid right to the face of the "Passaic Cyclone," Battling (William) Hurley (Library of Congress, Prints and Photograph Division, LC-DIG-ggbain-04080).

the squeaking sound of iron wheels, and his body the aching from being jolted in every conceivable direction. His days of limited mobility and hunger finally came to an end when he was kicked out from underneath the car. Thankfully, by that time he had reached his destination.

Starved and in need of a roof over his head, Oscar jumped into his $12.50 suit and answered a "waiter wanted" sign he saw posted in the window of a nearby restaurant. Offered the job at $3.00 a week plus board, he accepted on the spot, prepared himself and began working.

"This restaurant was called the 'Ironside,' and I afterward learned that it got the name from the tough steaks which were served at 15 cents a throw," Oscar recollected. "It was a regular hash-slinging joint and I knew there was no chance for tips. The fellows who ate there were lucky to have the 15 cents which was the cost of a regular meal."[37] Only four days into the job, trouble began brewing. Oscar was falsely accused of stealing 15 cents, refused the $3.00 pay he had been promised, and was reprimanded by his manager, Bill Ashton, for not seeing to an ice delivery. This situation, as one might have foreseen, led to fisticuffs with his manager.

Standing an imposing six feet, Ashton lunged at Oscar with his fist. Ducking the assault, Oscar planted a shot to the jaw that knocked his opponent flat. Ashton then grabbed a catsup bottle as he rose and lunged again at Nelson. Oscar relieved him of the bottle and then planted another shot to the jaw. After repeated bottle attempts, the manager then opted for a four-gallon milk pitcher, which he slung and caught not Oscar, but a table of customers. When the dust finally settled and the milk started drying, Ashton was left in a heap on the floor. Before Oscar could gather his things to leave, the owner of the joint came in and had both

The Promenade and Arlington Hotel in beautiful Hot Springs, Arkansas. The first Arlington Hotel, which opened in 1875, was later rebuilt (1892–93) and boasted of its Spanish Renaissance architecture (Library of Congress, Prints and Photograph Division, LC-DIG-det-4a08616).

combatants arrested. The following morning, the judge let Oscar loose and fined the manager $5. With stomach growling and few options available, Oscar returned to work at the restaurant.

"I put in my spare time around the several gymnasiums located in the bathhouses and was in pretty nice shape when things got going," Oscar called to mind.[38] The gym was Oscar Nelson's safe haven—he trained, performed and excelled within its confines. If he picked up a few bucks along the way, by disposing of some pugs or braggarts, then so be it. Practice makes perfect. Billy Maurice, of the Maurice bath, kind of took a fancy to Oscar and let him train in the gymnasium connected to his place. It wasn't long before Nelson managed the connections needed—individuals he had met who were prepared to underwrite his boxing ambitions—to quit his job as a waiter at the Ironside.

Oscar's contacts landed him an introduction to Colonel Andy Mulligan, who was operating the Vapor City Athletic Club. A friend of Mulligan's, Jack Frisby had a fighter—who had also worked as a waiter in town—he felt would match well against Nelson whose name was Elmer Mayfield. When Mayfield challenged Nelson, Oscar accepted; while he had wanted a fight at the twenty- to twenty-five-round distance, Nelson took it at ten. The event, held on December 2, saw Nelson surprisingly push his welterweight challenger—Mayfield had a twelve-pound advantage—around the ring with relative ease, especially during the final three rounds of the battle. Nelson won the decision, along with the hearts of a large group of regional boxing enthusiasts.

The day after Christmas, and in his final fight of the year, Nelson was matched against Christy Williams, a black man. Frankly speaking, little excitement was expected in the match as Nelson's experience far exceeded that of his opponent. But to steal a line from Alexander Pope, "Blessed is he who expects nothing, for he shall never be disappointed." The fight proved to be a barnburner, with Williams knocked down forty-two times to Nelson's nine. Williams, who was finally counted out in the seventeenth round, exhibited incomparable courage. And how he could have lasted against Nelson for that long a period of time continues to be a mystery.

As a result of his eleven fights in 1902, the Battler added eight wins, one loss and a draw to his professional record. He would fight for a total of seventy-eight rounds, seventeen of which occurred in his final battle against Christy Williams. Fighting in both the longest fight of his career, and the shortest, Oscar Nelson made 1902 even more memorable by making new friends, and enemies, in Hot Springs, Arkansas; accepting a fight challenge from the front steps of his home; and not making a match in Milwaukee.

1903

Oscar Nelson would view 1903 as the turning point in his career. "My success in defeating second raters in the several states visited had brought my name and prowess to the attention of the big fight promoters," he would later reflect, "and I found it an easy matter to secure bouts." His upward climb to fame, or "[39] the roped arena" as he called it, had begun.

Following a four-round no decision against George Brownfield on January 3, it was time, Nelson thought, to face a more competitive fighter. So officials at the Vapor City Athletic Club matched him against a western lightweight named Sammy Maxwell. A boxer who had displayed quick moves and solid footwork while training at the club, Maxwell appeared to fit the bill. The fight, planned for January 6, was precisely what Oscar had anticipated. California fighters had a reputation for stalling and fighting foul in clinches, so he sat back and observed until the fifth round, then punished Maxwell during the next five. The tenth-round knockout victory enabled Oscar to get that critical first win of the year behind him.

The first west–east transatlantic radio broadcast was made from the United States to England (the first east–west broadcast was made in December 1901) on January 19, 1903—it was a new link between two countries whose passion for the sport of boxing was unparalleled. Those involved with the fight game however, would have to wait nearly another two decades before this method of communication would impact their sport. Which is unfortunate for many, including Oscar Nelson, whose careers could have been bolstered through the medium.

Adam Ryan, a Philadelphia lightweight, was next to meet Oscar at the Capital Theater in Little Rock, Arkansas, on March 17. Ryan had drawn the likes of Eddie Santry and Ole Olsen, so Nelson knew what to expect. And Ryan, having seen Nelson fight, knew to avoid an inside battle and to keep a watchful eye on Oscar's dangerous left. Relentless in his pursuit of Ryan, Oscar just couldn't put him away, and the fight ended in a fifteen-round draw. Worth noting was that another Ryan was at the fight, namely welter and middleweight champion Tommy Ryan, who was Oscar's chief second and advisor during the bout. As for just how helpful Tommy Ryan was, or what advice he gave, Nelson would not elaborate. But the fact that he was in Nelson's corner speaks volumes about the potential he no doubt believed the fighter possessed.

Not quite twenty-one years of age, Oscar Nelson was still adventurous, still finding out just who he was and what drove him, so to speak. While employed at the Turf Cafe, at Hot Springs he met a potential business partner, and the two of them decided to buy out the owner of the restaurant—that's right, another boxer who thinks that just because he can afford to buy a restaurant, that means he can also operate one successfully. It was Oscar's first big business venture, and he was determined to make it both popular and profitable. But, in his words, "Somehow the fellows didn't seem to be quite so hungry that year as they had the season before, and the business was not near as big as the Waldorf, in New York," Nelson would confess. "As we weren't making much money, I would let my partner run the restaurant at night, and I would go out and fight to keep the thing going."[40]

On April 5, Oscar was scheduled to meet Jack Robinson, or as he would put it, "pull down a little dough to help the restaurant along."[41] But upon arrival at the club, he learned that the event was basically a six-round sparring session and was instructed that nobody must be knocked out. Oscar was livid. The $5 he received for the stint was a pittance, and the event a waste of time. When he hustled back to the restaurant, the fight having been held in town, he found some very peculiar looks on the faces of his employees. Oscar quickly learned that his partner had taken all the money, about $350, and left town. Overwhelmed, he basically handed the place over to his staff to operate. It was, as Oscar saw it, the only way he would be in a position to pay them. When the evening closed, the place was a wreck, as was the remaining owner. Then, just as Oscar was closing the doors and going uptown to search for another job, he received a telegram. Inside was an offer to meet Cyclone Johnny Thompson in Milwaukee on April 24. Having previously defeated Thompson, Oscar believed the offer was easy money. Doing this however, remained the question.

Not wanting to borrow money, nor particularly interested in staying in Hot Springs, Bat headed toward the Little Rock & Hot Springs Western railroad station. Seeing the fast train to St. Louis just pulling out, Bat ran to it, caught it, and assumed his position under the mail car. "I accepted the desperate chance, and though the trip was fraught with many dangers, starvation and pain," Oscar would remember, "I finally managed to reach Milwaukee in time for the fight."[42] Nelson, knowing that he would get hungry, had stuck two sandwiches from the restaurant in his pocket before he left. Although the price was still right, a stowaway risked the chance that they might fall asleep and have a foot drop out of place and into danger. Losing a limb, Oscar would remind himself, was as easy as losing a fight.

According to Oscar's recollection, the train rolled into St. Louis on the morning of April 23. As it backed into Union Station it became obvious that the brakes weren't working, so the end coach struck the steel safety bumpers and tossed Oscar from his iron-ribbed bed— located between the wheels—to the ties below. "The bumpers were strong and didn't give," Oscar gratefully acknowledged. "Had such not been the case I surely would have been ground to pieces beneath the train."[43] A car repairer, who Oscar would later learn was Mike O'Toole, happened to spot him on the ties and pulled him out from underneath the car. Covered in dirt, clothes tattered from every seam, Oscar tearfully pleaded with the angry man not to turn him over to the authorities. The old car greaser, as Oscar called him, felt compassionate and let the boy clean up in a nearby washroom.

As Oscar continued pleading his case, saying he was "Kid" Nelson the boxer, another moniker he had used, and was on his way to Milwaukee to fight Cyclone Johnny Thompson, the old man stood in silence, as if thinking. Suddenly he asked, "Look here, Kid, are you the boy that licked that Ole Olson out at Hegewisch?"[44] When Oscar said he was, a smile rushed across the old man's face.

Gathering a pair of overalls for Oscar, O'Toole even split his morning lunch with the lad before sending the youngster aboard a train bound for his next stop. "The old man even went so far as to tip off the fireman that I was 'Kid' Nelson, the great little Hegewisch boxer," Oscar would pleasantly remember.[45] While the journey didn't cost Oscar a dime, it took a toll on his health, as he was sore and fatigued. Recalling that he had stuck his five spot—the one he had earned as a result of his unexpected sparring session—in his sock, he then headed to his favorite steak joint, Flynn Brothers' restaurant. From there it was off to a ten-cent "flop house," over on State Street, and a bath before bed.[46]

The next morning, Oscar headed off to "Hoo-Dooville," Milwaukee.[47] Since Thompson last met Oscar, he had fought his way up the lightweight ladder in hopes of a big break. Now the odds-on favorite against Nelson, Thompson was "fresh as a daisy from four weeks' hard training on his farm at Sycamore." Both men met inside the ring, exchanged a few words regarding the odds, and got ready for battle.[48] As the bell sounded for round one, instead of staying back like he had done in their previous fight, Thompson went at his opponent. Both fighters tangled repeatedly until the third, when Nelson could sense the fatigue in Thompson. Taking the fight from that point forward, Oscar dominated the final rounds to take the six-round endeavor.

In Milwaukee, on May 22, Nelson met Stockings Kelly. Having heard that Kelly was a decent fighter, Oscar trained hard. The fight was fast paced from the start, but as Kelly slowed, he too became vulnerable. A half left hook to the jaw in the fourth round gave Nelson the knockout win. Milwaukee was slowly redeeming itself in the mind of the Battler, who had now posted two consecutive victories.

For Nelson, it was on to Fond du Lac, Wisconsin, to meet Young Scotty on June 16. In a fight only a Hollywood screenwriter could pen, well, I'll let the Battler explain, "I knocked Scotty out about a half dozen times, and, strange to say, every time I put him down and out the electric lights went out too."[49] Perplexed, Nelson could only assume that Scotty's head hit with such force that it was turning off the electric switch, putting a new meaning to the term "lights out." Scotty, to Oscar's amazement, was able to go the distance. In the end, however, the Battler took the decision and filled his pockets with $125. After the fight, Nelson would learn that the lights were being turned off to save Kelly, not to mention a slew of distance bets. "Nick Finley, who had won several small bets, handed me a crisp one hundred dollar bill, saying, 'You done great Bat,'" Oscar fondly recalled. "Even though they turned out the lights on you. You turned them out on Scotty a few times yourself.'"[50]

Three days later, on June 19, it was back to Milwaukee and Mickey Riley, the same boxer who took a six-round decision from Oscar back in April 1901. Nelson was beaming with self-confidence—three straight victories can have that affect on a fighter. Quite a character, Riley had exotropia—he was cross-eyed—a condition which endeared him to local sports fans but confused his opponents. He was so popular a fighter that his praises were literally sung in a popular early 1900s song titled "Hurrah for Mickey Riley!" and so influential that in 1904 he was featured in a large newspaper advertisement for "Swamp-Root," a liquid concoction, or magic cure if you will, that was "Indispensable for Kidney and Bladder Complaints." One only wonders just how indispensable. For Oscar, it was among those events that just felt peculiar. It was held in the same venue, with the same referee, and the fans looked like they never left. But the decision was different: a six-round draw.

The succeeding night—so much for recuperation time—Oscar was in Harvey, Illinois, where he knocked out Larry McDonald in the fourth round. The pace he was maintaining didn't seem to bother him much—having not lost a fight since January of last year helped.

A week later, Nelson drew Clarence English during a fifteen-round tussle in Kansas City. Which wouldn't have been so bad had he not fractured his left arm at about the midpoint of the contest. English was getting considerable press at the time, so Oscar initially wanted a crack at him in St. Louis to maximize newspaper exposure, but he couldn't swing it, even using St. Louis Browns pitcher Big Jack Powell as an intermediary. When Nelson's only option became Kansas City, he still took the fight. While the fracture slowed the Battler, it didn't stop him.

Mickey Riley was scheduled to meet Nelson again on July 15 at the Eagles' Carnival in Ashland, Wisconsin. Naturally, Oscar knew what to expect from the boxer, so he took the fight. Both fighters gave their all from the opening bell, but the police stepped in during the eleventh round and prevented what Oscar believed was going to be a clean knockout—he had cut Riley's eye and it was bleeding freely, making it hard for him to see incoming punches. Nelson's efforts earned him $150 and, as it turned out, a rematch—manager Poley LaPage of the fight club in Hurley, Wisconsin, loved watching both warriors and desperately wanted a final fight to settle matters. LaPage, to the delight of both boxers, offered up a guaranteed purse of $300 to fight the following week at his club. So Oscar, his new manager Teddy Murphy, and LaPage headed to Hurley the following day.

Ironically, when Nelson and Riley entered the ring for their rematch, they found there were no gloves. A scramble ensued before somebody came up with two pairs of skintight gloves. The gauntlets were believed to have been worn in the heavyweight title fight between John L. Sullivan and Paddy Ryan back in 1882. Taken aback, Nelson looked at the gloves and saw so much dried blood on them that they felt like iron. Maybe they were, Nelson thought. "Of course, the mere mention of the old time gladiators using the gloves stirred our blood up to a fighting pitch," wrote Nelson in his 1908 autobiography, "and how we did tear, maul and slam each other for fifteen rounds." Entertaining but inconclusive, the verdict was another draw.

As for the glove claim, well, when Paddy Ryan finally caved under public pressure and signed articles to meet Sullivan, their February 7, 1882, battle, it was under London Prize Ring rules—no gloves to be worn, of course—and held in New Orleans. As for Nelson and Riley, just the thought of the association was sufficient to enrich the battle. Oscar would always wonder what happened to Riley, no doubt to wage another challenge, or perhaps learn another trick: Mickey preferred to chew on a plug of tobacco rather than wear a mouthpiece while fighting—this gave him the option of using his opponent's eyes as a spittoon.[51]

On August 26, Oscar Nelson, substituting for a sick—or is it slick?—Eddie Santry, met Eddie Sterns in Michigan City, Indiana. Oscar had been relaxing at Pewaukee Lake following his Kansas City engagement when he found Santry there training—both Santry and Nelson were under the same management, and Oscar agreed to substitute for him. The scheduled ten-round fight, at 133 pounds, was a fiasco from the start. "We had $50 up for weight and appearance, but when my manager [Murphy] and I arrived in Michigan City, about noon," Oscar called to mind, "we found that Sterns had taken down his weight forfeit, and, being overweight, also refused to weigh in. Nevertheless, we waived the forfeit, and I went on and fought."[52]

Less than a minute into the brawl, Oscar knocked out Sterns. In fact it looked as if he did so every round up to the ninth. In each instance, Sterns was given at least fifteen seconds to regain his composure and Oscar a warning from the referee, "If you hit him again you will be declared loser on a foul."[53] Finally, a hammering right to the midsection of Sterns doubled the fighter over and he was out—Sterns was carried to his corner by his seconds and the referee and awarded the decision. Nobody could believe it, especially the Battler, and yet the worst was yet to come.

When Team Nelson went to collect their fight settlement, which was $125 regardless of outcome, plus two rail fares and payment for their hotel bill, they were handed only $50. And, even more insulting, he was asked to shut up and "leave town as quickly as possible, or be put into State's prison."[54] Shortly after their hotel bill was paid, Oscar and company, as infuriated as they were fatigued, headed to the train station—about 1:30 in the morning—and began the journey back home.

Just a few days after the fiasco in Michigan City, Oscar was in Flynn's Restaurant chatting with both Will Flynn and the actor Frank Daniels when the discussion turned to Oscar's latest rub. Whether or not Flynn and Daniels felt sorry for Oscar, or they wanted to try their hands at promoting, both put up a fight purse. "Dare Devil" Tilden, described as more of a circus attraction or a stunt man than a pugilist, was their suggestion for Oscar's next opponent. Oscar, intrigued by the description, accepted.

On September 3, at about midnight, those wise to the bout headed to Flynn's Hall on the northwest side of the city. Tilden drew first blood with his very first punch, a shot to Oscar's nose. That of course sparked Oscar, who began rattling off combinations. Before three minutes of fighting had elapsed, each boxer had scored a knockdown. In the second, Oscar fired shots that drew blood and put his opponent down for the count. Nevertheless, at the sight of blood, a female spectator began screaming, "Police! Police! Police!" The lights were doused, and everyone scrambled for cover. When the all-clear sign was given, the two pugilists were back at it, only to have the scene repeated. Later, everyone found out that it was Tilden's "sweetheart" who was responsible for the fight's interruption—humiliation, or is it love, always seems to come at a price. Anyway, referee Will Flynn finally ended the confrontation with a no decision declaration. Each warrior picked up $7.50 for the bizarre affair.[55]

No longer "Hoo-Dooville," Milwaukee, Oscar was back in the city to meet Charles Neary on October 16. Neary, whom Oscar called "the pet of the village," was part owner of the club in which the pair did battle. This, never a good sign, meant there was just one set of rules, his.[56] No outside fighter was ever allowed a victory from him in six rounds, despite whatever circumstances might arise. Oscar, whether on purpose or not, lost his face-off to Neary.

Coincidentally, as if anything in the fight game has ever been anything else, Nelson next met George Memsic, a rising star, in a six-round confrontation in Milwaukee on November 10. The bout would take place at the Badger Athletic Club. A scrapper, Memsic happened to be coming off some impressive battles against Young Corbett, at that time the featherweight champion, and Jimmy Reilly. Milwaukee promoters of the fight thought for sure Memsic would send Oscar to the Promised Land, but they would be mistaken. In six hard-fought rounds, the Battler simply destroyed Memsic and all the associated talk of him becoming the next Young Corbett. This fight, however, would be less known for the victory than for Oscar's effectual use of his trademark "left half scissors hook," the punch having now, through its victims, garnered some attention.

In the final fight of the year, on December 28, Oscar Nelson laced 'em up against Clarence English in St. Joseph, Missouri—the English team's headquarters. In a rematch of their June 27 draw in Kansas City, Oscar hoped to be able to get the better of his opponent. With the odds in English's favor at 3 to 2, Nelson was more than happy to collect the fifteen-round victory. For his troubles, the Battler left with $1,500—that included both his purse and side bets—all of which he sent home to his mother.

Oscar just wanted to spend the remainder of 1903 resting in Hegewisch, which he did and enjoyed every minute of it. To his delight he also received an invitation from the public school to talk to the boys on physical culture. At twenty-one years of age, it marked, at least in his own mind, a departure from one stage of his life into another.

In the busiest year of his professional career, Oscar Nelson had appeared in 16 fights, which included a trilogy with Mickey Riley. In over 140 rounds inside the ropes, he added seven wins, one loss, four draws, two no decisions and two no contests to his career totals. (Since the Tilden affair has not been noted in recognized record books, we will not include it in Nelson's total.) Maturing both as a man and a fighter—despite a few childish pranks and a couple of ridiculous business decisions—Oscar Nelson was also learning in the process. And, let's face it, it is much easier to recoup your losses while you are younger.

Three

1904

Positioning for the Title

> Battling was handed me when I was born, the selection of the splendid name falling to my daddy. I was such a scrappy, lusty lunged, busy child that he decided that there was but one name for me "De Battler" or Battling.
> —"Battling" Nelson[1]

On January 12, 1904, Henry Ford stepped into his automobile and set a land speed record of 91.37 mph; just over a month later, the United States added a commercially crucial piece of land to its control, the Panama Canal Zone; and on April 8, Longacre Square, in Midtown Manhattan, was renamed Times Square after the *New York Times*. Everything seemed faster, bigger and brighter.

Oscar Nelson rolled into Milwaukee on January 16 to take on Artie Simms, or "The Artful Dodger," as Nelson called him.[2] Simms, a lightweight, had been working out of the Midwest, tackling fighters like Tim Kearns and Otto Sieloff. The fight would take place inside the Milwaukee Athletic Club located on the top floor of the Wells Building, or as Oscar put it, "as near heaven as I have ever had a boxing match."[3] Simms, who was taller—only by an inch—and heavier, persisted on rushing his opponent and taking the battle inside during the early rounds. Oscar let himself be pushed around the ring during the first round, but having had enough by the middle of the second, he then turned to the role of aggressor. In round three of the six-round contest, the Battler dropped him not only once but twice, the last time being for good. Oscar hit him so hard that he didn't wake up until the following morning—a concern that worried everyone who witnessed the beating. Such a dramatic conclusion can take a toll on a fighter, and it did on Simms—he would win only five of his next sixteen recorded contests.

Oscar's final Milwaukee appearance of the year, and next to last appearance ever, came on February 5 against Philadelphia featherweight Jack O'Neil.[4] Having won three of his last four fights, O'Neil was quick and packed a powerful punch for a fighter his size. Nobody would understand that better than Oscar, who was delivered to the mat by a right to the jaw not long after the opening bell. Although Nelson was up in a flash, O'Neil insisted on trying to finish him off. Oscar held his ground, and by the sixth round O'Neil was so fatigued he could barely stand. It was Nelson who would take the six-round decision.

Following the fracas, it was off to Utah and the "glorious golden west" as Oscar saw it. There he hooked up with S.J. Kelley, matchmaker of the Salt Lake City Athletic Club, to

Pictured is Henry Ford, founder of the Ford Motor Company, participating in the manly art of chopping wood. This type of activity was often used by the sport of boxing to garner media attention (Library of Congress, Prints and Photograph Division, LC-DIG-npcc-04714).

make his presence known. Kelley was in need of a substitute to meet Spider Welsh, so Oscar took the twenty-rounder purse—to be split 60 and 40 percent—scheduled for April 6.[5] Welsh was quick on his feet, clever and armed with quick straight jabs. "We went sixteen of the speediest and most vicious rounds of fighting the good citizens of the dear old Mormantown ever viewed," Nelson boasted.[6] It was in the sixteenth that Oscar turned up the heat, but he just couldn't put Spider on the floor. "In about the middle of the round, fearing I might kill him, I refused to punish him any longer and appealed to the referee (Willard Beam) to stop the fight," the Battler stated. "At the same time William Lynch, Chief of Police, jumped into the ring to stop the slaughter, and to prevent what looked like the ruination of one of the gamest fighters that ever put on a glove."[7] Welsh was then led to his corner where he collapsed in his chair—the battle was scored as a sixteen-round knockout by Nelson.

It was then time for a quick break, so Oscar took a trip to the copper district known as Eureka and tangled in an exhibition with Tommy Markham. For most fighters, these side trips are easy money and lots of fun, not to mention a great way to increase a fighter's exposure. After the battle with Welsh, fight clubs from all over the country began contacting Nelson, and he believed he was finally at a point where he could set his own terms.

Soon, Alex Greggains, of the San Francisco Athletic Club, offered Oscar a match with Martin Canole.[8] It was the lightweight Canole, as Nelson was aware, that put on an excellent showing in his defeat of the pet of the Golden West, Jimmy Britt. Naturally Nelson bit at the offer, and he, along with his manager Teddy Murphy, started for San Francisco. The fight was scheduled for twenty rounds on May 20. Upon his arrival and signing of the agreement, Team Nelson set up training quarters at the Beach Tavern. Needing a competent trainer, the Battler turned to Frank Newhouse to work with him in his preparation for the clash. Newhouse, a baseball umpire and ex-journeyman lightweight, would later catch headlines in the *New York Times* when he hit New York first baseman Fred Merkle, of "Merkle Boner" fame, over the head with his mask during an exhibition game in 1913 in Zanesville, Ohio.

The evening of the conflict found odds at 10 to 2½ against Nelson. Just after the opening bell sounded, Nelson was greeted at his corner by Canole. There, his opponent launched a left to the jaw that dropped him flat on his back. In Oscar's words, "I thought I had been hit by the Brooklyn Bridge."[9] Irritated, Nelson recovered quickly and it was on with the battle. But by the third round it was evident that Nelson was being outclassed and outpointed by Canole, so obvious in fact that Spider Kelly, who was in the audience, got up and along with about one hundred others left the building. It wasn't until the seventh round that the tide changed thanks to a powerful crack to Canole's liver. Not only hurt, but mad, Canole was now out for blood. "Before he left his corner he rubbed his gloves in the resin, expecting to cut me up by jabbing his gloves in my face," Nelson explained. "That is an old trick of fighters."[10] Notwithstanding the ploy, Nelson dropped his opponent on four or five occasions in the rounds that followed, only to have him saved each and every time by the bell. Finally, in the eighteenth round, a stiff left to the jaw sent Canole down for good.

Nelson would note the battle not for the knockout, but for what he saw as his first temptation or an inclination to "go out with the boys" for a drink. "Something kept saying to me, and it was like the voice of my old mother in Hegewisch," Nelson would clearly recall, "Now, Bat, because you are successful don't go out and make a fool of yourself."[11] The powerful reminder kept repeating in Bat's heads, so much so that he went back to his training quarters for a period of meditation. Finally fighting off the temptation, he went to bed and slept peacefully.

The recent victory prompted the handlers of Eddie Hanlon to challenge Nelson at 130 pounds, or three pounds less than where he was when he battled Canole.[12] Nelson made weight, and the fight was scheduled for twenty rounds at Woodward's Pavilion on July 29. "Not since the Corbett-Britt battle has the San Francisco sporting element been so on edge in anticipation of a fight as is the case today on the eve of the contest between Eddie Hanlon and 'Battling' Nelson, which is to be decided tonight before the Hayes Valley Athletic Club," wrote the *Roswell Daily Record*.[13]

"In one of the fiercest battles ever witnessed in this city, 'Battling' Nelson of Chicago last night defeated Eddie Hanlon of San Francisco in the 19th round," was front page news in the *Rock Island Argus* the following day.[14] After the fifteenth round, the tide shifted to Nelson. Hanlon then struggled. Badly beaten by the eighteenth, Hanlon was saved by the bell. His adversary barely able to answer for the nineteenth, Nelson had the fighter at his mercy. Hanlon was so helpless that the spectators came to his rescue, begging the referee to stop the fight. It was Nelson, by knockout in the nineteenth. Along with several nice side bets, the Battler picked up $1,250 for his efforts.[15]

Dubbed the "Battling Dane" by sportswriter Waldemar Young, the sporting public, along with sports managers from all around the country, were starting to take that Nelson kid very seriously.[16] One such person was Billy Nolan, a crafty matchmaker for the Butte Athletic Club. Wiring Nelson's manager Teddy Murphy, Nolan offered a $1,000 purse for a Labor Day twenty-round battle with Aurelia Herrera. Murphy, like any good manager in this position, did not immediately reply. Instead he started a bidding war between Nolan and Uncle Tom McCarey of Los Angeles.[17] Following three days of debate, Nolan's high bid of $3,500 plus transportation—from San Francisco to Butte, then to Chicago—was accepted.

Herrera—whom many labeled as Mexican, not realizing he was born in San Jose, California—was tough, damn tough.[18] He had defeated every antagonist he had fought in Butte, the site of his conflict with Nelson, and that included fighters like Jack Clifford and Benny Yanger. Ironically, or luckily, depending on your perspective, Herrera had been employed by Nelson as a sparring partner back in Chicago. That's right, for $10 a week he was routinely beaten by the Battler. Both fighters felt this situation would work to their advantage. So the stage was set for what was sure to be a memorable melee, at an open-air arena built exclusively for this event on the flats of Butte. Held in the afternoon of a national holiday, Labor Day, one might anticipate a throng of fans, and one would be correct, the largest crowd ever to see a boxing match in Montana.

In 1908, Nelson would praise Herrera as

> The greatest whirlwind fighter that ever lived. He could hit like a trip hammer and he was so fast that his arms worked like piston rods on the New York Central "Twentieth Century Limited" engine going at the rate of one hundred miles an hour. When least expected his fist would shoot out like the head of a snake and down you would go.[19]

Oscar believed he could beat Herrera if he could stand off his powerful rushes, which he felt certain would take place in the first two rounds. Oscar also knew Herrera could take a punch, and he remembered how surprised Terry McGovern was when he hit Herrera on the point of his jaw and it did nothing. McGovern said, "My mitt bounded off like a pebble and he came right back at me."[20] Nelson needed to remember, to be as cautious as he was determined.

If Herrera had a weakness, it was his lack of training, cigars and whiskey. He seldom trained, ran with a cigar in his mouth, and took a belt of whiskey whenever he felt the calling. With a stocky build, huge shoulders and a chin like cement, he fought his fight his way, often a death warrant for his opponents.

Nelson arrived early for the fight, around 2:00 p.m. There had been talk, as there often was in a match like this, that the authorities might stop the fight. When he arrived, Herrera was already there puffing on a cigar. Both fighters were full of confidence and exchanged a friendly handshake.

Following a brief delay, one of the boxing officials informed each participant that everything had been worked out—confidential covenants not rare occurrences in fight promotions with the state authorities—and that the fight could take place as scheduled. With this word, both fighters lost little time getting to the enclosure.

Herrera was first into the ring, to the applause only a favorite might bring. Nelson followed soon after to a much milder cheer—the Hegewisch hopeful viewed as an outsider.

Bat kept his distance right from the start, but following a clinch in the fourth round, he was struck squarely on the top of his head. "I felt as if somebody had hit me with a sledge hammer," Nelson grumbled. "I turned a complete somersault and fell flat on my back, my head hitting the mat first."²¹ When Oscar opened his eyes, all he could see was Herrera standing over him like a vulture, this while he was taking the count. Regaining his footing, Nelson tried to compose himself as Herrera rushed toward him. But Oscar stood firm and even managed to deliver his left half scissors hook into his opponent before the bell. "I did my best, but I could not succeed in knocking him out," Nelson asserted. "The latter rounds were all my way, and at the end of the twentieth I had piled up such a lead that I was handed the decision on a silver platter."²² As referee Duncan McDonald made the incontrovertible announcement the crowd cheered in affirmation.

Nelson v. Corbett II, November 29, 1904

After the fight, Oscar hurried over to the local poolroom where he had placed $1,000 on himself. Collecting nearly $2,500 on his bet, plus the fight purse, left the fighter feeling rather well. Oscar, along with Teddy Murphy, a string of sparring partners and trainer Frank Newhouse, then boarded a special Pullman bound for San Francisco. On the train, conversation centered on Oscar's next prey. Now in direct line for the championship it was time to pursue the best the sport had to offer. When the train pulled into San Francisco, Team Nelson learned that Young Corbett, who had lost his title to Jimmy Britt, was in town, but Oscar wanted to fight Britt, so off they went to find the hometown lightweight.

When Nelson's contingent discovered James Edward Britt, he made himself perfectly clear: "Go and get a reputation for yourself."²³ A cruel statement from some perspectives, but this was boxing and Britt was in a superior position, or to borrow Thurber's yet-to-be-coined line, "the catbird seat." There was simply no way Britt would fight Nelson until he licked Corbett.

Hitting a dead end, it was then time to find Corbett. His delegation wasn't uncooperative, but they were exasperating, as were club officials. Finally, an agreement was worked out to fight on November 29, at Woodward's Pavilion in San Francisco.

As for the details, "They are to fight for 55 percent of the gate, to be split 60 and 40. The fact that Nelson insisted on 40 percent for loser shows that he realizes that he has a hard task before him. They are to weigh in at 6 o'clock on the night of the battle and each must make 130 pounds."²⁴ By the time most of this information found its way into the papers, Team Nelson had been in Chicago and were planning to leave for the coast as soon as possible. Teddy Murphy actually had a bit of a scare when he heard a rumor that the fight was off— so scared in fact that he wired a long telegram to Billy Roche, the matchmaker of the Hayes Valley Athletic Club to confirm that the fight was still on. Murphy was advised to keep cool and pick up his railroad tickets that had been ordered. As for the fighters' training, Corbett will do his at Sheehan's and Nelson will work at "Smiling" Metzner's in Larkspur.

William H. Rothwell, or Young Corbett II, entered the world on October 4, 1880, in Denver, Colorado. Turning professional in 1896, Corbett²⁵ hit center stage—although he was a well-known Colorado powerhouse—when he defeated the great George Dixon, "Little Chocolate," on August 16, 1901, in Denver. To put the triumph in proper context, Corbett was just coming off victories against Eddie Santry and Oscar Gardner, both sound fighters, while Dixon, having dropped two defeats to Terry McGovern, had recently battled Benny Yanger and Harry Lyons. Dixon went right out against Corbett, but his aggressive style was subject to a barrage of body shots. Targeting Corbett's eyes and head, "Little Chocolate" considered them his most vulnerable areas. The tremendous pace of the fight, not to mention the inflicted damage, left both fighters a bloody mess by the tenth round. The controversial decision, as some may have anticipated, went to Corbett.

This victory put Corbett in direct line with reigning champion Terry McGovern. On November 28, 1901, Young Corbett II would meet Terry McGovern at the Coliseum in Hartford, Connecticut, for the world (126 pounds) featherweight title. Before the term "trash talk," or insulting or boastful speech intended to demoralize, intimidate, or humiliate someone, there was the swaggering resonance of "Corbett Chatter," or, as Terry McGovern experienced, the ridiculous rhetoric of an arrogant hopeful—no doubt affected by the thin mountain air of his hometown—screaming insults regarding his mother at the top of his lungs outside his dressing room door.[26] Corbett fought McGovern's fight, or a successful retaliation that put his opponent within perfect range. In the second round, Corbett floored McGovern, who got up and floored Corbett, before a vicious skirmish ensued, or what many would call one of the greatest rounds ever seen, until a fabulous right hand by Corbett ended McGovern's night. It was a stunning upset. Corbett also stopped McGovern in the rematch on March 31, 1903 (KO 11). Corbett would defend his featherweight world title at 130 pounds, but Abe Attell was now recognized as the true world featherweight champion at 122 pounds as the dynamic world of boxing classes turned. Jimmy Britt would take Corbett's title, and with that it is now back to Nelson v. Corbett.

To no surprise, Woodward's Pavilion was jammed with fight fans, and the betting, often an early indication of any foul play, was brisk—the heaviest of any contest since the Britt—Corbett battle a year ago. With no championship on the line, what was certain was that the winner would meet Jimmy Britt in San Francisco the following month. Corbett, who had undergone a severe course of training since coming into camp at 146 pounds, weighed in at 130 pounds. Nelson also weighed in precisely at the 130 mark. Corbett was the odds-on favorite, and even money had him disposing of Nelson in from 12 to 15 rounds.

Corbett's team included manager Harry Tuthill and seconds Frank McDonald, Billy Otts, Benny Carson and Tim McGrath. Team Nelson included manager Teddy Murphy and seconds Frank Rafael, Dan Danziger and Jack Kelley.

At 9:46 p.m., the announcer introduced the "hardest nut to crack" in the fighting game, Battling Nelson, followed by "one of the best boys in the West," Young Corbett. The latter, to no surprise, garnered the popular ovation. Jimmy Britt was then introduced and announced that he was ready to meet the winner of the contest. Bill Roche, formerly of New York, would referee the evening's feature. The final introduction, or the protocol announcement, was that of Mike J. Fisher, manager of the Tacoma baseball club, winners of their league championship. "Though I felt confident when I stepped in the ring with the great slugger," Oscar admitted, "I knew that I had a job before me."[27]

At 9:55 p.m., following the traditional fight photographs, both men went to the center of the ring for instructions by the referee. They then returned to their corners and awaited the clang of the bell for round one.

A glance at the battle in five-round stages. Round one was uneventful as both fighters spent a majority of their time sizing each other up; Round two saw some nice exchanges, many at close quarters. Nelson had drawn first blood as Corbett was bleeding from the mouth when the bell sounded. The fight according to most remained even. Round three began with each fighter exchanging a left to the head. Nelson then landed a strong combination with Corbett now on the ropes. Corbett winced following a combination to his head and it sparked retaliation by the fighter, featuring two heavy rights to Nelson's jaw. The pace of the round was much faster. Round four opened with a Nelson right to the head. Corbett then missed a selection of punches before being forced to the ropes, then around the ring. Nelson was now in control of the fight. The men exchanged some vicious combinations before the end of the round. When the bell sounded, Nelson looked a bit dazed. Round five saw the exchanges slow a bit. Again, Nelson put Corbett to the ropes, but the latter fought his way off. Two lefts to Corbett's face, near the end of the round, started his nose bleeding.

Round six began at close quarters. Again, Nelson forced Corbett to the ropes, and again, Corbett battled his way off. Nelson drew blood from Corbett's nose and mouth, then followed with a solid blend of punches. Corbett was fighting back wildly, while Nelson was landing at will. As the bell sounded, a series of Nelson combinations to Corbett's face drew blood from his nose. Round seven began at close quarters with the advantage all Nelson's. Corbett did manage a nice right to Nelson's jaw, but the Battler returned two for one. Corbett kept coming back strong until Nelson caught him with a right to the jaw that left him groggy. It was then into the ropes for Corbett, who now had blood streaming from his mouth and nose. Corbett was so weak when the bell sounded that it was difficult for him to get to his corner. Round eight broke again at close quarters, Nelson raining blows at Corbett's face at will and opening afresh his wounds. Corbett missed several desperate swings as Nelson pegged away mercilessly at his face. Nelson did take a solid right to the face but fired back a crushing right to Corbett's jaw. Nelson's uppercuts were savage as he continued to batter his opponent's face. Just before the bell sounded, Corbett landed a right to Nelson's jowl. Round nine opened with Corbett missing a combination but receiving a solid one in return. In the mix Nelson kept driving his left to the face and his right to the body. Once more, Nelson forced Corbett to the ropes, then toured the ring, landing punches at will. Corbett looked helpless and was having difficulty protecting himself. Nelson was landing some ruthless combinations to the face of Corbett when the bell sounded. It looked, according to some, like Corbett was motioning his seconds to throw up the sponge. As the tenth and final round opened, Nelson went right at Corbett, who had no other choice but to hang on to his opponent. As Corbett fired back wildly, Nelson again took him to the ropes while throwing a heavy blend of punches to the face. At this point, the crowd started yelling, "Stop it." As Nelson went for Corbett, who was now barely standing, his seconds threw up the sponge. Corbett, with blood streaming from his nostrils, mouth and ears, was then carried to his corner in utter defeat. As the crowd cheered, a triumphant Nelson left the ring with scarcely a mark.

It took only four rounds with Young Corbett for Oscar Nelson to realize that he could win the championship if given an opportunity. Corbett was, as Oscar saw it, a slugger, a terrific hitter, a smart boxer and one of the greatest fighters this country has ever seen. Corbett's strength—no better exemplified than with his battles against Terry McGovern—was his ability to intimidate his opponent. If, Corbett believed, he could take his opponent out of his fight plan, he could reduce his mental efficiency. A fighter who reacts physically—throwing ill-timed or wild punches, often from a position of weakness—loses his strategic advantage.

"You can take it from me that Corbett gave me an awful fight for the first few rounds," Nelson elaborated. "If the decision had been given on points at the end of the fourth round

I guess he would have been the victor."[28] It took that amount of time for Oscar to discover Corbett's weakness, his wind. Corbett did not have the endurance to beat Nelson.

Oscar's strategy was to take the fight to Corbett's body with shots to the ribs, then, when possible, a left half scissors hook to the liver. Once bent over, a crack to the ear would throw Corbett off balance.

Corbett's strategy was to rush his opponent, "shooting his arms out like piston rods."[29] While in close he would then begin his strategy of intimidating remarks, such as "Whoever told you that you could fight?" or "Why, you're a joke."[30] His strategy did not work with Oscar "Battling" Nelson.

Nelson v. Britt—December 20, 1904

His desire to lick Britt "was because he wore a high hat and a Prince Albert coat," Nelson somewhat fictitiously remarked. "It may sound like a 'kid,' but, on the level, it made me awful sore to see a prizefighter going around in those swell togs, and I made up my mind that some day I would bring him down to the class where he belonged."[31]

"In those days," Oscar continued, "it was somewhat of a job for a fighter to lick Britt because he always fought on the coast, and to get a decision over him on points out there was like trying to slip the Washington monument through the eye of a needle."[32] Which was a pretty good analogy.

James Edward Britt joined the world on October 5, 1879, in San Francisco, California.[33] Turning pro in 1902, he stood five feet five and half inches tall, with a reach of sixty-five inches.[34] His accession into the ranks of the lightweight division was brisk and impressive: on May 29, 1902, he defeated George "Kid" Lavigne in San Francisco, the *Los Angeles Times* reporting that Lavigne's left arm was broken in three places; on November 26, 1902, he knocked out Frank Erne in the seventh round to claim the "white" 135-pound title and disposed of Young Corbett II in March.

In his last fight, on October 31, 1904, he met the legendary Joe Gans at Mechanic's Pavilion in San Francisco. With the world lightweight (133 pounds) title on the line, Britt dropped Gans four times; however the final time he hit his opponent, it was as he was rising, and thus he was disqualified. Nelson believed that "the minute he [Britt] saw the black fellow [Gans] in the ring he practically threw up his hands and admitted defeat."[35]

Although Nelson thought Britt didn't hit hard, he did have a worthy punch. It was a low left-hand swing that was half uppercut, half hook, and it could rip into a fighter's body and destroy his incentive.

The weigh-in was to take place at Harry Corbett's, on Ellis Street, at 6:00 p.m., but it attracted such a large gathering that it had to be moved to the Hamman baths. Britt balanced the machine at the 132 pounds notch, while Nelson, who was naturally lighter, tipped in at 131¼ pounds.

At 9:45 p.m., it was announced that the fighters were en route to the ring. Leading the way was Jimmy Britt, who received a loud cheer, followed by his seconds: "Spider" Kelly, Tiv Kreling, Curtis Richardson and Frank Rafael. Then came Nelson and his seconds: Teddy Murphy, Stockings Kelly, Marvin Hart and Eddie Santry. The fighters shook hands and went to their respective corners to "glove up." A half dozen posed images followed as part of the traditional pre-fight photo shoot. Dressed in a high silk hat, tuxedo and white silk vest, referee Billy Roche entered the ring as if it was his wedding. Introduced as "the famous Bowery boy," he smiled as he removed his fashionable white gloves—he took a good-natured chaffing from the crowd to which Roche answered with an arbiter's grin.[36]

The powerful voice of Billy Jordan then carried over the crowd as he announced the participants: "The Chicago crackajack, the hardest nut in the profession to crack, 'Battling' Nelson." As the cheering just started to subside, "The champion of champions, Jimmy Britt."[37] Cheers quickly restored to a roar, but slowly subsided with the announcement of provocations.

As challenges were read from Jabez White of England and Jimmy Gardner of Lowell, not to mention some lesser-known lights, the crowd grew restless until they spotted the familiar sight of Young Corbett. To cheers of his name, the little fellow then entered the ring to an incredible ovation. Corbett also challenged the winner and shook hands with the participants.[38]

Called on to say a few words, Corbett addressed the crowd: "Ladies and Gentlemen," causing a laugh to arise as there were only a handful of the fairer sex ringside, "I am glad to have friends left. I suppose you have to lose to find that you have friends. I will, if I get a chance, try to win back my title."[39] Again, more cheers.

The fighters were then called to the center of the ring for instructions. Jordan then announced, "The men will fight straight Marquis of Queensberry rules, break by order of the referee and protect themselves in the break-away—let 'er go."[40]

Bell sounded, fight on.

In a nutshell: Jimmy Britt outboxed Oscar Nelson from the start and was able to go the full twenty rounds by refusing to engage Nelson at his strength, that of infighting.

The early rounds were marked by Britt's willingness to hold at every opportunity. Since he certainly didn't need to, one can only assume Britt was trying to take Nelson out of his rhythm, or trying to find a comfortable pace for himself. Britt's ring generalship was evident from the start, always maintaining his composure despite the circumstance—far different from his battle against Joe Gans. After the first few rounds, and definitely by the tenth round, it became clear that Britt could not knock out Nelson—his combinations to the fighter's jaw were ineffective. And Britt just couldn't accept it, so he delivered an attack on his opponent's head in the twelfth. The attack again proved fruitless. Nelson took the assault and then waited. As soon as he was certain his opponent had expended his energy, Nelson turned on the Californian and nearly put him away. Britt was hanging on the ropes when the bell sounded. Nelson, whose bulldog tenacity had always been an asset, followed his target like a cat watches a birdcage. And Britt knew enough to stay out of range.

Britt's plan, or at least that of his corner, was to systematically outpoint Nelson. He saw what happened to Corbett when he tried to mix things up with Nelson, so that didn't make much sense. Staying out of reach made far more sense.

One newspaper account claimed, "Up to the seventh round Nelson had not landed an effective blow, although he was never idle for an instant in all that time."[41] It was then that Nelson sent a right to the jaw of Britt that appeared to hurt the fighter. Seeing this, Nelson commenced an attack that left Britt badly off before the end of the round.

Nelson's plan was to wear down his opponent, something he appeared to have accomplished by the eighth round. The ninth round was all Nelson, as was the tenth. Britt held as much as possible in the eleventh to gain a slight respite from the beating he was enduring.

As mentioned, Britt picked things up in round twelve but was lucky to be standing when the bell sounded. In the thirteenth, Britt effectively targeted Oscar's nose, which began to bleed badly. Nelson slipped to the floor during one of the mix-ups, but he was up in an instant.

From the fourteenth on, both fighters presented a gory appearance. When Britt rushed in at the opening bell, Nelson butted him over the left eye and cut him severely. Using his left, the Battler focused on the head but wasn't landing. This while Britt was using his left to keep Nelson's nose bleeding.

Britt again targeted the head in the fifteenth—did I mention that Britt failed to accept that he could not knock Nelson out? To no avail. Nelson continued to bore in. When Britt ducked one of Oscar's wild swings, he lost his balance and fell on his back. Up in an instant, Britt then tried to hold off Nelson. It was then that one of Nelson's blows went low and nearly stopped Britt in his tracks.

From most accounts, the sixteenth round was an act of desperation for both fighters. Nelson sprang from his corner to bombard Britt, backing him into the ropes before assaulting him with combinations. When Britt slipped out, both fighters stood in the middle of the ring to exchange blows. "I had been walking into Sir James without ever guarding a blow, trying to get him to swap punches, and this was my first opportunity to get him," Oscar would affirm.[42]

The seventeenth round opened like the sixteenth, only Britt did a better job avoiding the punishment. Nelson was shaken by a combination to the head, but Britt couldn't take him down.

Britt pulled back in the eighteenth, staying out of Nelson's range and dancing out of danger. This said, he did manage a devastating left to the body and a right to the head that would have stopped an ordinary fighter, but the Battler was far from ordinary.

Certain by the nineteenth was that Britt was playing for a decision. This action was dangerous if he wasn't convinced of the scoring, despite knowing that he was far less impressive in the earlier rounds. Nelson took three hard rights from Britt this round but just shook them off. Just before the bell, the Battler sent Britt back with a right to the head.

As is almost always the case, when you are playing for a decision, you must come on strong in the final round, this in order to leave a lasting impression on the judges. Though Nelson delivered a sound combination to Britt's chin, the round belonged to Britt, who seemed to land twice as many punches as his opponent.

When the final bell sounded, referee Roche led Britt to the side and pointed to him as the winner. There was no demonstration with regard to the decision.

As for the reactions, we will begin with the winner on points:

> I figured I could win from Nelson the way I fought him. Now, what is the use of a man being in the fighting business if he does not fight the way he knows he can beat a man? I knew I could beat him in such a battle and I carried out my plans accordingly. Nelson is a great slugger and an aggressive man. But, I think I could have outslugged him if I cared about fighting that kind of battle. My friends had their money on me and I wanted them to cash, so I took no chances. Nelson is a great fighter and the pace he makes is terrific. You can judge for yourselves if I don't look like I can go twenty rounds more. The cut over my eye was caused by Nelson's head. It was not from his glove. I was never in any danger at any time. As a fighter Nelson deserves credit and it will take a good man to beat him. —James Edward Britt[43]

As for the referee:

> I declared Britt winner because he was entitled to the decision. He did the cleaner fighting and outpointed Nelson in every round. Nelson was aggressive throughout the contest, but this does not entitle a man to a

victory if the other man does the cleaner hitting. Britt and Nelson were equally guilty of holding. I had my hands full trying to separate them and did not attempt to give either man the better of the breaks. A few wild swings landed on me. I never saw such speed and cleverness as Britt displayed. He is a great boy. Nelson is also a wonder of aggressiveness. Where he gets his vitality is a marvel to me. I would like to see the winner fight Young Corbett, provided Corbett is in condition. I am glad the public approved of my decision. It was an honest one and was given to the man that earned it.—Referee William Roche[44]

As for the loser by decision:

I am not the sort of fellow to make a holler, but at the same time I want to put myself right. I really believe I was unjustly treated by Roche. I chased Britt all over the ring in every round and fought every moment of the time. I never was in danger and took all his punches without flinching. The best he did was to jab me. I roughed it continuously and did everything in my power to fight a winning battle. I am willing to meet Britt again under the same conditions, only I positively insist on George Siler as a referee. I think he is the only man in the business who really knows how to judge a fight on its merits. I am willing to fight Britt again for a $5,000 side bet, but not with Roche in the ring with us. I will knock Britt out if we ever come together again. —Battling Nelson.[45]

Oscar's wounded feelings dissipated somewhat when the officials handed Teddy Murphy a stack of greenbacks totaling $5,600, the most the fighter had received for one fight up to that point. The fight, like any contest of this caliber, would linger in his mind for some time, constantly replaying itself to Oscar's indomitable self-evaluation.

The following morning it was time to settle up with Teddy, so Oscar set out to find him. When his efforts failed, the fighter grew concerned. Only recently, Murphy had a problem being timely with Oscar's earnings, and this looked like a repeat of that scenario. When the fighter finally found him, Murphy spilled excuses like a drunk on a bar stool, but both agreed to meet the following day. Well, when Oscar went to the designated spot the next day, Teddy never showed.

Nelson then figured that Murphy was at the ferry seeing off Eddie Santry on his departure to Chicago. That proved correct, as both Santry and Murphy were checking their trunks. A bit shocked to see Nelson, Murphy then delivered a tale that he was there merely to see Santry off. Oscar, having an evening dinner appointment, couldn't cross the bay with the two, so he headed over to Harry Corbett's for his mail. Whether Murphy told Nelson he had a payment there or not is uncertain, but the fighter did find an envelope on the top of a cash register with his name on it and in Murphy's handwriting.

Upon opening the envelope, Oscar found a note along with a hundred dollar bill. The note stated that Murphy had been called home due to a sickness in the family, along with a few other excuses that Oscar just wasn't buying. Now certain that Murphy took off with his bankroll, Nelson took off for the police station. At the precinct, Police Chief Burnett wired instructions to Stockton, California, advising the authorities there to arrest both Santry and Murphy. Detective Taylor then brought Santry and Murphy back from Stockton. Upon their arrival at the hall, the judge ordered Santry released on his own recognizance. Murphy was released on $4,000 bail, which was quickly furnished by Zack Abrams and David Sullivan.

The money, which was placed in charge of the property clerk at the Police Department, became a bone of contention with Nelson who wanted the cash now. Murphy contended that Nelson was entitled to between $3,500 and $3,700 dollars; the rest, as he saw it, belonged to him. The issue was eventually cleared up, and it was then that the fighter broke all ties with Ted Francis Murphy.

In Nelson's autobiography, he printed a letter written by Professor Mike Donovan to

George Siler. The latter, for whatever reason, then mailed the letter to Nelson in Hegewisch. In the note Donovan asserts that Nelson's climb, though meteoric, could also have been a tragedy. He then bisects Nelson, telling of two primary objectives as reasons for fighting: "to pay his mother's home on Superior Avenue in Hegewisch, and to win back the love and admiration of his father, brothers and sister."[46] Donovan then confirms—how he would happen to know is not stated—that Oscar has always had the love of his mother, this despite her not approving of his occupation for fear of him getting hurt. As for Oscar's father, the fighter did not want him to worry about debt. By eliminating this concern, Donovan thought Oscar was thinking, his father could focus on the education of the other children and keep them away from the fight game. It was an interesting observation from the former middleweight boxer of the bare-knuckle era and boxing instructor. Donovan also included a poem of admiration from poet John Wallace Crawford. As for its inclusion in Oscar's memoirs, one can only assume Oscar Nelson liked the letter.

Enlightening is the end of the year assessments that were commonly found in every newspaper during the month of December. The *Saint Paul Globe* published one such piece in which they interviewed veteran boxer Billy Edwards. So, who is the real featherweight champion? "I can't understand how Young Corbett or Jimmy Britt or Battling Nelson ever had any claim upon it. They are too big. I think the real title holder has never been beaten at the weight, 122 pounds, and that if he can still do 122 pounds at ringside he is still the featherweight champion."[47] Of course this refers to Terry McGovern, who went out of his class to meet Young Corbett. Just because McGovern lost to Corbett doesn't, in Edwards's mind, relinquish the feather title.

Edwards then goes on to provide his history of the weight class distinctions and adds an interesting personal account: "I remember well that when I won the lightweight championship by beating Sam Collyer, in 1868, the lightweight limit was established at 112 pounds, ringside at that. You see, among such very little men a difference of two pounds, or even one pound, is a very great handicap, and if a fellow who naturally weighed 114 pounds could starve down to 112 three or four hours before going into the ring and then eat a meal and put on a couple of pounds he would have a great advantage over a man whose natural weight was only 112."[48] In his day anyone who weighed more than 112 pounds was called a lightweight. When Edwards won the lightweight championship, he weighed only 120 pounds, while Collyer was only 124.

"A new arrangement of classes among fighters was made about twenty years ago [around 1884]," Edwards continues. "It was ridiculous to make a 120-pound man fight as a lightweight against a 130-pound man, or 140-pound man against a 155-pounder as a middleweight. So the best men in the boxing game got together and arranged these classes: bantamweight—anything up to 112 pounds; featherweight—anything up to 122 pounds; lightweight—anything up to 133 pounds; welterweight—up to 144 pounds; middleweight—up to 158 pounds; all above that heavyweight."[49] Edwards then speaks to the possible formation of the light heavyweight division scaling up to 165 or 170 pounds. "It is very necessary, too," Edwards continues, "for the cleverest 170-pound man in the world wouldn't have a chance with that wonderful champion, Jim Jeffries, who fights at 230 pounds."[50]

Edwards then refreshed everyone's memory regarding McGovern's victories, over Palmer at 115 pounds and over Dixon at 118 pounds. "McGovern was beaten, but he was beaten by a lightweight. Therefore, he could not lose his championship in that battle. How could he?"

Edwards contends.[51] "No one," he states with conviction, "fighting above 122 pounds can be the featherweight champion."[52] There is simply no point in discussing anyone weighing 133 pounds as the featherweight champion, when the real champion is Terry McGovern.

Edwards, who provides this fascinating viewpoint, was born in Birmingham, Warwickshire, England, on December 21, 1844. A standout lightweight of the late 1860s and 1870s, he began boxing at the age of 14 and was quick to find success. Edwards registered a 34-round win for the lightweight championship of America in 1868 with his defeat of Sam Collyer. He then retained the title in a rematch with Collyer, drew Tim Collins, and lost on a foul to Arthur Chambers. Fighting a couple more times, he then lost to Charlie Mitchell in 1884. Following the Mitchell bout, he retired from the ring but remained close to the sport by training John L. Sullivan. Edwards died in Brooklyn, New York, on August 13, 1907.

At a glance, boxing's seven weight divisions were filled with outstanding champions in 1904—all but one division, that of the bantamweights, was occupied by a member of boxings' elite class.

Atop the heavyweight division is James J. Jeffries, who on August 26, 1904, put away Canadian Jack Monroe in the second round of their title fight in San Francisco, California. For Jeffries, the battle with Monroe would be his seventh and final title defense.

Ruling the light heavyweight division was that of Robert James "Bob" Fitzsimmons. In 1904, he would fight only one battle, against Joseph Francis Hagan (better known as Philadelphia Jack O'Brien). Fitzsimmons would put away his opponent in the sixth round of their battle at the Baker Bowl in Philadelphia, Pennsylvania, on July 23.

At the front of the line in the middleweight division was Tommy Ryan. Fighting eight times in 1904, including bouts against "Philadelphia" Jack O'Brien and Jack Root, Ryan did not lose a battle—the contest with O'Brien ended in a no decision, while the battle with Root was a no contest. Still impressing many, though coming to the end of his career, Ryan knocked out five of the eight he faced.

Still impressing many, though coming to the end of his illustrious career, middleweight Tommy Ryan knocked out five of the eight he faced in 1904 (Library of Congress, Prints and Photograph Division, LC-DIG-ggbain-08063).

The welterweight championship was held by Barbados Joe Walcott.[53] Fighting eleven times in 1904,

Walcott would experience one of the most memorable years of his life. He defeated Charlie Haghey, then fought a no decision—although the newspapers believe the fight went to Bill— against Black Bill, before meeting the Dixie Kid to defend his championship. Walcott was disqualified for a kidney punch against Kid—although Walcott had been landing them throughout the battle with no warning of foul—so the contest entered *The Ring Record Book and Boxing Encyclopedia* as a loss by foul. According to the latter source, the two warriors met again on May 12 and fight to a twenty-round draw. Walcott then drew Sandy Ferguson before getting knocked out by Young Peter Jackson in June. Finishing the month of June with a victory over Mike Donovan, Walcott then drew Larry Temple and Sam Langford before fighting to a no decision against Dave Holly. In the final conflict of the year, Walcott battled Joe Gans to a twenty-round draw. Then, on the final day of the year, Walcott accidentally shot himself in the hand, effectively ending his days as a top prizefighter.[54]

The incomparable Joe Gans sat on his throne over the world lightweight championship having gone undefeated in thirteen battles during 1903. Winning ten consecutive bouts before a no decision to Dave Holly, he would draw Joe Walcott before winning by foul over Jimmy Britt.[55]

In the often confusing featherweight division, four fighters did their very best to position themselves as champions: Abe Attell, Young Corbett II, Jimmy Britt and Tommy Sullivan. Attell defeated Harry Forbes, Corbett defeated Dave Sullivan, Britt defeated Young Corbett II and Tommy Sullivan beat Abe Attell, putting Sullivan, in the minds of many, at the top. Thankfully, Abe Attell cleared matters up by 1906, to place himself firmly above all.

A stadium boxing exhibition between two of the greatest boxers ever, Young Corbett (left) and Abe Attell (Library of Congress, Prints and Photograph Division, LC-DIG-ggbain-26892).

Frankie Neil held the bantam crown until October 17, 1904, when he was defeated in London by Joe Bowker. As the first non–American to hold this title, many see Bowker's victory as the most remarkable event in the sport during the year. Bowker would quickly outgrow the bantam class the same year, leading Digger Stanley of England and Jimmy Walsh of Boston to claim the title—as one might expect, each country claimed their own champion.

Taking a look back on the year: in eight fights (not including exhibitions), Oscar Nelson fought 112 rounds and added seven wins, and only one loss to his career total. He fought two twenty-round battles—his longest fights of the year—and his shortest fight of the year was four rounds. For the very first time he would meet a member of boxing's elite, a member of the International Boxing Hall of Fame, Young Corbett II—a big step in any fighter's career. The police would stop one of his bouts, and for all intents and purposes also stop Oscar from removing the head of Teddy Murphy—the fighter eventually severing ties with his manager. During the year, Oscar met one of the hardest hitters he had ever experienced in Mr. Aurelio Herrera, and one of the most foul-mouthed in Young Corbett II. Half of his fights were fought in San Francisco, California, a city he would grow to love as much as they loved the Battler. And it would be the first year the national newspapers really recognized him as a bona fide contender for the championship. As a contender, the terms and conditions of Nelson's matches took on greater priority, exemplary in negotiations over length of bout, weight and purse percentage.

Assessing Nelson's talent, the *Salt Lake Tribune* stated,

> Nelson's meteoric flight to the top of his division had been marvelous to say the least. Two years ago he was an unknown quantity outside of Chicago and its immediate vicinity, while today he is considered the best of his weight in the country. His victory over "Spider" Welsh of San Francisco brought him some recognition in the far west, but he was not taken seriously until he had beaten Martin Canole and Eddie Hanlon. His defeat of Hanlon gave him his present standing and the opportunity of meeting Corbett. The latter had his doubts as to Nelson's right to engage him in battle despite his decisive victories over Canole, Hanlon and Herrera, but when Britt took on Gans and later refused to meet Corbett, there was nothing left for the Denver boy to do but take on the "battler."[56]

Ironically, it took until 1904—at least in the major newspapers across the country—before someone questioned what they believed was Nelson's moniker. The *Havre Herald*, of Havre, Montana, stated, after the child's birth, "his parents pondered duly before giving him his name, but his mother, who has a brother Battling and wished to do him honor, insisted that her third son should bear it.... Probably the original Danish name is not spelled that way, but that is as near as the English title approaches the original."[57] The article went on to attest that the name prompted his entrance into the fight game, and that his Danish roots worked to his advantage. "The family is of the thrifty Scandinavian type, the kind that makes good citizens, good Americans. The father, Nels, a carpenter, works at Indiana Harbor, Illinois. The mother, a little women of forty-five, takes care of the cottage and takes immense pride in her children."[58] The article was a stereotypical snapshot and, unfortunately for society, as common as a cold.

Four

1905

Five Memorable Lightweights

> Matthew was tacked on by my mother. She probably named me after the Famous Father Matthew founder of the well known temperance order. True to this good name I have followed the principles of this man all my life. I don't drink intoxicants, don't chew tobacco, nor do I smoke.
> —Oscar "Battling" Matthew Nelson[1]

In 1905, with the average wage in the United States at about twenty-two cents an hour and the average worker taking home between $200 and $400 per year, it's not hard to understand why a youth might be attracted to the fight game. While you certainly could push yourself and try to become an accountant or dentist, and that could boost your annual salary to between $2,000 and $2,500, you could also develop a trademark punch that could land a year's salary in a single night. At a time when 90 percent of all doctors had no college education, a youngster certainly had options.

For Oscar Nelson, he would exercise five options during the year in hopes of a crack at the title.

Nelson v. Corbett II, February 28, 1905

What wasn't envisioned, certainly not after their first fight, was an act of desperation by either combatant, nor could one foresee a battle where the inevitable outcome was apparent to most spectators by the fourth round, but that's precisely what happened at Woodward's Pavilion on February 28, when Battling Nelson once again met Young Corbett II.

Corbett, with his notable muscular physique, entered the ring first and was accompanied by Frank McDonald, Joe Gans, Spider Kelly and Tim McGrath. Ten agonizing minutes then passed before Nelson entered the ring, followed by Billy Nolan, Fred Landers, Martin Murphy and Rawhide Kelly. Announcer Billy Jordan introduced Nelson as "the hardest nut in the profession to crack," and Corbett as "one of the best boys in the world." Taking center stage next was Jimmy Britt, who confirmed his willingness to take on any man of his weight, before shaking the hands of Nelson, Corbett and Joe Gans. The latter, to nobody's surprise, received the biggest ovation when he was introduced as "the lightweight champion of the world." While there were calls of "speech" from the crowd, Gans would only state, "I'll keep quiet for a while and let these boys do the fighting."² A telegram from the East was then read affirming Eddie Hanlon's desire to challenge the winner.

"In all the history of athletics from ancient times down to the present that intangible quality called vitality has played an important part, although it can neither be seen or located. Corbett presented a splendid muscular appearance, but the vital spark was gone and when heavy drains were made on his nervous energy he fairly collapsed and made a pitiable showing against the implacable Dane," was how the *San Francisco Call* interpreted Corbett's display.³ The fighter pounded and pounded on Nelson's head—as he had done before—before smacking his jaw and pummeling his body, and still Nelson stood firm.

Early in the contest, Corbett's strategy of clever boxing fell by the wayside when Nelson's crushing rights began accumulating damage—destruction enhanced by Corbett's rushes. Also, Corbett failed to cover, choosing to take a blow to land a blow. It was this accumulation of damage that would result in the outcome.

> The blows which finally ended the unequal contest were not so hard as many which each man had landed during the fight. Corbett was in a bad way early in the ninth round, after getting a right and left to the head. Nelson followed this with a hard left to the jaw and was pressing Corbett about the ring. He suddenly caught Corbett a quick jolty left on the jaw and with almost lightning like rapidity he shot over a right. Corbett fell on his back like a log.⁴

And there he was, in the center of the ring motionless. Five long seconds—that felt like hours—ticked by, and finally something gave him the strength to recover his senses. Standing, it seemed, was not an option, but at the count of nine he somehow staggered to the ropes. Clearly helpless, hands at his side, Nelson walked at him like an executioner ready to flip the switch. As the sponge flew in, referee Welch quickly scrambled to grab Nelson and lead him into the middle of the ring. It was over and Nelson the victor.

As far as any foul play, early on there was a tendency to hold by both fighters. Corbett apparently attempted several head butts, and Nelson lowered his head and caused some sharp collisions. In the eighth round referee Welch thought he may have seen Corbett throw some foul blows so the fighter was given a warning, but that was all that was noted.

Early on Corbett was using his jab effectively to keep Nelson off balance, and it worked. But he did not maintain the approach. He lost his mark, or his ability to judge distance. When that happens, a fighter typically panics, realizing that he must now rely on a fight-ending punch, that one powerhouse blow that will conclude the event. The conundrum, however, was that his opponent was not susceptible to such a sockdolager.

Taking it by the rounds: When the opening bell sounded Corbett was first into action and first to land. Anxious from the start to plant a fight-ending blow, his anxiety seemed to find a home in his prolific feinting.⁵ The crowd hissed Nelson for his holding tactics. Nelson typically held high and at a strong angle, always concerned about the break. A left to the head by Nelson shook Corbett.

In the second, Corbett again was the first to take action, in this case a soft combination that did no damage. He was also doing a nice job at holding Nelson at bay with the jab, something he needed to keep up if he was going to win this fight. Corbett's distance slowly tailed off a bit, so when his punches connected, they did so with diminished strength. At close quarters, Corbett was taking the worst of it.

Round three was a bit more cautious. When Corbett bored in, he was often blocked. And, as he tired, he would work to a clinch. Nelson continued to land with the left, often to the face. When the Battler landed two heart punches and a solid left, it sent Corbett to his knees. Up quickly, the Denver fighter delivered two good combinations, the last of which staggered Nelson. But Corbett's swings at the close of the round were wild, allowing the Battler to plant two good lefts to the body. In Corbett's corner, they were trying to calm their fighter, who appeared to overreact to Nelson's assault.

Round four opened with a mix in the center of the ring. Following a separation, Corbett landed a left to the head and a right to the ribs. A brief exchange by both fighters led to another clinch. Following this clinch, both fighters went at it, landing good blows to their desired targets. The pace was brisk, enough to tire both fighters, with Corbett sneaking in a left flush to Nelson's jaw just before the bell.

Corbett opened the fifth with a left to the head of Nelson, who returned a strong mix of punches. The Battler then landed a right to the face that caused Corbett's mouth to begin bleeding. Nelson then rushed the Denver fighter into the ropes where he fired several hard rights to the jaw, followed by an amalgam of punches to the face. As the bell sounded, Corbett appeared concerned yet relieved.

It was clear by the sixth that Nelson was in control and improving with each passing round. Corbett, however, was on the downgrade and suffering from fatigue. The Battler was relentless in the round, and the Denver fighter had no choice but to keep on backing away. Corbett was wrestled to the floor but was quick to rebound to his feet. The end of the segment found the Denver warrior helpless in the ropes with Nelson firing and striking at will, some reports later stating that Nelson held off finishing him, which he clearly could have accomplished.

Corbett's tank was empty by the seventh round. Nelson, like a puppeteer, played with him through an assault of combinations. Corbett, however, did come close to landing a terrific left to Nelson's jaw, but it was too high to be effective—again, the Denver pugilist was missing his mark.

The eighth round found Nelson firing machine gun strikes at his opponent. None of the assaults did terrific damage, but the aggregate was taking a toll on his adversary. Corbett was panicking, compelling the referee to warn him about low blows and butts.

As a tactician, Nelson could be intimidating, as he was in this round, matching Corbett blow for blow. Nelson moved Corbett with ease, and again into the ropes. The Denver combatant did manage to fire two straight rights from out of nowhere to Nelson's jaw, but they did no damage. Corbett rallied briefly before being targeted to the center of the ring where he was struck with a straight right. Down for the count went Corbett. Although groggy, he did manage to stand up long enough to watch his seconds throw up the sponge. Battling Nelson was then given the decision.

Words from the winner: The Dane is After Britt.

> Well, I guess he knows now that I can punch some. I waded in and won just as I did before and just as I told my friends I would do this time. His wallops never hurt me. After the fifth round I knew I had him. Those old comebacks did not bother me, for I could see that he would blow up. I took my time and when I saw a chance I went in and landed. Now I am ready to talk to Britt. I have signed a contract to meet him and posted my $1,500 forfeit. He has not covered it yet. I am still waiting. As soon as he shows the color of his money I will feel happy, for I am going to beat him next time.[6]

Words from the loser: No Excuse to Make.

> Nelson beat me fairly and squarely. I have no excuses to offer and I do not want to detract from the glory coming to him. I was in as good shape as I ever was in my life before. Nelson simply wore me down. I

thought I had a chance in that eighth round when I waded in and brought rights and lefts over fast as I could steer them. I had him worried and I really believed I was going to put him out. But I could not last. I was worn down and all my strength left me. I was game to the last and never wanted to quit. No, I will not quit the game. I will keep on training and show the public that I am capable of coming back from a beating.[7]

Less than two months after the fight, Nelson found himself over at Harry Corbett's office in San Francisco chatting with the fellas. As usual, the subjects ranged from the latest winners at the horse track to Nelson's prognostications on fights and fighters. The Battler's stock was rising, and anything he did, or did not do, was news. When the topic turned to boxers and their vices, one of the beat writers took out his pen and began jotting some notes. "Just think here was a prizefighter (Nelson) who didn't know a race horse from a goat; did not drink intoxicating liquids and a fragrant cigar has no fascination for him. How many other prize-fighters who are famous can say: 'I don't play the races; I don't drink or smoke'? You can count them on one hand."[8]

Quickly the names of fighters surfaced faster than a hungry lake trout. "Jeffries smokes and drinks but doesn't play the races. Jim Corbett enjoys a glass of wine and a good cigar. Tommy Ryan drinks an occasional glass, but does not smoke or gamble."[9] The conversation then switched to more familiar characters: "Young Corbett has all three vices. Jimmy Britt tastes the cup that cheers, but does not use tobacco or play the races. Joe Gans has lost a fortune on the races. Kid McCoy drinks, smokes and plays the races. Tom Sharkey is known as a good fellow, though he does not drink to excess."[10] Watching the reporter take notes, Nelson listened attentively, interjecting only when he felt it was relevant. And in this case, relevant meant strategically important. "Frankie Neil follows the ponies, but that lets him out. Joe Walcott has often been 'skated' when fighting and he smokes a lot. Terry McGovern and Eddie Hanlon will make an occasional bet on a race, but won't lie awake nights doping the horses up. Jack O'Brien has no bad habits. Bob Fitzsimmons drinks some."[11] For a maturing Battling Nelson, a negative factor against an opponent was ammunition to use as he saw fit, an additional advantage to his growing arsenal.

Nelson v. Attell, May 22, 1905

The news traveled fast in New York:

Abe Attell and Battling Nelson were matched today over the long distance telephone to meet at Philadelphia next Monday night [May 22].[12] The conditions of the match call for six rounds, both boxers to weigh in at 130 pounds at 6 o'clock on day of fight. Willie Lewis was originally scheduled to meet Nelson, but the New York boy could not make the weight demanded by Nelson and the match fell through. Attell is in good shape and ready for a hard fight. Nelson has been hard at work training since his arrival in Philadelphia and says he will be in fine fettle for his battle with Attell.[13]

Lewis, a combination craftsman, had been demonstrating why he was one of the best lightweights in the east, defeating twenty-four men in the last seven months, most along the knockout path. "His last victory was over Martin Canole, whom he knocked out in nine rounds, a feat Jimmy Britt failed to do in twenty-five rounds, and which took 'Battling' Nelson eighteen rounds to accomplish."[14] When the match was originally made, it was at catchweights, so Nelson likely had second thoughts.[15] Considering the caliber of fighters, news coverage—

obviously the short distance contributed to the indifference—of this fight fell short of expectations, even if Attell was a last-minute substitute.

The *San Francisco Call* stated, "In view of Nelson's announcement that he is 'a fighter, pure and simple,' fight fans view his action in the Lewis matter with suspicion."[16] It was Nelson's first appearance in a Philadelphia prize ring, and one would have thought it might attract more than the few lines in the following morning's newspaper. The *New York Times* scoffed, "It was the old story of the finished boxer against a fighter."[17] The clever Attell, the former, in control from start to finish and moving the fight at his pace, while Nelson, the hard-hitting fighter, relentlessly ground forward.

Attell was strong from the opening bell, and through the first four rounds he jabbed Nelson in the face and stomach without a return blow. In the second and third rounds, Nelson managed to catch Attell several times with blows to the jaw, but they inflicted little harm. Both the fifth and sixth rounds ended favoring Nelson, although it was noted, "In the latter part of the sixth, however, Attell recovered himself and was hammering Nelson with rights and lefts when the bell sounded."[18] For two fighters of this caliber, six rounds was barely enough distance to break a sweat, but just long enough to collect a paycheck. For both it was another no decision to add to their growing list.

Until the men actually set foot into the ring, it looked as though they would not meet, as there was a hitch over weighing in. Attell weighed in at 126, but Nelson refused to get on the scales, claiming that his contract did not call for it. Contractual shenanigans, Attell

Abe Attell, a clever fighter, was often in control of his battles from start to finish. He would become known for his six-year reign as world featherweight champion from 1906 to 1912 (Library of Congress, Prints and Photograph Division, LC-DIG-ggbain-08235).

thought, and refused to go on. Management then scrambled and decided to substitute Kid Herman of Chicago, until Attell finally capitulated. Nelson would later state in his defense of weight and distance, "As I was under the care of Dr. Charles A. Clinton because of my broken rib gotten during the Corbett fight, I found it impossible to fight for a few weeks. I went to the mountains hunting for a month on the doctor's advice."[19] Not entirely correct, but it was an admission to his injury.

Noting that the San Francisco sportswriters had done a great job at chronicling his "gallant victory over Young Corbett throughout the East," Nelson, perhaps to stimulate more local press, repeated his apprehensiveness about his ribs. He then confirmed that the Philadelphia Club offered him three fights, at $1,500 per fight, and conditions he could live with— six rounds, no decision and name your opponents. For Nelson, it was a deal only a fool would ignore.

Clearly on his way to the featherweight crown, Attell was destined to be a division force. He had not lost in his last eight fights. Having recent victories over Harry Forbes, Eddie Hanlon, Tommy Feltz, Harlem Tommy Murphy and Young Erne, Attell would have been a dangerous selection had the contract not covered Nelson's considerations.

Nelson v. Sullivan, June 2, 1905

The first week of June found Nelson in Baltimore, Maryland, tackling "Kid" Sullivan of Washington.[20] Scheduled for six rounds, it would enter the history books as a draw, but it was a battle fought from two different perspectives. The morning's sports offering in San Francisco read, "Nelson and Sullivan Go Six Rounds to a Draw," contrasted against a subheading of "Battling Dane Is Hammered Hard by Washington Lad, Who Rains Many Blows on Head." To those viewing the clash, "Sullivan seemed to have much the better of it, landing on Nelson's head and neck repeatedly and usually getting in a stiff punch in breaking from the frequent clinches." In the fourth round, Sullivan even knocked Nelson through the ropes. "Nelson's blows were nearly all delivered at close quarters and he showed an inclination to hold more than the spectators thought proper."[21]

To Nelson, however, things were a bit different:

> [Nelson was] the unsuspecting victim of a prize-ring trick, one that may have ended his championship ambitions. As a rule, the public knows very little about the underhand methods that are sometimes resorted to in pugilism, and a little expose right here might be interesting. At the time, Al Herford was running a club at Baltimore and at the same time managing Kid Sullivan. He matched Sullivan and me at his club and agreed to pay me $1,500, guaranteed, win, lose, or draw. Herford, thinking he could put one over and gain fame for one—Kid Sullivan—felt very much enthused over the match.[22]

On the eve of the battle, according to Nelson, Herford—with club, fighter, and timing under his control—demanded that if both men were still standing at the end, it would be called a draw. Then the guileful Herford decided to amend Nelson's payment to $1,000. Livid, Nelson, who should have walked at this point, just bit his tongue.

On a mission, the Battler entered the ring with a vengeance, and after the first three rounds of the fight, the battle looked clearly in his favor. Sullivan's handlers, Herford, Joe Gans and Peter Jackson, became uneasy, and fearing a knockout realized that desperate times called for desperate measures, and that is exactly what they resorted to. At the end of the third, when Sullivan went to his corner, his seconds smeared belladonna or some drug on his gloves.[23] The goal then was to have their fighter deliver it to Nelson's eyes, thus blinding him.

When Sullivan failed to deliver the treatment soundly to Nelson in the fourth, it was back to the corner for a heavier dose. "In the sixth and last round we both stepped to the center, and, as is customary, shook hands," Nelson recalled. "This time the dope had been applied heavily and he succeeded in rubbing the besmeared gloves to my face. In a moment, I was almost totally blind."[24]

Nelson could no longer tell Sullivan from the referee, and in fact he accidentally hit the arbiter at one point. Thankfully he lasted the round and the fight ended in the agreed-upon draw. "Billy Rocap, the referee, failed to notice that Sullivan's gloves had been doped until the finish of the fight," Nelson firmly stated. "I was then totally blind and had to be led to my corner. Rocap asked what was the matter, and when I told him he immediately went to Sullivan's corner to try and get the gloves, but Herford, fox that he is, hustled Sullivan away and refused to give up the mitts."[25]

The reason for Herford's tactics became clear on June 15, 1905, when his fighter inked a cozy financial deal to fight Jimmy Britt. Morris Levy, manager of the Hayes Valley Athletic Club, was responsible for securing the match—the fight to be held in Woodward's Pavilion on the night of July 18. Both fighters agreed to scale at 133 pounds for the battle.[26]

Nelson v. O'Neil, June 6, 1905

A fair-sized crowd before the National Athletic Club in Philadelphia—the same site as Nelson's battle against Attell—was treated to a furious clash between two warriors, Battling Nelson and Jack O'Neil, on the evening of June 6.[27] Nelson, having fought and defeated O'Neil last February, was confident entering the ring. Since that time the prolific local fighter had become more of a welcome mat that a contender, having only won six of his last eighteen ring confrontations.

From nearly the beginning of the fray the Battler, living up to his name, took control.[28] Honors were even in the first, but O'Neil took the second round despite a bloodied nose; Nelson took the third by delivering some solid punishment; O'Neil was staggered in the fourth by a powerful right to the jaw that left him groggy at the bell; the fifth round was a repeat of the fourth, and all Nelson; and, in the sixth, the Battler had tried just about everything to put away O'Neil but could not do it. The fight would enter the record books as a six-round no decision.

O'Neil was seconded by Jack McGuigan, Jim Jeffords and Buzzy Ingram, while Nelson had in his corner Billy Nolan, Kid Howard and Johnny Loftus. O'Neil would fight until 1916, but he never meet Nelson again.

Having just disposed of O'Neil, a member of the press suggested—not in an insulting manner but as a sincere proposition—that Nelson should give the stage a try. As other pugilists had expanded their horizons beyond the ring, should not the Battler consider honing his thespian talents? Needless to say, the sheer thought initially petrified Nelson, who could think only of his attempt at making a speech following his fight with "Cross-Eyed" Mickey Riley; that incident parodied the quip "putting your money where your mouth is." Nevertheless, seeing dollar signs over stage fright, Nelson decided to give it a try. "I got a telegram from Harry Farren, manager of the Columbia Theatre, in Boston, offering me $700 for a four nights' engagement, in addition to two round trip tickets from Philadelphia to Boston," Nelson corroborated. "I accepted immediately and started for Boston."[29]

Still wondering why he ever accepted the offer, Nelson, filled with anxiety struggled, to craft his speech on his journey to Boston. But attempts at the address, and there were many, just weren't working. It wouldn't matter anyway, as once the Battler saw all the folks staring at him, his stage fright returned and he froze. An intent audience, fixed on Nelson's sparring over locution, quickly encouraged him to pick up the gloves, and as soon as he did his fear dissipated. And sparring he did, much to the delight of repeated packed houses. Honestly not knowing how to explain the phenomena, he countered his stage fright with a week at the Trocadero Theatre in Chicago on his way back west. Hey, for $1,000, why not?

Approaching the time he had to be back on the West Coast, this to sign the final articles for his fight with Jimmy Britt, Nelson began to get nervous. A special clause in the *temporary* agreement stated that Nelson must be on California soil by July 1, so he hustled back to San Francisco, arriving on June 30. On July 1, both he and his manager headed over to Harry Corbett's place, where the forfeits had been posted, to meet Britt and his manager. Once there, Nelson learned that Britt had been matched to fight Sullivan instead of him and that he had pulled down his forfeit. Nelson was enraged. Admitting that he was "again sidetracked for more easy game by the elusive son, Sir James Edward [Britt]," the Battler quickly considered his options.[30]

Certainly, Nelson thought, the public wouldn't stand for Britt's nonsense. So Oscar, having accumulated his fair share of print favors, pulled a few from his back pocket to begin "spinning" Britt's obvious avoidance of the Battler.

Next came the battle between rival promoters, all of whom were eager to land Britt versus Nelson in the ring before the end of September. By the second week of August it looked as if the promotion was between Morris Levy, who held a contract to fight before the Hayes Valley Club, and James Coffroth. Levy

The right-handed Oscar "Battling" Matthew Nelson saved all his poses for photographers, as during a contest he was always too busy attacking his opponents to ever look up (Library of Congress, Prints and Photograph Division, LC-DIG-ggbain-01717).

sent a representative to meet with Billy Nolan, who was now handling negotiations for Nelson. Nolan demanded that an equal offer, equal to that of $30,000 made by manager Jim Coffroth, be made before he would entertain Levy's proposition. Levy, however, didn't see this as an option. Nolan was also insisting that the fight be held in San Francisco, at Mechanics' Pavilion, the only venue he felt could manage such a large gate.

The newspapers were having a field day covering the negotiations, as daily they were fed information from all sides in an attempt to force certain issues. For example, it was printed on August 9, 1905, in the *San Francisco Call* that "Sam Berger [from Britt's camp] told Nolan that Britt will insist on a $10,000 side bet. Nolan said he would gladly put up that or a larger amount if a forty-five round fight is arranged. He said he would not bet it on a twenty-round affair."[31] It was all hype, and the readers loved it. James W. Coffroth would eventually become the promoter of choice.

"Early in August my manager and Britt's brother, Willus, got together in Coffroth's Belvidere and discussed the details of the match," Nelson called to mind. "Jimmy and I were not present and the managers wrangled for three days before a final agreement had been reached."[32] The Britts were negotiating from a position of strength—everyone understood this—dictating nearly every phase of the negotiation. The Britts wanted forty-five rounds at 133 pounds, and a $10,000 side bet. Winner takes all.

"Evidently the Britts didn't figure that they were playing right into my hands when they named the forty-five round route," Nelson would later claim, "which the San Franciscans have since named the 'Battler's route,' because I can go over the long course like a Derby horse over a Derby route."[33] Such hyperbole must be viewed with skepticism, as Nelson's team—overly anxious to get Britt inside the twenty-four-foot ring—was conceding points faster than a Derby horse.

"After agreeing to all the conditions named, even to a percentage of the gate, the Britts balked," claimed Nelson, "demanding a $20,000 guaranteed purse, with the privilege of 65 percent of the gross receipts."[34] Hearing this, Coffroth nearly fell off his seat. It would be, the promoter made clear, either one condition or the other—a $20,000 flat guarantee or 65 percent of the gross receipts. Nolan flinched, thinking Coffroth just broke the deal. When it looked as if all the negotiations were off, Nelson's camp weakened. The Battler would guarantee the $20,000 purse—posting $10,000 to make it good—and, in Nelson's words, "willing to gamble on a percentage basis for my end."[35] In other words, Britt insisted on a $20,000 purse or 65 percent of the receipts at his option, but refused to concede the same choice to Nelson, who is only to receive the percentage if he wins.

The next negotiation to tackle was that of a referee. "After wrangling and fussing around from 2 o'clock yesterday afternoon till midnight, Willie Britt and Billy Nolan left Manager Coffroth's office without having agreed upon the man who is to referee the Britt-Nelson fight," reported the *San Francisco Call* on August 27, 1905. "According to the agreement they are supposed to have forfeited the sum of $2,500 to Coffroth, but the manager graciously consented to extend the time limit till 7:30 this evening, when the rival managers will probably get together and agree on Eddie Graney as the third man in the ring. Both are satisfied with him, but each is waiting for the other to mention his name. The other will then accept."[36]

Since there was so much money involved, the choice of a referee by either side would be dealt a tremendous degree of cynicism. Both parties sat at opposite corners of the room—each knowing fully well what arbiter they wanted and who would work to their advantage—

casting dagger glances at one another before a slew of names were thrown out and argued over. Minutes, which seemed like hours, passed before the process was repeated. An occasional sarcastic remark was thrown, but these were only jabs, not serious punches.

"Most of Nolan's choices were Eastern men and, of course, Britt would not stand for any of them. He wanted local men, but none of the long list of names he presented looked good to Nolan," the paper reported. Meanwhile, Coffroth—who if he so chose could simply take the $5,000 already deposited—listened and did not speak. That is, until he had no other choice but to issue an ultimatum.

> I, therefore, will extend the time for the selection of the referee until 7:30 o'clock tomorrow evening, August 27, 1905. If at that time the men cannot agree upon a name, I will name a referee myself, subject to their approval. If they disapprove my selection, the contest is off and I will claim their forfeits. At this time, I will add that sum mentioned, $5,000, will not reimburse me for the expense to which I have gone.[37]

All the newspapers knew it would be Eddie Graney, as both fight camps kept his name in their back pocket. "Britt was for Jeffries, but Nolan would not stand for the big fellow. Then Britt named Colonel Brady, Jack Kitchen, Phil Wand and Jere Dunn, but as none of them suited Nolan the gloomy session set in once again and monotony reigned for another while," the *Call* noted. "The mystery as to why Nelson, a fighter, refuses to accept Jeffries, a fighter, who would appreciate the style of milling, is a mystery."[38] Nelson's camp actually agreed briefly on Jeffries, but changed their mind at the last minute. "The reason was Nolan, who had heard of a few things that were to come off, and being determined to take no chances, we point blank refused to stand for the big boiler maker to act as the third man in the ring," claimed Nelson.[39] In the end, Eddie Graney appeared to be the solution.

Meanwhile, the Battler was in Colma preparing for the fight at Joe Millett's training quarters. Both fighters entered the ring at 133 pounds, with Oscar an inch taller at five feet seven inches. Nelson also picked up an inch and a half advantage in reach at sixty-seven inches. Both fighters had equal size necks, biceps, and ankles, while Britt had a larger, by an inch, chest. Oscar's waist at twenty-five inches was three inches larger than Britt's, his forearm an inch thicker, and his wrist ¾ inch larger. As far as legs, it was all Oscar, whose thighs measured a half inch larger and his calf an inch wider.

Nelson v. Britt, September 9, 1905

They got to Colma on September 9, every which way they could, from automobiles and buggies to saddle-horses and bicycles. In a state with only 1.4 million people—the 21st most populous state in the union—there was probably a good likelihood that you knew someone else who was going to the fight. So if they were lucky enough to have a car—there were only 8,000 cars in the United States, and only 144 miles of paved roads—you might be able to get a ride with them to Colma. But you also had to give yourself plenty of time as the maximum speed limit in most cities was ten mph. And you likely had to arrange your transportation in advance and in person, as only 8 percent of the homes had a telephone. Most, as it would turn out, would turn to rail transportation.

An estimated 10,000 people journeyed to the park with hopes of witnessing the battle, or at least to listen to the cheering spectators. Manager George Chapman, of the United Railroads,

A panorama of the Battling Nelson versus Jimmy Britt prize fight on September 9, 1905. The victory allowed Nelson to pick up the world white lightweight title (Library of Congress, Prints and Photograph Division, LC-USZ62–52812, LC-USZ62–52813).

coordinated the service. It included 110 electric cars, each running a minute apart. Moving, by his estimation, 10,000 people by electric car, he serviced his customers without delay or accidents. Some individuals had special cars; for example, James J. Coffroth used the private car Hermosa to carry money and employees of the Yosemite Club to and from ringside.

"The Southern Pacific Company did not fare as well, instead of stopping its train in front of the coursing park the engineer in charge won the enmity of the passengers by taking them down to Colma and forcing them to walk back. After the fight the train was fully an hour late in starting, and many sacrificed their tickets and came home by electric car."[40]

That it was something of a society fete could be gleaned from those at ringside, including Abe Ruef, judge; Dr. Whitney; Sandy Smith, the turfman; ex-supervisor McCarthy; Jack and Frank Crane, the Merced horsemen; Jack Sullivan the politician; Phil Wand, the athlete and referee; Mrs. James J. Jeffries; Mrs. William Delaney; Fred Evans, supervisor; Jim Miller, the architect; Harold Magill of Oakland, one of the original Jordan shouters; Jack Suits, the promoter; Dan Carter, the cigar man; Assemblyman Lumley; Senator Dick Welch; Postmaster Fisk; Tom Cogan, a Cincinnati attorney; Colonel Martin Brady; Yosemite commissioner Jack Wilson; Charles W. Clark, the Montana millionaire; Jack Sheehan, the tailor; Senator Shortridge of San Jose, who arrived late and seemed disconcerted over something; internal revenue collector John C. Lynch; and Judge Hubbard and J. Downey Harvey of the Olympic Club, who, like a few others, made the trip in automobiles. Also Jim Jeffries and his old friend and manager Billy Delaney sat together in a box. And Billy Carroll, an old-time pal of the Considine brothers, was there. Billy, who would take a chance on a scrap to be pulled off at the North Pole if the ice was cracking right, made the trip all the way from Jackson, Michigan, just to see Britt win.[41]

"Britt entered the ring at eight minutes to 2 o'clock. He was clad in a red sweater, gray suit and a gray overcoat. As 'the pride of California' took his seat in the corner of the arena the crowd gave a lusty cheer." Britt's seconds followed: "Spider" Kelly, Tiv Kreling, Curtis Richardson, Frank Rafael, Sammy Berger and manager "Willus" Britt."[42] The usual tin bucket and water bottles were at hand, but so was a mother's clothes boiler—the latter, which had everyone ringside speculating on its contents, was assumed to be Britt's lunch.

As Britt's corner began preparing their fighter for battle, the crowd was growing impatient, as there was no Dane. Then the voice of Willus Britt rang out. "He says he won't take Jeff. We won Mr. Jeffries on the toss. We are in the ring ready to fulfill our part of the agreement—ready to fight. Anyone who is against Jeffries wants to turn a trick and I am against it."[43]

Manager Coffroth, seething mad, then entered the ring at 2:17, twenty-five minutes after Britt, and told announcer Billy Jordan to invite champion Jim Jeffries to enter the ring. Jeff complied and entered through the ropes, to a hearty cheer led by Britt's corner. As the applause drew to a close, an announcement was made.

"Gentlemen, Mr. Nelson refuses to come into this ring unless they select some other man than James Jeffries for referee."[44]

The crowd instantly ignited into hoots and jeers; cries for "money back" came from every corner of the arena. Jordan then confirmed, "Mr. Britt will not stand for anybody but James Jeffries." And, before the house volume was raised again, "Gentlemen: the only undefeated champion of the world, who has retired from the prize ring for the balance of his life—James Jeffries."[45] The crowd stood in adoration when Jordan called for three cheers for the boilermaker.

As the noise briefly subsided, cries of "Speech!" arose, and Jeff said, "Gentlemen: All I've got to say—I thank you one and all from the bottom of my heart." Again, more cheers. During another delay, Britt received a few telegrams wishing him luck before another announcement was made. "Gentlemen: Nolan is outside and he will accept George Siler or Eddie Graney for referee." To the throng of tired spectators this seemed like a good compromise and was applauded. Willie Britt then said, "The differences we had with Graney were purely personal and had nothing to do with his honesty. For the sake of bringing the fight off, we will take Graney."

A big cheer went up, and it looked like everything could proceed. Jordan announced George Siler, who was ringside, and confirmed that he was not there to referee, followed by a statement that Graney had been accepted. As cries of Graney could be heard, he was seen consulting with Jeffries and asking for his approval. Dressed in a gray suit and a straw hat, Graney finally entered the ring and headed to Brit's corner. Shaking hands with Britt, Graney promised the fighter a "fair deal."

Nelson was currently in sight and accompanied by Billy Nolan, his manager and chief second, along with Martin Murphy, George Gardner, Harry Foley, Fred Landers and three or four other camp followers. Nelson was in street clothes.

"The timekeepers took their places at the ringside and everything was ready for the 'slugfest.' Billy Gallagher held the watch for Britt; Jim Neal, father of the ex-bantam champion, did a little service for Nelson and George Hartling, the famous timekeeper, represented the club.

Nelson was then introduced as "the hardest nut in the profession to crack," followed by his opponent who was "a native son of the Golden West and the pride of California, Jimmy Britt." Challenges followed: Eddie Hanlon, Willie Fitzgerald, Jimmy Gardner and Aurelio Herrera all let their intentions be known.

Graney then whispered to Jordan to announce that all bets were off—a decision due to the referee change and one that was applauded by some for its fairness. (By most accounts, Britt was favored 10 to 7.)

In Nelson's corner another squabble erupted, this time over a moving-picture guarantee in which the promoter was to award him $5,000 for his share in the moving pictures. With all the discourse of recent weeks, Coffroth was worried about two things: the quality of the fight and that of the film—a fog had now settled over the arena and threatened to impact the moving pictures. "I am in $2,000 now," Coffroth vented, "and I can't give you the guarantee.

However, if the pictures turn out good I will give $5,000 for Nelson's interest."[46] Both Nolan and Nelson agreed to the terms.

The fighters stripped for action: Britt in red and white trunks, marked by the winged "O" of the Olympic Club, Nelson in his customary faded green trunks. Both fighters, along with members of the press, were then invited into the center of the ring for instructions:

"When I say break you must do so. If I say, 'Let go, Bat' you let go, and if I say, 'Jimmy you are holding,' you must let go," said Graney.

"There is no fair holding at all," said Nelson.

"It is against the rules," replied Graney. "Now, boys, obey me, and don't make a monkey out of me before this big crowd."

"I am not going to do any holding," said Britt.

"We are to protect ourselves in the clinches?" asked Nelson.

"Straight Marquis of Queensberry rules," said Nolan, and Graney acquiesced.

"How about interference from the outside?" asked Nolan.

"I will use my judgement and give a decision," answered the referee. "There will be no interference; but I'll stop the contest if I deem that either man can't go on."

The boys then shook hands and went back to their corners. Nolan turned to Graney and said, "Recognize no one from the corner but me." This was to prevent anyone other than Nolan from throwing up the sponge.

"This will be a forty-five round contest, Marquis of Queensberry rules, and break by order of the referee," Jordan projected into the arena.

It was 2:45 p.m. when the opening bell sounded.[47]

In round one, Nelson shocked everyone by beginning the action with a light left to Britt's face. Britt, working the jab, then sent Nelson back with a left to the body. While this excited the crowd, it angered Nelson, who countered with a blow to Britt's nose that started it bleeding. Nelson caught Britt with a left to the head at the end of the round.

Nelson opened round two as the aggressor, but took some hard combinations by Britt to the head. A left to the head of Nelson nearly took him off his feet, but the fighter turned the table with a solid right that staggered Britt.

In round three, Nelson staggered Britt early, only to have his opponent retaliate with an old-fashioned right cross to the jaw that put Nelson down briefly. Britt then worked Nelson's now bleeding nose for the remainder of the battle.

Round four opened with a Britt combination to Nelson's head. The Battler then returned with a straight right to the head that pained his opponent. Britt fired a hard right to the jaw in return, followed by another to Nelson's nose. Britt then sent two huge lefts to Nelson's body that made the Battler wince in pain.

A free-for-all erupted in round five, as both fighters "threw all caution to the wind."[48] Both aggressors stood, with little or no regard for defense, and fired their arsenal.

Round six saw Britt go right for Nelson's face with a straight left. Nelson seemed more than happy to take blow after blow in order to work inside. Britt continued to cover well to avoid the damage. Nelson did manage to get Britt into a corner and pound him with combinations. Britt stood bewildered after the beating, but Nelson could not carry out the knockout.

Both fighters seemed fatigued in round seven. Britt delivered a good amalgam of punches to the head, followed by a right to the jaw. Nelson then returned a good right. Britt still went to Nelson's body with a strong attack that likely secured the round in his favor.

Had Nelson been more aggressive he could have won the fight in round eight. He back-heeled Britt by accident early in the round before staggering him with one of those vicious left swings to the jaw. Britt was obviously struggling, but Nelson let him recuperate, and at the end of the round Britt was doing the better work.

The impact of the previous round was showing on Britt's face in round nine. Sending a hard right to Nelson's jaw, Britt was met by a robust combination to the face. Annoyed, Britt fired back three rapid punches to Nelson's head that staggered the fighter.

Round ten was rather lackluster as both fighters looked to regain a second wind. In the eleventh, the pace picked back up with Britt taking considerable punishment from Nelson. Just prior to the bell, Britt landed a nice mix of punches.

Round twelve saw a much wilder Nelson—perhaps looking forward to landing the big one. Seeing this, Britt pounded Nelson's head while the fighter tried desperately to return and defend.

Two minutes into the thirteenth round, Britt was dazed from Nelson's assaults. Nelson pounded Britt's head before staggering him with a right. The two fighters then stood head-to-head in a slugfest, Britt desperately trying to come back at the sound of the bell.

Round fourteen looked to Nelson's advantage as it took Britt's seconds assist him in getting out of his chair. Britt was wobbled by a straight left but managed to connect with a solid left to Nelson's head. A right then found Britt, who looked as if he was about to collapse, but somehow the fighter found a way to rally at the close of the round.

Rounds fifteen and sixteen saw minimal damage, as both fighters looked to conserve energy. Referee Graney had a tough time getting both exhausted fighters to break. Britt did draw blood from Nelson's face in the sixteenth.

The seventeenth was an exchange of blows, Britt to the head, Nelson to the body. Britt was noticeably conserving energy by evading rushes and wasting no blows. Britt worked Nelson's nose like a speed bag and staggered him with a right to the jaw. The Californian did, however, land a late blow after the gong and apologized.

As if on cue, the sun came out in round eighteen, much to the relief of the picture men. Britt continued to drive solid lefts to Nelson's face. Nelson continued his ineffective attempt at coming inside, as Britt would shower him with combinations. Nelson landed a good blow to the face before Britt switched his lefts to an assault on the body. Nelson then managed a huge left to the stomach that doubled up Britt. The two came together. Nelson pushed Britt back to put him in range for a powerful combination to the jaw.[49] Britt dropped, rolled over on his stomach, and was counted out. Watching Britt grab for the ropes in desperation was proof of his exhaustion. As the cheers for Nelson grew, Britt's limp body was carried to his corner by seconds.

On hand to witness what he would note as the "Dane's perpetual motion more effective than Britt's mental superiority" was Jack London, whose printed account of the fight would appear in the *San Francisco Examiner* the following day.[50] The U.S. novelist, who also witnessed the Klondike Gold Rush of 1897 and used it as a springboard for his latest work, *The Call of the Wild* (1903), had become fascinated with man's struggle for survival, and nowhere would it be better depicted than in Colma on this day.

"In the first round Britt hit Nelson a half a dozen blows. At each blow Nelson was coming in. The blows did not stop him. He kept coming on. Then Nelson hit Britt, and Britt was staggered by the blow. The whole story of the fight was told right there," claimed London at the start of his printed examination.⁵¹ Yet London also saw the conflict as Nelson, a fighting animal, versus Britt, an intelligent animal with fighting proclivities. Or an abysmal brute against a more highly organized intelligent creature. (Bear in mind, London's next work, *White Fang*, is dancing in his head and would be published the following year.)

> By abysmal brute I [London] mean the basic life that resides deeper than the brain and the intellect in living things. It is itself the very staff of life—movement; and it is saturated with a blind and illimitable desire to exist. This desire it expresses by movement. No matter what comes it will move. It came into the world first. It is lower down on the ladder of evolution than is intelligence. It comes first, before the intellect. The intellect rests before it; and when the intellect goes it still remains—the abysmal brute.⁵²

London continues—unconcerned that his readers, or at least some, have been set adrift, and not realizing that two out of every ten U.S. adults can't read or write, so there are not as many people reading this as he thinks, and since a mere 6 percent of all Americans had graduated from high school, they will likely not follow him to begin with—by going a step further.

On hand to witness, what he would note as the "Dane's perpetual motion [being] more effective than Britt's mental superiority" was Jack London, whose printed account of the Nelson versus Britt fight would appear in the San Francisco Examiner the following day (Library of Congress, Prints and Photograph Division, LC-DIG-ggbain-00676).

> Here are you and I, average creatures, fairly normal and fairly rational. Our minds are clear. We reason. We conduct ourselves with the intelligent poise of mind. But a sharp word is spoken, a sneer is made, an insult is given. At once our poise of mind is gone. We are angry. The mind no longer dominates us. The abysmal brute rushes up in us, muddles out clear brain, takes charge of us.
>
> This is a moment of anger. We are temporarily insane. Reason is gone. The brute has charge of us. The difference between us and the man in the insane asylum is that the brute always has charge of him.
>
> It is the abysmal brute that we see in a man in a Berserker rage or in a jealous spell of anger.⁵³ We see it in a horse, tied to too short a rope, frantic, dragging backward and hanging itself. We see it in the bull, bellowing and blindly charging a red shirtwaist; in the strange cat, restrained in our hands, curving its hindquarters in and with its hind legs scratching long, ripping slashes.
>
> And now to return, Nelson is the lower type. Britt is the higher type."⁵⁴

London goes on to claim that, had Britt had Nelson's capacity to move, combined with his own intelligence, he would have whipped the Battler. London also reluctantly stated, "The best man won—according to the rules of the game."⁵⁵

Britt's intelligence, at least from London's perspective, won hands down with regard to all preliminary negotiations. With regard to appearance, "If Nelson looked the lean and hungry proletarian, Britt looked the well-fed and prosperous bourgeoise."⁵⁶ Of his battle assessments, a few ring true: "Had Britt received the blows he gave Nelson, Britt would have been out long before the eighteenth round"; "Victory was hopeless for him [Britt] from the first round"; and "Britt was not fighting with his mind, for he was fighting himself out, exhausting all his reserves of strength." While London finishes his piece by hailing both, he can't resist the finer points: "Britt is the finer human. Nelson is the finer fighting animal."[57]

Of Oscar's take on the piece, it was printed inside his autobiography. But, included there as well was a piece by Ashton Stevens, also from the *San Francisco Examiner* and titled, "Tragedy is Mirrored in Face of Britt's Father." While Stevens called the fifty-two minutes of actually fighting "the greatest matinee I have ever witnessed," he was also taken by the appearance of "Old Man Britt, pillowing the gore-flecked head of his heretofore undefeated first born."[58] It was a prize ring tragedy played out vividly at ringside. Stevens acknowledged that he was in Britt's corner right from the start, a result of an impressive interview the fighter gave him for the *Sunday Examiner*. Stevens noted that, "during the fiercest rounds, Mr. Britt was the only man that stood in the great open-air auditorium."[59] An act accepted by a crowd that routinely cussed such an action down. "But the Old Man stood, and even those directly behind made no murmur. He stood with his black hat in his hand, close against his black coat, like a mourner at a funeral," Stevens noted.[60] He saw both the fight and its crowd commentaries played out on the face of the father.

Stevens also noted the women in attendance. They endured a battle of their own. "Hoots of mock applause properly met the entrance of each." He then stated, "Man at a prize fight is not a polite animal. In fact, he has no politeness at all and is much more animal than man."[61] The writer noted the behavior of other professional men, including that of Jack London, and the failure of melodramatists to accurately portray the scene.

As Stevens saw it, "If we must have the fighter in drama let him be dramatized accurately. Let him have a "Spider" Kelley in his corner screaming: That's the candy, Jimmy! Once more where he bleeds! Draw more of the claret; I like to see it run! Go in, you tiger, you, and finish him before he faints on your shoulder!"[62]

Give them, the fight fan, what he demands. Stevens continues, "The real surroundings: the hooded telephone operators; the worried correspondents from all ends of the earth ... a Naughton on the stage, talking like a phonograph to his telegrapher, the news to be carried from ocean to ocean, from newspaper to newspaper.... A-couple-of-lefts-to-the-body-brought-Britt's-head-forward." Ending the piece Stevens confesses, "I saw a fighter kill a man in the ring, the picture was not half so sad as that of Old Man Britt."[63]

Speaking of fathers, Oscar's dad went to San Francisco to see his son fight Britt. However, he didn't quite receive the amount of attention as Britt's father, unless of course you are the one who relieved him of his bankroll after the fight.

As the winner saw it:

> I guess they will not tell you any more that Britt is the cleverest and hardest hitting lightweight in the business. I think I showed the people I can beat him at his own game. I told all my friends I could beat him, and I did it. I will say he is a great fighter, and as game a boy as ever donned a glove. He fought me every inch of the way, and I was puzzled for a while by the way in which he came back. I can't describe just how I knocked him out. I saw my chance, and waded in with rights and lefts. I am not sure which did the trick, but I got him, and that is all there is to it. I will admit he hit me often, but none of those blows had any steam behind them and they did not hurt me. I thought I had him in the sixth round, and again in the thirteenth round; but he was so game and so strong that I could not quite put him away. Jimmy has promised me we shall be good friends now, and I am glad of that. I am sorry that my friends could not cash in on me on account of the bets being called off; but Eddie Graney knows what is right, and that is all.—Battling Nelson[64]

As the loser saw it:

I fought Nelson in his own particular style of fighting. Of course, I used my cleverness. I was stronger than he was at the finish, and was gradually wearing him down. My hands were swollen, and had burst the adhesive bandages. I don't say it was a lucky punch, but Nelson was particularly fortunate in landing that punch at that time. All honor to the victor. He is a great fighter. I am not a sorehead. I have won many a battle, and have lost one. I have always won like a gentleman, and believe I can lose this fight like a gentleman. I would like to fight Nelson again. I am not hurt, nor was I hurt anytime in the battle. I was not exhausted when I got that punch in the eighteenth round. I have no excuses to make, but desire to give all credit to Nelson. He is a strong fellow and aggressive. Those who saw the fight know what I did to win, and I am sure I cannot be criticized for losing. I trust the public got its money's worth. The bruises on my nose are slight, and were really received in training and were reopened by Nelson's gloves.—James Edward Britt[65]

As the referee saw it:

It was the greatest lightweight battle of modern times. Nelson won decisively. He was too strong and too tough for Britt. After the third round I made up my mind that Nelson would be the victor. His boring-in tactics, capacity to take a beating and his power of recuperation led me to this opinion. Nelson reminded me of Bob Fitzsimmons. He is abnormally strong and keeps coming all the time. In the eighth round Nelson nearly had Britt, but Jimmy showed his gameness and fought his man to a standstill. Britt is the gamest boy I have seen in years. He took the greatest punishment a man could take and remain on his feet. Britt landed hundreds of blows on Nelson and was doing splendidly, but his vitality was oozing out. Britt's condition must have been perfect, otherwise he could never have stood the pace. I did not intend to speak to Britt if he won, but when he was beaten I felt it my duty to shake his hand and ask him to let bygones be bygones. The fighting of the boys was clean. I did not have much trouble handling them. I can't say what started Jimmy in the eighteenth round, but I believe he actually dropped through exhaustion. Nelson was too strong for him. It was a grand battle.—Eddie Graney[66]

As for the winner's manager:

I announced on Friday night that if Nelson had an even break in the ring he would knock Britt out, and my prediction came true. All I have to say is that the better man won and that the fight was refereed better than any battle I ever witnessed in my life. Britt could not hurt Nelson, for he had no driving power behind his blows. Jimmy is a great fighter and a game boy and I think that is enough to say about him. I knew I would win my point when I held out so long against Jeffries. Graney is the king of referees and I know every one who saw the fight will agree with me. They say I am crazy, but I think I emerged from this fray like a man with a very evenly balanced mind. I am glad the fight ended in such a decisive manner, for now no one can offer any complaint. Nelson can beat any man of his weight in the world today and will meet all comers. —Billy Nolan[67]

As for the loser's manager:

We lost and lost fairly. We have no excuses to offer. My brother was coming along with his usual spurt and was winning, when Nelson caught him a chance punch on the jaw. Jimmy was game and tried to get up, but could not do so. I would like to match Jimmy and Nelson again. We are entitled to a return bout. Nelson is a great fighter and a wonderfully game one. He took a terrific beating from Jimmy. I am a little disappointed at the size of the gate receipts. Britt and Nelson would have battled before a $70,000 house had Nolan kept his mouth closed. He gained nothing by disparaging Jeffries. I have no fault to find with Graney. All our differences were personal and we never doubted his honesty of purpose. Jimmy will rest up for a while and then I will strive to get Nelson to fight him again. Jimmy is undaunted by defeat. he went in to beat Nelson in quick time or get licked.—Willie Britt[68]

According to box office receipts, $48, 311 was taken for the fight. "The first day the sale of seats opened the advance was $13,000. The second day brought in $10,000."[69] When Nolan became suspicious of Jeffries, his statements to the press hurt sales—people stayed away fearing that the event would never take place.

Manager Coffroth, who made money, was disappointed at the take. The promoter was hoping for a $70,000 house, but it was not to be done. A ray of sunshine for Coffroth may come in the form of moving pictures, as he owns the lion's share in the films. Promising Nelson $5,000 if the pictures are a success, he hopes to net a pretty post-fight penny.

The Yosemite Club gave the fighters 65 percent of the gross receipts, with Britt bestowed a side bonus to make the match. For Nelson's share it was $18,841.29, with the possibility of the picture money, while Britt took $12,560.82, plus the side percentage given by the club and an interest in the moving pictures. Billy Nolan, for his inconvenience, pocketed 25 percent of Nelson's take, or $5,960.32. Each of the fighters paid E. Merwin Graney $500 for his role as a referee.[70]

Coffroth's initial reaction to the fight films was positive—thankfully, the fog cleared away as the bout progressed. For the fight, two machines were in operation from the time the fighters entered the ring till the final punch was delivered. The images of the first two rounds were quite ordinary, but as the sun came out and coincidentally the action heated up, the images improved. Miles Brothers, the operators of the big machines, reviewed the images in advance and approved the quality. Since Manager Coffroth of the club bought exclusive rights to show, or sell, the pictures all over the world, this enabled him to compensate for some of his disappointment over the gate. As mentioned, Billy Nolan sold Nelson's rights for $5,000, claiming he was too busy already just dealing with his fighter. Britt, however, kept his percentage and hoped to be able to reap an additional benefit from his performance.

Eleven days later, it was reported that a scrap had taken place between the Dane and one Willie Fitzgerald of Brooklyn at the Belvidere Hotel in San Francisco. According to the *New York Sun Special* service, in a story picked up by the *Minneapolis Journal*,

Willie, whose Hibernian blood was aroused at the thought of a Dane being champion, made merry at Nelson's expense to a crowd of mutual friends. The tales were quickly carried to Nelson. The latter vowed that he would square matters with the "Mick." Fitz was talking with friends when the Dane walked in. Without a word they walked together. Fitz seized Nelson by the nose and gave that member a vigorous twist. This so disconcerted Bat that he turned away. This move gave Willie a chance to land a few wallops. The first one staggered Nelson, who tried to get into a clinch with the wiry Irishman, but the latter kept him off with a half-dozen more blows. Nelson was down on one knee and bleeding badly at the nose and mouth when friends rushed in and separated the pair.[71]

Promoter James Coffroth bought exclusive rights to show, or sell, the pictures of the Nelson v. Britt fight all over the world, thus enabling him to make up for some of his disappointment over the fight's gate receipts (Library of Congress, Prints and Photograph Division, LC-DIG-ggbain-04500).

The Battler would learn quickly that his title was far more intimidating in the ring that out.

Still basking in his victory,

Nelson was in Kansas City on October 15. He was attending a football game, something he had never done before. Nelson stood on the sidelines and watched the Kansas City Athletics duel with the College of Emporia. While he enjoyed himself, he also declared it was the most brutal exhibition he ever saw. "Excuse Bat from mixing up with that bunch of murderers," he remarked, as about a dozen men went down in a heap on top of the ball. "See 'em pile on that poor guy; he'll be killed."[72]

Nelson commented that he'd rather take his chances in the ring than be on the playing field, and he just couldn't believe some of the antics a football player could get away with. The Battler also picked up a few laughs with lines like, "That referee is worse than Billy Roche," and "Say, I always thought this was a dude's game, but I guess I'll take off my hat to the chaps from now on. Wouldn't Tom Sharkey be a peach in this game?"[73]

If it is labor that preserves us from three great evils—weariness, vice, and want—then Oscar Nelson had too much time on his hands for Voltaire. This said of a man who had few vices but a preponderance of unfortunate incidents involving the opposite sex.

An article in the *San Francisco Call* on September 24, 1905, thirteen days after Nelson's victory over Britt, read, "Battling Nelson Flame Appears in Lawlor's Court: Celia Fay, who hypnotized the Dane, is instructed and arraigned on Grand Larceny charges." The article goes on:

> Clad in raiment that fairly glittered Celia Fay, Battling Nelson's flame, appeared yesterday in Judge Lawlor's court to be instructed and arraigned on a charge of grand larceny. Judge Lawlor summoned T. Fitzpatrick of the Bond and Warrant Clerk's office to find out whether he deemed the $500 bail put up by the Battling Dane sufficient to hold the fair Celia. Fitzpatrick declared that the bail was satisfactory.[74]

Fay, accused of robbing P. Bauer, a drummer, of $260, is the same damsel who caused the split between the Battler and his former manager Ted Murphy—a date with Fay that night likely the reason Nelson did not go after Murphy that infamous evening. Fay was released and ordered to appear for trial on Tuesday.

It is said, to quote Jane Austen in *Pride and Prejudice*, "A lady's imagination is very rapid; it jumps from admiration to love, from love to matrimony in a moment." Well, a boxer's imagination, especially those of a champion, can also shift at a moment's notice. A dispatch to the *Record-Herald* from Cincinnati on November 10, forty-seven days after the Fay bailout, stated,

> "Battling" Nelson, the pugilist, yesterday for the first time announced that he was engaged to marry. The lady who is in time to share his fortunes, is Miss Marguerite Bellangero of Fairfax, California, a small town near San Francisco. She is only 16, and Nelson wanted to marry her at once, but has agreed to wait.[75]

Bellangero was a slender blonde born in Italy, and as Bat says, "You can't beat her for looks."[76] She resided with her father, Giussepi Bellangero, and courtship with Nelson was arduous and persistent. While training for the Britt fight, Nelson would go horseback riding with her nightly. The relationship, however, did not bode well with Billy Nolan, who felt courtship an unessential element to fight training.

Thirty-seven days later, on December 17, 1905, it was announced in Toledo, Ohio, that Miss Gertrude de Milt, one of the stars with Fred Irwin's burlesquers, the Majestys, was engaged to "Battling" Nelson. The date of the wedding had not been set, but according to Miss de Milt, it probably would occur after the close of Nelson's engagement—Nelson had joined the company for a stint. The beautiful young woman, who caught the pugilist's eye, had had a short but successful stage career.

Members of the company, who had been quick to notice the actions of the couple, confirmed that both had talked of the engagement for some time, but some considered it only a joke. "When Miss de Milt appeared on the stage last Tuesday wearing a three-carat diamond ring on her engagement finger she was hard pressed for the truth, finally admitting today that the engagement was a fact."[77]

With the announcement comes the statement that Nelson will star Miss de Milt, who lives in Brooklyn, New York, in his own show next season.

Noting some of the changes in the sport in 1905: James J. Jeffries announced his retirement from boxing and relinquished the world heavyweight championship title on May 13; Marvin Hart knocked out Jack Root in the twelfth round on July 3 in Reno, to take the title. Hart, who was saved by the bell in the seventh, just wore his opponent out, and on December 20, Bob Fitzsimmons lost his world light heavyweight championship to Philadelphia Jack O'Brien on a thirteenth-round knockout in San Francisco. O'Brien then effectively relinquished the title soon afterward.

Those who remained champions from the previous year include Tommy Ryan (middleweight), Barbados Joe Walcott (welterweight), and Abe Attell (featherweight). Jimmy Walsh will take the top position in the bantam class after Joe Bowker vacated. Perhaps the biggest surprise of the year, if you don't look too closely at the Hart twenty-round decision over Jack Johnson, comes on October 18, when ex-bantam and ex-feather champ, Terry

James J. Jeffries announced his retirement from boxing and relinquished the world heavyweight championship title on May 13, 1905. Over five years after retiring, he made a comeback on July 4, 1910, at Reno, Nevada, in a match against champion Jack Johnson (Library of Congress, Prints and Photograph Division, LC-DIG-ggbain-04527).

McGovern, puts Harlem Tommy Murphy down four times to take a first-round victory in Philadelphia.

In a memorable year that saw five ring battles—if, of course, you don't include the aforementioned females—involving "Battling" Nelson, he would not take a loss. Instead he would pick up two wins, a draw and two no decisions to be added to his record. He would fight forty-five rounds, the longest the eighteen-round clash with Britt, the shortest being his three six-round affairs. Nelson would fight two members of boxing's elite, Abe Attell and Young Corbett II. The victory over Jimmy Britt enabled him to pick up the world white lightweight title. And, in Bat's own words, "that may not sound as big to you who read it as it does to me, but to have that title in front of a fighter's name means both fame and fortune, as well as the satisfaction of having conquered them all."[78] Mr. Nelson would learn later that it is not titles that honor men, but men that honor titles.

FIVE

1906

McGovern and the Fight of the Century I

> The worst evil that a young pugilist has to encounter is the tendency on the part of certain men connected with the game to make him dishonest.
> —Oscar "Battling" Matthew Nelson[1]

In 1906, the Dow closes over 100 for the first time; a young socialist named Upton Sinclair published the novel *The Jungle* at his own expense, horrifying Americans by his accounts of the conditions in meatpacking plants; and President Theodore Roosevelt popularized the term "muckrakers" in a speech alluding to Bunyan's *Pilgrim's Progress* and the man with the muck rake.

With a few bucks in his pocket, Oscar Nelson, a former meatpacking employee and now world white lightweight champion, transformed his fight purses into judicious investments. From real estate to even stage productions, it was his sound financial strategy that he believed would secure his future. Now well known, Nelson also became an unfortunate victim of muckraking. For boxing, seeking and publicizing scandalous information about famous fighters—even if it has to be in an underhanded way—will become, as unfortunate as it sounds, as much a part of the sport as a ticket.

Just five days into the new year, and the Battler was already on the defense. It seems Miss Lizette Howe, a pretty burlesque actress appearing at the Grand Theater in Butte, Montana, that week, had brought a suit for breach of promise. The intent was to upset Nelson's engagement to Miss Gertrude de Milt, if, of course, the law could help her. Answering the question, which ring has no corners? This appeared to be another tough fight for the Battler.

Miss Howe engaged the services of a New York attorney to look after her interests. Although she was currently in a production, she said she would leave the company and go east if necessary to prevent the marriage. Miss Howe also claimed that she was engaged to the fighter two months prior while he was appearing with the company in which she was one of the principals. According to her, it was a case of love at first sight, and both were together constantly for the ten weeks Nelson was with the company. Miss Howe also claimed to have handled his money for him and even worn his jewelry during productions.[2]

It was Friedrich Nietzsche, a German philosopher, who once quipped, "The true man wants two things: danger and play. For that reason he wants woman, as the most dangerous plaything." Perhaps it was time for Oscar Nelson to place a limit on his rounds of precariousness.

Five—1906: McGovern and the Fight of the Century I

As for Oscar Nelson, he was in Hot Springs, Arkansas, saying—or as the press saw and spelled it out, talking "something like a broken cigaret"—he would fight Kid Herman in the vapor city if it could be arranged.[3] Nate Lewis, Herman's manager, was in Chicago when he heard the news.

"Herman will fight Nelson at any time or place and under any conditions suitable to the Dane," Lewis vowed, "but, what is the use of them boxing at Hot Springs for $1,000, or so, when they have been offered a $15,000 purse by the Pacific Coast Athletic club of Los Angeles?" Lewis then footnoted his remark—"provided Herman beats the winner of the Corbett-Herrera battle which will take place at Los Angeles January 12?"[4]

Nelson had been performing with T.W. Dinkin's best traveling attraction, the Baltimore Beauties. The company, with its well-drilled chorus and entertaining vaudeville segments, drew considerable attention thanks to the Dane—notably his boxing

An illustration showing President Theodore Roosevelt as a boxer sitting on a stool with his arms resting on the ropes in the near corner of a boxing ring, waiting for a challenger to enter the ring and sit in the vacant chair in the "Democratic Corner" (Library of Congress, Prints and Photograph Division, LC-DIG-ppmsca-25853).

exhibition with his sparring partner Jimmy Potts. The stint, originally taken for the "easy money" on Bat's end, looked to favor the opposite end as well, or so it would prove.

By the end of January, more of Bat's love interests had surfaced and gone sour—some intending to sue him for breach of promise. Who was it that said, "Left to herself—or was it themselves?—a fiancée will always turn from bad to worse"? Already being contacted by numerous attorney's willing to settle their cases out of court, the Battler was a bit bewildered. Having seen and heard enough, Oscar contacted his father to have him meet him in Milwaukee, which he did. His legal counsel suggested immediate action, including press coverage, in an attempt to defuse the situation. On January 26 the *San Francisco Call* reported, "Nelson Deeds Away Property, Takes Precautions against Soubrettes Getting Coin or Real Estate."

The Battler had, just as reported, nearly all of his money and real estate deeded over to his father—for some who viewed the father's signature, it was the first time they realized the family's name was Nielsen instead of Nelson, as it was generally accepted.[5]

"You know a guy in my place cannot tell when some of these stage fairies are going to steal him," said the Battler, "and I thought it best to take no chances. There is only one girl for me, and when I get ready there will be a merry wedding far away from these parts."[6]

Despite all the muckraking, Oscar didn't detest the press. He simply—as professional athletes can attest to—had his moments with them. For the most part, he handled them well, which was a delicate balance of giving and taking away information. Seeing his name, picture, or an article he authored in the newspapers was often a thrill, but not under the current conditions.

Not quite twenty-four years old, it was hard to believe that Nelson had been fighting for almost eleven years. His ascension into the ranks had been slow and steady and seemed to have served him well. However, he was quick to point out other pugilists who, he felt, didn't pay their dues, beginning with Jimmy Britt. Leaving the amateur ranks, Britt managed himself onto some impressive undercards, the increased exposure serving to accelerate the popularity of the pugilist.

> Fortune was slow in opening up for me, and now that I have won the [white] lightweight title I intend to cling to it until some fellow, superior to me, beats me to the floor unconscious. Many fellows who have won fortunes in the ring squandered their money. But not for me. I was down and out long enough, and now that I have a snug sum stowed away I will hang on to it, for I can't always be able to fight for a living. When I leave the ring, I will be so fixed financially that my old days will be spent in peace.[7]

Nelson's obsession with money, an intimidation factor used successfully by many a pugilist including John L. Sullivan, would slowly begin defining him more than his fistic prowess—a dangerous proposition that can lead many to question a fighter's sincerity.

"I have earned about $110,000 by the use of my fists," Nelson claimed. "The most of this amount was amassed during the past three years. From fighting for $5 purses to receiving $1,500 a week for a few minutes work each day with a show is quite a step."[8]

Nelson credited his ability to amass such a fortune on clean living, or never using liquor or tobacco in any form. Sleeping regularly and eating well were paramount to his lifestyle, but he also admitted to indulging in an occasional sweet, such as a pastry or candy. He would immediately clarify his remark by stating that he would never enter a ring unless he was physically fit.

For the first time in his career, Battling Nelson complained about the notoriety brought by being a pugilist, specifically a champion. "No matter where you go you cannot get away from the public," Nelson complained. "Speaking from my own experience, I cannot appear on the street without being followed by a crowd of people who want to shake hands with me."[9] Nelson then pompously compared his notoriety to that of Sullivan, Jeffries and Corbett, then eluded to his own experience with the latter during an appearance at a Chicago theater—he too wanted to shake Corbett's hand, or the man who laid John L. Sullivan low.

Could the notoriety be costing Nelson money? Well, he thought so and recalled a recent story: "When in Philadelphia a couple weeks ago, I was surrounded by a large crowd of salve merchants," the Battler stated while adding that he sought cover in a saloon. "The proprietor closed the doors to keep the crowd out, but in the mix-up to gain entrance a large plate glass window was broken."[10] Unimpressed by the incident, the saloon keeper compelled Nelson to pay $175 for the damage, which he did.

A mere forty days from his next big fight, Nelson turned his attention to Terry McGovern. Admitting that most of the public thinks he will have no problem with the fighter, Nelson took the middle ground, stating, "Maybe I will and maybe I won't."[11] Then he went on to verify that McGovern's speed and punching power were obstacles he must overcome, but he contrasted his remarks with, "I don't think it will go the six rounds."[12]

Commenting on current events, Nelson boldly stated, "It looks as though Young Corbett was on the pugilistic dump heap for good now."[13] A comment he attributed to Corbett's fifth-round loss to Herrera on January 12, 1906. Nelson added, "Dissipation in Corbett's case is a good example of what a fast life will do for a boxer."[14] Confirming that Herrera was a devastating puncher and the toughest warrior he had swapped whacks with, Nelson added, "He can unbuckle a stinging wallop from any hand."[15] Recalling their confrontation in Butte a couple of years back, Nelson upheld his claim that he would never forget the pounding he took from the Mexican. (Herrera, as mentioned, was born in California.)

Possibly feeling guilty of the distraction caused by his promiscuous behavior, the Battler then turned his attention of his manager, Billy Nolan. "Nolan is a shrewd business man and is absolutely on the square," he validated. "When he gives his word you can depend on it."[16] Nelson admitted the mental strain Nolan had endured—the contract negotiations, referee debacle, and thousands of screaming fans yelling to get the fight underway during the team's recent confrontation with Britt. He then added, "When Coffroth told Nolan that unless I got in the ring within two minutes he would take my $2,500 forfeit money, Nolan coolly replied: 'All right, you have already spent $3,000 in getting up this fight and unless the battle goes on you will lose that amount. If you can stand to lose $3,000, I can stand to drop $2,500.'"[17] For Nelson this was an act of contrition, knowing full well that his behavior had impacted his training, and more importantly his relationship with his manager.

Joseph Pulitzer hired a gentleman by the name of Robert Wadsworth

The very popular Terry McGovern was nothing short of a fighting machine. He won the bantamweight championship on September 12, 1899, when he knocked out Pedlar Palmer in one round. McGovern then relinquished the bantam title and captured the featherweight championship from George Dixon (Library of Congress, Prints and Photograph Division, 2014635693).

Edgren as sports editor of the *Evening World* in 1904. Edgren, born on January 7, 1874, in Chicago, Illinois, studied at the Mark Hopkins Art Institute and at the University of California at Berkeley—where his track prowess led to his competing in the discus and shot put for the American Olympic team at the 1906 Summer Olympics in Athens—and began his journalism career in 1895 at the *San Francisco Examiner*. Though hired as a "handyman," Edgren's prefight publicity for the historic 1897 world heavyweight championship between Bob Fitzsimmons and "Gentleman Jim" Corbett launched his career. Taking a job with the *Evening Journal* in New York as a political cartoonist, he gained tremendous exposure for his coverage of the Spanish-American War in 1898 and became nationally recognized. Working now for *The World*, he grew to love the sport of boxing, along with many of the participants—he was later appointed to the California Boxing Commission by Governor James Rolph—including Nelson, who he figured was always good for a story.

Less than a month before Nelson's duel with McGovern, Edgren ran a rather engaging piece in his regular column that he titled "All about Battling Nelson, Told by His Sparring Partner." In a subtitle, Edgren declared, "Battling Nelson can't block a punch that comes within two feet of his jaw because of his bad shoulder," then stated, "McGovern has a first-class chance to knock him out." Again, keeping in mind the timing of the article, he interviewed Young Donohue, Battling Nelson's sparring partner, whom he titled "the crack New England lightweight," and whose resume included victories over Unk Russell and Young Erne, along with two draws against Harry Lewis. Edgren caught up with Donohue in New York while he was training at Brown's gymnasium with Matty Baldwin, another of "the crack's" victims.

While Donohue was quick to agree that Nelson was indeed tough, could endure a lot of punishment and took good care of himself, he also noted that the fighter didn't work as hard anymore, his arms were flabby and his neck looked fat. Donohue then admitted, "I was surprised when I found out how easy it is to hit Nelson on the jaw."[18] He then stunned Edgren by stating, "The trouble is that he has a bad shoulder. He can't double up his right arm far enough to let him guard in close."[19] This made it easy to shoot a right to his jaw because he can't block it.

"He turns his head to the right and takes a punch as he comes in," Donohue noted. "He hooks his left, and then, if he gets in close, he brings the right up."[20] Then the employee took a few cracks at his employer's façade: "The left side of Nelson's face, is all beaten up and his left ear is pounded out of shape."[21] He then substantiated that Nelson took far too many punches and didn't care how hard he was hit, as he loved mixing it up in close.

Then the conversation switched to manager Billy Nolan, or the cat watching over the mouse. "One day we all went into a candy store. Bat picked up a piece of candy and was just putting it into his mouth when Nolan saw him. Nolan knocked it out of his hand and began roasting him. 'Next thing you'll be wanting to go out on the town,' he said, 'eating candy, hey?'"[22] A story was then told about Nolan chasing down Bat in the theater only to find him in the wings with a showgirl.

"McGovern," Donohue then confirmed, "has a first-class chance to knock Nelson out."[23] He then went on to pontificate about Nolan before closing with, "He [Nelson] would rather fight than box any day."[24]

Reading between the lines, the article—fight propaganda at its finest—was published by Edgren for a reason. Was it to convince McGovern that Nelson was vulnerable? Overconfidence, as most understood, was a common downfall of many a pugilist. Or was it to draw

Five — 1906: McGovern and the Fight of the Century I

McGovern inside, which would leave McGovern susceptible to a powerful Nelson right? Or was it as simple as Edgren wanting to tarnish a bit of the Dane's reputation, perhaps in retribution for an action or comment? Billy Nolan was a crafty codger who always had one hand on his wallet, so it certainly wouldn't have been beyond him to beguile Donohue into speaking to Edgren.

Eleven days later, the Battler was spending some time in Huntington, Virginia, prior to heading to Philadelphia to train for his battle with McGovern. While taking a walk, Nelson noted Mrs. Frank Howard and her two children on a buggy ride. All of a sudden the horse became frightened and bolted. Noting the situation, and well aware of the peril facing those in the carriage, Nelson darted after the animal. Leaping for the horse's neck, Nelson managed to successfully stop it, but only after he was dragged a considerable distance—a behavior Oscar was certainly familiar with from his days cutting ice. While Nelson was bruised, his injuries were not serious. Observers who had read Edgren's article would have noted that the right-handed Nelson used his right shoulder during the incident.

Edgren, like any good editor, was always looking for a clever slant, so he decided to send a famous athlete to visit Nelson's training camp. Just four days before the fighter's next fray, he ran the story in the *Evening World* but didn't reveal the name of the athlete. The article provided an interesting glimpse into Nelson's fight preparations, along with the opinion of a fellow athlete that the Dane was indeed ready for battle. Astonished at the Battler's commitment and hard work, Edgren's athlete was immediately impressed by Nelson's daily regimen. The fighter greeted the new days at 7:15 a.m., ate a light breakfast, and then waited until 9:30 before starting his roadwork. Following a ten-mile jaunt, the fighter got a rubdown, then had some lunch. Following his midday meal, he took it easy, shared a few stories with friends and perhaps a select visitor, but made no attempt at strenuous work. Being watched in camp by 125 spectators did not bother Nelson in the least, as he seldom, if at all, interacted with them. The Battler then played a game called ROKO, which he believed quickened the eye and improved his footwork. The game was essentially a speed bag, with elastic cords attached to both ends of the bag. The opposite ends of the cords are then attached to supports above and below. (A version of the game, or equipment if you will, is sold today as part of light commercial boxing stands.) At 3:00 p.m., it was into the gym for some sparring with three carefully selected partners—each chosen to improve a certain element in Nelson's arsenal. Skipping rope and bag work followed, before another rubdown. Now it was 4:45 p.m., and it was time for a quick walk before dinner. After his final meal of the day, about 7:00 p.m., it was another short walk, followed by some correspondence to both friends and family. Watching the time, the fighter then tried to get to sleep within an hour. The public, especially those in Philadelphia awaiting the fight, was so impressed with what they read about Nelson that much of the money slated for McGovern then turned to the Battler.[25]

Days before the fight, the conflict had already been dissected from nearly every conceivable perspective—something, by the way, that both fighters enjoyed. Everyone associated with the battle was given a forum. Billy Nolan, Nelson's manager, insisted that the fight be governed by straight Queensberry rules—no Philadelphia flavor added. This stressed that an opponent must battle his way out of clinches, hitting and protecting themselves at all times. While they must break at the order of the referee, the official cannot put a hand on either man. If a fighter doesn't break when requested, he could be disqualified. In the event of a knockdown, the man who delivered the blow must return to his corner until the count is finished or the man being counted regains his footing. The counting will be done by the official timekeeper at the edge of the platform, with the official timekeepers for each fighter by his side. This was to ensure a proper count.[26]

Both McGovern and Nelson had to be at the ring at 10 o'clock sharp, with the weigh-in to commence at five minutes past—the weight would be at the lightweight limit of 133 pounds. Both fighters would bandage their hands in the ring, with dressings supplied by the referee.

The Battler worked out hard on Saturday, did some roadwork Sunday, and tried to take it easy on Monday, March 12. Standing at 131¼ pounds, he was as confident as ever and eager to enter battle.

Up along the Harlem, McGovern too was confident.[27] And, quite frankly, he should have been, as he was one of the finest fighters in the sport. Born in Brooklyn, New York, on March 9, 1880, Joseph Terrence McGovern stood five feet three inches tall, with a reach of sixty-five inches. McGovern was coming off three impressive knockout wins in his last four fights. Holding victories over Harlem Tommy Murphy, Jimmy Briggs, Aurelio Herrera, Frank Erne, George Dixon, Tommy White and Joe Gans put him in a class all his own.[28]

McGovern was nothing short of a fighting machine. He won the bantamweight championship on September 12, 1899, when he knocked out Pedlar Palmer in one round. Relinquishing the bantam title, he then moved up in weight and captured the featherweight championship from George Dixon by a knockout in the eighth round and then lost his crown when he was stopped by Young Corbett II in two rounds on November 28, 1901. Though the battle with Nelson would be at a higher weight for McGovern—having captured his titles at 116 pounds and 118 pounds, respectively—he was not the least bit bothered.

As far as the tale of the tape, or the pre-fight measurements made of the combatants, it could be summarized as follows: Nelson was younger, taller and had a four-inch reach advantage. McGovern had a larger

"I am in prime shape, feel as well as ever in my life and am sure of winning," spoke McGovern. "I will do my very best. I intend to fight in my old-time style, but I won't be careless. If I can put Nelson out in the first round you can depend on it that I will do so" (Library of Congress, Prints and Photograph Division, LC-USZ62–116813).

Five—1906: McGovern and the Fight of the Century I

neck, expanded chest, waist, thigh and calf. The fighters' forearms were identical in size. How someone might weight the value of each measurement would be a subjective analysis at best and best left to oddsmakers.[29]

The fight was scheduled for six rounds at the National Athletic Club at Eleventh and Catherine streets in Philadelphia on Wednesday evening, March 14. The bout would be refereed by Jack McGuigan of Philadelphia.[30] The timekeepers were Lon Duriacher for the club, Paddy Sullivan for McGovern, and Eddie McBride of Buffalo for Nelson. The fighters used five-ounce gloves.

Looking at incentives, Nelson would take 45 percent of the gross receipts, while McGovern would take 33.3 percent. The estimated receipts were about $24,000, with Nelson's end about $10,800 and McGovern's about $7,500.[31] "It is expected to be the largest sum of money ever paid by the public to see two boxers in a six-round contest anywhere in the world," wrote the *Albuquerque Morning Journal* on March 14, 1906, beneath a header that read, "McGovern and Nelson Will Make $708 a Minute in Their Battle."

In their final statement before entering the ring, both fighters were confident. As for McGovern's "depend on me" attitude,

> This is the last statement before I got into the ring with Nelson tonight. I am in prime shape, feel as well as ever in my life and am sure of winning. I will do my very best. I intend to fight in my old-time style, but I won't be careless. If I can put Nelson out in the first round you can depend on it that I will do so. I realize that Nelson has the same idea and confidence and that he too, is in good trim. But, he can't outpunch me, and that is why I feel so confident. As I shake hands with Nelson in the ring I will say to him, "May the best man win" and then, go in with an effort to prove myself the best man. After the fight, it's hard to figure just what I will do. You may feel sure I'll fight anybody who wants to meet me.[32]

As for Nelson's "I am going to win" confidence,

> I realize I have a hard fight on my hands, but I am going to win it. I have given McGovern credit for everything. Still I can't see how he can defeat me. He may be trained to perfection and he may have his old-time punch, but you can bet it won't hit me in the right spot. I don't want to be understood as saying I can't be knocked out. I can, the same as anyone else, but Terry won't be able to do the trick. I feel physically perfect, and my years of clean living are responsible for my condition. I have never dissipated, have never smoked or taken intoxicants of any kind, so my confidence in my own ability is not unfounded. One thing everybody may depend on: This fight will be decided squarely. I've never faked anything in my life.[33]

As for an assessment from James Edward Britt,

> If Terry McGovern is anywhere near his old-time form he has a great chance to hold Nelson safe for six rounds. I think Terry is quicker with his hands and feet and can hit harder than the Dane. Nelson cannot knock anybody out in six rounds if his opponent is in any kind of physical shape. Nelson has, according to newspaper reports, framed a set of rules to suit himself, but unless Nelson butts with the head I think the rules are as good for McGovern as they are for Nelson. I have boxed with McGovern, and if he is as good as he was he will outfight Nelson in the clinches. It is a question in my mind whether or not Terry can stand the punishment. If Terry can I look for him to give Nelson a good walloping for the entire six rounds. I will fight the winner in Philadelphia on a week's notice. I will get on a train if the winner is willing to fight the night I get there. I hope the battle pleases the public.[34]

Bat's father, Nels Nelson, made an unexpected trip from Chicago to see his famous son battle "Terrible Terry" McGovern. And the Battler couldn't have been happier, leaping on his father when he entered the training facility. The two were just bursting with excitement. The entire team then headed to Philadelphia to set up quarters.

Nelson v. McGovern, March 14, 1906

The fight had every look and feel of a championship affair, as the rebuilt arena of the National Athletic Club began filling early, about 6:00 p.m. Rumor, and there was always speculation on the day of a noteworthy fight, had it that security might be casual during the later hours of the event—ticket or not, you might be able to work your way into the venue. But that proved unfounded. Security saw to it that not a single spectator could get within fifty feet of the building without showing their ticket.

Robert Edgren would note,

> It was the cleanest and best behaved crowd that ever saw a fight in Philadelphia—the best dressed crowd, and it smoked the best cigars. It was a crowd made up entirely of men who could afford to pay championship rates for their tickets. There was millionaires as thick as plugs in a pudding. John W. Gates, they say, paid $500 for ten tickets, and brought his friends.[35]

All modes of transportation saw to their delivery, hundreds by automobile. By 7:30 p.m., the galleries were packed and the ringside seats full.

Time passed fairly quickly thanks to three preliminaries. The first was routine, but it didn't seem to matter; the second witnessed local Grover Hayes destroy Johnny McKeever in two bloody rounds; and the insipid third was a mirror of the first. At 9:58 p.m. the scales were brought carefully into the ring accompanied by security. This was followed by a wave of photographers, maneuvering and securing their tripods by the ropes before pouring their flashlight powders in anticipation.

The exhilaration inside the venue was ignited by the appearance of Nelson, who climbed through the ropes at 10:20 p.m., followed quickly by McGovern.[36] This as the first loud cheer swept across the crowd standing in appreciation. You could see spectators pointing to their favorites, turning to those around them and staking their claim. McGovern's seconds fidgeted about, led by the ever-agitated Sam Harris, who began carefully arranging Terry's corner. Meanwhile, Charlie Maywood escorted McGovern around the ring like a chaperon with his prom date.

In the Nelson corner, the staidly champ sat and glanced periodically at Billy Rodenback, Joe Humphreys, Johnny Birdick and Terry Lee. Nelson then peeled layers and tipped the scales at 131¼ pounds—a weight that included an undershirt. McGovern, "in a state of nature, barring a pair of socks," then took his turn. The beam was motionless.[37] As the bandaging of hands followed, Humphreys couldn't resist the opportunity to throw a quick jab at Nelson: "Might as well put on plenty of tape, he would need it before Terry got through with him." Nelson, like a cat outside a birdcage, simply grinned.

"I kept Terry McGovern waiting in the cold on the raised platform for about three-quarters of an hour," Nelson admitted, "knowing that McGovern was very, very nervous and easily 'riled,' I took my time in putting the tape on my hands purposely to get his goat. I also brought an extra shoe lace, knowing I was going to break the one I had in my shoe accidentally—on purpose."[38]

As Humphreys went around reading a telegram from John L. Sullivan, Nolan, now in the ring, tended to his fighter, handing Nelson his old fighting shoes that he wore when he whipped Britt. "FOR IRELAND'S SAKE PUT OUT THE DANE. EVERY INCH ON THE LEVEL," Humphreys concluded loudly before reading the name, "JOHN L."[39] Unfazed by the

Five—1906: McGovern and the Fight of the Century I

pronouncement, Nelson stood to adjust his green trunks, in great contrast to McGovern's pink britches—the colors of the silks no doubt a bit confusing to the Irish ringside.

The ring then cleared, as McGuigan took charge. Earlier, Jack had taken a bit of ribbing for wearing his best blue jersey, complete with a large diamond pin, but this time nobody seemed to notice. Then an eerie silence fell over the ring as both fighters stepped forward, separated only by a layer of cigar wreaths that masked the ten feet between them. As the combatants stood face to face, McGovern's manager yelled to Nelson that there would be no hand shaking. The Dane stared right through McGovern like he didn't exist. As the corner chairs dropped, the gong sounded.

Both fighters engaged with a single punch, then came to a clinch. A minute, which felt like five, passed as the crowd, quickly reminded of the Queensberry rules, stood waiting for someone to punch out—each fighter patiently waiting for a display of tactics by the other. How they split would determine fight strategy. The corners waited, as did the crowd. Both fighters broke and threw a punch or two before clinching again. The referee warned McGovern about holding. The process would repeat three times before the end of the round.

According to some reports, the second round was worse than the first. While McGovern was scoring some to the body, he was also doing most of the holding. Nelson was cautioned about using his shoulder. The crowd hissed in disapproval—the fight did not leave a six foot radius at the center of the ring. With the look of a second-rate wrestling match, McGovern's corner grew more confident—they need their fighter to go the distance and not be battered in these earlier rounds.

In the third, McGovern's tactics changed, and he went after Nelson. A left into Nelson's body was met with a clinch, followed by a clean break, then a McGovern recovery. Nelson saw the change and bored in. A good mix found McGovern taking a right but returning a shot to the jaw. Annoyed, Nelson fired back combinations. In another mix-up, Nelson took a right to the chin that sent him in reverse. Gathering his composure, Nelson again came charging and landing. A jolting right to Nelson's body angered the fighter. Following another clinch, the Battler, in a show of strength, shoved McGovern across the ring and into the ropes. McGovern then retaliated with a right. Nelson followed with a vicious right hook to the jaw that shook McGovern. Then more mixing as McGovern's perpetual rights were matched blow for blow. The men were clinched at the gong.

Round four opened with McGovern misfiring wildly, allowing Nelson to send a left to the face before a clinch. In tight, Nelson was hammering the body before sending another left to McGovern's face. McGovern's retaliation was off center, and the fighter looked weakened. Before the gong, Nelson delivered a combination to the jaw that slowed McGovern. It was the first round in which the crowd approval noted any real fighting.

McGovern opened round five with a left to Nelson's chin before entering a mix. The round was fairly even after the first minute, but then Nelson took over. A heavy shot from the Battler sent blood from a cut on the bridge of McGovern's nose—the only bloodshed of the entire event. A clinch followed, with McGovern holding Nelson's left glove under his arm while enduring kidney punishment from the Battler's right. Nelson then broke the clinch, shoved his confused opponent back in trademark Battler style, and delivered a quick combination to McGovern's jaw. It was the perfect time for a knockout punch, but Nelson couldn't deliver. McGovern followed with a few more blows, then went back into a clinch. Nelson delivered a final uppercut to McGovern's chin to end the round.

In the sixth and final round, Nelson missed with a right before the two clinched. McGovern then telegraphed his fatigue by two rights to the wind. Nelson too missed with a couple of shots before driving McGovern into the ropes and delivering some choice body punches. As the gong sounded, McGovern looked like he was almost out.

As seen by the majority of the newspapers, the fight belonged to Nelson, but it would enter the record books as a no decision. It became very clear with this fight that the Battler was not a six-round fighter, nor did he own a devastating knockout punch. This said, it was also obvious that nobody was going to outbox him at this length. And the longer the fight, the less chance any opponent had against the Dane.

In the words of the winner:

> My victory over McGovern was no surprise to me. I must say it came rather easy. I was surprised at Terry's style. I had been led to believe that he was a terror, but I didn't find him so last night. Maybe he has gone back. He was vicious enough early in the fight, but after the third round I knew I had him. His punches didn't bother me any, and if he hadn't held me so much I would have knocked him out.[40]

In the words of the loser:

> I think I earned at least a draw in my fight with Battling Nelson last night. For three rounds, I did all the forcing and landed the cleanest of blows. In the last three Nelson tried to rough it, but he had no advantage. I never was in danger and I think in a longer fight I would have a better chance. Nelson hit me on the jaw, but he never hurt me. He is a tough proposition however.[41]

In the words of the referee:

> There seems to be a lot of talk about my not breaking McGovern and Nelson while they were locked during the fight. It was understood that I shouldn't place my hands on either, and didn't want to do anything that would violate that agreement. The fight might have had a different result if I had separated the men after they failed to break when I told them, but that's problematical. Further than this I can say nothing.[42]

At the Cafe Reynard in New York—"The Terror's" old headquarters at Seventeenth Street and Third Avenue in Brooklyn—an overflowing crowd of over 2,000 rooters, including McGovern's mother, congregated to hear the ticker's report of the fight. The mob became so large that it blocked the Third Avenue traffic for twenty minutes until the police arrived to clear the situation. According to *The World*, "There was plenty of McGovern money in the crowd to cover any Nelson bets at 8 to 5. Even along in the battle when the odds straightened to 2 to 1 the Terror's friends snapped that up."[43]

McGovern's mother, described as "big and belligerent," was rather vociferous before the fight, predicting victory to anyone who would listen. But, as the fight progressed her exuberance gradually dissipated—by the third round she had wrapped herself in a shawl and was silent. As the fifth-round returns were being read, the tears could no longer be contained and poured from her eyes. After the battle, those around her did their best to console her—even giving three cheers for Terry—but nothing was enough to do so. She then expounded, "My boy was up once, but he lost by his own carelessness and when a man once gets down it's hard to get up again. I was afraid he'd not be able to do this trick. This Battling Nelson is the winner. I want to congratulate him. Terry was beaten fair and square. I hope he'll acknowledge it."[44] She then answered a few more questions before turning and heading home.

Immediately after the clash, McGovern went back to his wife and baby who were staying at a friend's home in Philadelphia. Unable to hide his disappointment, he retired early to bed. The following day, McGovern would return to his fallback, that of the stage—he was appearing in a performance at the National Theatre of Philadelphia and one that would have run longer had he been victorious over Nelson.

Later in the week, a bit of pandemonium reigned in the train shed at the Broad Street Station. Prior to the departure of the New York train, Mrs. Terry McGovern tried to finish what the Battler had started. She dragged her husband about the outbuilding casting combinations to his face. According to reports, on the evening of March 19, Terry "joined a merry party of friends and became so absorbed in expressing his admiration for a pretty blonde show girl, that he failed to note the approach of his better half."[45] Let's just say that the quandary did not sit well with Mrs. McGovern. As the pair, and their son Joe, waited for the New York bound train, the combinations flew, and since there were no Queensberry rules in place, nearby trainer Joe Humphreys was unable to break the pair apart. The Battler chuckled at the subtitle of one report that read, "Wife of Little Prize Fighter Objects to Attentions to a Chorus Girl."[46]

Following the McGovern fight, Nelson was quickly matched with Aurelia Herrera at Los Angeles before Tom McCarey's club. McCarey put up a purse of $20,000, in which Nelson would receive a $4,000 bonus, then cut the remaining $16,000 with Herrera at a split of 60 percent for the winner and 40 percent for the loser.

Team Nelson, along with Bat's father, took a little time off and headed to New York City. The pair, who were staying at the Metropole, attracted considerable attention, constantly playing off one another orally, with "Hey, Dad, look over there," and the return of "Yes, Sir," a prefix the father used for the son.[47] The old man with his broken English bore the brunt of Bat's carefree jocularity—a dry as dust humor that few seemed to understand. When the younger Nelson spoke, it was either about the father or the fight. Nothing else seemed to matter much. The father, who now equated fights to houses, was quick to comment to one reporter that every cent his son made in the ring was invested in real estate—at least the portion Bat gave him. The elder Nelson also commented on the pair's intent to head to Europe and visit Copenhagen, Denmark, the place the family left twenty-two years ago.

Meanwhile, rumors ran rampant on the fistic front. Coast to coast, speculation ranged from the Pacific Athletic Club offering a trio of battles including two world championships (an affair that would include Nelson), to James Coffroth's $120,000 offer to Jeffries to fight a sextet of heavyweight fighters—Hart, Burns, Kauffman, Fitzsimmons, O'Brein and Ruhlin. But everything came to a shattering halt on the morning of April 18, 1906, when the most disastrous earthquake in American history shook San Francisco, California. In less than one minute, the quake, whose worst damage was caused by the fire that raged in its aftermath, killed over 1,000 people; 250,000 thousand people were made homeless, and property damage was said to be $250 million. Combined, both disasters killed an estimated 3,000 people and left half of the city's 400,000 residents homeless.[48]

The city was laid waste as far as the eyes could see. Survivors slept inside tents in city parks, waited in long food lines, and prayed for the survival of their loved ones. Food, water, tents, blankets, and medical supplies came in the weeks that followed, but for most it simply was not enough. In Los Angeles, on April 21, Battling Nelson sold newspapers on the street to raise money—having already given $1,000, the peddler added another $188—to turn over to the relief committee at the Chamber of Commerce.[49] Ever since coming west in the spring of 1904, Nelson had grown to love the Bay Area—he cherished the water, mountains, clean living and those around the fight game. It broke his heart to see the city a victim of such destruction. Owing to the disaster, Tom McCarey postponed Nelson v. Herrera until the end of May.

The last thing Battling Nelson needed this time was to open up the newspaper on May 18 to an article titled "Ladies Admire Battling Nelson, Fair Sex Out in Swarms to See Little Dane Train for Mexican Wonder." The article was a reference to the growing popularity of the Nelson training camp at Baldwin's ranch—the pilgrimage quite a fad amongst the elite of Los Angeles society. It was there that throngs of women gathered to watch the Dane during his afternoon sparring sessions. Bat was coming off a recent boxing benefit, where he toyed a few rounds with Eddie Robinson for a San Francisco relief fund. It was at this charity event that the Battler's "sunny smile and cheerful courteous manner" seemed to attract more than his fair share of attention by the opposite sex.[50] So, when the ladies found out he would be training at Baldwin's ranch for a *possible* Herrera fight, they couldn't resist the opportunity to view the fighter in action.[51]

Up to this point, Baldwin's ranch had only been known as a facility that turned out more than one Derby winner—in fact, four Derby winners—called the beautiful stable in the Santa Anita Valley home. Now it had been transformed to a rather comfortable training facility complete with gymnasium and a tent capable of holding over a thousand people.

By the end of May, some of the speculation—which the Nelson camp had been monitoring—finally made it into the press. "In Aurelio Herrera's refusal to weigh in at the stipulated time, local fans today accused the Mexican and his backers of entering a plot to clean up thousands of dollars on his fight with Battling Nelson," stated the *Minneapolis Journal*.

The belief—an opinion that many believe was supported by a sudden influx of thousands of dollars wagered on Herrera just prior to the event—was that backers would send their fighter into the ring weighing over 140 pounds, almost certainly to bring him a victory. Nelson's manager Billy Nolan, with an ear for the rumor mill, claimed he had proof Herrera's friends agreed to pay the weight forfeit in order to get their heavier fighter into the ring. Nolan, who insisted that Herrera weigh in while he was present, saw Herrera balk and called off the fight. While Bat was disappointed in the way the fight was handled, or as he put it, "the way the Mexican crawled out of the twenty round contest," it wasn't the end of the world.[52] He then decided to head back to the Midwest, specifically Iowa and Illinois, with the vaudeville company he owned.

By July, and while playing in Omaha, Nebraska, Nelson had finally had his fill of exhibitions and decided to head to his headquarters in Ogden, Utah, to hunt, fish, and perhaps rest. "I will whip the trout streams and hunt the sage hen and grouse until the open season arrives," Nelson confided. "We are in negotiations with clubs east and west and thought we would go where we get the best offer."[53] Before boarding the Union Pacific with Billy Nolan, the Battler acknowledged that people wanted to see him battle Herman, so that would likely be his next fight. After two weeks of hunting and fishing, Nelson went to Salt Lake City for a three-round exhibition with Willard Bean, a Mormon minister and pugilist.

Bat was an outdoorsman through and through. Whenever he had a chance to talk to friends back home, if it wasn't about a hook in the ring, it was likely about one on a line, as in fishing. Often spouting, "You don't know what a big fish looks like," the fighter would go on to brag, "Some of you manage to catch a six-inch perch in Lake Michigan, or land a half-pound bullhead in some nearby stream, but when it comes to yellowtail, the big boys which make you hang onto a line as though a cow is pulling at the other end, you must take your hat off to me."⁵⁴ Bat would then go off on a fishing tale that would typically include a boxing comparison such as, "Why, I caught fish out at Catalina Island as big as any lightweight in the business. Think of it, a fish as big as a man."⁵⁵ Naturally, leaving Ogden, a tale or two followed—his prowess as an outdoorsman rivaling, at least to him, that as a pugilist. Meanwhile, promoters scrambled to try to put together the ultimate card—Bat versus lightweight champion Joe Gans.

According to Nelson, Gans had been following him for some time, showing up wherever he could, from theater stages to the office of the *American*, a newspaper in Boston. "My first reason for holding him off was that he was looked upon as one of the crookedest fighters the prize ring has ever seen or ever will see," the Battler vehemently stated before referencing Gans's fights with Terry McGovern and Jimmy Britt. "For all of that he was a wonderful fighter and I refused a meeting with him on grounds that I had never been mixed in a scandal of any kind whatsoever, and knew the minute I signed articles I would be accused and called as guilty as he."⁵⁶

Mr. E.L. Van Buren, manager of the Hoffman Club in Sacramento, California, sent duplicate telegrams to the management of both Battling Nelson and Joe Gans on August 5, 1906, that read,

HOFFMAN ATHLETIC CLUB SACRAMENTO OFFERS FORTY-TWO THOUSAND FIVE HUNDRED FOR NELSON GANS FIGHT. BATTLE TO TAKE PLACE IN OPEN SEPT. 3 FIGHT TO BE TO A FINISH CHECK FOR ABOVE AMOUNT ON DEMAND.⁵⁷

The action was the result of five prominent members of the Sacramento community each putting up $10,000 to ensure the contest.

"We want the fight here and we propose to use every endeavor to get it," Van Buren firmly stated, "I have no doubt but we will succeed. The bid we put in today, $42,500, is the highest yet offered, Goldfield, Nevada, having pledged $30,000 and San Francisco $40,000."⁵⁸ The club manager then supported the bid: the location's superiority in hotel accommodations, which was not the case with Goldfield; that the open-air contest would be held in Oak Park, on the edge of city limits; and that the contest would be forty-five or fifty rounds, as state law does not permit a fight to the finish. Van Buren also noted that he would send a check in the amount to the *San Francisco Call*, "the only paper in San Francisco which has given this important sporting event the prominence it deserves."

But despite some attractive offers, Billy Nolan had given his word to the Goldfield Club—the deal would be considered done when the $30,000 in gold offered by the Goldfield club was deposited with the newspaper. Clearly, as many thought, the amount offered by the Goldfield bid was only the tip of the iceberg. It just had to be. Otherwise Nolan wouldn't have been so quick with his word. Nelson's manager believed he would be heading to Goldfield that week to meet with one "Tex" Rickard to iron out the details.

George Lewis "Tex" Rickard, was born on a Missouri farm around 1870. He found himself in Sherman, Texas, because his family moved there when he was just a youth. By the time he reached his teenage years, he was already on his own, living, and acting, like a cowboy. Elected as town marshal of Henrietta, Texas, while still in his twenties, the peaceful town was far from what most might think of as a cowboy town. Life was slow, gunfights rare, and wild dogs abundant. He wouldn't find a fortune in Henrietta, but he did find his first wife, Leona Bittick, whom he married and had a child with. When his wife and baby died, Rickard pulled

According to legend, or perhaps fact, Rickard had done a bit of promoting as a bartender and even became good friends with a popular referee named Wyatt Earp (Library of Congress, Prints and Photograph Division, LC-DIG-ggbain-32373).

up stakes and headed to Circle City, Alaska, a mining town on the Yukon River. Originally attracted to the area by the price of flour and not precious metal, Rickard delighted in the discovery of pay dirt and the Klondike Gold Rush of 1897. Staking a claim in the tent city of Bonanza Creek, Rickard picked and pawed, with either some or no result, depending on the tale he spun, until he sold his claim and headed to the thriving town of Dawson in the Klondike. There, his betting moved from the mine to the roulette table by opening a saloon or gambling house. When local prospectors turned their hunting to Rickard's tables, they turned the tide of the proprietor, who was soon back tending bar in the Yukon. From there he went to Nome and essentially repeated his behavior—from nest egg to saloon (the Northern Saloon) to back on the streets—before finally leaving Alaska at age thirty-one to again seek his fame and fortune. Following a stint as diamond miner in South Africa, Rickard returned to the American West in 1904—this time to open another Northern Saloon, but in a new town, Goldfield, Nevada.

Goldfield, the name alone a prospector's dream, was everything it sounded like and more. It quickly became another boomtown thanks to some substantial strikes—from the banks to the brothels, business was thriving in every direction. But even a town as lucky as Goldfield would need a business strategy to sustain itself. As a saloon owner, nobody knew more people in town, or tossed more from his property, than Tex Rickard, and when he suggested a prizefight during a meeting of local businessmen, it seemed like a solution to their long-term problem. And it would not be just any prizefight, but an event, a showcase to put the town on the map, like that of a world championship. Within a very short period of time, Rickard had not only persuaded the group to form the Goldfield Athletic Club but also to establish it soundly with a dowry of $50,000. It likely goes without saying that Rickard was expeditiously designated as club treasurer and promoter—and why not? According to legend, or perhaps fact, Rickard had done a bit of promoting as a bartender and even became good friends with a popular referee named Wyatt Earp. Unfortunately, that was as far as his contacts went in the game. At least until now, as a $50,000 bankroll can buy you lots of friend in the sweet science.

President Abraham Lincoln once remarked, and Rickard more than once remembered,

A feature prizefight between the first black to win the lightweight title and the world white lightweight title holder put Goldfield, pictured here in 1909, on the map (Library of Congress, Prints and Photograph Division, LC-DIG-ds-03082).

"How many legs does a dog have if you call the tail a leg? Four. Calling a tail a leg doesn't make it a leg." Calling Goldfield the metropolis of the American West, Rickard understood, wouldn't make it a leg. He needed a strategic plan to attract people to the town, something that would draw national attention. And at the center of that plan, at least in his mind, was a boxing championship.

While Rickard was busy targeting fighters, the town got busy with reality. Special rates were being negotiated with the railroads, even special trains from New York to the desert mining center of southern Nevada. A preliminary wrestling bout was being arranged, and an outdoor ring was to be constructed.

After days of both primary and secondary research, not to mention a bit of intuition, Rickard's first targeted fighter was Joe Gans. The black champion was not only the best fighter on the planet—having dominated both lightweights and welterweights—but also broke, a corrupt manager having seen to both. Rickard soon found Gans in San Francisco and wired him an offer for $20,000. No questions asked, Gans accepted, not knowing whom he would be fighting.

Rickard then targeted, and obtained, the services of Battling Nelson. Thirty thousand dollars, or the remainder of the club's treasury, would be the cost.[59] Goldfield now had a feature prizefight between the first black to win the lightweight title and the world white lightweight titleholder.

The town was so excited over the prospects of the fight that the local bank agreed to spotlight the event by representing the purse, $50,000, in stacks of gold coin in their front window. It seemed there was not a city in the country that didn't run a photograph of the display.

Meanwhile, on August 7, Oscar Nelson was making his second visit to a copper camp in Bingham, Utah. He toured the camp before the evening festivities, which featured him in an exhibition, at Canyon Hall. The preliminaries included Joe Green versus Kid Ophie, local favorite Spider Welsh versus Roy Wolf, then the Battler. Nelson would spar two rounds with local Roy Conde, followed by four rounds with Salt Lake's Terry Davis. Following the exhibition, a reception and dinner was held in Nelson's honor, making the entire day a success for everyone involved. While Oscar ate, Joe Gans was arriving in Goldfield to sign for the fight and begin training. Tomorrow, Nolan would arrive, followed soon after by the Battler.

As the press descended on Goldfield, every stage of negotiation, preparation and production prompted a thorough detailing, or a 250-word account, in the following morning's paper. The exhaustive coverage fed the excitement for the event and the hopes of every citizen in Goldfield.

Rickard, quick on his feet, defused any fires lit by the press. He immediately countered claims about Nolan's difficulty during negotiations. For example, weight, along with the weigh-in times, were an understood concern for the Nelson camp following the Herrera debacle. Following negotiations, both camps agreed to a three-time weigh-in, at 12 o'clock, 1:30 and 3:00 p.m. on the day of the fight, and not to weigh more than 133 pounds at any of the times specified. It was also stated that the Goldfield Club would select the referee, and the $5,000 posted by the principals bound both parties to abide by any referee selected.

Nolan acknowledged that both George Gardner and Jack Clifford would be joining Nelson during training. The Battler settled into his training facility on Wednesday, August 15. His first week of work was slow and easy, leaving the boxing for the following week. Veteran writer R.A. Smyth even found time and space to jab Nelson for his recent attire: "The Battler looks like a matinee idol. He wears his watch in his outside coat pocket and has also acquired the habit of wearing a jaunty malacca cane."[60]

Now joined by his wife at his headquarters in Columbia, Gans was doing some light workouts. Frank McDonald had also arrived to assist Gans with his training. Both fighters were given access to automobiles—Rickard not taking any chances with his investment—so that they would not have to walk in or about town.

Nelson v. Gans, September 3, 1906

The town of Goldfield, Nevada, would awake on the morning of September 3, 1906, in a frame of excitement that it had experienced only once before, when gold was discovered there four years ago. And perhaps, as many thought, it would be discovered again. Located about 240 miles southeast of Carson City, its remarkable production of the precious metal drove its population to new heights, and now they wanted to keep it there. The late summer dawn was filled with sunshine, smiling faces and the bustle of an event so large that few could genuinely appreciate its relevance. Goldfield had seen fights before, but not just with fists. Wyatt and Virgil Earp came to Goldfield in 1904, with the latter becoming its deputy sheriff in January 1905. Virgil kept the peace until he contracted pneumonia and died on October 18, 1905. Wyatt left shortly thereafter. And Goldfield just continued growing, strike after strike after strike.

The sounds of bands filled the air by 9:00 a.m. as an estimated 4,000 visitors, many having arrived in town on late-night trains, filled the streets, some waiting in restaurant lines so long they weren't sure if they were having lunch or dinner. The town wouldn't realize it until years later, but on this day it would reach the pinnacle of its population.

Even while the fighters' camps were serving breakfast, rumors flew. The first, out of Nelson's camp, was that Gans was offered $30,000 to lose the fight.[61] Not an uncommon accusation on fight day, but one perpetuated by the recent act of Larry Sullivan severing managerial ties with Gans. It's these last-minute impact statements that can buffer enthusiasm, create havoc with oddsmakers, and produce a level of apprehension that is difficult to counter.

At noon both men weighed in promptly, with neither man moving the beam set at 133. Gans wanted Nelson to weigh in where he could see it, but Referee Siler said it was unnecessary. Nelson then made a comment under his breath and Gans responded, "I'll attend to you when you get in the ring and you can attend to me."[62] Both men retired to their dressing room until 1:30, though Gans waited until everyone left the ring and reweighed himself naked, the beam now falling to 131½ pounds.

Five—1906: McGovern and the Fight of the Century I

It looked to be a sold-out crowd, and the number of women in attendance—estimated at about two hundred—couldn't help but be noticed. Ringside onlookers were quick to spot celebrities, like Jimmy and Willus Britt; Charles Clark of Montana; Harry Corbett; Jimmy Cofer; Nat Goodwin, the actor; Jack Grant and his brother Peter; Eddie Graney; and Eddie Hanlon. It was still hard for many to believe how quickly the special arena—the facility having cost promoters $15,000—had been built. Located down on the flats, two blocks from the main street, the edge of the fence extended directly into, of all things, a graveyard.

At 2:00 p.m., a preliminary bout was held between Bob Lundie of San Francisco and Jack Clifford of Montana. The $1,000 purse went to the latter, who put away his opponent by knockout in the second round.

Between the preliminary and the main event scheduled for 3:00 p.m., fans wandered about, glancing, gossiping and gambling—Nelson money was scarce, with odds 100 to 70 on Gans. The orderly crowd, many from the East, delighted at the appearance of the deputy sheriffs mingling dressed in their slouch hats, vests, and corduroy trousers. Goldfield, at least to some, was still the Wild West, despite the fact that the frontier was officially closed in 1890.

At 2:35 p.m., it was clear that the timekeeper selected wasn't going to make it, so an alternate needed to be selected. This caused a bit of rub with Nolan who immediately protested against any Californian. Burt Ullmer, a local, was then selected. Jack Welch would keep time for Gans, and Charlie Dixon would count the seconds for the Battler, both men from San Francisco.

At 2:54 Nelson entered the ring with his seconds, Billy Nolan, Johnny Reid, Tim McGrath, and Young Kid McCoy. Next came Gans, who was looked after by Frank McDonald, Bob Turner, Kid Simms and Eddie Hanlon. The Gans team immediately objected to Ullmer as the timekeeper on grounds of inexperience. Gans, who was concerned about a foul by one of his corner men, also addressed the newspapermen, making it clear that no member of his team could throw up the sponge for him. Only the referee could determine if he'd had enough or was counted out. As Gans had won the toss, he selected the southwest corner, by which the sun would be at his back. Short blue trousers and shoes without socks trimmed Gans. Nelson was in his light green trousers entwined with red, white, and blue ribbon.

Telegrams were read, including one from Big John L. Sullivan that stated,

REGRET CANNOT SEE FIGHT. IT OUT TO BE A CORKER. REGARDS TO ALL MY FRIENDS RINGSIDE.

Gans, who was seen with $2,000 in bills in his hand, began taunting Nelson to choose the odds. Nolan, who was objecting that Gans did not weigh in with his bandages, then distracted Nelson. Theses actions were taking place just before ring announcer Sullivan stated that President Roosevelt's son was ringside. The crowd applauded in approval as an onlooker yelled, "Show yourself and turn your face to the moving pictures."[63]

Following the introduction of club president Tex Rickard, announcer Sullivan paused, cleared his throat and then spoke: "Ladies and gentlemen, this battle will be for the lightweight championship of the world." A brief warning about jumping into the ring, followed by three cheers for Tex Rickard, preceded the customary challenges and ring introductions: Jimmy Britt wanted a crack at the winner; Eddie Hanlon, Eddie Graney, and Frankie Neil were all introduced; and finally, referee George Siler. Nelson then asked Sullivan to announce that he shared Gans' views with respect to throwing up the sponge. The cheers for both men sounded evenly divided, as the ring was cleared while both fighters posed for photos. The contest would be fought under Marquis of Queensbury rules with five-ounce gloves.

It was 3:22 p.m. when referee Siler called both men to the center of the ring for instructions.

Time was called at 3:25 p.m., fight on!

For a sense of fighting styles and strategy, it is important to take a detailed look at the first ten rounds, round by round.

In round one, as the bell sounded, Gans cued the artillery immediately and began delivering a plethora of good punches: two light lefts to face, a right on body, a combination to the face, a right to the face, two rights to the face, two rights to the jaw, a left to the face, and multiple combinations to the face. Nelson, clearly sizing up his fighter, or asleep depending on your perspective, delivered only a combination to the jaw. Blood flowing from Nelson's ears was the damage assessment. It was an overpowering display by Gans.

In round two, both fighters were up quickly. Gans delivered two right uppercuts; two punches to the jaw that jarred Nelson; nice short-arm rights to Nelson's face, two close-quarter uppercuts, a stiff right to jaw, two short rights to the face followed by a short belt to the ear, and finally a hard left to the jaw. Nelson sent only a powerful right to Gans's face, the rest of his assault not worth noting. Gans, who was in control, kept an eye on Nelson's ear while inflicting minimal damage. Nelson, clearly impervious to punishment, bored in despite his role as a punching bag.

In round three, Gans sent an immediate right to Nelson's ear (obviously told by his corner to work the damage), two uppercuts to the chin, a combination to the head, and a right to the stomach. Nelson dispatched a high right to the eye of Gans, then a left to the face and finally, as the bell sounded, a good right to the face. As far as damage, Gans drew blood from Nelson's nose. It was another round for Gans.

In round four, Gans posted a combination to the face, another combination to the face, a solid shot to the jaw, two rights to the face, and a stomach shot at the bell. Nelson drove Gans into the ropes where he delivered a strong combination to the head, but he was bleeding from the nose. Nelson was a bit more aggressive in this round, boring in with his head. This was the best round of fighting thus far.

In round five, Gans directed a left to the nose, a nice combination to the face, a terrific shot to the nose, a right uppercut to the jaw, and a stiff right to the face. Nelson managed only a right to the ear of Gans and a good right to the kidney. Nelson's nose, bleeding again, was now a prime target and took considerable damage this round. As the bell sounded, Nelson was spitting blood. Betting ringside was two to one in favor of Gans.

In round six, Gans discharged three rights to the face, a right to the jaw, several rights to the face, and at the end of the round was landing freely. Nelson managed only limited counters. Nelson, again bleeding from the mouth, was also cut on the face. The damage to Nelson was clearly evident, leaving many to already speculate on the outcome of the fight.

In round seven, Gans dispatched combinations at will to the face. Nelson offered only a right punch to the body and a few blows to the face but was often missing his mark. As Nelson retired to his corner, he was bleeding from both the nose and mouth. Seven rounds into the fight and Nelson had made no headway against Gans.

In round eight, Gans consigned solid rights to the kidney, a combination to the face, a right to the jaw, and then a strong combination that delivered Nelson to his knees. Nelson offered no offense worth noting during this round. Although Nelson was back on his feet quickly, he was noticeably groggy and fatigued.

In round nine, Gans struck immediately with a combination to the face, followed by a short-arm assault to the jaw. He then delivered rapid combinations to the jaw just prior to the bell. Nelson sent two lefts and a right, at close quarters, and a combination to the jaw of Gans. Nelson, who was taking punches at the rate of four to one, was bleeding only slightly at the end of the round.

In round ten, Gans directed a left to the face, then two rights to the face followed by a succession of lefts to the same target. Nelson saw a nice combination to the jaw of his adversary, followed by some strong punches that sent blood streaming from the mouth of Gans. Nelson began to show signs of life during this round, but he had a long way to go if he was to even the fight.

In rounds eleven through twenty, the pace of the fight slowed, as both fighters utilized tactics to revitalize themselves, clinches and holds becoming more frequent. Offensive tactics, such as boring in, were countered with avoidance techniques, such as staying out of a fighter's range. Frustration, too, began to emerge, often prompting warnings by the referee.

Glazing over the punch details, here is a look at a damage assessment and warnings: In round eleven, Nelson dispatched two hearty right uppercuts to Gans's mouth that started blood flowing. A request to stop Nelson's head-butting was made by Gans to referee Siler. In round twelve, Nelson slipped to the floor while forcing Gans against the ropes—it was noted that Gans held out his hand to help him up. In round thirteen, the mouth of Gans was bleeding again, and there was a bit more wrestling this round than in the last few, initiated by Gans. In round fourteen, Nelson fell back through the ropes by accident, and again Gans offered to assist. But by the end of the round, both fighters were kicking each other and needed to be separated. In round fifteen, Gans forwarded a straight right to Nelson during a breakaway that sent him to the floor, but he arose quickly. Nelson transmitted both an elbow and a head butt that were noticed by Siler, who then gave him a warning. The men fought at such close quarters that it looked more like wrestling. In round sixteen, both combatants were fatigued, and at one point Gans wrestled Nelson through the ropes, and in falling, Nelson pulled Gans back on him. They were both then pushed back into the ring. As Gans went back to his corner, blood was streaming from his mouth. Much of round seventeen was a wrestling match—a style that favored Nelson. This is the first round where Siler cautioned Nelson for hitting low. In round eighteen, Nelson addressed two lefts to the face of Gans before being warned about using his head. Both fighters did not hear the bell and had to be separated. In round nineteen, Siler was really becoming irritated with Nelson's butting and issued a warning, even going so far as to place his hands on Nelson's head twice as a reminder. Nelson sustained heavy damage in round twenty and looked like he was saved by the bell. Siler again warned Nelson about boring in with his head.

Rounds twenty-one through thirty saw Nelson force Gans to the ropes often, but he could not penetrate his opponent's defensive tactics. At this point, both fighters were conserving energy, if and when they could, while managing their frustrations.

In round twenty-one, Nelson's left eye was badly swollen, and his right eye was discolored. In round twenty-two, it was more about wrestling than boxing. In round twenty-three, Siler again warned Nelson about boring in with his head. Nelson brought the crowd to life by staggering Gans, then sending him into the corner with a powerful right hook. In round twenty-four, Nelson received corner instructions to finish Gans, but he could not do it and Gans fought back admirably. In round twenty-five, Nelson took the first portion, but Gans closed strong. In round twenty-six, both men appeared tired, and it was getting harder to predict a winner. Round twenty-seven saw some vicious exchanges as both fighters became exasperated over the other's assault tactics. In the twenty-eighth round, Gans took it to Nelson, leaving him groggy at the bell. Nelson revived himself a bit in round twenty-nine, while Gans kept enough distance to conserve energy. Referee Siler again warned Nelson about leading with his head in round thirty. The frustration was building inside of Nelson, as he deliberately hit Gans after the bell.

Rounds thirty-one through forty fell into a rotation of a round of rest, followed by a round of action, certainly in the case of Gans. Nelson still could not penetrate the defense of Gans, though he was relentless in his attempts. As usual, Nelson was repeatedly warned about leading with his head. In round thirty-one Gans turned defensive to expend less energy. Again, Siler warned Nelson about leading with his head. Gans kept his distance in round thirty-two, as Siler warned Nelson repeatedly about his head. Nelson's left eye was badly swollen and almost closed. Gans landed some impressive shots near the end of the round, but Nelson managed to stay alive. Nelson's left eye was entirely closed in round thirty-three. And the fighter exhibited some weariness for the very first time. It was later claimed that Gans turned his foot during this round. Both men were exhausted in round thirty-four as evidenced by their wrestle, stall, wrestle, stall cycle of performance. Rounds thirty-five through thirty-nine were essentially a repeat of the previous action.

Both fighters did very little fighting in round forty but a bit more in round forty-one. Round forty-two began with a Gans straight left to the face, followed by a clinch. As both men withdrew from the clinch, Nelson deliberately struck Gans low. The fighter doubled over and slowly sank to the floor. The blow was clearly seen by everyone ringside, and there would be no debate with the conclusion: Gans wins on a foul.

It was reported over the wire as "Nelson Deliberately Fouls Gans." Most saw it as, "Nelson had his head on Gans shoulder and his arm down. Several times he hit Gans below the belt, apparently feeling for a vital spot. At last he drew back his right arm and hit Gans a vicious blow square in the groin."[64] Gans then sank to his knees and rolled over to his back. Without hesitation referee George Siler ordered Nelson to his corner and awarded the fight to Gans on a foul. There was unanimous approval of Siler's decision. As for the referee, he did an incredible job of maintaining his control and composure, especially with regard to Nelson's repeated butting. When he was asked about it, Siler confirmed that Nelson had used his usual tactics all through the fight. While Siler knew that Nelson was butting whenever he had an opportunity, he did not disqualify him because he believed it was not hurting Gans, and no other referee had ever disqualified Nelson for doing the same thing.

Everyone was well aware of Gans' athletic prowess, but his endurance on this day really surprised those in attendance. His incredible boxing skills proved even more impressive when it was learned that he broke his right hand in the thirty-third round; Gans confirmed that when everyone thought he had turned his foot because of the way he was hobbling, it was actually due to his injured hand. In addition to knowing that he was intentionally fouled, Gans stated, "He could finish Nelson, as he [Gans] was comparatively stronger and Nelson was growing weaker all the time."[65] Gans also confirmed that he would gladly meet Nelson again in two weeks—nearly impossible and highly improbable—if it could be arranged, and

Five—1906: McGovern and the Fight of the Century I

that he was sure he could whip him. A favorite with the people, Gans's gentlemanly behavior won the admiration of the Goldfield community.

On a positive note, the Goldfield Athletic Club did a marvelous job in promoting the fight. President Rickard stated that the preliminary receipts for the fight amounted to about $78,000—the greatest amount of money taken in for a prizefight in the history of the ring.[66] On an unfortunate note, it was announced that the films, or moving pictures, became exhausted after thirty-eight rounds. As a result, there would be no concluding rounds.

> The official box office statement of Nelson-Gans finish fight at Goldfield, Nevada, before the Goldfield A.C., September 3, 1906, as follows: 927 (tickets) at $25 = $23,175; 130 at $20 = $2,600; 400 at $15 = $6,000; 1,760 at $10 = $17,600; 4,062 at $5 = $20,340, totally 7,285 = $69, 715. There were about 500 entered without paying admissions, including newspapermen, deputies and special officers, making a total of almost 8,000 people in attendance. There were about 1,500 women in attendance from all parts of the world, Signed T.L. Rickard, President, W.S. Elliott, Secretary.[67]

So what exactly did the battle demonstrate? An interesting commentary by Salt Lake writer W.D. Rishel—the area and newspaper had an interest in the Battler ever since he knocked out Spider Welsh back on April 6, 1904—added some insight:

> Now that the fight is over there is none who will not give the negro full credit for winning. The accounts of the fight received in this city only too plainly tell the story that for once in his life Nelson was up against a man who is equal, if not his superior. In Gans, Nelson found a man who could withstand those rushes for over two long hours and still be in as good condition as the heretofore never-tiring Dane. Where other fighters have been slowly worn down by the steady and never-ceasing onslaughts of this remarkable Dane,

Following the 1906 lightweight boxing championship, Goldfield's population slowly declined, leaving behind relics of a lost era (Library of Congress, Prints and Photograph Division, LC-DIG-fsa-8a13229).

> Joe Gans proved by yesterday's battle that he is a gamester who can himself absorb more punishment than any other fighter of the present day, unless it is Nelson himself.[68]

Rishel, not unlike most, believed that Gans did not own a Nelson knockout punch and that Gans played a waiting game with the Battler. This said, he also claimed that Nelson did not have a Gans knockout punch. And, at 133 pounds, Gans could beat the best, and was his best.

So where does this leave the championship? According to Rishel, nothing has changed. Gans was still the lightweight champion of the world, and Nelson was still the white lightweight champion of the world. Despite what anyone thought, the outcome was not decisive.

To sum it all up,

> One must give Gans credit for being the greatest fighter of the day, in science, cleverness, punching and the ability to take punishment combined. Nelson still stands before the world as a fighter whose whole stock in trade is a constitution so remarkably rugged that no man has yet stepped into the ring who can hit hard enough to make him stop.[69]

Three days after the fight, it was reported in New York that banker Henry Clews had received confirmation of the rumor that Battling Nelson was dead. This certainly stirred the wire for some time until finally reports out of Salt Lake City reported that the Battler was alive and well and had gone on a fishing trip. Nelson was "recovering rapidly from the grueling he received while Gans seems to be in almost as good condition as he was before the fight."[70] Nelson would later joke about the rumor—his mother naturally alarmed over the reports—to his New York friends while also bragging a bit about his latest acquisition, a gold mine. Located twenty-three miles from Reno, the Battling Nelson Mining Company was now as busy below ground as their owner was above it.

While the Battler was casting lines in the water, others were casting lines at him through editorials that appeared in newspapers throughout the country. On September 9, 1906, the *Minneapolis Journal* had a field day criticizing the Nelson Team: "Nolan showed himself up for about as much of a sportsman as a green goods operator"; "The fight was one of the dirtiest ever recorded in American ring annals. Nelson 'fought foul' almost every inch of the distance"; and as for Gans, "He slashed and stabbed the South Chicago product until his face [Nelson] looked like a bowl of scrambled plums and fought him to a stand-still for a long time while he nursed a broken hand—broken upon the jaw of the 'durable Dane.'"[71]

And, if all that was not enough, there were also reports around the conflict. On September 20, two men were shot dead and another severely wounded in a Hammond, Indiana, saloon, during an argument over the Nelson versus Gans prizefight. "Patrick Golden and Ferguson Lauden had been discussing the Gans and Nelson fight for some time, when both men became angry and used abusive language. Lauden drew a revolver and fired twice at Golden. As Golden fell dead Lauden aimed his weapon at James Blenn, a porter, shooting the latter to death. Detective John Bellamy interfered and was shot in the leg. Lauden escaped."[72]

By October, Nelson was healing while his memory was fading. "I don't think I hit low at all. I only hit a punch about eight inches with the front of my hand on his liver."[73] The Battler also confirmed that he had sent Gans four personal telegrams asking for another match, but he said he (Gans) would have to give Britt a chance first. In reference to a rematch and telegrams, Nelson asked reporters, "Does that look as I was duck soup to him?"

Nelson also couldn't resist the chance to defend himself regarding the kicking incidents with Gans. He stated very clearly that Gans said "insulting things about my family." He then continued, "Now you can use your own judgement if I was justified in doing what I did or not. You know it is bad enough to have a white man tell you such stuff let alone a coon."[74] That such a deplorable and insensitive remark be cast, and printed, was another testament to the racism that infected a sport and permeated a nation. For every progressive step the sport took, such as allowing a black man to fight a white man, it seemed to always take two steps back.

It was announced in Cincinnati, Ohio, on October 16 that Battling Nelson "has succumbed to the tender passion and was this week engaged to Miss Edna Hall, leading woman of the Bon Ton Burlesque Company," which was playing an engagement in the city. Nelson, whose company was appearing at another theater, confirmed that the pair became acquainted only about a week earlier in Indianapolis, and it was "love at first sight."[75] This as theaters, especially those in the West, were featuring the Nelson versus Gans fight films. Billed by one theater as "The only original life like reproduction of the greatest battle ever fought in the history of the prize ring. Most marvelous accomplishment of modern photography. Every move plain and distinct. Amount of purse fought for $33,500. Amount of gate receipts, $69,715. Prices for this engagement: Entire lower floor, 75 cents, First row in balcony, 75 cents, Remainder in balcony, 50 cents."[76] No comment was made regarding just what portions, or rounds, a viewer might see or in what order.

As for the moving pictures, a controversy between Billy Nolan and Tex Rickard—over the receipts from the Gans-Nelson prizefight—was thrown into the federal courts by James E. Fennessy, manager of the Empire Theatrical Circuit Company on November 19. It was inevitable, as the fight contract negotiations seemed to gloss over the filming. Empire held the concession for exhibiting the films in their theaters.

An unfortunate scenario indeed, but nevertheless necessary once negotiations between Nolan and Rickard collapsed—both failed at any compromise and nearly landed in a fistic duel over the issue in Fennessy's office. Following the dispute, as if matters couldn't get any worse, Rickard wired Ben Selig, of San Francisco, for authority to have Nolan arrested for alleged embezzlement of $15,000.

Five days later, Nolan was arrested in Cincinnati. A warrant had been sworn out in Chicago and brought to Ohio by Sergeant Duffy. It charged Nolan with embezzling $6,000, a dollar figure less than Rickard had hoped for, but nevertheless equally of concern. One would hope that a compromise befitting both ring contributors would be in order.

In December, while in St. Paul, Minnesota, Nelson, along with road manager Abe Pollack and a few friends, visited the state capitol. There they paid the champion of Minnesota politics, Governor John A. Johnson, an hour's visit.

Both politician and pugilist seemed to hit it off quite well, with the Battler claiming, "It has been one of the greatest pleasures of my life to meet you, and now I can think of only one thing that would please me more."[77] The governor just had to ask, "What is that?" "I want a chance to fight for you," Nelson stated. "They tell me you are going to run for president. Well, if you do, I will promise to knock out more enemies for you than I have ever met in the prize ring."[78] With that promise, the two shook hands, and the Battler went on a tour of the new state building.

On the morning of December 26, in New York City, Battling Nelson set sail for Europe aboard the liner *Majestic*. The steamer would arrive in Liverpool a week later. The fighter was meeting up with his manager Billy Nolan—his match with Rickard now resolved—in London, and from there the pair would head toward the east of Europe and wind up in Copenhagen, where Nelson would join his father. Also engaging in some theater dates while in Europe, Nelson hoped to stay until another good fight could be arranged.

Notwithstanding the Gans versus Nelson fight in Goldfield, there were a few other notable conflicts in 1906: Tommy Burns took the heavyweight crown from Marvin Hart, while the light heavyweight title remained vacant. Speaking of vacant, Tommy Ryan vacated the middleweight division, while Billy "Honey" Mellody moved atop the welters. Abe Attell (featherweight) and Jimmy Walsh (bantamweight) stayed in the top slot of their division, and we certainly know where Joe Gans rested his feet.

In 1906, Battling Nelson engaged in two ring battles, fighting a total of forty-eight rounds but not recording a single victory. Instead he would pick up a no decision and a loss by foul to add to his record. Boxers often fought to the level of the competition, and in 1906, Nelson met two of the very best—Terry McGovern and Joe Gans—both considered among the top fifty greatest fighters ever. Nelson's fight with Gans was an epic battle: a record gate for the era, one of the last scheduled fight-to-the-finish championships held on U.S. soil, and the longest clash to end on a foul. The Herrera fiasco was a learning experience, but that's

On the morning of December 26, 1906, in New York City, Battling Nelson set sail for Europe aboard the liner *Majestic*. The steamer, pictured here, would arrive in Liverpool a week later (Library of Congress, Prints and Photograph Division, LC-DIG-ggbain-34327).

boxing, and if it were not for a problem with a weigh in, it would have likely been something else.

Hitting the Battler squarely between the eyes this year was reality outside a prize ring. First, there were his female exploits. Any damage to his reputation from these escapades wasn't front-page news, but it was news and he had to find a way to control it. The cost of his multiple engagements is not known, nor that of any settlements, but the Dane certainly paid a price. Secondly, there was the San Francisco earthquake. When more than half of a city's population, some 400,000, are left homeless, it has an impact. Nelson, true to form, not only saw the devastation but did something about it.

Income from both Nelson fights was easy to total, as well as for his theater appearances, but the value of what he had learned and experienced during the year appeared much greater. They say memories aren't lost if we remember them, and Oscar had a year with his father that he would never forget. Watching the old man light up like a candle while visiting New York, or kidding with him in camp and even ringside, always brought a smile to the loving son's face.

Six

1907
Repositioning for the Ascent

I am not Irish, but I certainly do love the green.—"Battling" Nelson[1]

The steamer *Majestic* pulled into Liverpool, a city in Merseyside, England, on the eastern side of the Mersey Estuary just after the start of the New Year. Nelson enjoyed the trip and often sat marveling that only "ten years before [he] had been riding on the trucks of a train and slinging hash at a cheap restaurant."[2]

Dressed in his city finest, Nelson was met by a committee of English sports and escorted to London, where he found solace at the Hotel Cecil. A grand hotel built in 1890, the Cecil rested between the Thames embankment and the Strand in London, England, and was named after the Cecil family—they occupied the site in the seventeenth century.[3] The mansion was lovely, and Nelson felt pampered during his brief stay. From there, he accepted an engagement at one of the big music halls at Newcastle upon Tyne, or Newcastle, a city in the metropolitan county of Tyne and Wear in northeast England. The Battler drew an enormous crowd—his popularity a pleasant surprise—as he showed in conjunction with the Gans versus Nelson moving pictures.

On January 9, 1907, Battling Nelson was tendered a banquet by the Honorable Louis Zollner, Danish consul at Newcastle, in the banquet hall of the Northumberland café. The notables present included the Lord Mayor of Newcastle, Count J.M. Oubridge and Major Harvey Scott, also Chas. F. Donoghue, R.W. Johnson, J.B. Radcliff, and B.J. Sutherland. A number of speeches were given welcoming Nelson before the diffident Dane was called on to address attendees. Nelson was able to thank all those in attendance but reiterated that he was a man lost for words. The party then retired to a private box at the theater.

Nelson's success in the United Kingdom resulted in a twelve-week contract in the city of London, playing on the Holborn-Empire circuit. "Under my contract I was to receive $1,000 per week to show in one house at a time," the Dane confirmed. "I only worked a week when the Artists' Federation went on strike."[4] Since the federation consisted of almost all the actresses and actors working in England, Nelson refused to work until an agreement was settled; unless the strike is settled, Bat "will lose $25,000, and he is liable under the terms of the contract to pay a forfeit in an equal amount."[5] When it became clear that the matter would take some time to resolve, the Battler crossed the English Channel to spend a week in Paris, France.

Stereoscopic image of the Hotel Cecil and the Hotel Savoy with Cleopatra's Needle and the embankment along the Thames River, London, England (Library of Congress, Prints and Photograph Division, LC-DIG-ppmsca-06812).

Upon his arrival back to the United Kingdom, Nelson was served a notice at the Hotel Cecil to appear in court and answer a charge of breach of contract by the theatrical association with whom he had signed. Thankfully for Bat, the suit was eventually settled. The following week found him at an independent house, the Palace Theater in Manchester. While in the city, Nelson stayed at the Midland, a grand hotel in Manchester opened in September 1903; it was built by the Midland Railway to serve Manchester Central railway station, its northern terminus for its rail services to London St. Pancras. Bat was given the royal suite that King Edward used when visiting the city. Nelson marveled at the hotel—designed by Charles Trubshaw in a highly individualistic Edwardian Baroque style—and identified his quarters as the most beautiful suite in all of England. Following this run, he decided to head home via Ireland, visiting Cork, Dublin, the Killarney Lakes and finally Killarney Castle, where he kissed the Blarney Stone. Departing from the coast at Queenstown, Nelson spent his last evening in Ireland at the Queen's Hotel. The fighter would depart the following morning aboard the steamship *Lucania*, arriving on the evening of March 3 in New York City.

Met at the docks by a throng of friends, sportswriters, and well-wishers, all eager to learn of his plans, Nelson eagerly engaged. He mentioned that both he and Nolan managed to pick up some easy money in England—to the tune of $15,000 in 60 days. Some people drop names, Oscar dropped dollars. He also said that he and his entourage would be leaving in the next few days for Hot Springs, or possibly Mexico. Both Nolan and Nelson raved over their treatment in the United Kingdom and stated they intended on returning in June. Nolan was also preoccupied with a boxing carnival he had on his mind, to be held at the National Sporting Club. "He will take over with him, besides Nelson, a good heavyweight and a man to meet Joe Bowker—Abe Attell the likely choice," according to press reports.[6]

Following his visit to New York, and despite the comments he made to the press regarding his plans, Nelson headed home to Hegewisch to visit with his friends and family—where, of all things, he managed to reach Gans who was showing at the Trocadero Theater. Challenges and terms flew, as did a robust discussion over which fighter had the greater drawing power, but in the end there was no contract. Gans had knocked out Kid Herman on New Year's Day in Nevada and was, as Nelson understood, in no rush to leave the easy-money circuit.

While home, Nelson learned some disturbing news that was quickly confirmed by an article title: "Hegewisch Wiped Off the Map; Battling Nelson on the Warpath," a story that ran in various news outlets.[7] Just as Mr. Nelson had so graciously put his hometown on the map, it was taken off. The Battler, never one to duck a punch, appeared with an alderman and fifteen Hegewischians at the office of the corporation counsel to protest the name change. Hegewisch had been swallowed up by the village of Burnham (in the town of Thornton), as Chicago's boundaries continued to expand. "The post office, where a large crayon of 'Battling' flanks a smaller one of President Roosevelt, is all that is official of what once was Hegewisch," the newspaper pronounced.[8]

Perhaps in a move to establish a bit more clout behind his disapproval of his town's new name, the Honorable Mr. Oscar "Battling" Matthew Nelson, banker, financier, political leader and philanthropist, would assist the directorate of the First State Bank of Hegewisch, now capitalized and prepared for its modest entry into the arena of finance.[9] To some the Battling banker was spreading his wings; to others he was spreading them too far—taking risks in areas where he did not belong. Thankfully, soon he would return to the ring.

Articles, or an agreement outline, signed by three managers—Willus Britt, for Jimmy Britt; Billy Nolan, for Battling Nelson; and Alex Greggains, for the San Francisco Athletic Club (SFAC)—took place on the evening of June 7, 1907. Details of selected articles included the following: the SFAC agrees to promote a twenty-round contest between Britt and Nelson on the night of July 3, 1907 (the date of the fight would be changed to July 31); the SFAC agrees to give Britt and Nelson 60 percent of the gross receipts of said contest, the same to be divided by the boxers, 60 percent to the winner and 40 percent to the loser; the contestants agree to weigh 133 pounds at 6:00 p.m. on the date of the contest; the contest to be conducted under strict Marquis of Queensberry rules; referee to be selected by contestants 10 days before the contest; both men must appear in the ring no later than 10:00 p.m. on the night of the contest; the SFAC, Battling Nelson and Jimmy Britt to deposit the sum of $2,500 each with stakeholder (the *San Francisco Call*) to bind them to the agreement. Many of the fine points still needed to be fleshed out; for example, as of the signing of the agreement, a site for the battle had not been selected. Nelson, who had arrived in Los Angeles on the evening of the signing, was delighted when he heard the news and stated he would arrive in San Francisco the following day.

As the ink was drying on the agreement the press was already hard at work presenting their perspective on both fighters. "As he [Nelson] defeated Jimmy Britt decisively at their last meeting he [Nelson] would be expected to repeat this performance by the majority of the betting men had it not been for that 42 round meeting with Joe Gans at Goldfield last Labor Day," noted the *San Francisco Call* about Nelson. Then there was this: "Some of the critics are pointing out that Britt's showing with McGovern (a ten round mandatory no decision) in Madison Square Garden, New York, was a disappointing one." Let the wagers, not[10] to mention the analogies, begin.

Nelson v. Britt, July 31, 1907

Both fighters weighed in at 6:00 p.m. at the Central Billiard Hall, on Ellis and O'Farrell Street, in San Francisco, on July 31, and both made the specified 133 pounds easily. Following the event, Nelson went to Thompson's Cafe for dinner, while Britt was driven to his brother's house for an evening meal.

The crowd was unruly all day, and by 9:00 p.m. every seat in the auditorium (skating rink)—which covered the length of the entire block from Fillmore Street to Steiner, along Page—had been taken, while 1,000 people moved about the floor and in the gallery. Before the first preliminary went on, the police had little choice but to stop admissions, and the decision did not sit well with the hundreds gathered outside. As this was the first top-notch fight pulled off in the city since the earthquake and fire, interest was enormous.

"The turning out of all the lights, but the four central arcs makes the ring stand out in a blaze of white light midway in the darkened smoke-curtained hall," was how one paper described the scene.[11] It was a breathtaking view for the various observers in attendance.

In the preliminary contests, George Martin, of San Francisco, knocked out John Conkey, of Milwaukee, in the first round, while it took four rounds for Dale Gardner, of Seattle, to kayo San Francisco fighter Joe Elliott.

The ring was cleared at 9:25 p.m. as the crowd took their designated positions and awaited the combatants. Photographers flocked to ringside, setting up tripods, filling flashes and positioning themselves for the pre-fight images. Fifteen minutes later, a man attired in a tuxedo and opera hat suddenly provoked the attention of the audience, and a huge reception began to unfold. It was Joe Gans.

The native son, Jimmy Britt, arrived first in the ring dressed in his street clothes and followed by his seconds, Dave Ernst, Tiv Kreling, Spider Kelly and Sam Berger. The crowd roared to a standing ovation.

Two minutes later, Nelson, in his fight trunks, arrived followed by his seconds, Eddie Madison, Red Corbett, Tim McGrath and Billy Nolan. As soon as Nelson entered the ring he went over to Britt's corner and shook hands with his opponent.

It was now time for announcer Billy Jordan to clear his throat, take a deep breath and begin the introductions: "A native son of the Golden West and one of the gamest boys that ever entered a ring, Jimmy Britt," and the "hardest nut that ever stepped into a prize ring, Battling Nelson." The ovation, which was large for both fighters, then shifted to the cheer of "Gans, Gans, Gans, Gans." It was then that Gans entered the ring to Jordan's call of, "The only lightweight champion of the world, Joe Gans." Answering cries for a speech, Gans said, "I thank you gentlemen for the reception. Only one thing brought me here, and that is to challenge the winner. Thanking you kindly, one and all."[12] Time was called at 10:04 p.m., fight on!

Looking at the highlights of the first five rounds: In round one Britt opened with a right to the jaw, followed by a combination to the face and a left to the body. Nelson, who nearly went to the floor with the right, regained composure, smiled at his seconds, then delivered virtually no offense. In round two, Britt posted a left to the stomach, followed by another left to the stomach, before sending two lefts to Nelson's right ear. Nelson mailed two right uppercuts to the body, a right to the face, two lefts to the stomach, and a combination to the face. Nelson's ear was bleeding when he returned to his corner. In round three, Britt consigned a

The popular announcer Billy Jordan loved to introduce the Dane (left) as the "hardest nut that ever stepped into a prize ring, Battling Nelson." In this posed training photograph, Nelson's head—seldom higher than his opponents—would have been an easy nut to crack (Library of Congress, Prints and Photograph Division, LC-DIG-ggbain-01715).

potent combination to the jaw, a left to the stomach followed by a right to the face, and two powerful lefts to the stomach. Nelson directed a left to the face, three rights to the kidney, a left to the face, followed by two more lefts to the same area. As for round four, Britt mailed two straight lefts to the face, a right to the ear, a left to the jaw, and two blows in the face.

Nelson directed a combination to the face and some nice short-arm assaults. Britt was bleeding from the nose. And in round five, Britt sent two lefts to the face, two more lefts to the face and some impressive short-arm assaults. Nelson dispatched a combination of uppercuts followed by two lefts to Britt's mouth that drew blood and also delivered some quality short-arm assaults.

A quarter of the distance had now passed. Round six saw Britt address a left hook to the head, a hard left to the body, and many short-arm assaults. Nelson forwarded multiple jabs to the mouth, three terrific left uppercuts to the jaw and had Britt throwing punches to the wind near the end of the round. Britt's nose was now bleeding. Round seven opened up with both exchanging lefts to the jaw before more serious infighting. Britt transmitted nice combinations to Nelson's face. Nevertheless, Nelson was forcing Britt around the ring at will. At the end of the round, Gans stood and yelled, "Good boy, Jimmy!"[13] Round eight witnessed Britt convey some subtle left hooks and some impressive short-arm rights to the jaw. Three hard lefts by Britt drew blood from Nelson's muzzle. Britt then began scoring at will with combinations. Nelson managed only to withstand the assaults and shake his head to verify he was unhurt. As round nine opened, the crowd cheered Britt as he arose. Britt sent two lefts and a right to the jaw, followed by a crushing left to the jaw, two lefts and two rights to the face, and a left to the face. Nelson managed only two lefts to the face, as his own countenance took a tremendous beating. Britt was clearly in control and favored by the crowd. Round ten opened with Britt keeping his distance and firing two rights to the head, followed by three lefts to the same place. Nelson dispatched a right uppercut. Britt then drew blood from Nelson's nose with a battery of lefts. At the halfway point of the battle, Nelson was clearly outpointed.

As the second half of the fight opened, the crowd was wondering when Nelson would really start to fight. Britt opened with two rights to the face and controlled Nelson with his jabs. Nelson then began forcing the fighting but Britt wisely kept him at a safe distance. In Round Twelve, Britt posted four to one cuffs at close range. Every time Nelson forced the fight, Britt delivered a solid mix in return. Nelson mailed a solid combination to the face, before slipping to his knees. By the end of the round, Nelson was hanging on and butting, both of which earned him warnings. As the bell rang Nelson spat blood on his way to his corner. In Round Thirteen, Britt addressed two lefts to the stomach, followed by another left to the stomach and a left to the jaw. He then followed with two rights and a left to the jaw. Nelson sent a robust right to the jaw during a very weak offensive. He also slipped again, but regained his balance. In Round Fourteen, Britt dispatched a couple lefts to the head, followed by a firm mix of shots to the face. He then followed with a terrific right, accompanied by another solid combination to the face. Nelson forwarded an elbow to Britt, which floored him, although not for long. As the bell sounded, Bat sent a hard right to Britt's body. Nelson's fruitless assaults were not wearing down Britt, who always was able to slip away. Nelson began Round Fifteen by chasing after Britt. Three lefts by Britt completely turned the Dane around. Britt then fired his lefts at will while trying again to stay out of range. Britt was dominating the fight, and no matter how loud Nolan yelled at Nelson it was doing no good.

The final quarter of the conflict began with a Nelson uppercut and head butt. Britt then posted a left and wasn't hesitant to deliver a good combination whenever Nelson tried to bore in. Nelson mailed a nice amalgamation to the face and fought strongly throughout the sixteenth round, but it wasn't enough to win the segment. In the seventeenth, Britt addressed a left to the jaw, a combination to the jowl, a left to the face, another left to the face, and another solid combination. A powerful left to Nelson's face sent blood streaming from his mouth. Nelson directed only a right to the stomach, while his attempts to bore in on Britt failed. Britt opened the eighteenth with a left to the ear and a right to the nose. Britt then transmitted a left hook to the mouth to start Nelson bleeding again, followed by a combination to the face. As Nelson tried forcing things, he was met by a left uppercut to the mouth. Three targeted shots to Nelson's mouth forced the fighter to cover up and stall. Britt then sent combinations at will without retaliation. Nelson's right eye was nearly closed by the end of the round. When the bell sounded for round nineteen, Britt sent a straight left to the mouth, which Nelson answered with a butt. As Nelson tried to move Britt about, the Californian controlled him with a respectable mix of punches. Britt was in total control, always cautious to remain at a safe distance. Both warriors shook hands at the start of the final round. Nelson drove a left to the jaw, then appealed to the referee about Britt's holding on. The two mixed it up before Britt drove Nelson to the ropes with several fierce blasts. Nelson appeared helpless and Britt went to him, nearly sending the Dane through the ropes. The bell saved Nelson in the nick of time. As Nelson went to his corner, he was vomiting as a result of the pounding.

Britt was given the decision at the end of the round, referee Walsh having given Nelson only two rounds out of twenty.

The observations were valid: Nelson did the greater part of the leading, Britt was far more clever, Britt stayed away from Nelson, Britt's defense overpowered Nelson, and Nelson's hitting power was slowly diminished. One of the better summations ringside was, "Let's call it 'Battling Britt' and 'The Enduring Dane.'"[14]

After the fight, Nelson went to his dressing room and hurried into his street clothes. "I drove to Burns's baths in our automobile, where I retired for the night a very sick but much wiser young man," Nelson recalled.[15] The Battler blamed part of his loss on his pre-fight steak dinner, but this sounded like more of an excuse than a reality. "I knew the cause of losing this fight; knew in my heart that I shouldn't have lost, therefore would not give in, but was willing to start from the bottom and fight up the championship again," he admitted.[16] Despite the fact that he was willing, or so he claimed, to start again from the bottom—which is a bit of an exaggeration considering his ring experience—this would mean putting this loss behind him, and that would not be easy. Like any fighter in this situation, Nelson would need some time. To first reflect on his career, followed by the possibility of implementing a new fight plan. If he really intended to start again, it would mean rededicating himself to the task and avoiding the distractions. It might also mean forgetting about the past, something Nelson had never been good at.

On September 20, Battling Nelson, amid everything else he was dealing with, traveled to Butte, Montana, for the sole purpose of having arrested and prosecuted Harry O'Neil, a man who skipped out of town three years prior with money that belonged to the Dane. He did so because the county attorney's office refused to prosecute O'Neil unless Nelson paid the costs. The story goes back to September 1904, when Nelson came to Butte to battle Aurelio Herrera. There was someone tending bar for the M & M named Harry C. O'Neil. It seems Harry was rather popular in town, owned land and knew the right people in the right places. Since O'Neil was also well known in sporting circles, Nelson gave the bartender $350, or $375 depending on which source you believe, to place a bet on him against Herrera. It seems that less than an hour after Nelson won, O'Neil hitched a ride on the bumpers of a freight car, then headed south. Later, O'Neil was discovered tending bar in El Paso, Texas. Nelson said, "All I want is revenge."[17] Ironically, the incident, which is rather confusing to follow, led to the discovery that Billy Nolan was working harder on his own behalf than that of Nelson. So, Battling Nelson discharged Billy Nolan from his duties.[18]

Following the fiasco in Butte, Nelson went to Minot, North Dakota, to do a little duck hunting. Guest of landlord C.H. Parker of the Leland Hotel, the Battler couldn't resist the chance of shooting a few wagonloads before they all flew southward. Of course, the local press flocked to the sportsman. Nelson, using many now familiar lines with reporters, praised Minot for its hospitality.

In between a little rest and relaxation, and perhaps to not feel guilty for his lack of training, Nelson picked up some pocket cash from three four-round exhibitions. On October 19, he sparred with Tom Freebury at Red Lodge, Montana, then four days later took to the ring against Charlie Berry in Billings, Montana, before wrapping up his quick tour with a display against Mark Nelson in Minot, North Dakota. Towns like Red Lodge, with its 4,000 people—a plethora of miners, gamblers and saloon employees who contributed to the town's rather violent reputation—including countless Scandinavian immigrants, welcomed exhibits of the sweet science. It was violence in a controlled environment, and for some, the first they had observed in a while.

On December 9, the *San Francisco Call* couldn't resist the opportunity to print a photograph of Nelson, kneeling with his hunting partners, just in front of his trophies. The caption read,

> Battling Nelson and the members of his hunting party as they appeared near Williston, North Dakota recently. The 18 deer they secured bear mute testimony to their skills with a rifle. Two of the deer and one coyote made up Nelson's contribution. The members of the party include: The camp cook, Harry Hayes, Charles Loey, Horace Peck, William Jarbis, Nelson, Ed Cole, Clarence Parker, Arthur McGahey and Charles Hewitt.

The division championships shifted a bit in 1907, as the versatile Stanley Ketchel took over the middleweights and Mike Twin Sullivan the welters. Everyone else at the top of their divisions stayed put, in a year that had its fair share of surprises. Take for example the Ketchel versus Thomas battle in Colma on September 2. Thomas floored Ketchel in the twenty-seventh round with a right to the chin, but champion Ketchel came back to floor Thomas four times in round thirty-two before kayoing him with a left hook to the jaw. Also at Colma was the July 4 battle between Tommy Burns and Bill Squires. Scheduled for forty-five rounds, Burns caught the unbeaten Squires perfectly and dropped him at the 2:09 mark of the first round to retain his title. And, finally, there was Jack Johnson breaking Fireman Jim Flynn's jaw on the way to an eleventh-round kayo.

It was a strange year for Battling Nelson, having not had a year with just one recorded fight since 1897—or, for that matter, a year where he lost his only ring battle. The Battler had traveled the world, slept in rooms reserved for royalty, kissed the Blarney Stone, expanded his banking horizons, watch his hometown disappear, fought Jimmy Britt for the third time, chased down an old gambling debt, fired his manager, and shot some ducks, deer and even a coyote, all while trying to figure out exactly where he stood in the boxing world. If things were going to improve in 1908, he needed to begin anew, and it starts now.

1908

The Battler began the new year in Minneapolis, where he had recently received two "black hands," or extortion letters, demanding $500. Although he wasn't worried about the correspondence, Nelson now insisted on carrying a revolver of large caliber. The firearm would accompany him to Ogden, Utah, where he would next fight Jack Clifford on January 13 at the Grand Theater, also known as the Grand Opera House. While many in town were happy to host the fight, Mayor Brewer went on record stating that this would be the last boxing match he would permit in Ogden during his administration—so much for presenting the Dane with the key to the city.

Nelson v. Clifford, January 13, 1908

It was quick and painless for the Battler as he scored a knockout of his Grass Valley, California, opponent in the fifth round of a scheduled twenty-round contest—Nelson fought at 135, two pounds more than Clifford. Put away with a short right uppercut to the jaw that sent him flat on his back, Clifford hit his head so hard—the blow could be heard from the gallery—that it took two or three minutes for him to regain consciousness.[19]

Hard fought and fast paced, the confrontation saw Nelson assume his now-classic rushing tactics right from the start—both left foot and left shoulder pointed toward the target, head down, then charge, like a drill boring into a mountainside. Clifford countered well early—winning both the first and second rounds, and nearly sending Nelson down with a blow to his "tin" ear. However, by the end of the second, Clifford was bleeding from the mouth.

In the third, Nelson delivered a left to Clifford's chin that sent his opponent tumbling to the floor—he remained there for five seconds before regaining his composure. Violent fighting followed, but the Californian was unable to inflict any damage. Clifford did manage to take the fourth round on points, however, even if Nelson looked stronger. In round five, Nelson rushed from his corner, and the two exchanged a nice volley of punches. Nonetheless, Clifford soon took a wrecking ball to the jaw and sank to the floor for the final time.

Afterward, Nelson shared a few words:

> It was a great fight. I knocked out Jack Clifford in the fifth round with a short right uppercut. I never got a scratch and feel, like the Battler of old, ready for all comers. After meeting Kid Scaler at Los Angeles on January 26 and Unholz in February, the date yet to be set, I will be ready to fight Packey McFarland, and if I win to meet Gans again for the championship. I will prove to the world that I am Gans's master and that I can make him quit once more if he has the nerve to take a chance. There is no stopping me now until I'm

Nelson's firearm would accompany him to Ogden, Utah (pictured here), where he would fight Jack Clifford on January 13, 1908, at the Grand Theater, also known as the Grand Opera House (Library of Congress, Prints and Photograph Division, 2007662825).

proclaimed undisputed lightweight champion of the world and Hegewisch. I will leave Salt Lake City for Los Angeles.[20]

Leave it to Bat to always plug the hometown, even if it had been swallowed up by Chicago's expansive southern boundary. Later, it was learned that Clifford had broken a bone in his left wrist in the first round. The news, as was frequently the case, fed cries for a rematch.

In a sign of Nelson's popularity, the Denver & Rio Grande Railroad, aka the "Scenic Line of the World," had run an excursion to Ogden to see the fight, or what they advertised as "The Big Boxing Exhibition." For a fare of $1 you could leave Salt Lake at 1:00 p.m., 3:30 p.m., 5:50 p.m. or 7:00 p.m., watch the fight and return 30 minutes after the contest. This accounted for the numerous visitors who found their way to the city and improved Nelson's reported yield of $2,000.

Nelson v. Unholz, February 4, 1908

Slated for Tuesday night, February 4, 1908, in Los Angeles, California, it was "The Dane versus The Boer," or "The Boer War," or Battling Nelson against Rudolf Unholz, the German-born lightweight pictured here (Library of Congress, Prints and Photograph Division, C-DIG-ggbain-11702).

Slated for a Tuesday night at the Cabin, or the Pacific Athletic Club Pavilion, in Los Angeles, California, it was "The Dane versus The Boer," or Battling Nelson against Rudolf Unholz, a German-born lightweight.[21] Nelson was in rare form before the bout, stating repeatedly that his opposition hadn't a chance to whip him. So confident was he that he even took in the racetrack to witness the inaugural of the California Handicap. This stirred concerns of complacency by his team. He did, however, look good in daily workouts and sparred hard with Kid Dalton and Eddie Kelly, but he seemed to take the odds, which were in his favor 10 to 8, a bit too seriously. Unholz, who had turned some heads by defeating George Memsic—some disregarded the victory believing Memsic was not at his fighting best—had been training hard at the East Side Club and drawing many spectators.

Under Los Angeles city ordinance, there was no decision at Tom McCarey's Pacific Athletic Club on the evening of February 4, but if there had been, it would have been in favor of Rudy Unholz, who pounded Battling Nelson and nearly missed knocking him out in the eighth round.

Nelson didn't like the intimidating style of Unholz; in fact he abhorred the

Boer, who laughed and danced as the Dane pounded him with everything he could muster. Unholz controlled Nelson with straight lefts, unless he was backed into a corner, when he would resort to charging out like a mad bull, swinging in every direction—one such swing caught Bat in the first round and sent him backward to the floor, but he arose quickly. Unfortunately for Nelson, a few of those initial blows caught his snout, and it bled throughout the ten-round contest.

The Boer rode the bike, or evaded his opponent, most of the night. Nelson chased after him but landed only a few solid chops to the head. By the fourth round, Nelson was frustrated with "The Joke," as he called him, and when he did capture his target he unloaded some powerful shots. However, to the credit of Unholz, he was able to defend himself. Three straight lefts to Nelson's face in the eighth staggered the fighter, and Unholz nearly put him away with a combination just before the bell. Clearly behind by the fifth, Nelson needed to compensate for the ground he had lost, but he could not. Later, despite everyone's interpretation, Nelson actually believed he had earned a victory.

The showing made by Unholz impressed many and there was talk, by a couple of promoters, of quickly matching him again in the city. There was even chatter of matching him again against Nelson—this time for twenty rounds, with an official judge to name a winner. Nonetheless, such would not be the case, for a number of reasons, although it would have made for an interesting battle.

Rudy Unholz would stumble, however, losing his next six fights—his losses included Joe Gans and Harlem Tommy Murphy.[22]

Nelson v. Britt, March 3, 1908

For the fourth time, and what would prove to be the final battle in their quartet of encounters, Battling Nelson would meet Jimmy Britt in a boxing ring. This time it was located in Los Angeles, California, at the Naud Junction Pavilion on March 3, where the two would fight for ten rounds under the laws governing the sport in the city. Since their last battle, Britt had grown more assertive, and Nelson had shown some signs of his old self. And since their last clash, Nelson had become much more cautious about his pre-fight diet—all kidding aside, the Battler still held firmly to the belief that this was the reason for his defeat the last time out against Britt.

The winner, it had been said, would probably be matched against Packey McFarland as soon as possible, likely at Sam Berger's Club in San Francisco, but that would remain to be seen. Realizing this, Nelson understood his pre-fight value and was holding out for some high stakes—he wanted a bonus of 15 percent in addition to the 50 percent, which naturally would be divided between the two fighters as their share of the receipts just to sign. This would be a bargain from his perspective, because if Nelson won, he intended to demand a 20 percent bonus. There would be other terms as well, such as insisting that McFarland weigh 131 pounds at six o'clock on the night of the fight. But that was putting the cart before the horse, and right now all his attention needed to be focused on Britt.

During their ten-round crusade at "the Naud," Battling Nelson outpointed Jimmy Britt. But it was the slightest of margins, and it didn't seem "fair to rob Jimmie of the credit due him for the showing he made," wrote *The Call*'s ringmaster R.A. Smyth.[23] Had the fight gone twenty rounds instead of ten, most agreed, including Smyth, that it would have favored Nelson by a wide margin. Nelson was in complete command the entire fight, while Britt had moments when it wasn't certain if he could grapple much longer.

The Battler was the Battler right from the start, boring in head first and taking the best Britt had to offer. Even if the Californian slowed by the ninth round and took a few jeers from the crowd for his noticeable retreat, he had given an admirable performance.

"As an indication of the closeness of the struggle, an attempt made at the ringside to keep count on the clean blows landed [found] Nelson a total of 71 to 64 for Britt," wrote Smyth.[24] Britt depended almost entirely on a left jab to the head and a left rip to the body to control Nelson; the only problem was that he didn't have the steam behind them to do any damage.

If there was a turning point, it was the sixth round when Britt was so severely beaten that most couldn't figure out how he was still standing. Nelson drew first blood, cutting Britt's right eye in the third round and there was a trace of blood from his mouth as well, but both were taken care of by his seconds. Nelson exhibited no damage following the ten-round skirmish.

"Tonight I think I have demonstrated to the sporting public the world over the only way I am all in, is in the ring fighting like a demon. I fought Jimmy Britt for the fourth time in four years, and beat him 10 rounds out of 10, and had him practically out in seven different rounds out of the ten, and had it not been for his holding, would have finished him for sure, as I had him badly punished and had him out, standing up and swinging in the air when he was not running," was Nelson's assessment following the battle.[25]

The Battler went on to say that he believed he would leave in a few days for San Francisco to fight Packey McFarland. "I am out for the championship as well as the money," Nelson continued, "and will never down until I have accomplished my sole ambition in life—to become the undisputed lightweight champion of the world beyond the question of a doubt—and then retire on my laurels and know that I have won them honestly and conscientiously and never had the finger of suspicion pointed toward me in regard to a crooked fight."[26] Following the battle, however, it would be Britt, not Nelson, who would battle the undefeated Packey McFarland.

Nelson's financial demands likely cost him the fight, but in retrospect may have saved his career. McFarland pounded Britt inside the Mission Street Arena in Colma, California, finally knocking out the fighter at 2:23 in round six of their scheduled twenty-round battle. McFarland looked indestructible and would go on to finish the year drawing Freddie Welsh, knocking out Phil Brock, and picking up decisions over Leach Cross and Harlem Tommy Murphy. While Nelson—thankfully in this case—would never face Packey McFarland, he would have to turn his attention to Abe Attell, the world featherweight champion.

Nelson v. Attell, March 31, 1908

Inside the Coliseum in San Francisco, California, on the last day of March, Battling Nelson intended to show his lighter foe, Abe Attell, what life was like in the lightweight division. Attell, who couldn't care less what Nelson thought, was plotting a move up in weight anyway and frankly was running out of competitive feathers to face. Scheduled for fifteen rounds, the non-title fight vowed to be one of the year's finest displays of pugilism. Eddie Graney was the intended referee, but an illness in his family forced him to cancel. Eddie Smith, of Oakland, would be the decided upon substitute.

How the combatants saw the fight:

"I expect to beat Abe Attell, drawing my conclusions from our fight in Philadelphia, where I had him practically out in the sixth round. Had it lasted another minute he could hardly have gone on. I am in better condition now, as for that fight I had only a few days' training after crossing the continent. I feel that I am better trained now than at any time in my ring career. If Attell stands up and fights me it will be over quickly, while if he runs I expect to catch him before the fifteenth round. Should I not be able to catch him I do not see how he can win by running away. He is the best man of his weight in the country, but he is up against it this time," spoke Nelson.[27]

"I figure I will beat Battling Nelson for the reason that I have the cleverness and the ring generalship. I have not been compelled to make weight and therefore I am stronger now than ever before in my long ring career. Let Nelson fight any sort of a fight he wishes and I will be there to meet him every time. My last encounter with Eddie Kelly proved conclusively that I have a punch. Nelson is a tough rugged man. I have met and beaten his kind before and I can do the trick again. I boxed him six rounds in Philadelphia and I know his style thoroughly. I want everybody to know that I am in the best of condition and ready to put up the fight of my life," stated Attell.[28]

"I figure I will beat Battling Nelson for the reason that I have the cleverness and the ring generalship," spoke a confident Abe Attell, "I have not been compelled to make weight and therefore I am stronger now than ever before in my long ring career" (Library of Congress, Prints and Photograph Division, LC-DIG-ggbain-08236).

The bets had been even money since first recorded, and most felt it would stay that way. While some claimed that Nelson, with his height and weight advantage, was the obvious choice, others considered it the speed and cleverness of Attell that would carry him to victory. One factor that was worth pointing out was that Attell had trained with Nelson and was thus very familiar with his style. The feather knew his weaknesses and the angles to reach him, but—and it was a big condition—if he could reach him, what, if any, damage could he then inflict? And what punishment from Nelson would he have to endure? Nelson quoted the sporting adage that "a good little man never beat a good big man," but then admitted he expected to be outpointed in the first few rounds.

The redesigned Coliseum, or adapted if you will for boxing, generated considerable excitement from fans. "Galleries have been erected on the Oak and Fell Street sides of the building and each will have a separate entrance. The main floor entrance will be on Baker Street. There will be an unobstructed view of the ring from all parts of the place which will accommodate a large crowd," wrote *The Call*.[29]

The fighters weighed in at 6:00 p.m. Regardless of the fact that there was no official announcement, it was generally known that Nelson was down as low as 131, while Attell weighed about 124.

With Attell's speed, it was expected that he would dominate the earlier rounds, and he did. As his skills as a fighter continue to be refined, Attell had shown he was every bit as clever as one might expect from a featherweight champion. He was agile, fast of foot, and smart enough to realize that he had to keep Nelson at a distance—which he did successfully until the ninth round. Attell's impregnable defense finally showed signs of weakness in the ninth, when he took a straight right to the stomach that almost shot him through the ropes. He quickly covered and absorbed some more shots from Nelson while he was trying to regain his breath. Once recuperated, he showered the Dane with combinations. It was the speed with which he managed to fire these selections that kept him out of trouble.

Nelson took charge in round twelve, forcing Attell around the ring, and following three hard lefts to his face, he let loose with a left to the jaw that nearly floored the lighter fighter. However, the "Little Champ" fought back gamely. Nelson easily took round twelve. Round thirteen proved just as vicious as any preceding round, as both fighters battled at close range. Attell, who had no intention of enduring Nelson's punishment at such close proximity, did so marvelously considering the circumstances—the use of his machine-gun combinations saved him from destruction.

By round fourteen Nelson was relentlessly battering Attell, but the little man took the punishment. Nelson just did not have a knockout punch to put him away. In round fifteen, the closing chapter for the pair, "Nelson, his face bleeding and his eyes swollen, fought like a mad man but could not land a vital punch." In the end, as the crowd roared in approval for both men covered in gore, referee Smith called the contest a draw.

Pardon the worn-out metaphorical analogy, but it was the old story of boxer against fighter: "The consensus of opinion seemed to be that, while Attell [boxer] by far landed the most blows and was the cleverer, this was to a great extent, offset by [fighter] Nelson's aggressiveness and the superior power of his blows," wrote *The Call*.[30] And that was exactly what referee Smith viewed.

On June 13, George Siler, "The Grand Old Man" of the prize ring, died at 10:30 p.m. at his home, 786 East Forty-Sixth Street, in Chicago. He had been unconscious all day and kept alive by stimulants. It was believed that heart trouble was his cause of death. Siler was sixty-one years of age. Siler had been stricken on June 4 while on his way to the train to report the Ketchel-Papke fight for the *Chicago Tribune*. While resting at his home, things took a turn for the worse, and his death was unexpected.

A well-known and respected referee, Siler wrote sports for the *Chicago Times* before becoming the sporting editor of the *Chicago Globe*. About two years later, he started working on the *Chicago Tribune*. George Siler will forever be associated with some of the sport's finest battles, including Gans and Nelson I, Fitzsimmons and Jim Jeffries, Fitzsimmons and Peter Maher, and Terry McGovern and Pedlar Palmer.

SEVEN

July 4, 1908
The Fight of the Century II

> I have long known that I could beat any man in the ring at my weight, but I have had a hard time convincing the public at large of my ability.
> —"Battling" Nelson[1]

It took promoter John J. Gleason to begin to put it all together, and it wasn't easy because events like championship fights take the right moment, the right people, and the right terms in order to make the deal. On April 3, 1908, as the sun set over San Francisco Bay, Gleason signed a short, four-condition agreement and slid it across the table to Battling Nelson, who signed on his own behalf and then slid the paper over to Ben Selig, who looked it over briefly, then penned his name on behalf of Joe Gans.

The agreement read,

> We, the undersigned, do herby agree to box 20 rounds under the auspices of the Occidental athletic club during the month of May 1908, in San Francisco, under the following conditions: First—Gans to weigh 133 pounds, stripped, ringside, Nelson not to be compelled to weigh; Second—Gans agrees to post a forfeit of $2,500 for weight and both agree to post $2,500 for appearance; Third—We hereby accept John T. Clark as stake holder; Fourth–We agree to meet Monday night, April 6, at 8 o'clock to post forfeits and sign articles.

The weight negotiations—a sticking point—had been conducted for a period of time, and Selig, who had little patience, was growing frustrated over Nelson's insistence regarding the issue. Finally, Selig landed a bombshell saying he did not care what Nelson weighed. Nelson jumped at the comment and agreed to let Gans weigh 133 ringside if he did not have to weigh. Understand that Nelson didn't pick up much weight while training, as he fought Attell at 131 and Britt at 133, but he felt in his heart that if he didn't have to make weight and picked up a few extra pounds, it would work to his advantage.

However—and let me remind you, there are always more *howevers* in a boxing agreement than comp seats ringside, or so it seems—by April 15, Gleason was hiring an attorney to bring legal action, restraining John T. Clark from surrendering that forfeit money. The negotiations had fallen apart. To bring two fighters this far along in the process only to have it breakdown was heartbreaking for a promoter, but it was part of the fight game. By May 18, both sides were eager to meet at Coffroth's Mission Street Arena on July 4, with the only hitch being a considerable guarantee for Gans.

During this period, the Battler had engaged Willus, also spelled Willis, Britt—that's right, Jimmy's brother—to act as his manager. Nelson, feeling somewhat overwhelmed by the whole event, needed to tend to a match he had made in Seattle against Kid Scaler, and he knew if anyone could work to his advantage, it would be Willis. As he worked out the final negotiations, or articles, of the Gans fight, Britt would wire Bat regarding any details. When the articles were finally signed, the fight was scheduled for Independence Day. Part of closing the Gans deal was that Nelson must declare the Scaler match off, which he did. As Nelson and Johnny Reed, the manager with whom he had signed the Scaler fight articles, were good friends, there were no hard feelings.

However, Seattle fight fans were disappointed, so the Battler made it up to them by appearing for four days at the Star Theater. A three-round exhibition, with his globe-trotting buddy Jack Grace, acted as an appeasement. It worked out great as Nelson filled the house and picked up over $1,000 for his troubles. Happy with the take, Nelson and Grace then showed for another week in Portland before heading back to 'Frisco to begin training.

The Battler felt it might be a good idea to spend the first week of his conditioning in Mendenhall Springs, California; the unincorporated community in Alameda County, California, is located nine miles southeast of Livermore, at an elevation of 1,818 feet.[2] He felt the higher altitude might do him some good, and the hunting wasn't bad either. Team Nelson now consisted of Jack Grace, Jeff Perry, Red Cornett, Percy Dana and manager Willus Britt. After "The Springs," it was back to Millett's training quarters at Colma, California, to fine-tune his preparation. It was there that Nelson once again worked the "ROKO" bag—now it's time for Nelson's brief sales pitch—to develop "speed, agility, as well as sharpness of the eye."[3]

The very handsome and well-dressed Oscar "Battling" Matthew Nelson, in 1915, who turned the heads of many a female admirer (Library of Congress, Prints and Photograph Division, LC-DIG-ggbain-23084).

As time permitted, Nelson would also turn his attention toward his investments. On April 24, 1908, *The Call* reported that he had arrived from Livermore, California, after closing a deal whereby he became the owner of one of the finest ranches in that productive valley. Nelson reportedly had deposited $1,950 to bind the bargain. The Battler wouldn't take possession right away, however, but he did intend to invite his brother Albert and his family to join him on the property when he did. For the very first time, Nelson also brought up retirement. Bending a reporter's ear just a bit more, he mentioned that he had toyed with retirement—a word every fighter hates to hear but at some point must accept—but that it still depended on his ability to secure noteworthy battles. Admitting he wouldn't mind settling down in his new home, he didn't fail to mention that he preferred not being alone—it has been rumored that the Dane was considering matrimony.

A month later, Nelson spent an afternoon on the moored battleships *Ohio* and *Georgia*, "where he amused the jackies of Uncle Sam's big ships with an exhibition bout with his sparring partner, Jeff Perry."[4] It was always quite a sight to see the ships roll into port as part of the "Fleet Week" festivities in San Francisco. Bat had a wonderful time, joking with everyone and kidding about the upcoming fight. Today's line had Gans a 10 to 6 favorite, but Nelson warned the boys about betting against him. The event seemed to lift everybody's spirits.

The Battler enjoyed training out in the country. The fresh breeze reinvigorated him and was far better than the stale air usually found inside a gymnasium. Another change was his use of his sparring partners, who in the past had a right to hit him at will. This was no longer the case, and as such Nelson didn't endure anywhere near the punishment he had to face in the past for the Britt fight. Nelson's sparring partner Freddie Landers just punished the Battler, who took it as mere preparation. Willis Britt initiated the change, and Bat assumed an offensive mode that now saw him disposing of sparring partners at three-minute intervals.

Impressed by Gans's use of a short uppercut, Nelson developed a version of his own. Adding the new punch to his arsenal, he believed, enhanced his infighting. Although the approach was a bit different, hopefully the results wouldn't be. The Dane tipped the scales at 135 on June 27 and expected to be 136 or 137 following his workout on June 28. The weight, as Britt often reminded him, had to be put on the right way as to not slow him down.

Joe Gans believed his knowledge of boxing and ring experience would enable him to defend his title successfully. "Gans has had on the gloves but twice up to the present time during this spell of training, and according to his plans the boxing he does this afternoon [June 28, 1908] at Billy Shannon's, near San Rafael, will be the last practice he will have before he enters the ring next Saturday at the Mission Street arena," according to R.A. Smyth's column in the *San Francisco Call*. Gans had worked the bag hard and would continue to do so. He had also turned to carrying half-pound dumbbells in each hand as he did his roadwork. Not troubled by making weight, Gans simply wanted to enter the fight as close to the mark as he could get without going over. Every ounce counted against a fighter like Nelson, and Gans knew this fact all too well.

Looking at the measurements: At thirty-three and eight months, Joe Gans had a sizable advantage in reach, by three and a quarter inches. Twenty-six years of age Battling Nelson had an edge in height, by three quarters of an inch. Gans had a bigger neck, by a quarter of an inch; biceps, by an inch and two-eighths; and forearm, by a quarter inch. Nelson had a larger chest (normal and expanded), wrist, calf and ankle. They were evenly matched in their waist and thigh measurement.

The media were enjoying the newfound relationship between the Battler and Willus Britt. Of course the pugilistic Britt family was well known to the sporting press, so they were familiar with Willus blowing his fair share of smoke about his fighter. "Well, now, what do you know about this fellow?"[5] Britt would be muse, as he walked the room waving his hand among the press. "Why, he eats 'em all up, like Bosco. Can't get anybody else to go on with him. Too bad I outweigh him twenty pounds or I'd like to entertain him for a couple rounds myself," Willus would spout off. One day, Bat having heard enough, he turned to Willus and said, "Grab a hold of a pair of gloves and we'll roll some."[6] Well, Willus damn near fainted, but he was too far into the discussion to turn back so he donned the mitts and they were off.

Willus showed a bit of the old smoke, snapping his trademark hooks at Bat, but he was huffing and puffing at the end of the round. It didn't stop him from throwing a few more jabs at the press: "Did you see me hook him with that left? That's the one that won me the amateur championship at the old Olympic Club ten years ago," Willus bragged. "I was a great kid then."[7] The press just smirked and Willus found another breath. "Watch me this time. I'm going to uppercut that Dane on the mush, and, believe me, he will get crazy. He can't stop me," Willus continued. "Jimmy never could."[8]

Meanwhile, the Dane had painted himself a stern face and waited for the bell. Willus came out dancing and tried a few times to uppercut his employer. "Then came a thud, a yell and silence—the bout ended. The Dane was smiling, Willus could not."[9]

The medical team came to his rescue, and they managed to get Willus back to his feet. Bat felt bad afterward, blaming it on a brief lapse of reality, thinking Willus was Gans. Willus bought the excuse and accepted his damage, which included a shiner, while Bat gave the press a wink.

Nelson v. Gans, July 4, 1908

Standing five feet six and a half inches tall, Joe Gans used his seventy-one-inch reach to his advantage. The "Old Master" had solid defensive instincts and could deliver an aggressive offensive assault with incredible precision (Library of Congress, Prints and Photograph Division, LC-USZ62-116814).

"There were some seven thousand people in Mission Street arena yesterday afternoon [July 4] and they paid all the way from $2 to $20 to see the championship pass from a man with a skin just a shade darker than brown sugar to a youth with a fair Danish coloring. The championship was long in passing. Seventeen rounds represents 51 minutes of actual fighting and there were 51 minutes of fighting, too. Seldom was there ever more fighting in that space of time," reported the *San Francisco Call*.[10]

The atmosphere was compared to that of a county fair or carnival, as thousands walked along the road leading from the car line to Mission Street to the arena. Cripples and squatters lined the route asking for charity, gamblers and gamers offered up forms of chance in trade for coin, and a pair of hawkers pushed sandwiches and scalped tickets, or whatever they could, to clear a dime.

Sailors, those lucky enough to have found a ticket and even some still looking for one, walked about chatting with visitors or members of the mounted police borrowed from the sheriff of San Mateo. The crowd was excited and congenial, most bantering around their betting choice, or the odds they were given.

A crowd of boys rushed when they spotted the large automobile transporting the reigning champion and his wife. It was impersonal but exhilarating to actually see one of the matinee heroes of the afternoon. Nelson's group entered in the same fashion.

As the crowd filed in, most of the amphitheater near capacity at 1:30 p.m., the men couldn't help noticing the ladies. "Among the women were many of color," penned *The Call*, "the brightest blue hat was worn by a dusky damsel, but the most gorgeous plumes were sported by a person who cheered for Nelson. Mrs. Gans was somberly clad in some dark stuff and she wore an expansive black hat and a heavy veil. She is a handsome woman, large and graceful, with great dark eyes of her race. Her complexion represented about the same fraction of white blood that the pugilist husband was."

The twenty-foot ring rose from the center of the arena snugly surrounded by the ringside seats that sloped upward and back. Between the big-ticket buyers and the bargain basement bourgeois, or $2 ticket toters, rested a barbed-wire fence, like that of a cattle pen, its connotations left to interpretation.

In the preliminary confrontation, Sam Nelson fashionably bloodied "Red" Cornett, one of the Battler's sparring partners, in a decision. Arbitrated by "Tiv" Kreling, also a member of the Dane's entourage, the cries to stop the barbarous display were ignored and Nelson given the decision.

The human megaphone, Billy Jordan, then took over festivities by announcing the ring celebrities, including Jimmy Gardner, the Lowell crackerjack welterweight, and Jimmy Walsh, the bantamweight champion of the world. As usual the impresario took his fair share of ring heat. To cries of speaking louder, Jordan crooned, "Take the cotton out of your ears; if I had said you were going to be hanged you would have heard." The protests quickly ceased.

The crowd stood and waved their hats as the panorama camera expert took a picture. Many couldn't help noticing that a corner of the ring had turned into a betting booth where Tex Rickard and Jim May were transferring assets quicker than a calf leaving a branding.

As it was Independence Day, it was only appropriate that on this day, 132 years later, both fighters appear wearing an American flag for a belt. Conducting the parade into the ring was promoter Jim Coffroth, followed by Nelson, and then Gans. Nelson's seconds were Willus Britt, Jack Grace and Ed Moe, while Gans had Ben Selig, Jim Griffin, Young Peter Jackson and Kid North. Having won the coin toss, Gans selected the southwest corner for his temporary home. Removing his robe and a small blue cap, one could see the champion dressed in black sateen trunks to his knees, while Nelson opted for a pair of white tight-fitting trunks beneath his familiar flannel shirt.

Jordan then led Nelson into the center of the ring: "The hardest nut in the profession to crack, Battling Nelson." The crowd roared. Then, "The great and only lightweight champion of the world, Joe Gans," and the placed erupted in cheers.

The seasoned arbiter for the event, "The Honorable Jack Welsh," a veteran of such previous battles as Gans versus Unholz, McFarland versus Britt, Attell versus Kelly and Neil versus Attell, was then introduced before Jordan announced that Young Ketchel and Jim Flynn would fight in the city on August 31. At 3:07 the battle began.

As for the fight highlights, here they are, by round.[11]

Both fighters shook hands, and Gans began round one with three smashes to his opponent's face, followed by a shot to Nelson's "tin" ear. Gans then sent a right uppercut, a combination to the face at close range, and a combination to the face again. Nelson, who rushed to close quarters and in doing so telegraphed his fight plan, dispatched only a notable left to the nose. As Gans went to his corner, his lip was bleeding slightly.

In round two, Gans posted two straight lefts to the jaw, three hard lefts to the face, two short right arms to the jaw, rapid-fire short swings to the jaw, a right uppercut, and a good combination to the jaw. Nelson spent the entire round inside almost embracing the assault by Gans.

Gans pulled back a bit in round three, wanting to work his reach advantage. He then addressed a combination to the jaw, landed multiple mixes at will, two hard rights to the face, a right hook to the face, and a nice combination to the jaw that started the blood flowing again from Nelson's nose. Persistently infighting, Nelson went to the floor from a well-directed swing but arose quickly. Managing only to consign a left to the face, Nelson's nose bled from nearly the beginning of the round. Three rounds into the fight, and it belonged to Gans.

Nelson began round four by rushing to close quarters. Gans controlled him with combinations—each fighter's modus operandi now clear to all in attendance. Nelson would give no ground regardless of how hard Gans tried. Gans directed powerful short-arm combinations, a nice right to the jaw and a lightning left to the head. Nelson forwarded relentless blocked combinations until finally landing with a right to the face. As the bell sounded, a bleeding Nelson walked casually to his corner as if he was headed to the corner store.

Nelson was quickly out of his corner in round five and into close quarters. Gans transmitted a combination to the jaw, a hard right to the stomach and two lefts to the face. Nelson conveyed only a notable right to the jaw while expelling what appeared to be fruitless energy. Gans went to Nelson's stomach this round and conserved his strength by letting his opponent do most of the work.

Round six opened with both men at a comfortable distance firing shots. Gans, with his extended reach, inflicted most of the damage. He then phoned a right to the kidneys, an uppercut to the jaw, and two hard lefts to Nelson's mouth that started some bleeding. Nelson wired a short right to the ear, a hard right to the face, an uppercut to the jaw, and a hard left to the jaw. By far the most equal round of the fight, Nelson appeared to have arisen from his sleep.

Nelson opened round seven with the now commonplace, and let me add tireless, wrestling about the ring. Gans telegraphed a right swing to the jaw that staggered Nelson, and followed it with a rally. Nelson delivered a sound right and two light lefts before landing a nice combination. As the gong sounded, the round clearly belonged to Nelson.

Round eight saw some excellent fighting by both boxers. Gans dispatched a combination to the face, then a straight right followed by a solid left uppercut to the jaw. Nelson posted a short-arm combination, followed by a hard right to the kidneys that staggered Gans, a nice right cross to the face, and three lefts to the jaw. It was a fine performance by Nelson.

Nelson was hungry in round nine, as he pressed Gans around the ring. An unrelenting Gans mailed a combination to the face, three rights and a left to Nelson's jaw, two right uppercuts to the jaw, and a wicked right to the face. From Nelson's corner you could hear, "Hold your head up," and when Nelson did so, Gans clouted him with a solid right.[12] So much for secondhand assistance. Nelson addressed a left to the face. He then sent Gans through the ropes with a vicious left that was followed by a volley of combinations. When Gans recovered, he looked very concerned. It was another round for Nelson.

Nelson again rushed in as the bell sounded, this time for round ten. Gans consigned two rights to the jaw, a nice combination to the mouth, another amalgam to the mouth, and near the end of the round staggered Nelson with what looked to be a right. Nelson directed some punches during the segment, but nothing worth highlighting. The end of the round saw the Battler's mouth covered with blood. Gans was seen as having the advantage.

Typical entrance for Nelson in round eleven as he immediately forced the action. Gans forwarded a left to the jaw, then followed with a similar punch that staggered Nelson. Transmitting multiple combinations to the jaw, Nelson sent two rights to the stomach that forced Gans to start covering up. It was a robust pace, with Nelson at a slight advantage.

Round twelve began with Gans just trying to slow the pace. He conveyed a straight left to the face, followed by combinations to the identical spot, then two rights. Nelson phoned a left to the jaw, then a right to Gans that almost put him through the ropes. Gans was in trouble, and even as his seconds threw water at him to get him revived, he dropped to his knees from a left uppercut and looked out. There, Gans then took a nine count, followed by another count. As the gong sounded, timely for the champion, Gans was assisted to his corner by his seconds—he looked as if he had nothing else left to give.

Nelson opened round thirteen as if he owned Gans. Telegraphing two lefts to the jaw, followed by more combinations, Nelson then floored the champion with a left uppercut to the stomach. Try as he might, Nelson could not put Gans away. Gans kept holding, stalling, holding some more—anything to make it to the bell.

Miraculously, Gans found some life in round fourteen and was first up and into close quarters. He wired combination short-arm jabs to maintain his stride. Nelson dispatched a right and two lefts to the jaw, three left uppercuts to the jaw, and a left to the jaw. As the closing bell sounded, both fighters were bleeding profusely.

Nelson opened round fifteen by rushing Gans to the ropes. Gans held on to try to negate the damage. Recovering, Gans posted two rights to the face, then rocked Nelson's head with two rights. Nelson mailed a number of short-arm combinations to the stomach, then repeated the volley to Gans's sore mouth. Nelson then sent another left to the stomach of Gans. With Gans again against the ropes, Nelson shot three short-arm jolts to Gans's stomach before the bell.

As Gans came out for round sixteen, he appeared trembling, as if he had a chill. Nelson chased him, trying to deliver some punches, but nothing landed. The Battler consigned an uppercut to the jaw, then finally forced Gans to a corner with a right to the stomach. Nelson then fought Gans back to the center of the ring, then into his corner. One observer said, "It looked as if Gans was trying to invite a foul."[13] A firm left found its way to Gans's stomach, and he dropped to a nine count. Advantage Nelson, as Gans hung on by a thread.

Round seventeen had an ominous feel right from the start. The thirty seconds saw both wrestling before falling through the ropes due to Nelson's stumbling. The Battler then forced his prey about the ring before sending him down with a right uppercut to the stomach. Gans then took an eight count. When he stood up, Nelson sent a hard right to the jaw. This time Gans stayed down for the full count. When he arose, it was too late. He had been counted out.

"In the excitement of the moment the spectators could not understand under what conditions Gans had lost. Referee Jack Welsh pointed to Nelson as the winner and the information gradually reached the men throughout the arena that Gans, while not knocked unconscious, was still unable to respond to the call of time and was counted out," *The Call* reported. "After the fight Official Time Keeper George Harting said that Gans had been officially counted out twice during the round, the first time there being so much noise and confusion that the result was not even known to the referee."

Pandemonium ensued as the crowd surged ringside to hail the new champion. Nelson's seconds were throwing towels in the air before lifting the Dane to their shoulders. Through the chaos, somehow Bat's father had made it into the ring to shake the hands of his son. Tears flowed as they took a few minutes to remove the Battler's gloves. Team Nelson then attempted to make their way through the cheering crowd and into the dressing room—it took them ten minutes to walk only a few hundred yards.

Inside the dressing room, Bat was simply ecstatic, asking, "Well, am I there, kid?" as he poked Willus in the ribs.[14] "I'm the real champ now, and none of them can take it away from me. Yes, you are due for some of the credit too Willus. You're the greatest manager of them all. And old chief Jack Grace here is the candy too. He can always have a job in my camp when I am getting ready to fight," the new lightweight champion of the world firmly confessed.[15]

One of the first to greet the new champion inside was his father. Again, the old carpenter shook the hands of his son with a look of pride as if his boy had been elected president of the United States. For a few moments they just stared at each other, no words needing to be said. Finally, Nels proclaimed, "Well, you did a good job of it, boy. You're the champion now and you won it on the square. No wonder I'm proud of you."[16]

Bat, being Bat, then confirmed, "You know how I told you that I would beat this fellow Gans. I knew it all along and tried to tell 'em all, but they would not believe me, but it's different now."[17]

Once dressed, Willus found their big red touring car, and the entire party climbed in and went back to their training quarters at Joe Millett's a couple of miles down the road, the journey slowed a bit by a few thousand people who cheered and accompanied their progress.

Meanwhile, Gans was sitting in his corner, head down in deep distress. Attempts to comfort him, by his wife and friends, appeared in vain. Some ringside reporters rushed to his corner but were pushed back. Gans would only answer questions from his second. A few of the reporters caught portions of his responses that included: "The old man started once too often…. Never again will I enter a ring, I'll have to find another way to bring the bacon home…. It looks like my time has come…. Fifteen years is a long time to stay in the ring and meet them all…. After the third round I told Benny Selig that I could not go the route."[18] Mrs. Gans was quoted as saying, "Napoleon met his Waterloo and now Joe's time has come…. Nelson was too strong and too young for him."[19] So, badly beaten, Joe Gans needed assistance climbing from his chair and down the short steps leading from the ring. Those who saw him could not fail to notice how he trembled uncontrollably, as if chilled to the bone.

In the words of the winner, "Dream Realized—Content with Honor":

> I have made good my promise to my friends, winning the lightweight championship of the world on my merits and on the square. My dream of the last five years has been realized now and I am happy. It is the honor and not the money that contents me. To go right down the line and beat every one of them without a scandal connected with any fight is what I fought for. Now that I have accomplished my purpose I am willing to rest for a while. There is no use in commenting on the fight. I proved that I am champion. I withstood Gans's punches and beat him down with my body blows. I knew that I had him in the tenth round. There was nothing to it from that time on. My friends stood by me to the end and I will stand by them, as I always have done.[20]

Seven—July 4, 1908: The Fight of the Century II

In the words of the loser, "Old Age Counts—Beaten on the Square":

Well, the old master has finally met his match after 15 years of fighting against the best they could trot out. It is all over now, for I am through with the prize ring forever. All credit to Nelson. He beat me on the square and I am not the man to make a holler after I am licked. I saw that he would knock me out eventually, so I deliberately stayed down the last time. What was the use of taking unnecessary punishment? I have been at the game too long for anything like that. Old age got me. There is nothing else to it. At Goldfield I stood Nelson off for 42 rounds and I was still good at the finish. Today 17 rounds was my limit. This means that the old man is there no longer and the best thing for him to do is to say goodbye to the old ring where he won so much money and so much glory while he lasted. Youth will triumph over old age all the time. I know this now.[21]

In the words of the referee, "Nelson Is Marvel of Modern Prize Ring":

I counted Gans out when he went to the floor the last time. He was not knocked out, but simply worn down from sheer exhaustion. He could not fight another round and he very wisely stayed down after Nelson had smothered him under a shower of blows to the face and body. It is the same old story of youth winning out over old age. Gans has not the steam behind the punches that he used to possess and he could not stop the rushes of Nelson. In the meantime, Bat kept coming all the time, and finally wore his man out. Nelson is the marvel of the modern prize ring. He is a great champion and he deserves all the honor that is justly coming to him. Always on the square, he promises to be a ring favorite for many years. I have refereed my last fight. Though I did the best I knew how, the soreheads were hissing and hooting all the time. I want no more of the game. Today I retire as referee.[22]—Jack Welsh

In a not so ordinary post-fight event, Charles Dixon, Nelson's timekeeper, was slashed with a knife—two painful wounds in the cheek and one under the arm—by none other than promoter Jim Coffroth. The scene of the stabbing was located in a back room at Coffroth's

Promoter James Coffroth (right), with his New York representative Charles Harvey, outside on a brisk day no doubt discussing their promoting strategy (Library of Congress, Prints and Photograph Division, LC-DIG-ggbain-04502).

saloon, at 1518 Ellis Street. Dixon, who was Nelson's representative at the gate, as well as his timekeeper, was assisting in counting up the receipts and was quoted as saying, "Drew a pretty good house," in answer to a casual remark.[23] Benny Selig, Gans's manager, was also in the room and commented about the prices. That's when Dixon remarked that had the ticket price been higher, so would have the take, by several thousand dollars he estimated. Overhearing the conversation, Coffroth asked Dixon what he meant by the remark, and Dixon replied, "Oh, that's all right." Then Coffroth wielded a knife from his pocket and rushed after him.[24] Chasing Dixon into another room, Coffroth then sliced his face twice, followed by a slash under the arm. Coffroth admitted to the row but denied the attack. Dixon was hurried away undercover from the police, and his wounds were confirmed by Dr. William D. Clark, who noted that they were painful but not life threatening. Dixon spent his recovery time in a Turkish bath, where he rested comfortably.

As for the take, there were 7,598 paid admissions of an estimated 9,000 spectators; total receipts were $24,031. The fighters received 70 percent of the receipts, amounting to $16,821.70. This broke down to Nelson's 60 percent cut, or $10,093.02, and Gans the remainder at $6,728.68.[25] Referee Jack Welsh took home $500, while promoter Coffroth's share was $7,209.30—the cost of the fight to be deducted from Coffroth's share.

Details regarding some of the heavy bets emerged, beginning with Reno's Jim May, who made three bets with Rickard, all of which he won: "He first bet $5,000 even that Gans would not win in twenty rounds, then bet $2,500 against $5,000 that Gans would not win the fight

Artifacts from the Nelson versus Gans era including trading cards (1910 E75 American Caramel Nelson, 1910–11 T9 Turkey Red Nelson, and 1910 E75 American Caramel Gans), program (September 3, 1906) and ticket (September 3, 1906).

irrespective of the distance it went, and finally $2,000 even that Gans would not win in 15 rounds."[26] For those at ringside, the straight betting went 10 to 3, with Gans the favorite.

"I may be a subject of Denmark, or better—was," Nelson crooned, "but I have no doubt been the subject of much worry for a band of ill-mannered ring followers and their breadwinners in this good ol land of the free—U.S.A." And speaking of Denmark, "Enthusiastic writers of late have been wont to call me 'the Peerless Dane,' 'the Durable Dane,' etc.... This is all very nice," the fighter asserted, "but I am simply Battling Nelson, of Hegewisch, Illinois, a champion boxer, that's all."[27]

Eight

September 9, 1908
The Fight of the Century III

> I have not been foolish with my money, like some former champions, but have invested it wisely, and today [1908] I would not sell all the property that I have for a quarter of a million dollars.
>
> —Oscar "Battling" Matthew Nelson[1]

"To much of a good thing can be bad," it has been said, but not in boxing, where there is never enough of a good thing. A quality match can often prove incomparable, especially when you have a scenario where both gladiators have defeated each other once. Such a course of events demands the requisite rubber match, or deciding event. Every boxing promoter in the country understood this, especially if a championship was put on the line. Employing strategies, even in advance to the second fight, promoters—like vultures over fresh roadkill—came out of the woodwork in hopes of grabbing the third segment of what would prove to be one of the sport's finest trilogies. A mere five days after the fight, Nelson agreed to give Gans a rematch—Tex Rickard offered a guaranteed purse of $30,000. Of this Nelson would receive $20,000, no matter what might be the outcome of the fight, the remaining $10,000 going to Gans. Rickard would post $10,000 with the First National Bank of Ely within ten days and the balance of the purse thirty days before the fight. The fighters had to post forfeits of $5,000 each to guarantee that they would fulfill their part of the contract. Both fighters agreed to be in Ely thirty days before the fight to train, and they also agreed not to engage in any fight prior to Labor Day.

Also negotiated was the moving-pictures portion, Nelson giving $5,000—from his initial share, which was $25,000—to Gans in return for his rights to the film. This would give Nelson two-thirds interest in the celluloid to Rickard's one-third. Both fighters had to agree on a referee, but if they could not, Rickard would choose one. If the promoter made the call, it would likely be among Eddie Graney, Eddie Smith or Jack Welsh. Of the articles, yet to be signed, were details regarding the finances, including binding and forfeits, as well as an agreement to box Marquis of Queensberry rules and to weigh 133 ringside at selected times.

Tex Rickard then went to work trying to schedule the fight for Ely, Nevada, which looked good—the promoter offering to post $10,000 for two special trains to the town—at first, but quickly turned when the required railroad transportation couldn't be worked out. Meanwhile, waiting in the wings was "Sunny" Jim Coffroth, who by July 24, the day after the Rickard deal tanked, had begun negotiations with both parties for a forty-five-round fight on Labor Day in the open-air arena at Colma, California. In the end, Coffroth won out.[2]

The derby-clad Oscar "Battling" Matthew Nelson amongst well-wishers. This photograph, similar to many that appear in this work, is part of the impressive George Grantham Bain Collection in the Library of Congress (Library of Congress, Prints and Photograph Division, LC-DIG-ggbain-04071).

Nelson v. Gans III, September 9, 1908

It was as conspicuous as it was unpropitious, and a vibrant assertion by a new champion:

BAT NELSON KNOCKS OUT VETERAN JOE GANS, FIVE THOUSAND PERSONS SEE OLD MASTER FALL LIMP IN TWENTY-FIRST ROUND[3]

With an attendance estimated at 5,000 inside Coffroth's Arena on September 9, Battling Nelson delivered a right hook to Gans's stomach that stopped the fighter in the twenty-first round. Fighting under straight Queensberry rules, Gans landed forty-eight hard swings flush on Nelson's jaw, any one of which might have dropped an ordinary lightweight. Nelson returned eighteen blows to the jaw of Gans but centered much of his assault to the stomach. Punch numbers can be deceiving, as in this case, where the greater number of blows ended in a loser's cut—the winner received 60 percent, while the runner-up 40 percent, of 70 percent of the gross receipts. The value to Nelson was estimated at $10,500, while Gans took $7,000.

No single blow put away Gans, only a terrific series of relentless body punches that endured over twenty rounds. When Gans sank to the floor in the twenty-first, he was unable to rise until after being counted out by the timekeeper. Gans fought superbly during the entire battle; however he had neither the energy nor the punch to defeat his opponent. "Every time Nelson was staggered he fell toward Gans, and every time he fell toward Gans he worked his sturdy arms like pistons," observed the *Evening Star* of Washington, D.C.[4]

The end of the fight was pitiful to recall, as Gans had endured a prodigious beating.

When the bell rang at the opening of the twenty-first round, Nelson bolted from his corner and delivered a multitude of combinations to his antagonist's jaw. Gans fruitlessly fired back, but the Battler was relentless. Following another series to the jowl, Nelson then turned to the stomach. Gans had no option but to cover, but for how long? Backing away toward the ropes, the "Old Master" was hoping to sustain himself a bit, but Nelson countered to the body with machine-gun strikes. Gans was crippled with exhaustion, as Nelson, smelling blood, would not capitulate. Gans's corner cringed as their fighter suffered with each passing blow. Finally, Gans winced and sank to the floor. As the seconds tolled off, his defeatist attempts to regain his breath painted a portrait of an erstwhile champion. When he got to his feet, it was too late. Referee Ed Smith, of Oakland, California, had declared him out. There would be only one knockdown during the contest, and that was the one that ended the fight.

As the "Old Master" regained his bearings, Nelson's seconds and admirers rushed into the ring to hoist the victor upon their shoulders and carry him to the dressing room.

Gans's statements after the fight mimicked those he had delivered before; he had indeed fought one too many fights with Nelson.

One of Gans's seconds, Willie Keefe, summed up the fight this way:

> Gans was all in after the ninth round. In the eleventh, I begged him to allow me to toss the sponge into the ring. This he would not consent to, saying he preferred to be knocked out and would fight as long as he had the strength to stand up. For eleven rounds Gans fought on his courage alone, as he could not land a damaging punch.[5]

In the words of the winner:

> Gans was tougher than before. He was in good shape and he fought me a different kind of fight. From now on I will never fight a colored man again. I shook hands with Billy Papke today and we made a compact. I hurt my right hand in the second round, but kept it going regardless of the pain.[6]

In the words of the referee:

> In the twenty-first both the timekeeper and myself counted ten, therefore making Nelson the winner. Gans, I believe, did not know he was counted out, but it is just as well that he was, for Nelson had him completely at his mercy and it was useless for the game colored man to take a further beating.[7]

Reality doesn't always meet expectations, as reports of the receipts were a bit disappointing. Some blamed the Moran versus Attell battle held two days before, which was likely true, as it was a featherweight title bout. The gate was slightly in excess of $18,000.

Both fighters weighed in promptly at 2:30 p.m. and at exactly 133 pounds. Time was called at 3:01 p.m.

A quick review of the highlights: Round one was all Gans, although Nelson forced the action and drew first blood from the nose of the "Old Master." By the fifth Gans was landing repeatedly with no return from Nelson—a performance similar to the previous fight. In a continuation of his protractive strategy, Nelson turned to Gans's body in the sixth. Gans took the seventh round, but Nelson the eighth and ninth stages. The tenth round was even, but the eleventh belonged to Nelson. Gans appeared fatigued after the eleventh, and his corner tried desperately to revive him. By the twelfth, it was all Nelson, with most ringside wagering centered on what round he would get the decision. Nelson drew more blood in round thirteen with a hard left to the mouth. Round fourteen was even and led to the best round of the fight up to that point—round fifteen.

Nelson pranced to the center of the ring, he quickly started with a right to the body but Gans more than evened it up with two rights to the stomach. Gans's mouth bled as Nelson forced him against the ropes. Suddenly Gans caught the Dane with a terrific right and left to the mouth and the blood went splattering. Nelson rushed in furiously landing a wicked left to the body. A terrible right uppercut followed this. They both spat blood freely and Gans appeared very tired. Nelson closed the round by landing a left to the body and rushed to his corner with blood flowing freely from his mouth. It was Nelson's round.[8]

Having shed more blood in this round than when Ethan Allen's Green Mountain Boys captured Fort Ticonderoga, both weary combatants benefited from their brief reprieve in their respective corners. As their seconds waved towels in a frantic attempt to revive their warriors, they shouted instructions with consternation. Both fighters realized they might have hit a turning point. Gans, to the surprise of many, took round sixteen, while the seventeenth was even. Both fighters appeared energized as the gong sounded for round eighteen.

Nelson landed a left to the face and Gans retaliated with a fierce left to the jaw. Gans slipped to the floor from the force of the blow and Nelson gallantly permitted him to rise. Nelson rushed in leading with a left to the face and hard rights to the body and put a right to the jaw, then two rights to the body. Gans stalled. Gans shot a left to the body at close range and they exchanged rights and lefts during which Gans staggered Nelson by landing two pile-driving rights to the jaw. The Dane, however, was not to be downed. He rushed Gans against the ropes and landed two or three solid punches to the face and jaw, but Gans rallied and just before the bell rang, evened up with rights and lefts to the stomach. The round was very fast.[9]

The eighteenth was very close, and some favored Nelson, while Gans came back in the nineteenth and staggered Nelson with several hard rights. But Gans shut down after the round, and it appeared that the fight belonged to Nelson. Gans somehow managed to stay alive in the twentieth, but the bell tolled, oh did it toll, in the twenty-first.

Boxing as a Reflection of Society

The reality of racism in America has had no better gauge than the sport of boxing. As unfortunate as this association may sound, recognize also that there has never been a time when a man of any color associated with the sport hasn't wanted to smash the mirror for what it reflects.

Although difficult to accept today, during the early part of the twentieth century, racial prejudice was there front and center. In Nelson's self-published book, *Life, Battles and Career of Battling Nelson, Lightweight Champion of the World*, delivered in 1908, he provides his readers a perspective into his world, as he saw it, experienced it, and felt it at the pinnacle of his career.

As Nelson's trilogy with the "Old Master" drew to a close, he felt a need to candidly reflect his views. As interpreted in today's world, it is a tasteless and illiterate point of view, yet it was reality. In chapter 18 of his autobiography, he adds the subtitle, "My Ring Experiences with the Negro Population," then provides some forthright remarks:

I feel proud of stating "No Colored Man Ever Conquered Me." Many of my readers may take exception to this statement, but it is nevertheless true. I demonstrated fully to the public on July 4 and September 9 of this year [1908] that I was this negro's master by licking, trouncing, beating and battering him into a mass of "black jung," if such a slang phrase may be used.[10]

Nelson then begins an overview of the "tough Negro scrappers" he has met. "It was in July of that season that I met the first Negro boxer—one Feathers Vernon, a man who was at that time looked upon as a pretty tough coon in and around Englewood, 'one of Chicago's beautiful suburbs,'" an older Oscar recalled. "Black Griffo lasted but three rounds, being cracked into dreamland with my favorite punch, a 'left half scissors hook' on the liver, where I usually have been getting them all ever since, particularly the negro boxing population." He then continues by humiliating, in a very repulsive manner, one "Mistah Edward Jackson Burley."[11]

Later, and to not ignore another ethnicity, Nelson writes,

> The Danes, as Burke's Irish history tells us so plainly, were the boys who populated and set at rest all war and strife in Old Ireland many, many "rounds" ago. Well, I'm a Dane all right, and as most of the Irish are no doubt related to me in one way or the other, through ancient descent, I have a feeling for most of them—that is the good ones. So when on St. Patrick's Day, March 17, 1901, when the Chicago papers announced the fact that Bat Nelson was going to meet Black Griffo again at the Sheridan Club, I had a spasm [Nelson 1908, 160].

Nelson was obviously concerned about how his Irish friends would feel about meeting a black fighter on the traditional death date of Saint Patrick (c. AD 385–461), the foremost patron saint of Ireland. For support he turns to his Irish friend and St. Louis American League pitcher[12] Jack Powell for support. "Bat don't hav' any broachins about Oireland an' yer bein' our cousins, an' not wantin' t' foight on Paddy's birthday, but go in me Batthler an' knock th' devil's head off th' coon. Ye' don't hate thim anny more thin Oi do."[13]

And finally, as your stomach churns and your blood begins to reach a boiling point, Nelson recalled, "The hardest battle of all the coons ... Mistah Christopher Columbus Williams. This coon had a jaw like the hull of the battleship *Ohio*, and it required seventeen grueling, slashing rounds to shove him gently into 'slumberland.' After Nelson sent "Christy over the ropes, down and out," the brass band ringside—unusual to a boxing event but a regular occurrence in Hot Springs—played the tunes, "All Coons Look Alike to Me," "I Don't Care If You Never Come Back," and ended with "Home Sweet Home" as the crowd filed out.[14]

These are the words of a Danish immigrant's son, twenty-six years of age and the 1908 world lightweight champion, a fighter born in

Photograph shows the memorial fountain in honor of black Canadian champion boxer George Dixon (1870–1908), which was dedicated on August 28, 1908, at the corner of Thompson and Broome streets, New York City (Library of Congress, Prints and Photograph Division, LC-DIG-ggbain-01523).

Eight—September 9, 1908: The Fight of the Century III

Copenhagen, Denmark, who has just defeated an older boxer born in Baltimore, Maryland, the latter the "Old Master" and easily one of the finest boxers the sport has ever known. One wonders—I'll say it for you—how these views might have changed had Gans won the majority of their confrontations. And, how would Gans have handled his retrospective accounts of his white opponents?

And while Nelson fought Gans, champion Jack Dempsey wouldn't dignify any Negro with a fight. The man they called "Kid Blackie," who had fought many black boxers during his ascension to the championship, later turned his back at the thought—this a recommendation from his manager and fight promoters. There would be no Dempsey v. Johnson, no Dempsey v. Wills, and no justice.

Even though slavery was abolished in the U.S. in 1865, which we all know, many black Americans still faced poverty and injustice, and we all understand this. Rampant racism and prejudice toward people of color was a recurrent reaction throughout the twentieth century—they faced it in the classroom, on the streets and in the prize ring. Many white fighters, not just Dempsey, refused to face black fighters, and conversely—something that must be remembered if we are to place both Gans and Nelson in the proper context.

Geographic pockets of bigotry also existed. Society in the southern states was almost entirely segregated, with the hatred perpetrated through the many organized hate groups. Racism was still a factor in the northern states, but segregation was not official policy as it was in the South. Many African Americans had only the option of hard manual labor or working in areas inherently dangerous, such as in foundries, so turning toward the ring was not such a difficult decision. In fact, the ring became an outlet for the hatred they felt and the intolerance they faced.

The imposing figure of John Arthur Johnson, born on March 31, 1878, in Galveston, Texas, commonly ranked by historians as one of the ten greatest boxers in the history of the sport (Library of Congress, Prints and Photograph Division, LC-DIG-ggbain-08094).

The Joe Gans versus Battling Nelson trilogy—the second fight of which took place exactly two years before "The Fight of the Century" between Jack Johnson, the "Negro's Deliverer," and Jim Jeffries, the "Hope of the White Race"—will be considered by most historians as one of the greatest trilogies in the sport of boxing. The word "trilogy," part of the boxing lexicon, has also become associated with greatness in the sport thanks to *this* confrontation, the oldest quality exemplar. Joe Gans was the lightweight's Jack Johnson, a fighter emblematic of his ethnic origin. Had he been as controversial as Johnson, and perhaps not died so young, Gans's epic series with Nelson might have been given the same attention as that of their heavyweight counterparts.

In the face of bigotry, it took a tremendous amount of courage for Joe Gans, regardless of his financial position, to accept a match with Battling Nelson. Also, ignoring the obvious foul by Nelson, Gans did not have to give the white fighter a rematch, yet he did. And Nelson returned the favor.

After Gans

There seemed to be a symbiotic relationship between the press and Nelson regarding his financial position, which seemed to always find a place in the papers. Days before a fight, like that of Gans, Nelson's habit of accumulating the coin was highlighted in many a trade—his reserve estimated at $100,000, on its way to twice that figure. Real estate was his overwhelming interest, and it had now left the shores of Lake Michigan for the rolling hills of California. Speaking of the latter, the Battler was about to combine his love of California with his ongoing fascination for the stage.

Three days after the Gans fight, Nelson signed a contract with proprietor and manager Ernest E. Howell for a boxing exhibition at the Central Theater. It was called "A Curse of Drink," ideal for the abstemious Dane. Nelson liked the stakes, $1,500 for nine performances and 40 percent over $3,500. Capitalizing on his new title and certainly no stranger to the footlights, the fighter proved an enormous draw in Frisco and Howell. The shows were held at the Central Theater, over on Market and Eighth Street. Matinees were scheduled for Saturday and Sunday with admission set at fifteen, twenty-five and fifty cents. All the Central Theater regulars would assist in the vaudeville performance, and moving pictures of the Britt versus Nelson conflict were shown between acts.

Charles Dixon, George Dixon's brother and the Battler's timekeeper, introduced Nelson to his audience on opening night. George Dixon, a gifted boxer, who was the first black man to win a world championship in any weight class and the first ever Canadian-born boxing champion, had passed away on January 6.[15] The ovation was thunderous for Nelson who followed the applause with a brief speech. In addition to his new title, the champion was also recognized for scoring the quickest knockout on record (Billy Rossler, Harvey, IL); having no less than three arenas built for him (Butte, Colma and Goldfield); the largest gate on record ($69,715); never "laying down" despite repeated offers; being the wealthiest boxer; paying taxes in Illinois, Ohio, California, Nevada and New Mexico; never losing in a financial deal; never tasting liquor or tobacco; and giving his defeated opponent a second chance at the championship.[16]

Nelson's homestead claim near Perry in Quay County was recognized on September 19, as was his announcement that he would be making his home in New Mexico Territory. Located west from the Texas state line, Quay County was named for Pennsylvania senator Matthew Quay, who supported statehood for New Mexico.[17] It was a growing community, about to reach the pinnacle of its population, and the boxer felt it ideal. The champion hoped to erect a hunting lodge, gymnasium and dance hall.

Not one to look for trouble, Nelson and a few friends boarded a streetcar with transfers. When the conductor demanded tickets from the group, Nelson's admission was refused—this same situation had happened to the fighter only days before, and his patience for the circumstance was growing thin. Nelson politely insisted that the transfer was completed properly only to then be ordered to "Get off before I throw you off" by the conductor.[18] Shocked, the Battler replied, "Do you mean it?"[19] And while the conductor made his move at Nelson, Bat powered a right that crumbled the conductor. More fisticuffs ensued, leaving a trail of two knockouts to be later sorted out. These were not the actions befitting a champion, a behavior modification Nelson had yet to enact.

Two days later, the press caught up with two members of the Nelson family in Salt Lake City, Utah, at the Kenyon Hotel. Nels, or Neils Nelson, Bat's father, and Arthur, one of Bat's brothers, were on their way home to Hegewisch following the Gans fight. Both were still reeling from Bat's ring performance and willing to share their enthusiasm with anyone interested. The Battler had been called immediately to Chicago for his theater engagement, or he would have gladly traveled with his family from Ogden.

Elder Nelson beamed as he stated, "Bat is good boy and has made a great deal of money and has put all of it to good use or placed it where it will bring him good income."[20] The father also confirmed—the railroad acronyms far easier for the elder to recall and pronounce—that his son "owns a piece of property between the tracks of the C.B. & Q. and C. & N.W. in Hegewisch, Illinois for which he paid $50,000 and for which he is now offered $150,000."[21] The report validated that the Nelsons, consisting of seven boys and one girl, were properly taken care of through their fighting brother's financial efforts. Elder also affirmed—a father's praise just a child away—that Charles Nelson, age twenty-one, was studying medicine at the University of California at Berkeley and was the fourth member of the Nelson clan at Bat's last fight.

Hegewisch—notice I don't dare say Burnham—was indeed eager to welcome the Nelsons back in town. The Reverend S.A. Dennis, an area Methodist minister, turned a few heads when he stated, "I hope to have Battling Nelson join the church. If he were to become a Methodist every man, woman, and child in the place would forthwith join the church. I have prayed unremittingly for the conversion of 'The Battler.'" Confirming the decency of Nelson and that his instincts were good, the Reverend Nelson stated, "He has promised me to give the question (Will he turn to the path of righteousness?) serious thought."[22]

Meanwhile, across the pond they too couldn't wait for the chance to greet Nelson, or an opportunity to greet an opportunity, if you will. While traveling through

The debonair Freddie Welsh, born Frederick Hall Thomas on March 5, 1886, in Pontypridd, South Wales, fought his first pro bout in 1905 (Library of Congress, Prints and Photograph Division, LC-DIG-ggbain-06621).

Europe and picking up some easy exhibit money, the ex-white lightweight champion Jimmy Britt dropped his brother's camp a note stating that a fortune awaits the Battler on the other side of the Atlantic. It was Britt's suggestion that Nelson travel there following his theatrical engagements. Nelson, now working at the Trocadero Theater at 414 South State Street in Chicago, took the idea under consideration as he sorted out his daily domestic offerings. Promoter Coffroth was pressing Bat for a Thanksgiving Day battle against McFarland, while Baron Long, manager of the Jeffries Club, was pushing the Dane to meet Freddie Welsh, the lightweight champion of Great Britain.

Wise not to take either of these offers but to sit and polish the crown, Nelson and Company would first take full advantage of every opportunity outside the ring. Besides, McFarland was disposing opponents at will and was clearly the most dangerous fighter in the division, having beaten Welsh once and drawn him in a rematch. Following his draw with McFarland, Welsh would defeat his next four opponents before the year ended, including a points victory over feather Abe Attell. To use the overused Chaucer line, "Patience is a conquering virtue." Nelson understood his position and desired to now exploit it for everything it was worth.

As soon as Bat heard the news of the death of R.A. Smyth he dispatched a telegram to the R.A. Smyth memorial fund that read,

> DETROIT, OCT. 9, HAVE MAILED CHECK FOR $250 FOR THE SMYTH TESTIMONIAL. I HOPE IT WILL BE A HUGE SUCCESS, FOR BOB WAS ONE OF THE GRANDEST MEN WHO EVER LIVED. LETTER ON WAY. BATTLING NELSON.[23]

While the committee was deeply affected, they were not surprised by Nelson's generosity, stating, "Bat is one of the kindest and most generous of men. His heart and his purse are ever open to those whom he likes and he will go to the end of his resources to do a turn for any man, woman or child who ever gained his friendship."[24] "Bob" Smyth brought the fight game into every sportsman's heart, and when he found Nelson, he found a gold mine. He understood that trying to package Bat into anything more than what he was, was like serving scrambled eggs and trying to pass them off as crème brûlée. The two seemed made for each other as Smyth was always looking for a good slant and Nelson never failed to deliver. The benefit for the mother and sister of the late Robert Assheton Smyth was promised to be an unbounded artistic and financial success and certainly delivered. The financial committee of the fund presented the mother and sister of the writer the sum of $5,031.55, the proceeds of the boxing and theatrical shows which were given.

Robert Assheton Smyth, the sporting editor of the *San Francisco Call* died at 4:30 p.m. on October 3 at the French hospital. The forty-two-year-old Smyth was born in Castle Martyr, County Cork, Ireland, the son of a prominent Irish huntsman. After a brief residence in Australia, the Smyth family headed to San Francisco. Bob attended the Lincoln School in the city, worked as a clerk for Wells Fargo Express Company and became a popular cyclist. After retiring from racing, he became a bicycle handicapper before entering journalism. Becoming sporting editor for *The Call* over the past ten years had become his passion, and he wore that ardor as a gentleman who lived a simple life. Living through an illness that eventually made him a mere shadow of a man, Smyth did so without complaint, perhaps knowing it would eventually take his life.

While in Detroit, Battling Nelson got caught up in the excitement of the Ford Model T, considered by many to be the most influential car of the twentieth century. As a boxing champion, Nelson had access to automobiles, but car ownership was still considered a rarity. Even though automobiles had been around for decades, their adoption as a popular form of transportation had been slow, primarily due to cost and availability. All that changed on September 27, when the first vehicle rolled off the Piquette Plant assembly line. Priced at $850, it became a viable option for many who never thought they could afford such a purchase. Now, comparatively speaking, these Tin Lizzies seemed to be everywhere in a city that would become the center of the U.S. automobile industry. In less than ten years, Henry Ford himself would watch as the fifteen millionth Model T Ford was produced.

Also while visiting Detroit, Nelson had occasion to take in the 1908 World Series between the defending Chicago Cubs and the Detroit Tigers.[25] The event, the first ever rematch of this young affair, promised to have all the excitement of a championship fight. And it had a fresh syndicated reporter covering the event. Fancying himself a genuine fan of the game, Nelson picked up a pen and began his writing career. With lines like, "Then the Cubs commenced to bore in toward the end of the round, little Evers scoring the knockout, running up another score for the day," the Battler—likely with more than a bit of advice shared by his fellow journalists—put his own unique spin on the game.[26] The friendly confines of Bennett Park, at Michigan and Trumbull, welcomed the Dane like he was one of their own. The champ took particular pride in penning the exploits of a young Tigers sensation by the name of Ty Cobb, who seemed to have some of the same fighting spirit Nelson had seen inside the ring. But even Cobb was not enough to stop the Cubs from clinching another championship. The champion summed up the game with a two sentences:

> The Tigers seemed to be utterly outclassed, with only one exception, which was in the fourth round, when they danced around rather cleverly, blocking jabs, swings, hooks, even the deadly uppercuts, but the Cubs seemingly a bit worried, took the Tigers by the tail, giving it a quick twist and making them squeal for help. From this time on they were outclassed from start to finish, and apparently never had a look-in with the champion.[27]

Following the event, Nelson was back on the circuit to complete the few remaining dates on his tour.

At the end of October, it was off to Boston as Nelson opened up a week's engagement at the Howard Theater. He was performing a bit that was written especially for him and included small speeches before and after a three-round exhibition. Attendance was good, an improvement over all his previous engagements at the Howard. Nelson took some time to head to New York to submit his autobiography, *Life, Battles and Career of Battling Nelson, Lightweight Champion of the World*, to the printers for publication. The book, like the author, had been a work in progress, constantly being edited with pieces selectively leaked to the press.

While in New York City, on November 6, a highly fashionable Battling Nelson, accompanied by a friend, became the second pugilist—the first being "Philadelphia Jack" O'Brien—barred from the Waldorf-Astoria, the luxury hotel in Manhattan. Under hotel rules, pugilists were barred from accommodations. One would think a luxury hotel would be more than happy to welcome a champion, but such was not the case for the Dane, who found it far more difficult than expected to find a place to call home.

The Battler just happened—as just happens to happen in boxing—to stumble upon Team McFarland as both were visiting the offices of a local New York newspaper. Hell-bent to raise a ruckus over why the two hadn't been matched yet, Packey went at Bat with some "neatly rehearsed and cleverly acted jawology."[28] The two engaged in some of the finest ring

On November 6, 1908, while in New York City, a highly fashionable Battling Nelson, accompanied by a friend, became the second pugilist—the first being "Philadelphia Jack" O'Brien—barred from the Waldorf-Astoria. The luxurious hotel in Manhattan is pictured here. (Library of Congress, Prints and Photograph Division, LC-DIG-det-4a08045).

hyperbole of the era, all in hopes of generating a bit of ink in the dailies, and obviously a bit of public pressure for the match. The noble Nelson was concerned that everybody in Gotham didn't know who he was, and he was right.

Returning home for the holidays, the Battler found himself preventing a death grapple between two bull terriers, of all things, inside city hall—probably not the best place for a fifty-six-minute dog fight, but at that mark was when the event drew to a conclusion as the trustees of the village of Burnham, along with a dozen armed deputies, stormed the venue.

An estimated five hundred spectators immediately scrambled for windows and doors in an attempt to escape the illegal action, one even jumping from a second-story window, breaking his leg. Deputies fired shots into the air in an attempt to slow the stampede, but they were unsuccessful. The helter-skelter flight of attendees was sheer chaos, many struggling to find a quick method of escape, be it by foot, carriage or even automobile. Amidst the mayhem, authorities managed to capture nine men as a statement of order.

The *Los Angeles Herald* reported the story on November 24: "Champion Battling Nelson escaped the same fate by what his followers might call a new exhibition of ring generalship. When the scramble began the Battler bethought himself of a deputy's star presented to him by an admirer last summer at his 320-acre ranch at O-Bar, New Mexico Territory. Pinning this to his coat, he mingled with the raiders and finally slipped from the place unobserved." However, Nelson was arrested the following day on warrants charging disorderly conduct and resisting an officer. He was released following the incident.[29]

The Battler, fresh from his discharge in the Burnham police court, was in front of the local transportation committee of the city council on November 25—the committee went to Hegewisch to look over the proposed right of way for the Kensington and Eastern railway by which the Illinois Central hoped to get an entrance into Gary, Indiana. "We people down here want the road bad," spoke Nelson. "We have no direct connection with the city now and this would give us one. It would raise the price of real estate and I own some lots here." The committee listened to Nelson, stated the need for a permit or ordinance, then got back into their carriages and departed. Both parties seemed rather unimpressed with each other.

In a stroke of serendipity, Nelson announced himself as a candidate for the Republican nomination for alderman of the Eighth Ward. Incumbent Patrick H. Moynihan had the necessary support of the political bosses in town, so Nelson's challenge wasn't taken all that seriously. However, Nelson made his points clear:

> Say, I am running for alderman down here. We want this railroad here. That's all—see? [Sounds like Cagney in *The Public Enemy*, still over two decades away (1931).] We'll drop over here and fix this thing up now. It's a big boost for father. I'll tell you guys another thing, when I get to be an alderman, this Burnham stuff don't go. Burnham is the junk they have thrown out of the drainage canal. This is Hegewisch and the home of Battling Nelson, and that goes. Don't forget.[30]

Speaking of running, Nelson also expressed interest in running marathons. "Haven't I often run for five hours at a time?" he said in a wire story picked up by the *Evening Times* of Grand Forks, North Dakota, "So I see no reason why I couldn't run one of these races." He then went on to expound on his physique, which he had precisely measured on July 27, 1908: "Height, 5 Ft. 7½"; Weight, 130 to 133 pounds (Trained), 140 to 145 (Normal); Reach, 67½"; Neck, 15"; Chest, 34" (Normal), 39½" (Expanded); Waist, 27"; Biceps, 10½" (Normal), 12" (Contracted); Wrist, 6¾"; Forearm, 10"; Length of Arm, 26"; Thigh, 19" and Calf, 14"."[31] Nelson seemed to find reassurance in the tale of the tape and, like any champion, would use it as an intimidation factor against his opponents. But measurements are one thing and narcissism is another, the latter of which he may have crossed by the inclusion of two medical opinions in his autobiography—the first apparently solicited by himself, the second by a newspaper.

According to Dr. Sargent, the greatest physical culture expert in the world, "Battling Nelson is a perfectly developed man, both physically and mentally, and a human battering ram." His assessment was so noteworthy that Nelson included it in his autobiography. The highlights of Dr. Sargent's thorough examination of the 1908 lightweight champion of the world are as follows: "Nelson has the best heart and lungs I have ever examined"; "His brain is of normal size—there is nothing extraordinary about it, except that he can think quicker and act faster than most persons"; "Nelson's jaw puzzled me more than any other part of his anatomy. You can catch him a good hard uppercut on the point of the jaw, and you get no response"; "He has smaller hands and feet than the average person, but that is no odd characteristic"; and "His endurance is wonderful."[32]

When it comes to the medical field, it always pays to get a second opinion, so the *Evening Tribune* of Oakland, California, secured the services of Dr. D.D. Crowley to examine Nelson in the presence of H.A. Herrick, the paper's news editor. Here are some of his conclusions about the Dane: "Battling Nelson was a specimen of that *rara avis* in the world of fighters—a man with a perfect nervous system"; "Within 15 or 20 seconds (following a strenuous training session) his heart beats which were more than 85 were reduced to 52 beats per minute"; "Battling Nelson is a wonder and an abnormal man to the loss of much that goes to make life endurable—a pure fighting machine which nature has lavishly bestowed with an unusual gift"; "Not beyond the normal in anything, but singularly a well muscled man"; "Nelson is an egotist. One born to the condition and one in whom it is part of the natural heritage of birth" and "He is easily the most picturesque of all the champions—more, in fact, like those olden-time fighters who braved dangers of the ring from the impelling innate desire to rule."[33]

Beyond the need for a physical evaluation by the champion in 1908 was also that of an audit. Nelson felt a need to gauge his success, or at least set the bar at a certain financial level, for future champions. The insights the twenty-six-year-old shares are indeed intriguing and paint a picture of the champion at the pinnacle of his career. During his twelve-year ascent to the 1908 world lightweight championship, Battling Nelson received $231,886.80, which breaks down as follows: fighting professionally, $121,486.80; theatrical tours, $45,400; side bet winnings, $15,000; business ventures, $50,000. Interesting averages include revenue per fight (92), $1,320.50; revenue per round (710), $171.10; average revenue per year (12), $19,323.90.[34]

How that ring revenue separates by year: 1896–1898, $21.50; 1899, $25.00; 1900, $182.50; 1901, $606.73; 1902, $724.50; 1903, $2,307.50; 1904, $13,303.00; 1905, $25,591.00; 1906, $35,271.50; 1907, $10,500.00 and 1908, $32,965.57.[35]

Up to 1908, only ten men had handed the Battler a loss: Charles Berry (2), Pete Boyle, Jimmie Britt (2), Joe Gans, Joe Hedmark, Charles Neary, Joe Percente, Mickey Riley, Eddie Santry and Eddie Sterns. A calculating champion also claimed: "On September 9, 1908, I found after a bit of study that I had been fighting just 4,386 days, or twelve years and six days. Each and every one of those days was fraught with many trials and tribulations. Still I am happy withal, even though I own the brow which wears the crown."[36]

And there were more crowns in 1908: Jack Johnson became the first African American world heavyweight champion by defeating Tommy Burns in Sydney, Australia, on December 26, in one of the most memorable events of the year. Dropping Burns in the opening seconds of the battle, Johnson then toyed with his smaller opponent until the bout was stopped in the fourteenth. World middleweight champion Stanley Ketchel lost his title on September 7 to Billy Papke by a twelfth-round technical knockout at Vernon, California, but regained it on November 26 at Colma, California, where he knocked out Papke with a left hook to the jaw in the eleventh round. Mike "Twin" Sullivan vacated the world welterweight championship, Nelson had his crown, Abe Attell retained the feather crown and Jimmy Walsh continued his reign over the bantams.

Six fights, amounting to three wins, two no decisions and one draw, are added to the record of the new world lightweight champion in 1908. Battling Nelson fights seventy-eight rounds averaging thirteen rounds per fight and not only wins the title, but defends it against the former champion. Fighting two members of boxing's elite, Attell and Gans, he adds one of the greatest trilogies the sport has ever seen into the record books and concludes a quartet of impressive battles with Jimmy Britt. Speaking of the Britt family, the Battler was now under the watchful eye of Willus Britt who helped guide him through this championship period. Commanding top dollar inside the ring, allows the Dane to expand his real estate holdings, as well as play to packed houses during his theatrical performances. The durability of the Dane was also

A full-length portrait of Jack Johnson and his wife Etta, wearing winter coats. The couple's interracial lifestyle unfairly reflected on the boxer and made him so unpopular that Jim Jeffries came out of retirement to battle the "Galveston Giant." (Library of Congress, Prints and Photograph Division, LC-DIG-ppmsca-31941).

exhibited during the year, as he managed his way out of a couple of legal tussles, proving that if you can't beat them in one ring, try another—even if the boxer would never become the alderman of the Eighth Ward, he certainly managed to shake up a few politicians.

NINE

1909
Retaining the Title

> My first theatrical tour put $21,400 into my pocket, my second $11,000 and the odd theatricals another $13,000 during my twelve years of fighting.
> —Oscar "Battling" Matthew Nelson[1]

Boxing champions aren't born. They're made. A reflection of both their time and surroundings, they are shaped by their experiences. They seize the moment because they understand that it is their time. And they will stay champions for as long as they think, and act, like one—something the young Battling Nelson needed to be reminded of, even if he didn't always listen to his manager.

Expected to win, champions understand that the ring is their domain. Transformed by their confidence, this realm has only one thing to offer them, victory. But this realm also has parameters, such as opponent skill, length of battle, or risk of title, that must be constantly evaluated against reward. And this balance is not a simple task.

Great pugilists also acknowledge their past. Following in the footsteps of lightweight champions such as Jack McAuliffe, George "Kid" Lavigne, Frank Erne and Joe Gans suited Battling Nelson just fine, but these were big shoes to fill. And to do so, would take untold hours of commitment.

Understanding that the small wins gave them the credence to win their title, champions endure because they did not become complacent or overconfident. Champions see their life as a gift, not an obligation. This is tough for some boxers, who may not love every minute of the journey, every photograph with a fan or autograph during dinner, but they are conscious that attitude fashions skill, or polishes the bust of a Hall of Fame fighter.

So, what separates the great champions from the good ones? Their faith is greater than their fear. It is their passion and purpose that will overcome any challenge they may face, and that is completely understood. They grow from their miscalculations to become stronger, wiser and better fighters. And they don't make excuses when they don't win—something Battling Nelson had been guilty of, and something that needed to be altered.

The best days of their life, champions know, are always in front of them. Oscar Nelson believed that; Battling Nelson needed to live it.

So, what kind of champion would Oscar "Battling" Matthew Nelson be in his first full year wearing the crown?

Tour talk, and even routine discussion, while the champion was out and about always seemed to waltz back to the Battler's destruction of Gans, tales of champions past, automobiles and even the 1908 presidential election. Nelson, like many of those he encountered, was shocked that current president Theodore Roosevelt had stuck to his public declaration that he would not run for reelection in 1908. When "TR" backed his secretary of war for the Republican nomination, it appeared to many as a guarantee, especially to the Democrats, who viewed it as a compulsory succession to the presidency. Nevertheless, when it went to the cards, William Howard Taft had won by a comfortable electoral margin—providing his opponent the worst loss in three presidential campaigns—even if he garnered only 51 percent of the popular vote over William Jennings Bryan.[2]

Many eyes looked to the pages of *Life, Battles and Career of Battling Nelson, Lightweight Champion of the World* early in the year, thanks to advanced excerpts printed in numerous newspapers. Believed published in 1908—it mentions the Dane's visit to the White House on February 14, 1909, on page fifty inside the piece, while his actual visit was on January 14—the introductory matter of the work begins thus[3]:

RICHEST PUGILIST IN THE WORLD TELLS HOW HIS PROWESS IN THE RING HAS BROUGHT HIM WEALTH—PROUD OF HIS RECORD OF 100 PER CENT AT ALGEBRA IN SCHOOL—SHREWD INVESTMENTS OF HIS EARNINGS—BORN ON DANISH INDEPENDENCE DAY AND BEAT GANS ON THE GLORIOUS FOURTH—HERE'S A SCRAPPER WHO SEEMS TO BE A PRETTY LEVEL-HEADED BUSINESS MAN[4]

President Theodore Roosevelt, twenty-sixth president of the United States, 1901–09, working hard in his office. The inserted portrait is that of his secretary, William Loeb, Jr. To the right of both images is the dustcover of Nelson's autobiography (Library of Congress, Collage, Prints and Photograph Division, LC-DIG¬hec-15452; LC-USZ62-76768).

The narcissistic self-published work claimed Nelson as not only the happiest man in the world, but also the richest of all pugilists. The boxer whose hallmark punch, the left half scissors hook, ended the reign of the "Old Master" painted his adversary as a ring deity who systematically disposed of his opponents. That is, until Nelson.

In addition to the Battler's own stories of his life, he registers the aforementioned story, "My Ring Experiences with the Negro Population," along with a synopsis of the two foremost cartoonists of the world: T.A. Dorgan, known as TAD, sporting cartoonist of the New York *Evening Journal*, and Robert Edgren, known as Bob Edgren, sporting editor and cartoonist of the New York *Evening World*. Naturally such adulation led both artists to contribute lampoons to the autobiography. And, as we will see, Nelson had more than a passing interest in the art of cartooning.[5] While the satires were indeed interesting, as were the fighter's self-assessments, not so funny was the depiction of Battling Nelson's "Colored Morgue." The crude drawing, given "To Bat, with compliments, CAD Brand, [of the] *Milwaukee Sentinel*," stands as a testament to the racist indignities faced by so many fighters.

Other wordsmiths also surface within the work, even Jack London who pens the unmemorable "How Different People View Fighters. Brain Beaten by Brute Force," or "Nelson, 'the Abysmal Brute,' Beats Britt, the Intelligent Creature," which was dissected earlier.[6] The book, which had a planned publication by November or early December, had been subject to the champion's schedule. Several thousand copies of the finished work, as anticipated, would follow the Battler along his future path, be it inside or outside the ring.

On November 16, 1909, *Los Angeles Herald* gossip columnist Jay Davidson summed up the books arrival—possibly through reading excerpts or proofs—by stating how proud the sporting public was in Nelson and that the fighter's anticipation of a large demand for it was certainly accurate. Always treating "the public—and himself—fairly and honesty," Davidson added, "no suspicion, even, of a frame-up ever entered into the consideration of the merits of a battle where he was one of the principals."

The introductory of *Life, Battles and Career of Battling Nelson, Lightweight Champion of the World* was also quick to quote the figure of a quarter of a million dollars as the Dane's worth, and that he did not care if he ever saw a glove again. While there was little argument with the former, the latter was a bit harder to believe based on the boxer's actions both in and around the fight game.

As champion, Nelson was being "called out" routinely, much of it during the month of January by the "Welsh Wizard," Freddie Welsh. Welsh, having signed articles, announced that he would claim the title by default unless Nelson agreed to sign for a match within thirty days—Welsh was calling for a ten-round no decision bout. Such are the trials and tribulations of those ascending the thrown—Welsh would however end up the British lightweight champion by year's end. And, as fate might have it, a day would come when Oscar would be spending much of his time throwing down the gauntlet to Welsh.

A Visit to the White House

The word from Washington, on January 14, was that Battling Nelson didn't need a press agent, but anyone following the sweet science could have told you that. The new champion dropped in on President Theodore Roosevelt to congratulate him on his ninety-eight-mile gallop through Virginia—the ride from the White House to Warrenton, then back—during a blinding downpour of sleet and snow. Bat's visit, or photo op, just happened to coincide with the president's excursion. For "TR" it was time to congratulate the latest champion, and perhaps add a bit more machismo to the Roosevelt image. Clearly both were capitalizing on each other's notoriety, though Roosevelt was a genuine boxing fan.

The prelude to the president's journey, just before he was prepared to leave office, was this: army officers were complaining at a Roosevelt directive that they must be able to ride 90 miles in three days. So he went out to prove them wrong, and only needed seventeen hours—bully for him!

Truthfully, Roosevelt always enjoyed the company of a pugilist. As a youth he had learned to box in order to defend himself. John Long, an ex-prizefighter, became his first real mentor. "TR" would often recall viewing the "colored pictures of the fights between Tom Hyer and Yankee Sullivan, and Heenan and Sayers, and other notable events in the annals of the squared circle" that adorned the fighter's office.[7] Roosevelt carried these skills to Harvard where he did a great deal of boxing and wrestling, then on to Washington where his verbal self-defense replaced the need for physical prowess.

Nelson also spent time with Secretary William Loeb, Jr., an old friend he had met in Montana. In the White House, Loeb served as assistant secretary to the president from 1901 to 1903 and then succeeded George B. Cortelyou as secretary to the president (1903). Roosevelt's right-hand man, the bespectacled and mustached assistant even looked a bit like the "TR." Loeb stayed by the president's side for the rest of Roosevelt's time in office and gradually became one of the era's most powerful figures.

The modern champion also fielded questions saying that California shot-putter Ralph Rose could be convinced of fighting Jack Johnson. Rose was the first shot-putter to break fifty feet and stood a mammoth six feet five and a half inches.[8] As for his taking on Johnson, Nelson confirmed that wouldn't happen, but he would fight any other man of his own weight.

The president would later recall the visit in his autobiography: "Battling Nelson was another staunch friend, and he and I think alike on most questions of political and industrial life; although he once expressed to me some commiseration because, as President, I did not get anything like the money return for my services that he aggregated during the same term of years in the ring."[9]

When Nelson arrived back in Chicago on January 16, he confirmed to the *San Francisco Call* that he thought Roosevelt was "all right." The fighter also noted that he was eager to pick up a little theater money before fighting again. "Why shouldn't I? I'm not afraid of anyone. What's the use of taking a chance unless the money is there?"[10]

Exhausted from the craziness caused by all the fight speculation, Nelson announced in early February, "I am through with the game until spring. I may consent to fight some time in March, but I hardly think so. April, however, probably will find me back in the ring."[11]

Nine days later, on February 13, an article with the header "'Fighting Dick' and Bat Nelson Matched" appeared in the *San Francisco Call* stating that a Nelson fight was imminent. "Fighting Dick" referred to none other than local favorite Dick Hyland. Catching everyone by surprise, it was rebuffed by many. As for Nelson, well, he was on tour, having resumed his travel. That was until he briefly suffered a severe cold at the end of the month that sidelined him. Spending some time at the healing Hot Springs replenished Nelson, who was then off to San Jose before going back to the Bay Area.[12]

Back in San Francisco in early March, looking the same rugged fighter that he was when he left some six months ago, Nelson ducked a few questions regarding his next opponent, only stating that an announcement was forthcoming. Claiming to have beaten all the good lightweights in this country and needing new fields to conquer, the Dane then turned his attention to Great Britain. "There are five of these Britishers who have been causing so much talk lately. These men are Jem Driscoll, Freddie Welsh, Owen Moran, Johnny Summers and Jabez White," the champion confirmed to the *San Francisco Call* on March 2. "I don't think that any one of them can give me a fight, and just to show everyone that I can beat them I will take on the whole bunch next Fourth of July."[13] Of course, the champion was just *being* the champion with these egotistical remarks, as the logistics involved with such a proposition were out of the realm of even the finest promoters. Nevertheless, it made for some good press and was picked up by all the hungry beat writers. While on the peninsula, the Battler even donned his tuxedo and sat for a special photography session for the newspaper—the timely image was featured predominately inside their Tuesday, March 2, editions. Coincidentally, the following day a lightweight championship battle was issued and signed for May.

In a poetic spin, Nelson's press agent Jack Densham had been creating daily verse as a way to communicate about the Battler, for example, "Thursday, Battling Nelson wants to fight, Fifteen Britons in one night, He is feeling out of sight, [signed] The Press Agent."[14] Densham understood not only that his boss appreciated poetry but that it made for good press, so why not add another twist?

Speaking of prose, St. Louis newspaperman J. Ignatius Finnegan, through his attorneys, was preparing the necessary legal papers to compel Battling Nelson to get an accounting of the proceeds of his autobiography. Finnegan claimed in Chicago on March 19 that he was the author of the book. Nelson denied those claims and stated that Finnegan acted as a stenographer and typewriter, but nothing more.

A week later, Finnegan penned a letter to a Chicago daily emphatically claiming he wrote every word of *Life, Battles and Career of Battling Nelson, Lightweight Champion of the World*. "Nelson did not write or compose one paragraph in the whole book," asserted Finnegan. "I secured most of the early dope of his career from George Siler, who knew him well. Nelson merely paid my expenses while I was with him."[15] The newspaperman then went on to claim a partnership with Nelson and that the champion had been ignoring him ever since the book's release. The issue then went to Finnegan's attorney who would ask for an injunction against the publisher.

When George Bernard Shaw quipped, "Imitation is not just the sincerest form of flattery—it's the sincerest form of learning," I doubt he considered its application to the sport of boxing, but such could certainly be the case. It seems that two men had been using the Battler's name in cities throughout New Mexico and Texas as part of swindling operations. The champion found out about this through the Chicago police on April 1. The worst hit had been El Paso, but other towns had also been schemed. The police issued letters to all the associated cities in these two states seeking the arrest of the men.

In part of a different operation, this time out of Joplin, Missouri, one "Charles Eagan" was charged with having secured $1,500 in this district while posing as Battling Nelson's advance agent. "Eagan arrived [in Joplin] three weeks ago and began boosting a moving picture show. He secured a theater and for two weeks sold tickets. He attempted to advertise in the newspapers, but his advertisements were refused. He then secured cards and posted them in saloons and billiard halls and sold many tickets."[16] Eagan was eventually caught passing a forged check.

After two hours of wrangling, champion wrestler Frank Gotch and his opponent grappler Fred Beell from Wisconsin decided that the only man worth acting as a referee in their title match was Battling Nelson. The two would meet in Denver on May 6, and Nelson's appearance was sure to keep the battle within the rules and perhaps sell a few tickets.

Ah, such is the way of a lightweight champion.

Nelson v. Hyland, March 29, 1909

Nelson's second title defense was scheduled for Saturday, May 29, inside Coffroth's now familiar Mission Street Arena (in present-day Daly City). The outdoor event would begin at the printed ticket time of 2:30 p.m. inside the squared-off facility. Promoter Coffroth had priced ringside at $10, near ringside at $5, followed by a $3 section and the remainder of the floor priced at $2. Bleacher sections that surrounded the venue had all seats priced at $1. The match was announced as a 45-round event, a more or less arbitrary number, used only because "fight to the finish matches" were nominally illegal.

Another revenue source, as we have seen, was film, as major prize fights—this ever since Veriscope's Corbett-Fitzsimmons fight (1897) became one of cinema's first major attractions, ushering in a new era—were now placed on celluloid. But it too came at a price. Filmmakers, now a ringside staple, also calculated that if a fight went 20 rounds, they would lose money, because the film was so expensive.[17] Coffroth understood this, as did Nelson.

At 11:30 the gallery doors opened, followed by the main entrance an hour later. Any remaining tickets, Coffroth informed patrons, should only be purchased through direct sources and not through the scalpers mingling about. The ten-round preliminary fight would see Nelson's sparring partner Jeff Perry battle Frankie Smith, a speedy lightweight. The champion would meet, at least according to some, "California's Greatest Lightweight," Dick Hyland, who hailed from 140 Wool Street in San Francisco, California.[18] However, to some outside the Bay Area, it was "Dick who?"

So one of the stories goes, a gentleman by the name of William Uren, born on October 20, 1885, or possibly September 12, 1887, substituted for an amateur fighter named Dick Hyland. In a situation that would also confront the future Walker Smith, the name stuck. This story, confirmed by both the *Tacoma Daily News* on November 13, 1908, and the *San Francisco Call* on August 15, 1907, casts a bit of speculation regarding the true identity of Nelson's opponent. If that were not enough, in November 1908, the Tacoma paper also noted that there was a Dick Hyland impostor fighting in Seattle, and yet another imitator battling in both New Orleans and Little Rock only a few months later. Taking this into consideration, it's time to meet the real Dick Hyland.[19]

Standing at a height of five feet four inches, with a reach of sixty-six inches, William Uren, aka "Fighting" Dick Hyland, was a legitimate boxer.[20] Many knew he had fought out of Alex Greggain's old San Francisco club gymnasium down on Sixth Street, which was *the* school for fighters. As neighborhoods were often branded by cable routes, Hyland was a "South of the Slot" fighter—an area known for giving rise to such scrapers as Abe Attell,

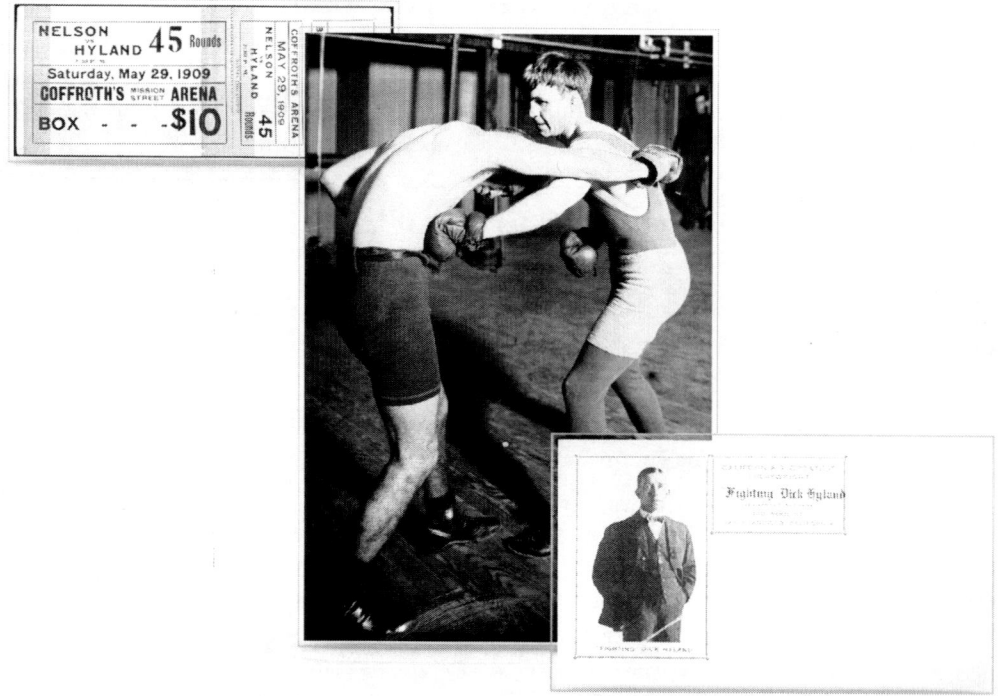

Nelson in a posed photograph of him delivering his trademark "left half scissors hook" to his opponent. Also pictured is a ticket from the Nelson vs. Hyland bout on Saturday, May 29, 1909, along with a commemorative souvenir envelope featuring "Fighting Dick Hyland" (Library of Congress, Prints and Photograph Division, LC-DIG-ggbain-01716).

Monte Attell, Eddie Hanlon, Frankie Neil, and Willie Ritchie. Hyland wouldn't shine immediately, so it was said, but he did gain a bit of recognition along his journey.[21]

The day before the fight, Hyland tackled a bit of morning roadwork before spending the remainder of the day relaxing with friends at Croll's Gardens—famous for quartering the likes of James J. Corbett, Bob Fitzsimmons, Jim Jeffries and Jack Johnson, to name only a few—in Alameda.[22] Ready for his encounter, the fighter's main concern, as was often the case on fight day, appeared to be holding his weight at 133 pounds.

Hyland would enter Mission Street Arena at 35–12–1 having in January lost a ten-round, anti-climactic decision against the dangerous and undefeated—don't let me fail to mention that he owned a 50–0–1 record—Packey McFarland. Hyland however, had been very inconsistent of late, winning only two of his last six fights. Nevertheless, he had also fought some very tough fighters leading up to McFarland, including Kid Goodman and Leach Cross. Having taken a solid beating against Young Corbett II back in April 1906, many felt the fighter had matured. So, this Dick Hyland, Nelson's opponent and promoter Coffroth's gamble, was certainly a boxer.

Following the two Gans fights, it was easy for some to view "Sunny Jim" Coffroth as nothing more than an opportunist. And I'll tell you something. There was a bit more to this circumstantial exploiter; he was also a clever businessman. According to many boxing historians, James W. Coffroth was the first large-scale boxing promoter.[23] Born in Sacramento, California, on September 12, 1872, James Wood Coffroth was the son of a printer turned state politician.[24] His parents settled in San Francisco when he was still an infant, and he was raised during a time when boxing was gaining in popularity. Coffroth worked first as an office boy in a firm of local attorneys, then as a clerk in the Surrogate Court in San Francisco. It was there—he was also a member of the Olympic Club in San Francisco—that he developed an interest in law, politics and boxing, as if, in some minds, there is a distinction between the three.[25]

Traveling east to witness sparring matches from some of the best in the sport of boxing, Coffroth became friendly with New York promoter James C. "Big Jim" Kennedy. Possessing razor sharp instincts, it was Kennedy, partnered with Patrick Powers and James Brady, who promoted major Madison Square Garden events like the "Six-Day Bicycle Race." "Big Jim" also handled a stable of prominent lightweights such as Frank Erne, ex-lightweight champion, and Buffalo middleweight Al Weinig.[26] Friendship between the two soon led to fight promotions on the West Coast. As might be anticipated, the young Coffroth received a solid education from Kennedy. And it was through this knowledge that Coffroth was able to secure a permit to stage boxing events in San Francisco, not to mention a bit of help from Abe Ruef, the local political power broker. Ruef was known to most as the political boss—or master puppeteer if you will—behind the administration of San Francisco mayor Eugene Schmitz during the tragic 1906 San Francisco earthquake.

The major feather in the Coffroth/Kennedy cap was the heavyweight championship match between James Jeffries and Gus Ruhlin on November 15, 1901. Held in the Twentieth Century Athletic Club in San Francisco, the fight is remembered by most for one particular incident. Ruhlin's manager tossed in a corner sponge, between the fifth and sixth rounds, to indicate an unconditional surrender—this the first time in American boxing history that a fight had ended in that manner. Setting a precedent for scoring, it entered the record books as a fifth-round knockout.[27] Furthermore, the championship fight also established a level of notoriety—needed in order for the promoter to compete successfully at this echelon of the fight game—for Coffroth.

When Kennedy died in 1904, Coffroth acted quickly to establish an even stronger hold on "Bay Area" promotions.[28] To avoid both the attention and influence of the San Francisco and Daly City authorities, Coffroth began another arena in San Mateo County—in the unincorporated town of Colma.[29] As a promoter, in a city noted for its corruption and misbehavior, Coffroth also became identified for his resilience, dodging accusations like a prizefighter. Nevertheless, even the best fighters can't elude every punch. On March 1, 1906, during a bantamweight bout between champion Harry Tenny and challenger Frankie Neil, Tenny took a beating that found him unconscious in the ring. He was reported dead the following morning. All the parties involved, including Coffroth, were arrested.[30] Although not convicted, his arrest in the case, along with a grand jury indictment of political power broker Abe Ruef, seriously impacted his public perception.[31]

While Coffroth certainly had become known for some classic promotions, like Corbett–Jeffries (1903), Bob Fitzsimmons–George Gardner (1903), and Battling Nelson–Joe Gans (twice in 1908), he was now dealing with obstacles he had never before encountered. Yes, he had gained a degree of popularity through his financial practices, like paying fighters a percentage of the gate receipts, but these small milestones were constantly being overshadowed by the unpredictability inherent to the sport. Although the immediate priority was Hyland versus Nelson, looking beyond boxing, he thought, might have to be a consideration.

According to numerous accounts, the fight drew one of the finest crowds in the history of the Mission Street Arena. With automobile ownership still a minority, area residents didn't leave town, so gate expectations were enormous and often met—a blessing for promoters. Fans, both inside and outside the arena walls, could feel the intensity and sense a memorable ring confrontation. Small groups met to claim the best viewing positions possible, often both at or beyond their ticket purchase, while fight predictions were as common as cigar smoke. The champion closed a 10 to 4 favorite, with Hyland money scarce beyond the twenty-fifth round.[32] The fight would not be viewed from any choice seats sold on this day as most had been disposed of the night before. Local media praise for the challenger remained strong, with the *San Francisco Call* stating, "Hyland is one of the most rugged of the little fellows that the modern ring has known, barring Nelson."[33] These accolades from sources aware of Hyland's recent inconsistencies.

Nelson had also spent a relatively quiet day prior to the fight, completing his usual morning roadwork before lunch. A bit more restless in the afternoon, he toyed with equipment, talked strategy and played a few games before shutting down camp and setting up quarters at the Sultan Turkish Baths at 624 Post Street. He felt good, looked great and retired early in prime physical form.

The Sultan Turkish Baths (the Andrews Hotel today) was a gentleman's sauna and recreation establishment, in many ways perfect for a fighter like Nelson. There was a restaurant on the ground floor; a saltwater plunge, tiled hot room, and a rubbing room on the second; and a barber, a chiropodist, and a bar and lounge on the third floor. Beyond the third floor were sleeping quarters, the third and fourth floors complete with steam room. And visitors like Nelson could rent one of numerous apartments, each containing a bedroom and a parlor, on the sixth and seventh floors.[34]

As Battling Nelson made his way down the center aisle, the crowd erupted in cheers. The 3:00 p.m. bout found promoter Coffroth ringside eagerly awaiting the opening bell. Nelson entered between the ropes first, at five minutes to three, followed by Jack Grace and Willus Britt. Nelson also had in his corner his hometown friend Abe Silverman and Jeff Perry. In his custom regalia, the Battler looked as confident as ever. Standing in the southwest corner of the ring—the corner Gans occupied when he lost the title—had no visual or psychological effect on the champion.

Hyland followed only minutes after and was accompanied by his manager Jack Perkins, Frank Schuler and numerous seconds including his brother. Standing only in a pair of black silk running breeches, Hyland appeared in peak condition.[35]

As both fighters adjusted their hand bandages in preparation for gloves, a representative from both corners participated in a coin toss to determine corners. Hyland, wanting the sun at his back, chose the southwest corner. The Battler comfortably occupied the opposite side.

In a bit of irony before the fight, Dick Hyland made an error and chose Battling Nelson's gloves—Nelson had penned the number "23" instead of this name inside the gloves—rather than his own. A gentleman by the name of Sol Levinson made each fighter's gloves to order—a common ring etiquette expressed in promoter Coffroth's venues. A few days before the bout, Levinson would do his measuring of each fighter's hands, then construct three or four pairs for possible use. When Hyland found the pair he initially wanted, he penned his name inside. But at the fight, Hyland placed Nelson's gloves securely on his hands. When confronted by the champion of the mistake, Hyland remained with his choice.[36] Nelson then remarked, "If you want my gloves you can have them, but I hate to knock you out with your own gloves."[37]

Over eight months removed from the last Gans fight, the new world lightweight champion entered not only the same venue and the same ring as before, but stared into the identical eyes of the same referee, Eddie Smith. Unlike Nelson, Smith had remained ring active over the past eight months. He had refereed seven "Bay Area" fights since Nelson's coronation, including heavyweight Sam Langford's devastating first-round knockout of favorite Fireman Jim Flynn. It was back on December 21 of the previous year, when Flynn tried to mount an aggressive first-round attack—"gloves up" charge—against Langford. Ever cautious to size up his opponent, Langford stepped back from the assault, then delivered a powerful right to Flynn's jaw. Staggering backward, Flynn then found his antagonist's left hook that sent him crashing down to the canvas. It was arbiter Smith, an area resident (Oakland), who would count "The Fireman" out at 2:14 of the first round.

In 1878, Edward J. Smith was born in New York. In his younger days he found fame as a bicycle rider, taking part in numerous relay events on the San Leandro triangle. His ring interest, one that would include a fascination for rules, was attributed to his time as an amateur fighter. Believing in a fair and equitable contest, he began his career in ring arbitration on June 21, 1901, at the Reliance Athletic Center in Oakland, California.[38] Quick to impress those around the fight game, he worked his way into a solid rotation of area umpires. Tireless inside the ring—even tackling three fights in a single day if necessary—Smith often led by example.[39] Having worked the Nelson v. Attell battle last year, Smith knew precisely what to expect from the Battler, and vice versa.

As expected from most, and calculated by Nelson, the early rounds belonged to Hyland. The *Los Angeles Herald* viewed it this way: rounds 3, 4, 16, and 18 for Hyland; rounds 11, 19, 20, 21, 22, and 23 (knocked out Hyland) for Nelson; and rounds 1, 2, 5, 6, 7, 8, 9, 12, 13,14, and 17 even or too close to call.

Nelson's body blows, which he had consistently thrown throughout the fight, had a cumulative effect by the twentieth round. The champion, clearly sizing up his opponent—not unlike Langford battling Flynn—even took punches on the ropes to fatigue his challenger. Surprisingly, when Hyland displayed noticeable exhaustion, Nelson made no attempt to close in and take his opponent by knockout. Instead he continued to box, wearing him down through further punishment. This was definitive Nelson, taking the heart out of his opponent before the final assault. But—and there always seems to be one "but," or discreet fact, in a fight of this nature—it is worth noting that Battling Nelson, besides fighting, was also acting as a film director. Having contracted with Miles Brothers to film for a specific number of rounds, the Battler instructed them *not* to record images unless he gave them his approval. Having shut the cameras off in the seventeenth round, Nelson, confident of a conclusion, gave them an order to continue in the twenty-first round.[40]

The turning point, as predicted, did come in the twenty-first round. Hyland opened up strong, by rushing his adversary and trying to avoid the champion's clinches—his corner assuming Nelson's clinches were nothing more than a stall tactic. But the champion found an opening and "shot his right squarely over the heart," and Hyland dropped for a five count.[41] Regaining his footing, a stunned ringside bore witness to the dazed look on Hyland's face. Meanwhile, a cocky pugilist turned director motioned to the ringside film crew to be ready for the knockout. In a whirlwind of combinations, topped off by a solid shot to the jaw, Hyland fell for a nine count. Miraculously, and much to the chagrin of the Battler, he was saved by the bell.[42]

In the twenty-second, Nelson swarmed his opponent and unleashed a multitude of combinations that seemed to last for minutes—there was, after all, only so much film available. Finally, in the middle of the round, a precise shot to the jaw sent Hyland down, but not out. Nelson at this point couldn't believe his eyes. Struggling badly from the blow, Hyland finally regained his feet at the count of eight. Following another assault, again he was dropped for a nine count, and again he was saved by the bell. The crowd stood in disbelief, as did Nelson—the champion now staring at his opponent and thinking, now what?

When the bell sounded for the twenty-third, nobody, certainly not at ringside, felt Hyland could answer, but somehow he managed. Nelson had had it by then. He rushed his opponent, who tried to fight back, and delivered a left to the jaw, a right to the body, and then a right to the head that sent his adversary to the canvas for a seven—or possibly eight—count. Once Hyland hit the canvas for the second time, referee Eddie Smith had finally seen enough. Nelson was waved off and declared the winner. It came at the appropriate time, as Hyland's brother, a second in his corner, was about to throw up the sponge, or whatever he could get his hands on. As it was, Hyland needed to be lifted from the floor and carried to his corner.

While some spectators had envisioned the champion falling, it simply was not to be. In reality, Nelson was rock solid, and in far better condition that he had looked. He had not only fought his battle his way and won, but he directed it; he took the best Hyland had to offer, withstood it and fit it into his fight plan.

Following the contest, Battling Nelson commented on his opponent's size and determination. "He fought hard all the way," claimed the champion, "and gave me a tougher fight than many other lightweights."[43] He also reaffirmed that he was in complete control of the bout and even stated, to the surprise of some, that he told his friends he would claim victory in the twenty-third round.[44]

As for the future, Nelson confirmed that he would be heading to Oklahoma in June. There he would match against a club-selected lightweight, which would later turn out to be none other than Jack Clifford. He also mentioned having a look at a young fighter from Michigan named Ad Wolgast, possibly in Los Angeles, but he wasn't sure.

Eddie Smith too wasn't shy regarding the clash, claiming after only a few rounds it was clear Hyland was in for a long and arduous punishing. Nelson's strategy to go to the body wasn't a surprise to Smith, but Hyland's endurance was. In Smith's mind, Nelson's body blow—Nelson's famous "scissors hook"—early in the twenty-first round was the punch that did the damage. "I stopped the fight after I saw that Hyland had no chance and was rapidly losing his strength."[45]

Putting a new spin on the Gans's line "bringing home the bacon,"[46] Nelson had reportedly completed arrangements with A.H. Poape of San Francisco to start a hog farm on his Livermore property. "I think I have a scheme that will prove a great financial success," Nelson professed. "I have been figuring on this venture for a long time now, and everything looks good."[47] The Battler was in San Francisco on June 6 and was planning on heading to Oklahoma City by way of Los Angeles and New Mexico—the stops along the way part of the marketing of his autobiography. Team Nelson figured this would give their fighter about ten days to prepare for his June 22 fight against Jack Clifford. As the champion head in one direction, Bill Russell and Chief Jack Grace, the globe-trotting trainer, would handle the moving pictures of the Hyland fight. Nelson trusted both to see to the proper preparation of the celluloid.

A week before the Clifford clash, and in testament to the unusual occurrences that beset a public figure such as a world lightweight champion, Neil Normandy, from Osseo, Minnesota, was committed to the insane asylum for his statements regarding the Battler—he was going to fight Nelson, and although he had never seen the Dane, he insisted he can give him a thumping. Delusions such as these weren't uncommon for the time. Nor was institutionalizing individuals incapable of dealing with everyday life. Regardless of the fact that the insanity boards of these institutions had medical training, most lacked the compassion and expertise to deal with mental illness. Unruffled by the event, the Battler remained focused on his book tour, and a bit on his next fight.

Nelson v. Clifford, June 22, 1909

A familiar face awaited Nelson on Wednesday, June 22, in Oklahoma City, that of Jack Clifford, a former sparring partner. The pair were scheduled to battle for twenty rounds. It was just last January when Nelson delivered a short left to the California fighter's jaw that sent him backward to the canvas in the fifth round. Clifford started his career in Montana before testing his skills in the West Coast boxing scene. It was in Nevada, in 1906, that he caught the attention of many when he kayoed Bobby Lendl, another of Nelson's sparring partners. This was on the undercard of the first Nelson versus Gans fight. Now he hoped to impress even more boxing fans by putting up a respectable performance against Nelson in their rematch.

Since their last meeting, Clifford had fought only twice and had not impressed. He managed to drop prosaic middleweight Joe McGurn in the first of a six-round battle on July 16, 1908, but couldn't finish him off. McGurn, only in his second professional fight, then drew the fighter. And on October 8, 1908, Clifford stepped inside a Marysville, California, ring against mediocre Charlie "Kid" Dalton. Fresh off two tough losses, the first a distance defeat to Frank Carsey and the second to Cyclone Johnny Thompson, Dalton was out for blood. In a fight arbitrated by Eddie Smith, Dalton kayoed Clifford in the twelfth round.

Talking about Dalton, he believed Bat had deliberately thrown him down in selecting Jack Clifford as his opponent. According to Dalton, and the *Los Angeles Herald*, he wired the Dane asking for the match, but it was too late—the Clifford deal was nearly done. While it was true that Dalton "whipped Clifford to shoestring" in their previous battle, the fighter also had a classless reputation that preceded him. Nelson, he believed, could readily dispose of "a punchless wonder" like Clifford, so why bother with the tougher and often unpredictable Dalton? Every participant in the fight game, especially those around a champion, understood that there was nothing arbitrary about the selection of an opponent. However, every contending fighter also knew the importance of a title shot. The art of intimidation, as a methodology of selection, had become routine.

Nelson found his way to Oklahoma via a number of train destinations including Los Angeles, most with scheduled publicity stops for his book. In the "City of Angels" he "exhibited with pride a contract with a northern firm to supply them [Team Nelson] with 10,000 copies."[48] Bat also declared that he would return to Los Angeles following the Clifford scuffle and begin training at Jack Doyle's South Side Athletic Club for his recently confirmed fight against Ad Wolgast.

A confident Nelson entered the ring no worse for wear from his travels. He had as his chief second Warren Zubrick, the former Buffalo lightweight who once tackled Frank Erne. Referee Dave Porteous, in only his ninth professional fight, stopped the fight in the fifth when it was clear Clifford could take no more—he had been knocked to the floor by a solid blow to the stomach but arose after the count of five. Later, Porteous would confirm "that a deputy in charge gave him the 'high sign' to stop it, and he did."[49]

For a time it looked like the contest might never take place. The district attorney viewed the contest as unfair for public consumption as Nelson had met and beaten Clifford before, and as mentioned he had used him as a sparring partner—but somehow a discreet adjustment fixed the circumstance. In retrospect, however, it probably shouldn't have taken place. When referee Porteous stopped the fight, angry spectators hissed and jeered at the participants before storming the box office demanding their money back. Searching for fight highlights, one could only recall a couple, Clifford drawing blood from Nelson's nose in the first, followed later by Clifford's valiant body assault on Nelson in the third round, which drew cheers from the crowd.[50]

Later, Nelson was denounced by the press for being more interested in his reputation as an author than as a boxer, and they were right. Despite the criticism, as soon as his books arrived he began contacting neighborhood bookstores arranging for their sale. At one store in San Francisco, where the books had been available for two days, the Battler decided to drop by and check on sales. Learning he had only sold one copy, Nelson began scratching his head in bewilderment. In an attempt to reassure the budding author, the clerk stated, "Why, Kipling only sold one a month." Bat then turned to Jack Grace, who had accompanied him, and asked, "Who is Kipling?"[51]

Book sales, be they poor or not, had little impact on the aspiring author, as he wasn't planning on quitting his day job any time soon, or was he? Nelson was beginning to use the word "retirement" with a far greater frequency, many believing it was because he had finally found a sweetheart and just wanted to settle down. "Oh, there's a girl all right, and she's THE girl too. She lives in Chicago and she's got so much money that I call her my 'Forty-Million-Dollar Girl.' I don't dare to say much because her dad don't think very well of prizefighters in general. No, I don't deny that I MAY get spliced. You never can tell what is going to happen."[52] The champion only dwelled briefly on the topic with the press before switching back to the ring, or his other financial endeavors.

Always good for a story, the press knew how, and when, to press Oscar. Retirement, to the media, meant settling down and likely having a family. Had the champion finally found a lifetime companion? And would he, after all his previous problems with relationships, go public with the details? Oscar took the bait, and while cautious about revealing THE girl's name, certainly narrowed the field with his dollar figure. When you love someone, you express yourself differently. A sensation comes over you and you feel safe confessing your adoration. The mention of the girl's father alone was an indication of Oscar's feelings—a depth chart, if you will. Knowing that the family's disapproval of prizefighters—not an uncommon view with Chicago's gentry at the time—would be an obstacle, Oscar would have to overcome if he was to take their relationship further. Wisely, Nelson concluded his commentary after his brief remarks.[53]

A week before his next ring battle, the Battler, along with some friends, were in Ogden and narrowly escaped being one of the victims of a robbery. The Bamberger railroad was looted by two masked thugs, who got away with cash, valuable papers and railroad tickets—the amount of cash was first reported as $700, but later replaced by a lower figure. Nelson had already missed two trains to Salt Lake before finally catching the locomotive at 10:45 p.m. It was right after his train pulled out of the depot that the robbery occurred. As for what the Battler was thinking on his return to Salt Lake, it likely had little to do with boxing.

Nelson v. Wolgast, July 13, 1909

In a battle that a ponderous lightweight champion should have never taken, certainly not using Clifford as a warm-up, an article header in the *Los Angeles Herald* on the morning of Wednesday, July 14, 1909, spoke volumes, "Wolgast Gives Battling Nelson thorough Beating in 10 Rounds."

"The Michigan Wildcat," the perfect moniker for Adolph Wolgast pictured here and born on February 8, 1888, in Cadillac, Michigan (Library of Congress, Prints and Photograph Division, LC-DIG-ggbain-11250).

Naud Junction arena in Los Angeles, California, was the place, and the Durable Dane's opponent was the heralded Adolphus "Ad" Wolgast.[54] With little regard for defense, the right-hander was as pugnacious as he was enduring—sound familiar? Hailing from the Great Lakes region of the midwestern United States, "The Michigan Wildcat" stood five feet four and a half inches tall with a sixty-five-and-a-half-inch reach. Born on February 8, 1888, in Cadillac, Michigan, he was the oldest in a family of seven. Wolgast, like some, had found boxing while in need of money—he convinced a young promoter that he was a talented amateur. Picking up a decision over a fighter nearly thirty pounds heavier, Wolgast's pugilist career was launched.

Fighting out of both Grand Rapids and Milwaukee, Wolgast established himself as an unbeatable powerhouse. Which is good of course, if you can find someone respectable to fight, along with a decent purse. Wolgast could not, so it was off to New York where he met with the much heavier (14 pounds) and more adept fighter Owen Moran, whose imposing record stood at 40–5–2.[55] In a six-round newspaper loss, Wolgast received a quick beating accompanied by a New York City education. Returning home, again the warrior headed for more fertile ground, this time in the opposite direction, west to California. Three quick local victories there found him facing the invincible Abe Attell, who stood at 50–5–14.[56] In a ten-round battle—both the *Los Angeles Times* and the *Herald* differed in their results, which was common for the era—Ad drew the talented Attell. The *Times* sports editor Ham Oliver stated, "Wolgast demonstrated that he has been sadly underrated." Following this conflict, he "stepped down" a bit in talent, even took a few out-of-state fights.[57] But by this time, Wolgast's image as a rough inside fighter—arms, shoulders and head constantly active—had been secured. Although he had taken a six-round newspaper loss to Tommy O'Toole in Philadelphia on June 19, 1909, he was confident entering his fight with Nelson.

Here's how the two measured up: Nelson was taller by an inch and a half (five feet seven inches) and heavier by eight pounds (133). Nelson had a bit longer reach, by half an inch, a larger expanded chest and a bigger thigh. Wolgast had a larger waist, biceps, wrist and forearm. The fighters had identical sized neck, chest (normal) and calves.

Climbing between the ropes at 9:55 p.m., Wolgast, donning his trademark mottled gray bathrobe, entered first, accompanied by manager Tom Jones along with half a dozen seconds. Two minutes later Nelson entered with Jack Grace and company and stripped to his tights, with a Turkish towel thrown over his shoulder. Both struck the traditional poses for the cameras before time was called at 10:09 p.m.

From the opening bell, the Milwaukee featherweight, then five pounds lighter than his opponent, gave the Battler a rather sound beating. The crowd was dumbfounded, as round after round an unscathed Wolgast chipped away at the champion. Nelson was wincing as blood poured from his mouth—a result of Wolgast's targeted blows. The featherweight had armed himself with an impressive arsenal of punches and feints that kept Nelson off balance.

When the wallops ceased, Wolgast had secured a newspaper victory. The bout, advertised as a contest for the world's lightweight championship, would enter the record books as a no decision because it wasn't a long-distance affair, nor was it a matter of a knockout or ringside decision. The *Los Angeles Herald*'s assessment of the scoring had Wolgast winning eight rounds, with two even.

Taking a closer look, when the opening bell sounded, Nelson, in characteristic form, rushed from his corner. After a clinch, with both working inside, the fighters split, then reestablished a more cautious distance. When Bat had his man in the ropes, he could only land soft lefts. Wolgast, who danced effectively, still took a few solid hits to the nose. When the closing bell sounded, the circumspect first round was considered even at most.

In round two, Bat once again bounded from his corner, and Wolgast met him with a face and body offensive. Knowing he was a smaller fighter, Wolgast wisely decided to "fight up," stomach to head, on the inside.[58] It's a sound strategy if, and that was a very big "if," Wolgast could take Nelson's solid kidney punches. Frustrated in a clinch, Wolgast then head-butted the champion, sending blood from his nose. An infuriated Nelson complained to referee Charles Eyton, but to no avail—a dose of his own medicine, he likely thought. At the closing bell, Wolgast was scoring to the head while a bleeding and disgruntled champion headed to his corner. Advantage Wolgast.

A confident Wolgast used his combinations effectively in round three, connecting solidly to the head. Noticeably more mobile, he managed to avoid Nelson's rushes and clinches by staying back and throwing sharp jabs. Clearly controlling the pace, Wolgast's tactics were working. This annoyed the Battler, who missed several hard hooks but did manage a robust right to the heart at the bell. Wolgast took the round.

Round four opened with a barrage of exchanges by both fighters. Wolgast, determined to match punches inside, clearly understood the danger. Moving out, Ad then danced at a safe distance while relying on his left jab to keep the blood flowing from Bat's muzzle. A confident and assiduous Wolgast seemed to be landing at will. A dual jaw exchange, near the closing bell, exemplified the intensity of both fighters. The round belonged to Wolgast.

A flurry of punches opened round five as both assailants tried frantically to connect with the ultimate blow. With the failed clouts nearly as impressive as the hits, the crowd delighted at the frustration exhibited by both fighters. Many spectators also reacted with hisses when Nelson struck solidly at Wolgast's kidneys—these types of punches have a cumulative effect on a fighter.[59] Coming out of a clinch, just before the closing bell, Ad rocked Bat with an amalgam of punches to the head. The late-round assault sent the advantage to Wolgast.

Left eye swollen, Nelson walked out for the sixth like a sacrificial lamb. For Wolgast, it was target practice, or precision strikes to Nelson's countenance. When the Battler swung wildly twice, Ad cast a self-assured smile. Wolgast then decided to move in and cover up with hopes of getting the indefatigable Nelson to slow. Ad was still delivering excellent combinations when the bell sounded. Again, the round went to Wolgast.

Wolgast opened round seven with a wild punch that was partially blocked, then danced effectively around his opponent. Surprising many, the champion still appeared strong despite some bleeding. Following four hard punches to Nelson's head, the round ended with each fighter staring at each other. Ad took this stage.

An opening clinch and an exchange of punches at the ropes began the eighth. Wolgast then missed a series of punches before going to the body. Nelson retaliated with his own shots at the heart. This round to most was too tough to call.

A tenacious Wolgast opened round nine with a solid offensive shot. Nelson then retaliated with a barrage of misses, to the entertainment of all. Smiling to his seconds, Bat shrugged off the blunder. Wolgast fired back with a combination to Bat's jaw, then sent him back with a solid hook. Still aiming at Nelson's impregnable head, Wolgast fired an amalgamation, hoping to keep his opponent at length. Nelson bored in, but took no ground. The round clearly belonging to Wolgast.

Touching gloves to begin the tenth and final round, both immediately came together to exchange blows. Pensive, both boxers then sauntered the canvas as if reviewing their closing strategies. Halfway into the round Wolgast began to position himself for a knockout. According to the *Los Angeles Herald* on July 14, "The final minute was one of the fiercest ever seen at Naud junction. Each boxer was hoping to land that one punch that would give them a decisive win, but it was not to be done. As the bell sounded, both needed to be separated."[60]

To his friends, fans, and team, Battling Nelson had disappointed—Wolgast had gotten the best of him inside the ring, his distractions outside of it. His nonchalance irritated his supporters. "I did not have my usual ginger," the champion admitted. "I noticed it in training, and think my 35,000 miles of traveling this year has dulled my speed." Nelson then admitted, "He [Wolgast] made a good showing and deserves his credit, so let it go at that." Clearly, Ad Wolgast had impressed everyone with his performance. A rivalry, and an impressive one at that, had been born on that day.

Self-absorbed, Nelson seemed oblivious to the ten-round affair with Wolgast, even if his appearance reflected differently. He left the West Coast for New York on July 22, where he intended to appear at a benefit for Gotham newsboys. Proclaiming to the press that this was his fifth trip that year to the coast, Nelson made his usual promotional stops en route. While in Philadelphia, on August 3, he asked a friend of his to check him into one of the finest suites available at the fashionable Bellevue-Stratford Hotel; the reason for the discreet request was that eight months ago the management had refused a room for the pugilist. The friend obliged and checked the room for a wealthy cattleman from New Mexico, which Nelson certainly was.

After a time enjoying his accommodations, the champion summoned a hotel stenographer and dictated a letter. Once the girl completed the task and was dismissed, she rushed to inform hotel management of the true identity of their houseguest.

Nelson was then called upon by management and vehemently ordered to remove himself immediately from the hotel grounds. The Dane refused and then escorted the hotel manager out of his room and locked the door. Hotel detectives quickly arrived, pounded on the door, and ordered the Battler to open it. Nelson then invited them to "chase themselves."[61] Obviously

The rich and famous, royalty and heads of state from all over the world, presidents, politicians, actors and famous writers have stayed within the walls of Philadelphia's Bellevue-Stratford, or the "Grand Dame of Broad Street" (Library of Congress, Prints and Photograph Division, LC-DIG-det-4a25331).

that did not go over well with the investigators, so, they called a locksmith. Nelson then felt it was time to issue an ultimatum: if he were not left alone, he would make it hot for someone. Intrusive activity outside his door ceased. The Battler then advised hotel management to anticipate a lawsuit. This was not the behavior of a champion even if he was trying to prove a point.

A week later, the unruffled pugilist was playing golf in New York on the Van Cortlandt Park links with his instructors. New to the avocation, Bat couldn't break the century mark yet insisted he would soon become an expert. The pretentious attitude, even if it drew the requisite press, was becoming somewhat overbearing, and honestly speaking, Harry Vardon never felt threatened.[62]

On October 13, the *San Francisco Call* stated that Nelson had received an offer to fight Ad Wolgast twenty rounds before the Mission Club in San Francisco the coming month for the sum of $10,000. Nelson's answer: "THANKS FOR OFFER. DATE TOO EARLY. CHRISTMAS OR LATER."[63] While fight fans had hoped for some Thanksgiving entertainment, such would not be the case. It was a prudent decision by Nelson, and certainly understandable to any fight fan who had witnessed his last travesty. The telegram caught the fighter at home in Hegewisch and on the very day he was heading to New York to take possession of the films that recorded his battle against Dick Hyland. The champion hoped to soon book the films at various venues in the East. Once that task was completed, Nelson would start for his ranch in New Mexico where he and pal Billy Benner planned on doing a bit of bear hunting. But plans, like lives, are dynamic.

William F. Britt, or "Willis," or "Willus," as he was known, died suddenly from hemorrhage at 4:30 p.m. on October 30, 1909. The boxing manager had been admitted to St. Joseph's hospital only the day before following a violent hemorrhage of the stomach. His wife, infant daughter and attending physician were at his bedside. The brother and manager of boxer James E. Britt, Jr., he was a well-known sporting man in San Francisco and a great contributor to many fighters, especially Stanley Ketchel and Battling Nelson. Willus was born thirty-three years ago on Market Street in San Francisco and graduated from Polytechnic High School. Garnering fame as a fighter, his battles with Billy Hogan and Jimmy Lawlor were well known, as was his capture of the Olympic Club bantam title.

Working for the newspaper, Willus moved quickly through the ranks to a reporter, where he became known for his exciting stories about the Klondike. He lived hard, enjoyed the ladies, the ring, and the bottle, and his unabashed behavior often preceded him—he sued the city for property damages following the 1906 San Francisco earthquake. Willis hooked up with Nelson following his fight with Joe Gans on July 4, 1908, and stayed with him through his trilogy with Gans and into 1909. In late 1908, Britt turned most of his attention to Ketchel, according to many the greatest middleweight champion ever.[64] Willus, who knew and practiced every pugilist trick in the book, earned plenty from the ring, something like $150,000, but he lived fast, enjoyed a wager or two, and left virtually nothing behind. Nevertheless, money never mattered much to Britt, who always believed that as long as the fight game existed, he could find a job. Everyone in the fight community, especially those in San Francisco, was grief stricken.

Combining the records of the fighters Willus worked with—Jimmy Britt (13–7–1–2), Nelson (59–19–19–33) and Stanley Ketchel (52–4–4–4)—you have an impressive 124–30–24–39 total, with two out of three of his gladiators members of boxing's elite class.

In the middle of November, the Dane decided to try his skills at promoting, wiring the managers of both Jack Johnson and Jim Jeffries offering them $85,000 to have the fight between the heavyweights settled on his property in Virginia City, Nevada. The Battler was willing to post a $30,000 binder with the only stipulation being that the fight shall be a finish fight.[65] The historic fight, as most know, would be held the following year in Reno, Nevada, without the assistance of the Battler.

As champion, his every move, or lack thereof, was scrutinized. And, there were a number of questions: If he was champion, then why was he not acting like one? When will Nelson turn his attention back to boxing? And what impact would Nelson's recent abysmal ring performance have on his popularity?

Nobody had the answer to the first two questions. As for the third, well, in Montreal he opened up with a week's worth of engagements at the Royal Theater. And, according to manager Oliver McBride of the Royal, "attendance eclipsed anything they ever had in town."[66] Quebec, Canada, still adored the Durable Dane. In the United States, it was much the same. In Schenectady, New York, for example, he played to more money in one performance than the average business of the house for six shows, and in nearby Albany, he did over double the regular average gate.[67] For as long as Nelson could draw on stage, he thought, why bother with the ring?

On December 24, a telegram to matchmakers confirmed that Battling Nelson would meet Ad Wolgast at the Vernon Arena, in Los Angeles, California. A February or March fight date would hopefully be announced at a later time. Win, lose or draw, Nelson would receive $10,000, with a side bet of $5,000 agreed upon. "I believe I will be able to polish him off," claimed Wolgast. "Every man must lose sometime and I believe that the time will come for the Dane when he and I meet."[68]

The holidays are a time for reflection, and Nelson hoped to do precisely that, if of course he had the time. In his first full year as lightweight champion, Battling Nelson fought thirty-eight rounds against three opponents, all with winning records. Of three boxers faced, only Ad Wolgast stands out as a "Hall of Fame" caliber boxer. Despite the fact that Nelson did not lose a fight in the record books, he does have the humiliation of the Wolgast newspaper decision—a scar, he knows, that can only be healed with a decisive rematch victory.

There was little change in division champions in 1909—only the dynamic bantams shifting claims. However, the year had its fair share of ring thrillers. On March 26, in a ten-round New York no decision, Stanley Ketchel floored light heavyweight champion Philadelphia Jack O'Brien four times, even leaving him out cold at the final bell. Two black heavyweight

Stanley Ketchel, aka the "Michigan Assassin," knocked out forty-one of his first forty-nine opponents in a career that rivaled the best middleweight champions ever (Library of Congress, Prints and Photograph Division, LC-DIG-ggbain-03987).

Nine—1909: Retaining the Title

contenders, Joe Jeanette and Sam McVey, battled in Paris on April 17 in the longest fight of the twentieth century; McVey was unable to answer the bell for the forty-ninth round. And on June 26, Dick Hyland floored Leach Cross fifteen times en route to a knockout in the forty-first round in the longest fight ever held at the Mission Street Arena in Colma, California. Colma was indeed the place to be if you were a fan of pugilism, as two other notable fights took place there. Fought during a thunderstorm on July 5, Stanley Ketchel dominated Billy Papke to pick up the victory despite a broken right hand, and after being floored by Stanley Ketchel, Jack Johnson knocked out the middleweight champ in round twelve of their October 16 bout.

Outside the ring, the year turned out to be one of the most memorable in the life of Battling Nelson. From visiting the White House not only as the reigning lightweight champion, but also as a friend of the president, to making numerous shrewd business deals including expanding his real estate empire, the view from the top suited the Battler just fine. He wasn't blind to the distractions—taking time off for a bit of touring, reporting, and even promoting an autobiography had cost him in the ring—he just had difficulty keeping them in perspective. A balanced lifestyle was still something Nelson hoped for, but hadn't mastered. If everything worth fighting for unbalances your life, he believed, then what is a reigning champion to do?

Ten

February 2, 1910
A Disappointing Loss

> Just ten years after, this, my first victory, I fought the first battle with Joe Gans for the lightweight championship of the world at Goldfield, Nevada, September 3, 1906. Ten years doesn't seem very long, but it made a difference in size of purses with me from $1 to $23,0000. Going up a bit!
> —"Battling" Nelson[1]

The year opened, just as it had closed, with fight promoter Sid Hester trying to secure a February match between Nelson and Wolgast. Tom Jones, Wolgast's manager, had been dickering with the promoter for some time and on the final day of the previous year rejected an offer of $3,750. For Nelson, who had already declared his willingness to accept Hester's offer, it was Wolgast who was now the stumbling block. Should the match be made, the promoter's next obstacle would be acquiring a permit to stage the event. And, if the match couldn't be made soon, Hester believed he would have to look elsewhere, perhaps Australia—the promoter mentioning the possibility of going offshore to hopefully pressure officials to grant him his permit—where he had received a few, in his words without elaboration, interesting offers.

"I felt sure that Wolgast was going to run out," Nelson affirmed to *The Call* on January 9, 1910. "I was in the midst of making plans for an immediate tour of the world."[2] This statement coming the day after the Battler had served as a referee at a women's wrestling match in Minneapolis; apparently a bit intrigued that the star of the show, Cora Livingston, could dispose of three women in fifteen minutes, Nelson couldn't resist the opportunity to personally witness the act. Born Cora Lingingstone, in Buffalo, New York, the female wrestler stood five feet five inches and weighed 139 pounds. Livingston, who would be seen as a pioneer of women's professional wrestling, was pressured into the activity by husband Paul Bowser, who was both a wrestler and a promoter. A hit from many perspectives, the show intrigued both wrestling and boxing fans alike, to say nothing of the arbiter.

While in Chicago, on Monday, January 10, Nelson signed for an eight-round no decision contest with southern lightweight Eddie Lang. Scheduled for January 21 at the Memphis Athletic Club, the battle would be refereed by friend and former champion Tommy Ryan.[3] Only three years removed from the ring, Ryan was still a popular drawing card and already considered one of the all-time greatest middleweight champions. Certainly if the fight didn't measure up to expectations, as some thought, viewing the former champion would.

By the second week in January, boxing promoter Billy McCarney stepped into the mix, trying to secure the Nelson v. Wolgast fight in Los Angeles.[4] McCarney took this action when it was learned that Hester could not acquire a fight permit—a forty-five round battle, which was Hester's desire, would not be permitted in San Francisco until the ordinance was changed to make long-distance fights legal. Not giving up on his quest, or the least bit concerned about the competition, Sid Hester began looking for sites outside the city.

Soon Richmond, a city incorporated in 1905 and located in the eastern region of the San Francisco Bay Area in western Contra Costa County, California, came into the picture. The conditions in the city were similar to those of Goldfield. Not yet five years old, Richmond was carved out of Rancho San Pablo and was seeking an identity of its own. When the city agreed to construct a 15,000-seat venue specifically for the event, it had Hester's attention. Impressed by Mayor Willis and a committee headed by Pat Dean, the fight promoter finally had his venue.

Nelson v. Lang, January 21, 1910

Having not had a ring battle since July of the preceding year, Nelson claimed to have signed the Lang fight just to test himself—in reality it was simply target practice. The choice bewildered many, who believed the Battler should have not only fought sooner but established a strenuous training regimen in preparation for his argument against Wolgast. Even a greater surprise was the choice of tomato-can Eddie Lang, who entered the fight with limited experience.[5]

In Lang's previous fight, just to shed some light on his vocation, he battled fighter Kid Taylor at Union Park in Cedar Rapids, Iowa. Taylor entered the fight having lost four of his last six fights. The *Cedar Rapids Evening Gazette* reported that Taylor was scheduled to meet Frank Whitney, who was replaced by Lang. The substitution infuriated Taylor, who nevertheless took the ten-round contest. But when the fight was declared a draw, Taylor had enough and cold-cocked the referee. A riot quickly ensued, and the arena was desecrated by spectators.[6]

Lang was about to face the lightweight champion of the world, who had not only a title belt but over ten times the ring experience. Although the quixotic Lang was determined to stay the eight rounds with the champion, it was far from a realistic endeavor. Nelson sparred for nearly seven rounds before dropping his opponent to the canvas. However, Lang was saved by the bell. The Battler reloaded, then took only a minute and a half to knock out his opponent in the eighth. Even if an overflowing crowd was entertained by the champion's ability—attacking his neophyte antagonist from every point in the ring, the champ put on quite a display—it was more of an exhibition, or pocket money, than a contest.

Following the bout, Nelson's entourage, which included new manager John R. Robinson, finally left for San Francisco and the championship bout with Wolgast. Their arrival was scheduled for about February 2, following a brief stay at the champion's ranch in New Mexico.[7] Once out west, Nelson confirmed that he intended to hunt and fish until the first week in February, then settle down for some hard training at Millett's, his Colma training site. Figuring that three weeks of training should do the trick, Bat chartered a course before requesting the assistance of his brother Arthur and Jeff Perry.

It was speculated by the media—when you have an inactive champion and deadlines to meet, beat writers often have a greater reach than most boxers—covering the Battler that one of the reasons Nelson hadn't responded to other offers was that he couldn't hear them. Word hit the newspapers at the end of January that Nelson was growing deaf. Fight followers that watched him train in Memphis over the past couple weeks expressed astonishment at Nelson's cautious and often apprehensive movements while sparring. The Dane, who was also quite nearsighted, denied the claims and noted that his corner had often tried a variety of ways to catch his attention, even hand signals.[8] This story hit the wire the same day as a bogus announcement stating that Nelson would meet Ad Wolgast on February 23 at Colma.

Speaking of conjecture and preoccupation, some members of the press felt that Nelson had been traumatized for nearly a week, ever since George Rawlings, a member of the Sewanees champion football club, shot-putter and all-round athlete, delivered a stinging blow to the Battler's jaw that sent the champion to the mat. The two were sparring inside the local YMCA gymnasium in front of a taken-aback group of spectators on January 21. A prelude to the inevitable, some wondered? Or simply a coincidence?

Certain of victory against Wolgast, Nelson, as mentioned, had already made plans for an around-the-world trip. He would be accompanied by Stanley Ketchel, "The Michigan Assassin"; John R. Robinson, his manager; and Chief Jack Grace, who would act as his experienced itinerary advisor. The tour would start in Ireland and cover all of Europe, and hopefully Australia a bit later. Both Ketchel and Nelson would take on all comers and give boxing exhibitions in every metropolis. "We intend to start," Bat verified, "some time about the middle of May or the first of June."[9]

The combination of Nelson and Ketchel caught many by surprise. Ketchel, viewed as an erratic fighter—careless about everything, save for a good time for himself—was in stark contrast to the handsome, shrewd and business savvy Dane. Nelson, the media concluded, knew a good drawing card when he saw it. And the "Michigan Assassin" was most certainly that, having only recently (October 10, 1909) battled, and lost, to Jack Johnson for the World Heavyweight Title. However, unbeknownst to all, Stanley Ketchel would fight only five more times before his tragic death later in the year.

Besides being matched inside the ring, Nelson was also being matched at home. Frank Weiland, secretary of the Hegewisch Improvement Club, announced that Bat would be appointed chairman of the committee. The group, strategically designed to include the area's most influential citizens, would visit the Chicago City Railway Company to demand better streetcar service, along with one or two extensions of the line. On a mission to attract visitors and new residents to Hegewisch, not to mention to protect housing values, the Battler's inclusion seemed only obvious.

Meanwhile, preparations of all kinds were being taken to ensure the upcoming championship contest. For the first time in the history of the regional fight game, the promoter's insured themselves against rain on the day of the fight. And, not only were the promoters protected against mother nature's elements, but also for the loss of the referee. In the event that referee Eddie Smith passed away before the afternoon of the fight, $5,000 would go to Nelson and a like sum to Wolgast. Even if this made sense to promoters, one just has to wonder how it made Smith feel.

Always appearing as if he was two steps ahead of you, with his piercing eyes, perfectly combed-back hair and cheek-to-cheek smile, was Nelson's astute manager, Jack Robinson.

He was the kind of guy you always took ice fishing because he instinctively knew how thick the frozen water was. Maybe that's why Bat liked him. Robinson was a graduate of the University of North Carolina and then pursued a career in journalism. Beginning work at a small daily, he covered a variety of topics before landing in sports. At the outbreak of the Spanish-American War, Robinson's restless spirit landed him in a recruiting office and then Cuba, where he remained throughout the campaign. Following the war, it was back in the newspaper business, where his experience quickly led him up the chain of command. Surprisingly, at least for many who felt him destined for tabloid glory, Jack Robinson joined up with the Battler. And, despite the move, he remained in good stead with his cronies. Media savvy, Robinson was an asset, but as a fight manager, his skills had yet to be seen.

Nelson v. Wolgast, February 22, 1910

Forty-five rounds, at 133 pounds, with virtually no bounds, that's what 15,000 (later reported as 18,000) spectators anticipated viewing on February 22: two superior gladiators, both willing to absorb a Herculean amount of punishment just to infiltrate their enemy's defenses, vying nearly unconditionally for the lightweight championship of the world.

And what they would witness was a battle ranked by many as one of the greatest title fights ever.[10]

Pre-fight expectations favored a one-sided affair, with the champion in complete control. However, the twenty-two-year-old Wolgast—as confident, committed and capable as he was tenacious, merciless and barbaric—was not to be underestimated. A mirror image of the champion himself, the "Michigan Wildcat" was indomitable.

Nelson's résumé spoke for itself. Any man who could beat Joe Gans in two out of three ring battles had to answer to no one. As for Wolgast, in his fourteen battles of 1909, he did not suffer defeat—he picked up wins over Harry Baker and Danny Webster

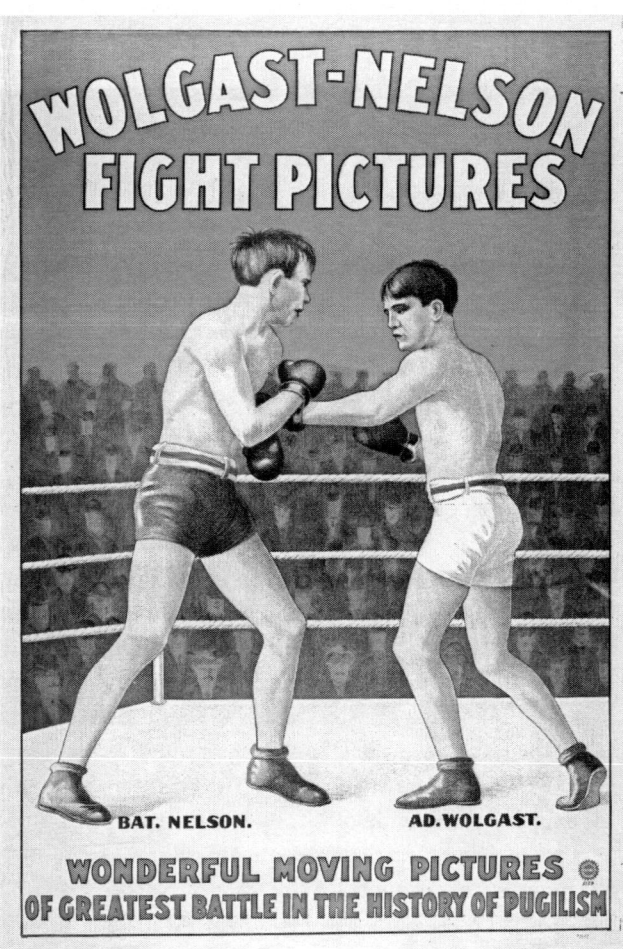

A great poster used to promote the film of the battle between Battling Nelson and Ad Wolgast, two of the finest lightweights ever (Library of Congress, Prints and Photograph Division, LC-DIG-ppmsc-03514).

and dropped Tommy Langdon in the first round. Although Wolgast's fight with Nelson the year before entered the books as a no decision, it was clear that he had outclassed the champ.

The news shook the boxing world:

> AD WOLGAST OF MILWAUKEE MADE PUGILISTIC HISTORY HERE BY DEFEATING THE REDOUBTABLE BATTLING NELSON IN ONE OF THE HARDEST FOUGHT CONTESTS SEEN IN THIS PART OF THE COUNTRY IN OVER TWO DECADES.[11]

At one time the peerless Battler presented a pathetic sight. His face was one mass of cuts and bruises. His eyes were completely closed, and blood streamed down his cheeks and covered his body. Nelson fought with the same gameness and spirit that had characterized all of his fights. He was the same old Battler when it came to rushing and taking punishment. He was, too, the same old Nelson who was willing to take five blows in order to get one punch. However, the old sting was lacking, for only once during the encounter was Nelson able to put the Dutchman down.[12]

In the opinions of the experts: "Nelson's gone back. He showed the effect of too many ring beatings. He was poorly handled by his seconds," according to Jim Coffroth. "Age told the same story," stated Jack Gleason. "Nelson was slower than of old, but Wolgast earned the title. He is a wonderful fighter," claimed Eddie Graney. "Wolgast beat Nelson at his own game and deserves credit. It was the greatest lightweight battle ever fought," spoke Tex Rickard. And referee Eddie Smith claimed, "I'd have been a brute to have permitted the fight to proceed."[13]

As the former champion sat among his training staff following the fight, he could hardly see or speak. His swollen eyes were gashed unmercifully, his nose shattered, his lips distended to a shapeless mass, and fluids ran freely from nearly every possible location, yet he insisted that he was okay. Those ringside during the final rounds sat in horror, witnessing a ruthless slaughter. Nelson, who was not knocked out, was simply so close that there was no choice but a fortieth-round intervention.

The confrontation had its moments, but they were limited for the champion. In the twenty-second round, Nelson sent a stinging punch to the jaw of Wolgast that staggered him, then repeated the assault in the middle of the ring and sent him to the mat for a count of three. Some spectators were so confident of the Battler's fighting prowess that they actually got up and left believing that the fight was over. It was not. Wolgast recovered and activated a fight plan of slowly wearing down the Dane—a strategy that was inconceivable. For the next dozen rounds, Nelson's armor was being chipped away, and even sadder, he seemed susceptible to the persistent assault. From the thirtieth round forward, it was difficult to watch as the left side of the Dane's face gradually degenerated into an unrecognizable countenance.

The Battler survived the thirty-seventh, but those watching would be hard pressed to explain just how he did it. By the thirty-eighth, the champion's corner was so devastated by the performance that the emotionally distraught Robinson made a move to throw up the sponge, but Abdul the Turk, one of Nelson's seconds, ripped it out of his hands. The maelstrom in Nelson's quarter was nearly as difficult to watch as the carnage in the ring. Thrashing about, Robinson was protesting to everyone within hearing distance that his fighter was beaten and had enough.

Referee Smith went to the Battler's corner before the gong for the fortieth and asked Nelson if he was done, and the fighter, unable to speak, simply shook his head negatively.

Ten—February 2, 1910: A Disappointing Loss

Thirty-seven of the longest seconds imaginable passed before referee Smith interceded and raised the glove of the new lightweight champion into the air. As Wolgast scampered around the ring in a victory dance, Nelson was carried from the crucifixion in the arms of his seconds. As Nelson's body passed through the crowd, some applauded and a few wept, but many turned their heads, unable to view the gore from such close proximity.

Let's take a look back at the first thirty-six rounds. Round one set the pace, which was fast and inside, both fighters comfortable at close range and measuring their artillery. Nelson worked short-arm combinations, as did Wolgast. Ad worked his opponent's face with punches that were sharp and powerful. Wolgast also exhibited a nice combination of uppercuts that hit their target. Both fighters failed to hear the gong. The bell for round two rang prematurely, so both fighters were sent back to their seats. Nelson was sending his opposer to the ropes almost at will, but Wolgast covered nicely. Still targeting the face, Wolgast landed at close range to begin blood flowing from Nelson's lips. Combinations were being exchanged almost evenly, with a slight edge to Wolgast. Nelson managed a good right that opened a cut under Wolgast's right eye. Both fighters bounded out for round three, with Nelson forcing the pace. Nelson bloodied his opponent's nose with a powerful right, but not before he endured three straight lefts to the face. Again, Wolgast was pressed against the ropes, and he efficiently covered. The pace slowed slightly at the gong. Nelson came out strong in round four, and although Wolgast fought back, he was staggered by a Nelson uppercut to the jaw. Wolgast's right eye was swollen, and both fighters were bleeding from the nose by the end of the round. Round five opened with Nelson again controlling the pace as both fighters exchanged fierce combinations. As the brawling moved into close quarters, both warriors took warnings regarding the butting of their heads. The round ended during an intense exchange that found Wolgast to the advantage.

As Nelson began battering his antagonist in round six, Wolgast was conversing with his seconds almost in defiance of the assault—even smiling periodically during the Battler's barrage. Near the end of the round, Wolgast moved his attack from the head to the stomach, where he landed two wholesome blows to the Dane. Round seven, Nelson appeared to have slowed a bit. Exchanges were returned repeatedly until the Battler nearly sent Wolgast through the ropes with a straight left to the jaw. The second half of the round then saw Wolgast landing two to one in the punch column. Again, Nelson forced the pace in round eight, but was met with potent combinations by Wolgast. The Dane also started the blood flowing from Wolgast's nose with his ceaseless mix of punches. For the first time, Wolgast looked tired. As the gong sounded, Nelson winked to his ringside friends as he took his seat. Wolgast broke ground first in round nine trying to take the fight aggressively to the Battler. All exchanges were met until Wolgast cut open Nelson's ear with a right. Blood flowed freely from Nelson's ear as he returned to his corner. His ear still bleeding, Nelson opened round ten by forcing the pace and sending Wolgast again to the ropes. Having the option to cover or fire back, Wolgast used both alternatives to his advantage. Even though Wolgast continued to pound away at the champion, he never winced. As the first ten rounds concluded, it had the makings of a duration battle—the indefatigable Nelson enduring Wolgast's tenacious assaults.

Wolgast came out smiling in round eleven and again targeted Nelson's face. Only this time he unleashed an onslaught of combinations that left Nelson's face in a mass of blood. As the champion took his seat, it was difficult for some to view. Wolgast was warned against holding in round twelve, before both fighters met each other's ordnance. Again, Wolgast bloodied Nelson's face before the gong sounded. Wolgast's manager Tom Jones opened round thirteen yelling "Good-bye."[14] Nelson's eyes, lips and mouth were swollen and he was spitting blood. As the Dane's relentless approach continued, his face was being cut to ribbons. According to the *Los Angeles Herald*, you could hear fight followers saying, "The worst beating the champion has received," as his corner frantically went to work following the bell.[15] Wolgast, clearly the fresher of the two, opened round fourteen with a right to the face, followed by combinations to the body. At one point, Nelson nearly forced Wolgast through the ropes, only to chivalrously assist him to the center of the ring. Nelson was again spitting blood when he returned to his corner. By round fifteen the betting money had it even, as both fighters battled with a bit more caution. Nelson just missed with a knockout punch, showing Wolgast that despite his beating he could still muster an offensive.

Wolgast carried on like a fighting machine in round sixteen, and Nelson continued to take his punches. Both men fought hard in round seventeen, with a left to Nelson's jaw causing the blood to flow afresh. As the bell rang, both fighters were blathering at each other. Round eighteen opened with a verbal exchange: "How do you feel?" asked Nelson. "As if I were a punching bag," claimed Wolgast.[16] While in his own corner, Wolgast slipped to his knees, but he was up in a flash. A right staggered the Battler before Wolgast deliberately butted him. Referee Smith then delivered a warning as the crowd hissed. Round nineteen opened with the now routine exchanges, Wolgast jabbing to the face with short-arm jolts, and Nelson fighting back when he was possessed to do so. Nelson tripped to his seat and was spitting blood as the round ended. Round twenty again was routine and ended in a similar manner. Twenty rounds now behind them, the questions were, How much longer could Nelson endure such punishment? And could Wolgast maintain the pace while continuing to answer?

Wolgast stated to the crowd, just before round twenty-one, "I'll close his eyes pretty soon."[17] This before a round of routine exchanges, many of which could have eliminated an average boxer. Following a minute of punch swapping in round twenty-two, Nelson suddenly staggered Wolgast with a clean right to the stomach. Follow-up punches, including the aforementioned stinging punch to the jaw of Wolgast, sent him to the mat for a three count. Although he staggered when he arose, Wolgast managed to regain his control. Nelson tried with everything he had to put him away, but he could not. Wolgast was given a shot of whiskey at the conclusion of the round. Nelson smelled blood in round twenty-three, but Wolgast retaliated against his punches, covered and clinched when necessary. Another shot of whiskey awaited Wolgast at round's end. In round twenty-four, Wolgast looked the fresher but then slowed, prompting the crowd to yell, "Fight! Fight!" While Wolgast looked to tire in round twenty-five, he managed to deliver four hard rights to the jaw of Nelson, followed by a half dozen lefts to the face.

The two fighters wrestled in the center of the ring in round twenty-six in a rather featureless few minutes. Again, the Dane went to his corner spitting blood. In round twenty-seven Wolgast changed tactics and rushed to battle shoulder to shoulder. While Nelson's eye was almost entirely closed at this stage, he managed to cover as needed. Nelson's left cheek was badly swollen as round twenty-eight opened. The pace quickened but was dampened by longer clinches and a failure by both fighters to break. At the gong, Nelson's mouth was still bleeding. Round twenty-nine saw both fighters deliver solid body punches — one left caught Wolgast over the heart, leaving him groaning. As round thirty opened, Nelson's left eye was completely closed. At one point Nelson looked to have delivered a low blow but wasn't

Ten—February 2, 1910: A Disappointing Loss

warned. Over all, it was a lackluster round. Thirty rounds in, and the two questions we had ten rounds earlier could still not be answered—rethinking this, perhaps the second one was addressed with the whiskey.

Round thirty-one opened with Wolgast still exchanging banter with his corner and smiling—it appeared that his corner was just trying to keep their fighter loose. In contrast, Nelson began the round cautiously and appeared to be conserving energy. In round thirty-two, the blows were diminishing in strength, as were the fighters. Few telling punches were landed until Wolgast let loose with a right that caught Nelson flush on the mouth and began the bleeding once again. Round thirty-three saw Wolgast pepper Nelson's face until he was half blinded, the Dane mounting little more than a moderate defense. Nelson had virtually no offense by round thirty-four. Appearing to be nothing more than a punching bag for Wolgast, Nelson was just trying to sustain himself. Round thirty-five found Nelson in full defensive mode. Each Wolgast combination appeared to rock the champion, who was saved by the bell. Nelson could hardly see his opponent as round thirty-six began. Wolgast, who wasn't strong enough to deliver a knockout punch, then danced around the champion injecting blows at will and avoiding any attempts by Nelson to stall. The crowd was yelling "new champion," at Wolgast who kept up a constant exchange of repartee with his fans. Such was the prelude to the aforementioned closing rounds.

Sitting in a box together on that Tuesday afternoon were James Britt, Sr., and Nels Nelson, the Battler's father. They watched together as the lightweight championship of the world passed to the younger Wolgast. As the sun set, as if on cue, behind the Golden Gate, one could only wonder their thoughts about Willus, and if he could have managed to avoid such a humiliation for his fighter. It was the elder Nelson who sought out Britt to be his guest at the Washington's Birthday Show, all the old scores between Jimmy and Bat long wiped away. Jimmy would do his best to console Nels as the disaster unfolded, not knowing that he himself would face his own tragedy in just over eighty days. The Britt family, having lost a sister to tuberculosis in 1906 and Willus in 1909, would soon, on May 14, 1910, face the death of Alice Britt, the eighteen-year-old daughter of Mr. and Mrs. James E. Britt. She too would die from the dreaded disease that took her sister, leaving "Jimmy" Britt his parent's only surviving child.

Needless to say, Nelson's defeat changed most of his plans. He was, however, surprised when Jack Robinson told him that despite his defeat, his theatrical dates back east had not been canceled. Thus, Team Nelson packed their things and headed to Chicago on February 25. No longer his handsome self, Nelson was praying that his face would miraculously heal before his opening on Monday night. A throng of admirers, many from his hometown, greeted the former champion and his team when they arrived. Bat's father was there to comment: "It was a bad mistake, a bad mistake. Battling should have trained down on the ranch instead of the mountains. He was not careful enough."[18]

"It was the only fight he has fought when I was not in my boy's corner," the elder Nelson continued. "We are all sorry, mother and me and there's the kids. Perhaps when Battling has a little rest he will be as good as ever. After this, I will go with him to take care of my boy."[19]

Arriving home, Bat was greeted by his mother who brushed away the tears and said, "This is the saddest moment of my life!" She then felt a need to proclaim to the press, "Nobody can ever accuse him of a dishonest act." She then paused and said, "I hope Battling will give up boxing now."[20]

March brought the healing announcement of the gate receipts "being $37,750" for the Nelson-Wolgast event. Win, lose or draw, Nelson was guaranteed $12,000, with $1,000 in expenses. Wolgast took a guaranteed $3,750 for his end. The estimated cost of the fight was about $20,000, leaving the rest as a healthy profit margin for the promoter. The stake was large enough for any fighter, including Nelson, to dismiss the wishes of a loving mother.

The moving pictures, of which Nelson had 35 percent, were also a quality concern, as nobody had yet viewed the images.[21] An anticipated viewing by the press was expected in about a week. Certainly they will not be bashful, Nelson believed, regarding an evaluation.

Since the loss, Nelson's performance had been dissected from every conceivable angle by the newspapers. One of which was a self-comparison of measurements—those from two years ago versus the recent Nelson. This yielded an increase in age, wrist, and waist, and a decrease in weight, reach, biceps, forearm, chest (both normal and expanded). The Battler's recent loss was attributed to old age, shortness of breath and an expanding waistline. A much younger Nelson surely would have prevailed over Wolgast, claimed the Dane's followers.[22]

In addition to theater owners not being shaken by Nelson's loss, word also came that many promoters were scrambling to get Bat's next fight. A match was trying to be made between Nelson and "Cyclone Johnny" Thompson. Haggling over the mill were promoters Louis Holt, Hester and Jim Griffin, all of whom were finding Jack Robinson still able to drive a hard bargain—Nelson even now expecting a 45 percent cut of the gross.[23]

Thankfully, reviews of the recent fight pictures were good—a screening was held in San Francisco during the second week in March. Some consolation, Nelson thought, for his efforts. The twenty-second round, when the Battler brought Wolgast to his knees, was the most exciting to many. But, as the sun began to set, it became harder and harder to follow the action—during the final round, when referee Smith grabbed Wolgast's glove and held it aloft, it was difficult to see any detail.

As for Nelson's critics, well, they had a field day penning articles regarding the passing of Nelson as a championship candidate. Many were concerned that he no longer had his greatest asset,

Featuring Battling Nelson, this poster was used to promote the film of the fight between Battling Nelson and Ad Wolgast, a rivalry for the ages. The two fought sixty grueling rounds during their trilogy that took place between 1909 and 1913.

that of endurance. Some thought that he had not been honest with himself regarding his conditioning, while others believed that in Wolgast, Nelson finally met a man after his own heart, pain free and indefatigable.

In the process of healing, his heart still intact, Nelson paid an unexpected visit to the jeweler. Confirming he was having a unique diamond and pearl necklace constructed, he would not affirm for whom. The forty-two-stone (largely pearl) display, with its three-carat centerpiece, had a brilliant appearance and a distinctive design. The Dane first hinted it was for his sister, but later denied that anyone would ever see it worn in Hegewisch. On the day of the visit, Nelson left $1,250—some accounts claim that was the purchase price, while others claimed it was only a payment—with the jeweler who was in the process of completing the piece. Of course, it didn't take long for the marriage rumors to once again surface, especially when it involved such an ornate and expensive piece of jewelry. Nelson, who was convinced that gemstones were a means to a woman's heart, often purchased such gift pieces during his courtships.

An interesting item appeared in the *Daily Standard* of Ogden, Utah, on Wednesday, March 23. In the wire article, "Nelson Has Won a Good Fortune," penned by Eddie Smith, it talked about the wealth the Dane had accumulated—something that many a published article had chronicled—but then contrasted it with the risks he had taken. This was one of the initial disclosures to note Nelson's financial vulnerability.

"There is no telling just how well fixed Nelson is at this time, but it is felt that he is not worth anything like $200,000, as per his claim," states Smith, who goes on to confirm, "There are a thousand and one ways that money slips through the fingers of a fighter and the Dane has fallen for many a bunko game that he has not let the public in on."[24] Smith then went on to detail some investments: the Dane's property in Hegewisch had dramatically slipped in value due to the rail routing, his vineyard (or possible hog farm) in Livermore was costing him a small fortune, his mining company had lost money, he fell for an investment in his ROKO training game he tried to popularize, and there was some sort of new washing machine that took him for a bath. Smith did admit that Nelson had become wiser due to his losses, and that he remained the same great guy everyone always knew—willing to help or lend money at the drop of a hat and still caring for his parents and siblings, including paying for Charles's tuition at the University of California, but the contrast was stark. Lifting the financial facade that Nelson had maintained for years put into question his long-term security and his pecuniary awareness.

Arriving at Philadelphia on April 5, Nelson began his run at the Gayety Theater. As always, one of his first stops was at a barber to grab a shave. While it is seldom that a well-known sports figure enters a public place and doesn't create a stir, this time was a bit different. Not immediately recognizing the former champion, the barber lathered up Nelson, then stopped. "Look here, you're Nelson the fighter," he proclaimed. "If you're not good enough to stop in the Bellevue-Stratford, you're not good enough to be shaved here. Get out!"[25]

Nelson, of course, thought the barber was only joking. "Get out!" the barber repeated. The Dane finally went to the washbasin and removed the lather from his face. Outraged, Nelson delivered a few unpublishable lines before leaving the premises. The entire situation disturbed the fighter, who decided he would finish his stage obligations then take a layoff back at his ranch. This hiatus, the Battler believed, would put him back into the proper frame of mind.

The Bellevue-Stratford Hotel, a landmark building that opened in 1904, was built at 200 South Broad Street at the corner of Walnut Street in Philadelphia.[26] The French Renaissance styled design was that of architects G.W. and W.D. Hewitt, and the structure essentially replaced two earlier hotels, the Bellevue and the Stratford—both nationally known for their high standard of service, elite clientele, and fine cuisine.[27] It was here, as you recall, that Nelson's manager had registered the fighter before his well-publicized confrontation with hotel management.

On April 7, a judge in the U.S. circuit court decided against Nelson in his suit for $10,000 in damages against the hotel for refusing accommodations. The hotel's defense was that Nelson "had persistently violated the laws of some states by fighting."[28] Nelson was quick to state that he engaged in boxing exhibitions and that the only real prize fight he had ever engaged in came off in Nevada, where there were no state laws against the sport. "If Nelson had violated the laws of any state which prohibited prize fighting," Judge Holland directed the jury, "then he would be an undesirable guest."[29]

To make matters worse, the following day, Nelson suffered some bruises and cuts when his automobile collided with a streetcar while he was traveling to a prizefight. Thankfully, nobody was seriously hurt, and the Dane received an ovation when he entered the clubhouse. In spite of the incident, he continued to field questions regarding his next fight, stating only that many names had been batted around, like "Cyclone Johnny" Thompson and even Methuselah "Matty" Baldwin.

Bumps and bruises somewhat healed, Mr. Nelson traveled to Washington, D.C., in the middle of May to appear before the House committee in opposition to the bill to prevent moving pictures of prize fights, or news results of such endeavors sent over the wire. "If you are going after boxing contests and the pictures taken of them," proclaimed Nelson, "why not make a good clean sweep and do away with racing news, stock tickers and accounts of football games."[30] The Battler then went on to criticize those who had never seen a contest, particularly one of his, for interfering with the game. The Battler was just starting to profess the sport's financial position when a call of the House broke up the committee meeting. Nelson smiled playfully and stated, "They rang the gong too soon on him, as he had not yet finished."[31]

Nelson also paid a visit to Joseph Gurney Cannon, a U.S. politician from his home state of Illinois and leader of the Republican Party. Cannon, who served as Speaker of the U.S. House of Representatives from 1903 to 1911, chuckled when Nelson told him he would have made a great featherweight. Cannon was already an extremely influential man in Washington and didn't need a boxing ring to execute his control over the House. He was, however, humbled by Nelson's remarks.

Nelson got a kick out of learning that Jack Johnson had discharged manager George Little of Chicago in favor of Billy Nolan. Like religion, resurrections are common in boxing. Thus Nolan would now try to keep the heavyweight focused on his training. Rumors were flying in the press regarding Little's attempts to keep Johnson out of his automobile and in a gym. Little believed it was Johnson's automobiling buddy, onetime bantamweight Sig Hart, who was keeping him from his training. Nevertheless, it took a squad of policemen to remove the stubborn Little from Johnson's training quarters—he was there taking tickets for a Johnson sparring session. Little then claimed that the fighter would not battle on July 4 against James J. Jeffries in Reno and that the $10,000 forfeit money belonged to him. Nelson, who had been resting at his ranch awaiting details of his return match with Ad Wolgast, was soon en route to Reno to cover the heavyweight fight as a member of the press. This he would do by way of San Francisco and Los Angeles where he would be making some promotional stops.

Lured out of retirement for all the wrong reason, Jeffries, with little more than courage to his advantage, withstood a battering by Jack Johnson. Taunted repeatedly during the fight, Jeffries allowed his corner to defend him orally while he did everything possible to defend himself physically. Dropping three times in the fifteenth round, Jeffries was powerless. It was Johnson by knockout. Ringside was Battling Nelson who had predicted the outcome and would open his July 15, 1910, account for *The Call*:

> NEGRO NOT EVEN MARKED, HUGE "MELON" FOR BOTH,
> Jeffries Gets $114,400 for Giving Up Title and Johnson Cleans Up $122,600 in a Day.

In his article about the fight Nelson claimed it "was the poorest exhibition of fighting for a championship that he ever saw." He then went on to claim, "The tenth round was the beginning of the end. Jeffries got a good hard left hook on the liver that made him reel like a drunken sailor." Of the loser Nelson would state, "During the whole fight Jeffries never fought with enough even to encourage his friends who bet on him," and "Jeffries showed absolutely nothing of the great fighting ability which made him famous in eight years." Of Johnson, whom the Battler had picked to win, "Johnson didn't show the ability he should to be popular with the fans. He is not aggressive enough to suit the bloodthirsty fightbugs." No Alfred Runyon—who by the way would move to New York City in 1910 and drop the "Alfred" in favor of "Damon"—when it came to a ring assessment, Bat intended to soon turn his attention to the great outdoors.

The Death of Joe Gans

Word came out of Baltimore, Maryland, that former lightweight champion Joseph Gans had passed peacefully at 8:30 a.m. on the morning of August 10, 1910. He was comforted by his family—his wife and foster mother, and friends. Tuberculosis, an infectious bacterial disease, put Gans to the ropes, as it had done with Peter Jackson and George Dixon, and slowly wore him down. On Argyle Street, outside his mother's home, fans gathered for a glimpse of the horsedrawn hearse that carried Gans's casket first to a church to be memorialized, then on to Mount Auburn Cemetery where he was buried at age thirty-five.

For the sport of boxing, it was a monumental loss of not only one of the greatest lightweight boxers ever, but one of its most lovable figures. Joseph Gans was admired for his ring prowess; execrated for his vulnerability to ring temptation; and then, given the strength to redress his issues, awarded the respect and admiration of men of every color. For those who had let the shame and repugnance of bigotry ravage their souls, there was no looking away, no dismissal of the great skills Gans possessed, no renunciation of his achievements, and no repudiation of a man beloved by the sport of boxing.

Born on November 25, 1874, Joseph Gant, or Joe Gans—a name fastened to him by a referee early in his career—began his pro career in 1891. Clever from the very beginning, or so it seemed, the "Old Master" fought out of the Baltimore area—like so many other pugilists from this era, his early record was incomplete. Working his way up, Gans was given a title shot against Frank Erne on March 23, 1900. But the champion was in his prime, and Gans was forced to stop in the twelfth round with a nearly severed left eyelid. For several years, his career fell into the wrong hands and Gans developed a reputation as a crooked fighter; his biggest ring folly came in 1900 when he laid down in the second round against Terry McGovern.[32] His behavior nearly cost him his career—a confession and a promise of honesty was his savior.[33]

Only four years before, Gans was a fighting machine, an incomparable ring deity. He won the lightweight title in a rematch with matinee idol Frank Erne on May 12, 1902, and did so with an impressive first-round knockout, becoming the second boxer in history to win a championship in this manner. He then fought a notable twenty-round draw with Joe Walcott for the welterweight crown on September 30, 1904, before turning his attention to Battling Nelson. His successful title defense against Nelson in the forty-second round of their September 3, 1906, match was the third-longest bout of the twentieth century. Gans would lose the title to Nelson when he was stopped in the seventeenth round of their July 4, 1908, rematch. According to the *Tacoma Times*, his physical downfall began with the advent of his trilogy with Nelson, "forced to tear needed flesh off his bones to meet the enormous conditions imposed by Billy Nolan."[34] Perhaps not quite that dramatic, but Gans did have to tip the scales at exactly 133 and that did require additional roadwork and sacrifice on his end—consuming "toast three times a day along with a tiny cup of tea."[35] Nelson stopped Gans again on September 9, 1908, this time in round twenty-one. Gans's final ring battle, a ten-round no decision, was against the Englishman Jabez White in New York on March 12, 1909.

The man whose career ring earnings topped $300,000, but whose gambling addiction was difficult to suppress, left an estate estimated at under a third of that figure; he also owned the heavily mortgaged Goldfield Hotel in Baltimore. Not bad for someone whose mother wanted him to join the ministry—in hindsight he felt he should have listened to her plea.

Gans brought a methodical if not pragmatic element to boxing; from his detailed competitive assessments to his limited defensive movements, Gans hit angles and targets with precision accuracy.

It was in Baltimore that Gans made his last public appearance on the stage of the Gaiety Theater. His health failing, it was his last night home before heading west to Prescott, Arizona. It was the hot dry air, he had hoped, that would rejuvenate him. Why the Gaiety? It just so happened Battling Nelson was playing there at the time, and the "Old Master" could not resist the opportunity to join his old friend—and yes, they were friends—on stage. The applause was deafening as he walked out on the dais and spoke briefly of his sorrow in leaving his hometown. His voice cracked slightly, the tears welled up in his eyes and though there was more he wished to say, he just could not.

Bat Being Bat

Following Bat's fight coverage of the Jack Johnson and James J. Jeffries fight in Reno, it was off to Yellowstone National Park for a month of bear hunting with his trainer and chum "Abdul the Turk." Located primarily in Wyoming, although it also extends into Montana and Idaho, Yellowstone, as these two fistic men saw it, would be the ideal spot to conduct some scientific research then publish their results; it seemed like Nelson had more energy for literature than he did for the prize ring. The Battler did state, however, that he intended to reenter the ring against Wolgast the following February. "This dub a champion? Forget it," boasted Nelson. "If I ever get the chance I'll tear his can off in a punch. There's only one champ and he's your friend The Battler. See?"[36] Following a brief stop in Salt Lake, the pair headed to Kansas City, where they would appear in a vaudeville theater for two weeks. No details were provided regarding the publication of their scientific results.

In Kansas City, Nelson chatted openly with the press about his current status, other fighters and rumors. "This Wolgast, McFarland and Thompson," the former champion jabbered, "who are they anyway? Did a Wolgast ever whip a Gans? Never. And, a McFarland never fought forty-two rounds under a broiling sun and finished stronger than the victor."[37] As usual, this was just Bat being his narcissistic self. Given a forum, he couldn't resist tossing out a ridiculous challenge or two to see if anyone would bite, like Nelson brawling both Wolgast and McFarland in the same ring, or even the Battler delivering a better show than Jeffries against Jack Johnson. Somebody pass me a grain of salt.

It took two hours and fifteen minutes to make the run from Kansas City to Topeka in a Great Smith automobile—a distance of about sixty miles as the crow flies. Accompanied by "Abdul the Turk" and E.C. Turney, a Kansas City representative of the Smith Automobile Company, Nelson delighted a crowd of well-wishers when he told them that he and his party planned on spending the remainder of the week in Topeka, visiting the state fair. Later, they would continue to tour in a Great Smith, stopping in Texas, New Mexico, Arizona, and Utah, before heading west to California. "There is no rush on," claimed Nelson. "Our party will drift along easy. We will take our guns and hunt along the way, and camp when we feel like it."[38] If time or demand permitted, he might train with Abdul or even give an exhibition, but that remained to be seen. This was really about the Great Smith line of automobiles and not about fight talk, but naturally tossing a jab or two at Wolgast was always an option for the Dane.[39] The group was registered at the National Hotel and welcomed visitors to take a closer look at the car, or the Battler.

Three days later, while Nelson and Fred Langley endeavored to make a record run from Topeka back to Kansas City, the two were thrown twenty feet into a field when their touring car struck a farmer's wagon and flipped over. As Bat got up and dusted himself off, he went to check on Fred, who was driving. Fortunately neither man was injured. The steering gear broken on their horseless carriage, both men weighed their future travel options.

In the fall, Battling Nelson was matched against Denver fighter Monte Dale.[40] The pair would fight ten rounds in Kansas City on the night of October 10. Hosted by the Grand Avenue Athletic Club, both fighters would not attempt to make the lightweight limit—Nelson weighed 157 and did not want to train down for such a short fight, and Dale stood at 135 pounds.

Nelson v. Dale, October 10, 1910

To the former lightweight champion, the fight, if you call it that, was a confidence builder or tune-up, but not much more. The Battler, who did not weigh in, entered the ring to a rousing reception and looked every bit as tanned and rested as he had claimed—most described Nelson as about five pounds heavier than his opponent, who tipped the scale at 133 pounds.

In round one, both fighters had a bit of trouble measuring their punches. Dale only managed to send a right to the heart and a soft left to Nelson's jaw. Nelson dispatched a solid left to Dale's left eye, a right to the jaw, and a couple of solid combinations before a solid left to the stomach sent Dale down for a four count. After the collapse, Nelson was landing a mixture of punches at will. When the gong sounded, Dale was bleeding from his eye.

Nelson charged out after the second-round bell sounded and took his opponent to a clinch before missing a right in the breakaway. Posting only a left to the eye and a right to the stomach, Dale spent considerable time retreating from his opponent. Nelson mailed a solid combination to the jaw and a right to the mouth before looking to the body. The bell appeared to have saved Dale.

As round three opened, it was clear that something was amiss. Dale was only using his right hand, having broken his left in the previous round. Despite the broken limb, Dale addressed several weak rights to the jaw, two rights to the head, and a stinging blow to Nelson's left ear. Nelson consigned a solid right to the chin and a couple of solid combinations before taking over the fight.

To save their fighter, Dale's corner threw up the sponge at the beginning of round four. The fight wasn't much to speak of, so nobody did.

"So certain is the Battler of his ability to keep going [after his recent victory] that he has accepted Promoter Jim Griffin's terms for a 10 or 15 round bout with 'One Round' Hogan or Anton la Grave on the evening of October 28," reported *The Call*.[41] Regardless of the fact that Nelson had accepted some of the terms the day after the Dale fight, some details still needed to be worked out. Nelson was holding out for a larger cash guarantee than Griffin was willing to extend. Since Hogan would draw better than La Grave, Griffin became concerned when Hogan was no longer available. Interest in a Nelson v. La Grave match was there, he believed, but only at a certain price point. Figuring that the final terms could be worked out in California, Team Nelson optimistically packed their things and headed for their training quarters in Colma, even canceling a scheduled Chicago business meeting with Ad Wolgast.

A local product, Anton La Grave had "been coming to the front right along, and when the opportunity for getting to the front came, La Grave's (new) manager seized it for his protégé," reported *The Call*.[42] Now handled by veteran manager Sam Fitzpatrick, his team was working hard over at Shannon's resort in San Rafael. Meanwhile, the Battler was over at Millet's under the watchful eye of Jack Grace.

Six days before the fight, the wagering opened at odds of 10 to 7 in favor of Nelson—a surprise to many who figured the Dane a 2 to 1 favorite. La Grave's two brothers had raised a purse of $2,000 to wager on their man's chances against the former champion. This of course prompted others to follow, including an influx of money on Nelson. "I have not touted my friends to bet on me," said the Butchertown lad (La Grave), "but they all seem to think that I have a grand chance, so I am glad that they are with me so strong."[43]

Often forgotten are the little things that make someone special. Much has been stated about Nelson's obsession with money, but he was not without compassion. The *San Francisco Call* newspaper had a fund for the orphans of Mount St. Joseph Asylum. During their fund drives, they would note significant contributors, one of them being Battling Nelson, who sent a check in the amount of $50 to the foundation at the end of October.

Nelson v. La Grave, October 31, 1910

"Anton La Grave Holds Battling Nelson to a Draw at 15 Rounds, Fighting Dane Another 'Has Been' Who Illustrates Again the Theory of the Man Who Can't Come Back—Punches of Former Champion Lack Steam, While La Grave Stands Up under Terrific Pounding without Flinching. Outlook for Lightweight Challenger Not Promising Unless New Blood Found"; again, the assessment in the following day's newspaper spoke volumes.[44]

Before the Broadway Club in San Francisco, Nelson displayed all his classic attributes, from boring in to not being able to deliver a knockout punch—only managing a fifteen-round draw against La Grave. The first three or four rounds were all Nelson, but when La Grave finally managed to calm his nerves, he steadily fought back—exhibiting little polish but a lot of heart, the Butchertown youth was strong enough to stave off defeat.[45] Clearly in command of the fight, Nelson could not capitalize on his opportunities. His distance was also an issue, as his punches often missed their target. To add insult to the Battler's performance, his opponent stood toe-to-toe with him in the final round, trading punches as if he was a lightweight contender.

Despite his performance, a very supportive Jim Coffroth thought it strong enough to try to match the Dane against English scrapper Owen Moran. "The Battler fought a good fight," said Promoter Coffroth, "and he will get better. He has been out of the ring for some time, and a fighter often gets a little rusty through the need of work."[46] Coffroth was hoping to sign both fighters to a twenty-round battle on the Saturday afternoon before Christmas, preferably in Blot's open-air arena on Eighth Street. Nelson, who did not like the sound of the initial conditions, stated that he might head to Kansas City, where he hoped to be able to find a decent match—this, of course, nothing more than a casual threat to pressure Coffroth to reach terms. Leave it to Bat to always have the last word.

Not wanting Nelson to leave town for fear that his fight negotiations would break down, Coffroth worked diligently to secure terms with the fighter. It took only until the following day, November 3, for the promoter to proudly announce that he had signed Battling Nelson and Owen Moran for a twenty-round dual before his San Francisco group, the Broadway Club, on the afternoon of November 26. His opportunity secured, Nelson canceled his engagements in Kansas City and decided to stay on the West Coast.

The Battler also took a few minutes to drop his friend Theodore Roosevelt a congratulatory birthday telegram, as a belated dinner was taking place in his honor in New York. It read,

> MAY YOU BE ABLE TO CELEBRATE MANY MORE GLORIOUS BIRTHDAYS AND AT THE SAME TIME HAVE AN APPETITE THAT WILL MAKE THE CHEF AT THE CAFE BOULEVARD WORK. I AM WITH YOU WHATSOEVER YOU DO ALL THE TIME. MAY YOU ALWAYS BE YOUNG AND HAVE A "BULLY GOOD TIME." YOUR FRIEND, BATTLING NELSON.[47]

The former president's birthday was October 27 and they were celebrating it a bit late in his birthplace.

Moran's team quickly wired Coffroth to inform him that they hoped to be able to arrive by the middle of November to begin preparations for the fight. Moran, having full knowledge of the significance of this opportunity, planned to train especially hard for the encounter. The confident Englishman believed he was a better boxer despite giving away a few pounds to the former champion. Unlike many of those who had fought Nelson at that distance, Moran also believed he could handle the twenty rounds.[48]

For the critics, and there were many, they believed that this was the contest to demonstrate whether or not Nelson was still a viable contender for the title. Some pundits had already written off Nelson for his inability to knock out La Grave, but those who viewed their battle knew better. La Grave was a much tougher boxer than many outside the Bay Area realized. Certain was the fact that a battle with Moran would test Nelson.

Style, What Style?

Durability and perseverance was the Nelson mantra. As for style, the Battler was a brawler, or "slugger." He was not the classic boxer or stylist, who always maintains distance between himself and his opponent. Instead, it was about boring in on his adversary, taking ground and never retreating. This, he felt, diminished any reach advantage an opponent might have, established control and pace, and impressed the judges. Nelson was not the type of boxer who enjoyed sitting out of range and toying with his opponent with the jab. The game, as he saw it, was inside, wearing down your opponent.

Without that single-shot power punch, he took down his opponents with combinations. The fact that he wasn't a slippery, defensive-style fighter—someone who often relied on the failures of his opponent in order to gain an advantage, be it on the score cards or more preferably a knockout—didn't bother him one bit. However, if his opponent advocated for such a defensive approach, it irritated the hell out of him. He wouldn't really toy with the jab as much as use it for measuring his punches. His jabs were good, his hooks exceptional and his uppercuts solid.

As a Brawler, Nelson lacked finesse and footwork—as an orthodox fighter, he would slide his left forward, dragging the right. Less mobile, more leverage and a stable platform suited him just fine. Leading with the head, staying low enough to press into his opponent's shoulders—watch some film of the bout with Moran and notice how low he managed to keep his head even against a shorter fighter—while using his hands in front to block his opponent's arms, he could then pivot his right foot and adjust his left for leverage. Nelson worked hard on the development of his short-range punches, especially for the Gans trilogy and chiefly the right uppercut.

Defensively, slipping, blocking with his arms and clinching were common, as was pushing his opponent back—he loved the latter, an intimidating action. Giving the idiomatic expression "to come to a head" a new meaning, Nelson's offensive and defensive strength was his skull. Impervious to assault and willing to endure enormous punishment, the Battler was truly an enigma.

Nelson v. Moran, November 26, 1910

"Two-seconds after the [November 26] contest had officially ended Nelson was on his feet, shouting that he did not hear the count," reported *The Call*'s William J. Slattery, "shouting that he was not out, clamoring for another chance at his victorious opponent. But it was already too late. The 'toughest nut in the ring' had been cracked and cracked decisively."[49]

Looking at the fight by rounds: At the sound of the opening bell, both fighters rushed together and fought shoulder-to-shoulder. It was evident from the start that both gladiators intended to assert their dominance at close range. Nelson scored first when he dispatched a clean hook to the jaw. Moran in return marked by sending a nice combination to the face of Nelson. Both fighters easily traded punches, and the round ended even.

Nelson danced to the center of the ring as the bell sounded for round two, as if to challenge Moran to break ground. Moran posted a solid right to the ribs, followed by several strong rights and some short-arm lefts to the head. Moran scored again with several straight lefts to the jaw, then a powerful combination to the body and face. Nelson, who had forced the pace, mailed only two lefts to the face of Moran and that was at the end of the action. Moran took the round.

Nelson forced his enemy against the ropes early in round three, but the Briton danced away. Addressing a sound right to the nose that drew first blood, Moran then turned his attention to Nelson's face. As an outscored challenger, Nelson went to his corner spitting blood.

As the gong sounded for round four, it was clear that Moran was in control of the fight. Measuring his punches with accuracy, Moran was scoring with combinations to the face of Nelson—his agenda clearly to keep the blood flowing from his opponent's nose. Every time Nelson scored with an amalgam, Moran would successfully counter.

Round five looked to be hectic as both fighters seemed to harness their energy. Moran immediately directed a straight right to the jaw followed by two flush rights that jarred the former champion. Nelson forwarded two shots to the face, then managed to bring the crowd to its feet by forcing Moran from one corner to another with solid combinations. However, the Brit quickly countered, managing to utilize short-arm mixes at Nelson's face with precision. It turned out to be the best round of the fight to that point, with honors virtually even.

Round six opened with a minute's worth of close quarters battling with little or no damage. Moran scored when he transmitted two good lefts to the face. Each Nelson rush was being countered with a Moran combination. The Battler conveyed a sturdy hook to the stomach, but not much more. Moran had the better round.

Nelson tried to retake control of the fight in round seven by scoring a quick combination to the face of Moran. Both fighters then went head-to-head, with Moran scoring just a bit better. The Briton then shot some machine-gun rights to the face that made the Dane wince. The round ended in Moran's favor.

Nelson came up smiling in round eight before reaching an exchange with Moran. The Battler wired several combinations to the face and body of the Brit that made him break ground. Nelson seemed to be going after his man, but again Moran took control with timed combinations to the face, one of which all but closed the Dane's left eye. Moran, having successfully targeted the face, was now reaping some benefit from the prolonged assault. It was Moran's round and, for that matter, battle up to this point.

At the opening bell for round nine, again Nelson came out with an agenda, that being to take it to the Brit. But Moran telegraphed a short right to the jaw, followed by a straight left. With the fight still at close range, Moran's combinations to the face continued to be effective. Nelson managed only a notable right to the kidneys; so much for planning.

If Nelson had proven anything by round ten, it was that he could endure Moran's punishment. But just enduring doesn't win fights. Nelson was being outboxed, and he knew it. Again at close range, both fighters were simply trading punches. It was a lackluster round with neither to the advantage.

When the bell sounded for round eleven, both men appeared alert and without distress. Nelson had driven Moran into the corner, but Moran cleverly broke away and turned the table on the Battler. As Nelson was pushing his opponent into the center of the ring, Moran unloaded an enormous right, using the full force of his body, by pivoting on his left foot. It was as effectual a punch as he had ever thrown. Nelson then tumbled to his back, nearly completing a back somersault. Rolling to his knees as Selig issued the count, Nelson was smart enough to stay there to try to regain his equilibrium. Nelson then began to rise but had to put his gloves back to the canvas for support. As he rose he staggered to his feet before going back to his back once again, this time to the edge of the ring. Selig pushed Moran back and began the count, this as Moran continued to hover close by. Selig again pushed Moran back as Nelson put his gloves on the mat again. Selig could not control Moran. When Nelson arose, he was hit once again and began tumbling forward against Moran until he fell to his knees, hitting his head on the canvas. Selig then turned to instruct Moran to move away, even pointing him in the proper direction. Nelson took the next count with only one knee down. Again, Moran hovered like a vulture before delivering three rights to the face and missing a fourth. The assault staggered Nelson before Moran attacked again, sending Nelson nearly to all fours. Backing himself up, Nelson rose again. Then Moran skillfully measured his distance before starting another assault to the face led by a terrific right. Again Nelson fell forward, this time to all fours. As Selig began his count, even holding Moran back with his left hand, Nelson managed to get to one knee and then squatted until he was counted "out." As Moran celebrated, Nelson was shouting at Selig. Selig reiterated his decision, even mimicking his count with his right arm. Nelson appeared dazed on his feet and did not move, even after his second placed a towel over his back. The crowd delivered a standing ovation as the once shatterproof champion, blood streaming from his face, stood defeated in the center of the ring.

Moran had the lead the entire battle—only three or four rounds considered even. The Brit had cleverly blocked and sidestepped Nelson's assaults with precision combinations, delivered with pinpoint accuracy. The pace of the battle was swift and the final round memorable, if not defining.

> It was fortunate for The Dane that the contest was not stopped after the second knockdown. Captain of Police Shea, who was sitting next to Promoter Jim Coffroth, made many wild attempts to jump into the ring, fearful of a fatality. But for the efforts of Coffroth, Shea would have succeeded and the spectacular finish would have been spoiled.[50]

Both gladiators shook hands after the fight and posed for pictures. Moran even celebrated by turning a few somersaults as part of his victory dance. No sooner had the fight ended than accounts of the battle hit the wire. Nelson was described as "a shadow of his former self," and "lacked the wonderful power of recuperation." Even, "Today he is a Jim Jeffries the second in everything but spirit." Moran was described as fighting "a great battle, the best in his career."[51]

An enormous crowd had witnessed not only a spectacular battle, but also the first pugilistic affair ever staged in Blot's arena—the venue had been built especially for the Kaufman-Langford fight, which got vetoed by Governor Gillett, as did the Johnson-Jeffries bout. An estimated 5,000 filled the bleachers as part of the largest crowd to witness a boxing contest since the Nelson-Wolgast fight held in Richmond.

"According to promoter Jim Coffroth, the receipts were $13,101. Of this sum Nelson received forty percent, or $5,240.40. As he bet $1,000 on himself, he is just $4,240.40 to the good," stated *The Call*. "Moran got thirty percent of the house for his end, amounting to $3,930.30, which is more money than he received in any other contest in which he ever took part. Promoter Jim Coffroth takes the remaining $3,930.30 as his bid for staging the event."[52]

In the words of the winner, Owen Moran, "Moran Is Proud of His Wallop":

> Next to the fact that I have the honor of scoring the first clean knockout from Nelson I feel happy over the fact that I have demonstrated to the American public that I have a punch. Before today, it was widely heralded that I did not have a winning punch. I know that I had one, and I am glad that I have had the chance to prove it. At no time in the fight did Nelson have me in distress. He kept coming as he has done in all his fights, but he could not come too fast for me. I think that those who saw the fight will admit that I took care of myself at every stage of the game and ably protected myself in the clinches, which is the game at which Nelson was supposed to be strong. I have chased Nelson all over the country for three years to get a fight, feeling that I could whip him, and the fact that I did makes up for all the trouble I have been put to in getting a match with him. But don't let anyone lose sight of the fact that Nelson is a "hard nut to crack." He is one of the gamest men that ever put on a glove. The way he tried to get on his feet and fight after repeated knockdowns in the eleventh round was one of the best showings of grit I have ever seen. Although Nelson is a whipped man today, he is one of the greatest fighters the world has ever known, and it will be a long time before a man in the ring will establish a record such as The Battler's.[53]

In the words of the loser, Battling Nelson, "Battler Says He Was Not Out":

> I was rising from the floor when Referee Selig counted me out, and I feel that I got the worst of the count. I am satisfied that I could have stalled the round out and come back strong in the next round with a chance of winning. When Moran clipped me on the jaw he put me down clean, but I always had my senses with me and deliberately took advantage of the succeeding counts in order to finish out the round. I distinctly heard Selig tolling off the seconds for the last knockdown, and was off the floor when he declared Moran the winner. I was raising myself from the floor and was clear of the canvas and ready to straighten up and fight again when the fight was taken from me. Selig only counted nine, and as I started to straighten up, he gave Moran the fight. I feel that Selig acted in accordance with his judgement and meant to be fair, but I think he lost his head in the excitement following the first knockdown and took away my chances to come back. Nobody can convince me that Moran is my master, and all I ask is another chance to show that I am not a "has been."[54]

In the words of the referee, Ben Selig, "Referee Says He Gave Nelson Best of It":

> Nelson was counted out fairly and squarely. If it had been anyone else but Battling Nelson, I would have declared Moran the winner after the third knockdown, when The Battler fell again without being hit. I was fully aware of Nelson's ability to take punishment and recover quickly, and I think that all fair minded people who saw the fight will agree that I gave The Battler all the best of it in the count. The fourth time Nelson went down without being struck, which should have disqualified him. I took into consideration the fact that Nelson might have overlooked this rule while dazed, and allowed the fight to continue. All this time Moran was begging me to stop the fight, so that he would not have to punish The Battler further. When he went down the last time I shouted the count in his ear, and as the timekeeper said "ten," I said "out." Nelson was not off the floor at the time. Nelson claims I did not say "Ten," which is true, but I substituted the word "out" for "ten," as is usual in such cases.[55]

The following day it was reported that Owen Moran, who had received several offers to appear on stage following his victory over Nelson, would head east. Once there, the fighter would sort through the stage propositions while his manager Charley Harvey bartered over the terms and conditions of a fight with Ad Wolgast. Following last night's fight, Wolgast offered his terms: a guarantee of $12,500 for himself plus the right to name a referee. Harvey thought the conditions were ridiculous and believed if Wolgast was worth $12,500, then his fighter's value was at least $15,000.

Nelson was also active, contacting Coffroth with hopes of a match with Wolgast. Nevertheless, the Dane's insistence that he could beat the champion was not heard, nor his pleas acted upon. Frustrated, Nelson boarded a train for Los Angeles on December 3, after which he headed to his ranch in New Mexico for an undetermined period of rest and relaxation. The break came at a good time, as not only was the press beating him to death about the loss to Moran but also taking Nelson to task regarding his investments. Another wire story hit out of Chicago on December 9 claiming, "Former Lightweight Champion Is Not Worth a Fortune According to a Close Friend," with lines such as, "Battling Nelson has more stock in enterprises that proved a failure than any man in America," "Nelson has more bum shares of stock than he has dollars," and "Nelson was a great money-getter, but he was a sucker for the smart fellows."[56]

As the year drew to a close, Nelson found his mind drifting to days past, reflections about his family, career and future. As champion, the title had brought him more than its fair share of rewards—perks to various aspects of his life. But without it, what would this mean? And when he thought about companionship, he thought primarily about Irma Kilgallen—she was THE girl, Nelson's "Forty-Million-Dollar Girl."

Irma Kilgallen

It had been claimed that Nelson was a boxer whose heart—there was no mention of his eyes—did not wander, regardless of circumstance. And it certainly hadn't drifted far

This Charles Dana Gibson drawing depicts four attractive young women, all reminiscent of the beauty of Irma Kilgallen, observing a diminutive man through a magnifying glass (Library of Congress, Prints and Photograph Division, LC-USZ62–25573).

from Irma Tracy Kilgallen. The Battler still believed it was love at first sight for the both of them.

In the 1890s, it was Charles Dana Gibson who gave us the "Gibson Girl," or a pen-and-ink illustration of the feminine ideal of physical attractiveness. However, had he not, we would have found it in the countenance of Irma Kilgallen, whose seductive innocence was captivating. Like a Gibson Girl, she had an exaggerated S-curve shape, achieved by her swan-bill corset, and was well proportioned. Her neck was thin, and when she wore her hair piled high upon her head in the contemporary bouffant, pompadour, or chignon, it accented her face perfectly. Her thin lips and nose drew little attention, as many couldn't get beyond her eyes. Always perfectly dressed in the latest fashionable attire, obviously appropriate for the place and time of day, she was American gentry through and through.

The trouble—at least for Battling Nelson, and soon the Kilgallen family—was that Miss Kilgallen, daughter of the multi-millionaire Chicago Steel manufacturer Martin H. Kilgallen, took the hand of Count Jacques Alexander Albert von Mourik de Beaufort, a Flemish nobleman, although his title wasn't recognized by the *Almanac de Gotha*, he certainly had been.[57] The two, having met in July 1909, were married in London on September 15, 1909. The new bride, along with her mother, then departed for the Kilgallen home in Chicago. Their wedding announcement, as was socially proper, came from Mr. Kilgallen on October 13, 1909—the same day the new bride went to meet her husband in New York.

A Turbulent Year

For the newlyweds, the year began slowly, acclimating themselves to marriage. The count was familiarizing himself also with the family and American customs, while the countess was proudly introducing her new husband to members of Chicago's high society.

On February 23, word—if there is one thing any member of Chicago's elite abhorred, it was bad news reaching the newspapers regarding their misfortune—reached Chicago that the couple, who were vacationing in Hot Springs, Arkansas, had encountered a problem. It seems the count's trunks—one containing his bride's trousseau—were being held and attached to an alleged $500 gambling debt. Mrs. Martin H. Kilgallen, like any good mother-in-law would do, immediately came to her son-in-law's defense.

> They must have tried to swindle the count and he refused to let them. The count did just what any American would do under the circumstances. It was a dispute over the price of the chips that were played on a roulette wheel. I was in Hot Springs for two weeks and I know that the count did not gamble for heavy stakes. While I was there we visited a few of the clubs and played a little of the usual stakes. The chips then were only ten cents each and undoubtedly is what those were worth that the count lost. His conduct pleases Mr. Kilgallen and myself, and it shows that he is up to our expectations. Because the count appears to be a foreigner is no indication that he is not well informed.[58]

Martin Kilgallen, having never had a son, proudly took the count under his wing with hopes that his son-in-law would follow in his footsteps. On March 17, 1910, it was announced that the count, now living in the Kilgallen home with his bulldog Jack, had gone to work as a puddler in the South Chicago steel mills.[59] On the first week of April 1910, the gambling debt incurred by the newlyweds while in Hot Springs was finally won in court by the couple. The dust had settled, or so it was believed, for the Kilgallen family. "Their summer passed quietly; at least without publicity."[60]

On to autumn and winter: On October 3, a report was forwarded from New York that the count had fallen from a horse while mounted and was near death—the first public announcement that the couple was no longer together. The countess hurried to the city where a reconciliation took place.[61] Despite the reuniting, it was this account that started the media frenzy.

Seventeen days later, it was reported that the Countess Irma de Beaufort had fallen down a flight of stairs at her father's home and had been taken to St. Luke's Hospital; as might be expected from a member of the haut monde, the family would not confirm or deny the claim.[62] It was also reported that the husband of the countess, Count de Beaufort (healed from his equestrian injuries) appeared with a bruised face. Later, it was learned that the countess was "accidentally pushed over a railing in the Kilgallen house," with Kilgallen himself "having beaten The Count and having kicked him from the house."[63] On October 23, the count was forced from the hospital, while trying to visit the countess, "and taken to Harrison Street under arrest, then released on bond."[64]

By November, the story was spinning out of control and the public was eating up every detail. The press, with virtually no concern for any member of the Kilgallen family, continued their unabated and insensitive pursuit. For the Kilgallen family, especially the patriarch, it was just an embarrassment. And they just couldn't defuse it. Finally, on November 13, it was announced to the press that the Countess de Beaufort was beginning a suit for absolute divorce from the count. The action claimed "continued cruelty, extreme physical violence on various occasions and many threats to kill."[65] Irma's father, who had also had his fill of the circumstance "denounced the Count as worthless and unwilling to work" and "charged the Count with deceiving Mrs. Kilgallen and Miss Irma as to his character and antecedents by sending them to designing friends in London prior to the wedding."[66] Mrs. Kilgallen blamed the count's temper for the bulk of the problem. "It led him," said Mrs. Kilgallen, "to strike the Countess in a hotel at Hot Springs last February, again while riding in her father's automobile in Chicago, and a third time at Bayhead, New Jersey, where they spent a part of last summer, and on several occasions at the Kilgallen residence."[67]

Four days later, on November 17, as the unmitigated salacious affair began playing out before a hungry press—to the delight of Chicago's gentry—other participants came into view, including Battling Nelson. In an overdue society item, sent by wire from San Francisco where the Battler was training for the Moran fight, it stated that he was once engaged to the young woman.

"'Irma engaged to Battling Nelson!' exclaimed Mr. Kilgallen, 'Impossible! I don't believe she knew him. I will not discuss it.'"[68]

Meanwhile, it was learned that Miss Kilgallen met the Dane in Hegewisch, back in 1905.[69] Young Irma, whose eyes at that time wandered toward the athletic set, was visiting a schoolgirl friend. In fact, she made numerous automobile trips to the Chicago suburb and each time saw Nelson. When the family, likely only Mrs. Kilgallen judging by her spouse's comment, learned of the démodé attachment, Miss Kilgallen was sent to London—she departed in early 1909.

"In London she was under the protection of Mrs. Damrosch, an American widow. She had an allowance of $300 a month and was soon marked in the fashionable tearooms as an American heiress."[70] It was then claimed that all memory of Nelson and Hegewisch was forgotten when she met Count Jacques Alexander Albert von Mourik de Beaufort in the tearoom of the Hotel Cecil. Apparently it took an astute Mrs. Kilgallen to "read between the lines of her daughter's letters in which she spoke of the young man with the continental titles."[71] It was then off to London, as Mrs. Kilgallen needed to do a bit of investigating before consenting to the marriage. Needless to state her due diligence was not comprehensive.

Frequently quarreling and separating, it appeared as if the couple's skirmishes—not to mention Irma's father who had thrown his fair share of uppercuts at Beaufort—may have garnered only slightly less press than the Battler.[72] As for his sentiments, Nelson had always admitted that it remained with Irma, with or without "Count No Account," as he called Beaufort.

Then, just when it looked like things couldn't get much worse for the Kilgallen family, they did. On November 18, it was learned that Count von Mourik de Beaufort and his trusted dog were booked for a week's engagement at the American Music Hall in Chicago.[73] Apparently Col. W.A. Thompson, manager of the venue, offered an appealing amount of cash to de Beaufort to perform what was being called the "trials and tribulations" of his courtship of, and marriage to, his wife, prior to his expulsion from the Kilgallen residence on Michigan Avenue, the latter occurring shortly after the countess sustained her broken arm and leg, yet before the count was arrested at St. Luke's Hospital. It is de Beaufort's hope that this event will somehow reconcile him with his wife and save his marriage. Now, this entire event leads to the obvious question: Where does the dog fit in? The dog, which could be a factor in the couple's divorce, performs tricks taught to him by his master. Should the show be a success, de Beaufort intends on entering the steel business to amass a fortune that would rival his father-in-law, or is it former father-in-law?

In its initial performance, the show was a hit. "De Beaufort sang, danced, gave a monologue and scattered flowers over the audience among the fair ones. Many a Chicago woman tonight cherished a flower from a real

Count de Beaufort, or "Count No Account" as Bat often called him, with his dog doing a bit of promotion for their stage show (Library of Congress, Prints and Photograph Division, LC-DIG-ggbain-02810).

live count," reported *The Call*.[74] The question then was, Will millionaire Martin Kilgallen allow his dirty laundry to play out upon a Chicago stage or will papa-in-law "come across" with some cash to prevent "The Count of His Account"?

On November 21, the count appeared in the initial performance of *Dear Little Maid of Chicago*, with his creditors—apparently the count can't count and his financial pipeline now capped, what's a guy to do?—getting the receipts. Two days later, the count and his dog were thrown out of both the Congress and the Blackstone Hotel.[75]

As the holidays approached, not everyone was in the Christmas spirit. On December 2, the count swore out a warrant charging his father-in-law with assault and battery. "The alleged assault," de Beaufort claimed, "took place in Kilgallen's office. The complaint says the millionaire summoned de Beaufort there and when the latter refused a sum of money to leave the country, the complaint says Kilgallen struck The Count in the face."[76] All this and the Kilgallen family didn't want Irma to marry a pugilist.

Adding insult to injury, on December 19, the count penned an article titled, "Why I Am Making a Fool of Myself." In the piece he states,

> I did not know whether her father was worth 10 cents, $10 or a million.... I loved her. She loved me.... They scoff at me for going on stage, but they forget the fact that what drove me to the stage was an honest desire to pay off my debts.[77]

Meanwhile, Countess de Beaufort, while in a hospital bed, formally renounced her husband Count Jacques Alexander Albert von Mourik de Beaufort, of the principality of Luxembourg, on December 20. The count, recently convicted of disorderly conduct, would not get a visit with his wife. The count became incensed by her refusal to see him and vowed to take the matter to the Supreme Court.

On Christmas Eve, the countess was secretly removed from St. Luke's Hospital and taken to her father's home on Michigan Avenue. This was to avoid the watchers hired by the count. The Kilgallen family has also retained the services of a guard to watch over her at the home.

The entire incident, which has now captivated an audience beyond Lake Michigan and even as far as New Mexico, will continue to play out in the months ahead.

Back to Bat

In 1910, Nelson fought seventy-seven rounds, twice the number of the previous year, against five opponents, two of which, Wolgast and Moran, are Hall of Fame caliber boxers. The Battler won two fights, drew one and lost two, along with his title. Perhaps even more important, for the first time in his boxing career he exhibited his vulnerability.

Not only was Nelson's title defeat, along with his fight with Moran, memorable during the year, but so too, that of boxing's first "Fight of the Century," which saw Jack Johnson knock out the "Great White Hope" James J. Jeffries in round fifteen to retain his world heavyweight championship title. Further battles included Frankie Conley's forty-second-round knockout—the longest title fight under Queensberry rules to end in a knockout—of Monte Attell on February 22 and Freddie Welsh's ten-round victory by foul over Jim Driscoll on December 20.

Ten—February 2, 1910: A Disappointing Loss

For the sport of boxing, the loss of Joe Gans left an enormous void, and there would be more. On October 15, 1910, Stanislaw Kiecal, aka Stanley Ketchel, was shot to death by a farmhand named Walter Dipley at a ranch near Conway, Missouri. Both Dipley and a companion named Goldie Smith were imprisoned for the crime. The murky circumstances that took place on the ranch owned by Ketchel's friend, R.P. Dickerson, were never fully explained. Ketchel's three brothers, John, Leon and Alexander, were so confused that they had his body exhumed for examination—the results found not only bullet holes but also evidence of a club having been used. Both Dipley, who was hired as a farmhand under the name of Walter A. Hurtz, and Smith, a ranch cook, were found guilty of murder on January 24, 1911.

Ketchel, the "Michigan Assassin," was born on September 14, 1886, in Grand Rapids, Michigan. Knocking out forty-one of his first forty-nine opponents, he became the only man to knock out twin brothers (Mike and Jack Sullivan) in consecutive bouts and even picked up a world middleweight championship in doing it. He lost then regained title to Billy Papke before defending it four times. Outweighed by thirty-five pounds, Ketchel then challenged Jack Johnson for the world heavyweight title. He was knocked out in the twelfth round. Ketchel then continued to defend his title, compiling a record of fifty-two wins, forty-nine by knockout; four losses; and four no decisions. What lay ahead for the Battler was yet to be seen. While he had lost his title, he had not lost his integrity, the latter a far more difficult item to reclaim.

Eleven

1911–1912
Mounting a Comeback

> I believe that all fights should be to a finish to determine which is the better man—this is called the "Battler's Route."
>
> —Oscar "Battling" Matthew Nelson[1]

1911

Planes were now landing on aircraft carriers, the first aboard the USS *Pennsylvania* stationed in San Francisco Bay; the U.S. Supreme Court declared Standard Oil to be an "unreasonable" monopoly under the Sherman Antitrust Act and ordered the company to be dissolved; and the first Indianapolis 500-mile auto race was run, with Ray Harroun in his Marmon "Wasp." Progress, and the pace at which it was being made, required parameters to keep it from spinning out of control.

For the sport of boxing, often defined by eras, we had passed "The Early Glove Era," 1890–1908; were now concluding "The White Hope Era," 1908–1915; and were entering "The No Decision Era," 1911–1920. As a sport, it was viewed as needing greater supervision and control—safety was a concern, gambling a controversial element. Many states, such as New York, sponsored legislation to provide such jurisdiction through a State Athletic Commission. Such a commission could license sparring exhibitions given by clubs, license fighters, nominate referees, require a fighter to have a physician's certificate, prohibit the sale of liquor during sparring contests, and even require an accounting of tickets sold and gross receipts. Legislation, in the minds of many, was the answer. Easy to say, if of course you do not make a living as a fighter. From 1900 to 1911, if a fighter fought in New York, the only way he could add a win to his record was by knocking out his opponent within the distance. This was because there was no judging allowed at the end of the contest. In 1911, the Frawley Act mandated no-decision bouts and set the maximum bout length at 10 rounds. If a fighter did not kayo his adversary, it wouldn't count, or would it?

Since betters—gamblers and boxing forever inseparable—despise a draw, they turned to newspapers for their decisions, and to sportswriters as their judges. Agreeing in advance as to which scribe made the final call lent confidence to a wager and gave sportswriters command over their kingdom—a dangerous thing. To some beat writers it added legitimacy to their craft; to others it was an alternative source of income—newspaper salaries were often low, wagers the opposite.[2]

Unable to secure a fight, at the level and terms—conditions many promoters felt unreasonable considering the fighter's status as a former champion—he believed he deserved, Oscar Nelson turned to his growing financial problems. He began restructuring his accounts to pay off debts, even portioning off his ranch. Advertisements ran in the real estate section of the *San Francisco Call*:

> Get a Ranch from Battling Nelson on Easy Payments, $350. $25 cash and $5 each month buys one of those rich, level, 2½ acre Home Farms in the famous Battling Nelson ranch; will build for you on the same terms. F.D. Burr Co., 968 Broadway, Oakland, Cal.[3]

It was not an enjoyable process, as humiliating as it was essential for the former champion.

Traveling as necessary, even back to Hegewisch in the spring, Nelson was keeping an open mind regarding his future. This while also trying to influence his financial interests. In Hegewisch, the Dane sang the praises of Carter H. Harrison and Alderman John R. Emerson during a Democratic meeting in South Chicago. While some accused him of having political ambitions, Nelson's primary concern was protecting his investments in the Eighth Ward.[4] However, if that meant running for office, the Dane might have considered it.

During this period Nelson was also having problems with John R. Robinson, not a surprise considering the circumstance; Robinson was more of a press agent than a manager and it was beginning to show.[5] If Nelson was indeed serious about a comeback, he needed to find himself in a title-driven market, facing genuine contenders, as part of a sound strategy. He also needed to eliminate the distractions and focus on what brought him the title to begin with. It was easily said, but not so easily done.

Down Went the Count

For the Kilgallen family, the saga of the count and the countess continued, as not only was it being playing out in real time, but also on theater screens. "Persons who attend moving picture shows will soon have a chance to see the Chicago romance of Count de Beaufort thrown upon the screens of 5 and 10 cent moving pictures theaters. The Count has posed for a picture story of his affair with Kilgallen heiress of Chicago and says he is going to get $25,000 and royalties for the venture."

The short picture has three scenes: the first shows the count and countess in the homecoming act, the second takes place at the hospital, and then somewhat of a surprise ending. "The last scene shows the Count literally rolling in wealth and two men with shovels such as are used by laborers in Pa Kilgallen's steel mills keeping the Count from being buried by a flood of gold."

Meanwhile, the count not only spends a majority of his time sorting through his numerous financial problems but also finds himself partaking in the manly art of self-defense. On February 27, the count entered a Chicago emergency ward with a black eye and cut forehead.

> While walking along the South Side last night, de Beaufort noticed two men walking behind him. He imagined they were following him for some direful purpose and challenged them to combat. They accepted, and their combined efforts did as much physical damage as Kilgallen and the Chauffeur used to do when they were "putting the boots" to the noble count.[6]

Almost a month later, on April 21, the count, along with Allen McCullough, Jr., the nineteen-year-old son of Allen McCullough, a wealthy banker, was arrested for fighting in

Chicago. The confrontation took place in front of the home of Mrs. George Dahlman, mother of McCullough's young wife, from which he had been separated, and who had filed a suit for divorce against him. "The young man had trailed de Beaufort to the house and waited there until 2 a.m."[7] And, to make matters worse, on May 2, de Beaufort was "named as co-respondent in the divorce suit filed by Allen Porter McCullough, who 'beat up' de Beaufort recently at the home of the parents of his estranged wife."[8] And the count was also sued for a $200 clothing debt. Throughout the year, talk of a reconciliation between the count and countess surfaced—the press even noting an accidental meeting between the two on a downtown Chicago street on April 7—but remained only rumor.[9]

Tending to his own set of financial issues, Battling Nelson also spent the first part of the year strategizing over his attempt to get back into the title mix. If he was spending time with Irma, or contacting her in any other manner, it was done—which was likely and later alluded to—discreetly.

The First Fight Back

To begin scraping off his ring rust, Nelson scheduled two six-round exhibitions during the first week of July—the first in North Bend, Washington, against Ned Whitman, the next in Bellingham, Washington, against Percy Cove. With his first real fight only a month away in Medford, Oregon, the Dane hoped to be in shape for his scheduled ten-rounder on August 4 against Tommy Gaffney.[10]

Nelson's opponent, or Spokane punching bag, took a merciless beating but managed to last until the fifth round. As soon as referee Russell Hanauer declared in Nelson's favor, Gaffney began claiming that he was repeatedly fouled. Gaffney's brother then turned his attention to Nelson and began jawing at him. The entire one-sided affair—the Dane outweighed his opponent by fifteen pounds—was not pretty and proved to be little more than a paycheck for Nelson. In a sign of just how far and how quickly the Dane had fallen, fight coverage, which used to be measured in columns, was reduced to only about two or three newspaper lines—this if you found a newspaper that covered the event.

While in Seattle, Nelson found time to meet with the Reverend Joseph L. Garvin, pastor of the First Christian Church. Garvin conducted an interview with the Dane for his newspaper column in *The Seattle Star*. The pastor's description of the twenty-nine-year-old former champion stated that he was "clean looking, neatly dressed, with a grip like a vise and an arm like a gnarled limb," and "His talk was slangy, but it was direct and well chosen." When asked about his religious life, Nelson commented, "My parents were Danish Lutherans. One of my brothers is studying at Berkeley, California for the ministry in the Methodist church. I go to church occasionally, it depends upon who I am with. But really I do not have any religion." In reflection, the pastor stated, "We parted friends, I came away convinced that 'Bat' was a good fellow in a bad business. Boxing on a gambling basis is a damning curse."[11]

Nelson would soon confront his religion but not on the terms he had hoped for. On August 10, his mother, Mary or "Mattie" Nelson was killed by a mail train on the Wabash Railroad at Burnham (Hegewisch), Illinois. She was returning from a shopping trip in nearby Hammond, with her friend Mrs. Annie Martin, and had just stepped off a Lake Shore & Michigan Southern train at the station. Nelson then waited for a freight train to pass before crossing the tracks. It was then that she was struck and killed by a mail train. Mrs. Martin narrowly escaped death and tried in vain to save the life of her friend. Nelson was only fifty-two years of age. Word reached the Battler while he and his brother Arthur were in Oregon. Nelson immediately canceled all his engagements in the West and prepared to return home. Telegraphing promoter James Coffroth, who had been working, or so the Battler believed, on matching him with Jimmy Britt, Nelson alerted him of the news and requested he postpone negotiations.

Following the events at home, Nelson headed east instead of west. He didn't feel he was being given the attention he deserved or the matches he felt that he had earned. A different direction, he believed, would mean a fresh start and hopefully in markets that would welcome him. While he had fought Eddie Lang in Memphis last year, he hadn't been northeast since his Philadelphia bout against Terry McGovern back in 1906. Perhaps it was time, he believed, to reconstruct the Battler, in a new set of surroundings north of the Mason-Dixon line. It was an enormous gamble that came with no guarantees.

Fifteen seconds after the bell sounded for the tenth round, referee Sheehan parted both boxers, then sent them to their corners. He then declared Nelson the victor over Cambridge boxer Billy Nixon, who was clearly nothing more than knockout bait by that time.[12] The previous rounds had been ugly. "The Battler did not box fair according to the rules," read the *Evening World*. "Nixon was examined by a physician after the bout and it was shown that he had been hit low in the ninth round."[13] While Sheehan thought the blow was clean, those ringside thought otherwise. Nelson had beaten Nixon by that time; the Cambridge fighter had insisted upon his suicidal approach of fighting close quarters with Nelson.

Nixon was not, however, without praise as he outboxed Nelson in some early rounds, and even managed some impressive combinations to the Battler's jaw. But Nelson was his relentless self and kept forcing his opponent about the ring inside the Armory Athletic Association in Boston, Massachusetts.

This day, September 19, saw another Nelson garner some press, as brother Charles Henry Nelson was said to be heading to Yale, from the University of California, to study medicine and perhaps become a professor. It seems Professor Elmer C. Moore, while renewing old acquaintanceships in California, sparred with Charles for exercise. When the professor left California, to resume his place at the head of the Department of Education at Yale, he invited Nelson to join him. The altruistic professor also defrayed Nelson's Yale tuition. The Battler couldn't have been happier for his brother and hoped to visit him if his travels took him to New Haven, Connecticut.

Fourteen Fights, Fast and Furious

The decision was made to set a grueling pace on the road to a comeback—bear in mind no former lightweight champion had charted such a course. The decision was made to divert the Battler's attention away from the recent loss of his mother and back to the ring. And done, understanding fully that a title can be replaced, but a mother cannot.

Two weeks later, on October 3, Nelson was back inside the same ring, this time against James Milburn "Young" Saylor.[14] The Indianapolis fighter was far from just a punching bag, as he had picked up newspaper decisions this year over some good fighters including Phil

Brock, Matty Baldwin, and Jack Redmond. The fight confirmed that the road ahead would be long: Nelson's head was no longer in the fight game, as his opposition fought at close quarters and held his ground. Taking all twelve rounds, Saylor was given the decision.

The accounts were depressing, but telling nonetheless: "Saylor held the upper hand every minute of the mussing and made Nelson look foolish at the latter's own game, infighting, when he battered the former champion all over the ring."[15]

Having twice defeated a tough opponent in "Knockout Brown," local fighter Willie Beecher was optimistic about his chance with the former champion on October 11.[16] And at the beginning of the fight it looked like Beecher just might have a chance. But the Battler, who took two rounds just to "warm up," then landed a destructive series of combinations to Beecher's face—drawing blood from his mouth and nose—in the third. Two lackluster rounds then passed before Nelson assumed complete control. By the ninth and tenth, Beecher looked as if he'd had enough; "it was the general opinion that Nelson had won handily."[17]

The fight, hosted by the Madison Athletic Club, was Nelson's first in New York City. The large Madison Square Garden crowd cheered the former champion, who was very touched by the response. Like many, Nelson was always mesmerized by his visits to New York. The memories came flooding back: his passage aboard the *Majestic* headed to Liverpool, England; being met by the English sportsman and his royal treatment; and being met again when he arrived home. It was hard not to get sentimental.

It was back to the Armory Athletic Association of Boston—the same site as the Nixon and Saylor fights—for the Battler, as he took on Philadelphia Pal Moore in a twelve-round contest on October 17.[18] Moore was a clever, fast and very accurate boxer, who was coming off a newspaper victory over Dick Hyland and two draws against Harlem Tommy Murphy. The Philadelphia fighter also held victories over Al Demont and Jim Driscoll and had both drawn and lost to Owen Moran.[19] Accounts of the fight had Moore landing blows at will. In typical Nelson style, the fighter took a beating before beginning his own offensive assault. But it was too little too late. Nelson, who had lost his sense of timing, was simply outboxed and Moore given the victory.

Two days after the Moore loss, Nelson, now 2–2–1 for the year, headed north to Augusta, Maine, for a six-round affair with "a second rater," as one newspaper described George Alger.[20] Alger, a Cambridge fighter, opted to stay out of range of Nelson. "Landing four punches to every one he received," Alger's hopes were to strike and back away before the Battler could return fire.[21] And it appeared to work, as most viewed the no decision as a loss for Nelson.

For the Battler, it was his first time fighting in Maine, and he wanted to extend his best wishes to the many fans who had traveled from Bangor, a city that had recently been devastated by fire. Nelson had witnessed such hardship in San Francisco after the quake and empathized with those who had suffered.

Word also traveled on this day that the preeminent New York State Athletic Commission announced that all fight contestants must break clean in the clinches. No longer in favor of fighters protecting themselves in the clinches, the move was part of the sweeping changes being made in the game. "Can it be true?" wrote boxing beat writer W.W. Naughton. "If so, farewell to loop-de-loop and the breast grazing uppercut."[22] The writer continues, "Furthermore, exit the Ad Wolgasts and Battling Nelsons and enter Matt Wells and Freddie Welshes. Welcome the straight left and sweeping right, and bid goodbye to the hundred and one little pokes and prods that can only be delivered when a fighter has his face flattened against his opponent's chest."[23] The order was seen as a benefit to English boxers, who favored the rule, but unfair to a generation of American boxers who had crafted their art under the old law.

Fighting the familiar face of Monte Dale on October 25, the Battler found himself next in Manchester, New Hampshire. Having knocked out Dale last year, in the third round of their battle in Kansas City, Nelson was hoping for a repeat performance. However, this time victory came via a slim fifteen-round decision and not a knockout. Dale, who had gone down four times to the count of nine, managed to make the fifteen-round distance. How he did it would be anybody's guess as Dale, who had fought six times since his last bout with the Dane, hadn't won a fight since December 1909, and that was a disqualification.[24] For Oscar, he was just grinding out a comeback, something he believed he had to do, even if there was no path to follow.

Watervliet (Troy, New York), located north of Albany, was known nearly as much for the sport of boxing as it was for being located on the main route of the Erie Canal—it was the home to two great prizefighters, John C. Heenan and John Morrissey. As part of his "comeback tour," Nelson found himself in upstate New York matched against Philadelphia fighter Frank Loughrey on November 6.[25] Scheduled for the maximum ten rounds at the Grogan Athletic Club, local fight fans were excited about the match. Loughrey, who weighed 133 pounds, rushed his catchweight opponent right from the start. It wasn't until the third round that the former champion really started to bore in on his adversary. "The crowd hissed Nelson in the sixth when he gave Loughrey the leg, nearly sending him to the floor," reported the *Evening World*. "Loughery was the popular favorite, and in the third the crowd yelled for a knockout when he landed several right and left jabs that shook The Battler."[26]

Following the no decision, and in a mark of pure sportsmanship, Nelson lauded Loughery for his efforts and predicted a great future for the boxer. A draw was how most spectators viewed the fight.

From one end of the Erie Canal to the other, as the Battler found himself in a Buffalo ring with Tommy Moore on November 10.[27] Although the fight would enter the record books as a ninth-round knockout win for Nelson, it was not a clean fight. In both the sixth and seventh rounds, Moore complained of low blows. And when he complained again in the eighth, the referee cautioned Nelson. By that time however most of the damage was done, and Moore could no longer answer. It was becoming very obvious that Nelson was getting frustrated with himself and his inability to routinely dispose of his opponents.

Fighting again inside Convention Hall in Buffalo, Nelson this time faced the French import Louis de Ponthieu of Paris.[28] Billed as the featherweight titleholder, de Ponthieu had won eight of his last ten fights before meeting Nelson on November 25. A protégé of lightweight champion (1899–1902) turned coach Frank Erne, de Ponthieu was a fast and very clever defensive fighter. Being thrown into the ring with a former champion like Nelson did, however, catch the fighter a bit off guard, as de Ponthieu couldn't believe the punishment his antagonist could endure.[29] It was the Dane's fourth no decision of the year, the third at the ten-round limit.

Frustrated by the inability to get a clean decision, Nelson crossed the border into Toronto, Ontario, and took on tomato-can Joseph Spero at the Agnes Street Theatre.[30] The November 30 clash, which was scheduled for a twenty-round distance, lasted only six. Spero, a Buffalo boxer who had never fought more than ten consecutive rounds, was given his ring moment of eternity, while Nelson settled for a check.

The first bout of December, on the 4th, matched the Battler against Andy Bezenah in Jeffersonville, Indiana.[31] When it was over, most saw the no decision as a rough, not to mention quick, ten-round draw. Hailing from Cincinnati, Bezenah was a veteran of over fifty fights, so it came as no surprise that he could make the distance. He had a solid following and was also a prolific fighter for manager John B. McKee of the National Sporting Club of Winnipeg, Manitoba. McKee was working—trying to establish relationships with certain fighters to perhaps convince them to fight in Canada—the Cincinnati market and hoped to match Bezenah again with Nelson, but next time in Manitoba.

Central New York hosted Nelson next as he took on hometown fighter Bobby Wilson in Utica, New York, on December 15.[32] Wilson weighed in at 135 pounds, while Nelson, who looked about seven pounds heavier, had taken the match as a catchweight contest. For the Battler, this time the warnings from the Referee were not about low blows but his butting tactics. Oneida County Athletic Club hosted the ten-round no decision, which was viewed as a win for Nelson.

From Utica, Nelson made his way southeast to Brooklyn, about 180 miles as the crow flies. There, on December 18, Nelson took on Willie Howard in a ten-rounder.[33] Howard, or ring sacrifice if you will, hadn't beaten a fighter with over ten fights' worth of experience, yet alone a former champion. Nevertheless, the Irving Athletic Club enjoyed watching Nelson easily defeat Howard in the no-decision event.

Three days before Christmas, "One-Round" Hogan was given the gift of outpointing a former champion in a ten-round no decision battle at the Madison Athletic Club.[34] The reality was painful; every New York newspaper declared Nelson's "comeback" essentially hopeless. Before one of the largest Brooklyn crowds in months, Hogan, a San Francisco fighter, was quicker, sharper and more prolific.

> Hogan gave the brittle-haired battler as severe a drubbing as Nelson has ever received in a limited-round contest. In the second round Hogan made Nelson's knees sag from the force of a right to the jaw, while in the tenth round Nelson was beaten back with a forceful left. Hogan was by far the cleverest boxer, for he landed his blows with precision, meeting the battler's rushes repeatedly with well-timed blows.[35]

Afterward—in another sign of a frustrated former champion, or poor sport, if you will—Nelson scoffed at the event, claiming he was never good in ten rounds and if Hogan was serious he would meet him on the West Coast in a twenty- or thirty-round event for $2,500 a side. Nelson fought at catchweight, while Hogan weighed in at 134 pounds.

On the final day of the year, Battling Nelson delivered a superb twenty-round performance against St. Paul boxer Jack Redmond.[36] For nine rounds Nelson waited patiently, taking numerous blows from his opponent, all with hopes that Redmond would punch himself out. In the tenth, however, the alarm went off in the Nelson corner, and the Battler went all out on Redmond. Had the confrontation lasted more than twenty rounds, many believed Redmond would have hit the canvas for good. And that's the same Jack Redmond who only a little more than a year ago unmercifully beat Ad Wolgast. Nelson's assault on his opponent's stomach found Redmond in a life-saving clinch during the last round, saving him from a knockout. The large New Orleans crowd—the event was held at the West Side Athletic Club in Gretna—was thrilled at the performance.

For Oscar Nelson, the holiday season was always a very special time, filled with love and laughter, and so many family memories. But this year, without his mother, it would be filled with far different emotions. Writing in his autobiography, "I am awful strong for Christmas at home and that hanging up the stocking thing still has a hold of me. Every Christmas as regular as a clock, I hang my sock, and my good old mother never fails to see that Santa Claus puts something in it."[37] This season he could not even bear to glance at the stocking. Add to this that many no longer saw him as a contender for the lightweight title, or a key player in his profession at the young age of twenty-nine, and you have some difficult obstacles for anyone to overcome.[38]

True to form, the former champion had attacked his issues with hard work and perseverance. Because he had always been a man of integrity, he remained popular with fans and a drawing card in virtually every market—something many former champions could not claim. In his heart, he knew he was a legitimate contender, and nobody was going to convince him otherwise.

Not taking into consideration his two exhibitions, Nelson appeared in sixteen fights in 1911, for a total of 165 rounds—an average of 10.3 rounds per battle. The last time he appeared in sixteen fights in a single year was 1903. As he increased his exposure, by fighting in new markets during his comeback, he did so by being matched with good, but not great, boxers. As a former champion he was breaking new ground, and defining, so he hoped, a comeback. Nelson added six wins, two losses and eight no decisions to his record, while also knocking out some debts.

The year saw a couple of other good battles: Ad Wolgast knocked out Owen Moran, for the very first time, in the thirteenth round of an Independence Day battle held in San Francisco, and Johnny Coulon took a twenty-round decision, and the bantam title, from the rugged Frankie Conley in New Orleans on February 26.

1912

In a year that found Albert Berry making the world's first parachute jump from an airplane, the RMS *Titanic* sinking at 2:20 in the morning and taking with her the lives of more than 1,500 people, and New Jersey governor Woodrow Wilson winning a landslide victory over Republican incumbent William Howard Taft, precariousness, in one form or another, seemed to be on the minds of many, including Battling Nelson, who was charting a delicate course through the lightweight division.

Following the holidays, Nelson was matched for ten rounds against lightweight Tommy O'Rourke in Springfield, Missouri, on January 9.[39] The fighter had been receiving favorable reviews, and frankly speaking, Nelson didn't consider it much of a challenge, so he took the fight. The no decision, however, favored O'Rourke who was said to have beaten Nelson "to a standstill."[40] Clear from the loss was that the Battler needed to get his head back into the fight game, but just how remained the question. Although last year's fight frequency was deemed too much by Team Nelson, it did keep their fighter's mind on boxing. They needed to find a balance between a serious assault on the championship mix and tending to their fighter's outside needs, so they set their sights on fighting at least once a month.

On February 26, it was off to Fort Smith, Arkansas, for a six-round scrap against Young Togo, the Japanese bantamweight.[41] Similar in style to Nelson, in that he could endure considerable punishment, Togo could also attract some media coverage, which was what the

Battler sorely needed. Although Nelson was given the victory, his inability to dispose of Togo actually worked to the Japanese fighter's advantage—the following day Togo was matched for a fifteen-round battle against Johnny Coulon, the bantam champion. Instead of being viewed as a contender, he was being viewed as a measuring stick for the role.

"I knocked him down so often I lost count of the exact number of times he was floored," claimed Bat. "In the sixth and last round I put him down five times, but he still came back with gameness of a fighting terrier, toeing the scratch."[42] When asked why he didn't dispose of Togo, the Dane responded, "because ... Eddie Robinson, who was also the promoter of the contest made me wear pillows instead of A.G. Spaulding No. 115 regulation [5 oz.] fighting gloves."[43]

While in Arkansas, the Battler couldn't resist the opportunity of throwing a few financial jabs at the press. It was time, he thought, to plant some positive notes regarding his finances. The press bit at the chance, and articles soon ran supporting "Battling Nelson, Big Financier." "For his six to 15-round bouts in the bushes, Nelson demands a guarantee of from $800 to $1,500 with a privilege of 30 to 50 percent of the gate receipts, and from $50 to $100 for training expenses," the *Evening Times* stated. "Nelson is today almost as popular a fighter as he was in his prime because he always gives the fans his best."[44] A question that should have been addressed and not ignored: Was Bat pricing himself out of contention?

On March 1, at the Dayton Gymnastic Club in Dayton, Ohio, Battling Nelson broke both of his hands during a fifteen-round draw against Columbus fighter Sammy Trott.[45] "I wore Spaulding's regulation gloves, and as Sammy was so easy to hit I put an extra amount of steam behind my blows and in the second round I bruised an old break in my left hand," Nelson claimed. "When the left was hurt I pulled Trott with it by jabbing and drawing him out for some good rights, which I turned loose with full force until the fourth round when I broke it."[46] As for making it through the fight, Nelson said, "although I was as harmless as a toothless dog I kept doing something all the time and Trott was too green and was kept too busy to realize I was harmless and he failed to grasp the golden opportunity. He is a good boy and has lots of time yet to learn and improve."[47]

Despite the terrible circumstances, Nelson appreciated the battle and respected the chance to appear before the Dayton Gymnastic Club.[48] Unprepared for the circumstance, the Battler really didn't know what to say, or what to do. Still believing he had a shot at the title, he added, "I guess I've about served my time and if I am forced to retire, may all my troubles be little battlers."[49]

Next stop for Battling Nelson, Youngstown, Ohio, and consultation with "Bonesetter" Reese about his mitts. With his comeback on hold, it was time for a damage assessment. While in town, Nelson had time to referee a fight between Tim O'Neil of Chicago and Tom McMahon of Spring Valley, Illinois. The Battler disqualified McMahon, whom he had warned numerous times, for "holding on" during the ninth round. It was a nice diversion for the Battler and one he seemed to enjoy.

Noticeably frustrated over his current health dilemma, it was reported out of St. Louis on April 15 that Battling Nelson had announced his retirement. "He said that the beating he received in the ring had impaired his constitution, and that he could no longer cope with the strong, youthful lightweights before the public." A bit presumptuous perhaps, but the article managed to run in a number of newspapers including the *Washington Times*.

Four days later, the *Albuquerque Evening Herald* ran an interesting article titled "Battling

Nelson Tells How He Was Bunged Up in Ring Career." Always good for a story, and now out of the ring, it was time for the Battler to pontificate. "Fighting," declared Bat Nelson recently, "is the only fun I have."[50] The article explained how the fight game has left him with "two cauliflower ears, two broken arms, two badly bunged-up hands, one broken thumb, and two broken ribs." The Battler then confessed, although some disagreed, "About the only thing that isn't changed since I took up the fighting game is the size of my head. Fifteen years ago, it was a 6⅞ hat fitted me. It still does today." The Dane then went on to discuss in detail each and every physical variation. The article concluded with details regarding a possible Nelson world tour. "I'll wind up my career in the greatest tour ever engineered by a pugilist," Nelson stated. "There will be six fighters, a picture machine operator and a business manager with the troupe. I have already entered into negotiations, which will net me $75,000, and I believe that before the tour is over I will have taken in more than $100,000. We will be gone for fifteen months."[51] As usual it was Bat being Bat, free press and putting the proverbial cart before the horse. In the days that followed, the ring would again lure him inside the ropes.

Well, John B. McKee, of the National Sporting Club, got his wish. He matched both Andy Bezenah and Battling Nelson for twelve rounds inside the auditorium rink in Winnipeg, Manitoba, Canada. On July 1, fight fans interested to see if Bat's mitts had healed properly, were treated to a compelling twelve-round display. Taking immediate charge, Nelson was the aggressor, forcing Bezenah to constantly break ground. The rugged no decision was seen in Nelson's favor.

The Battler opened slowly, trying to regain the feel in his mitts, before finding a comfortable rhythm. As his confidence grew, so too his lead, which was clear by the sixth. In the eleventh round, Bezenah managed to draw blood from Nelson's ear, and it made him angry. As mad as the Battler was, however, he couldn't reach Bezenah, who danced away. Both men fought like madmen in the twelfth and final round, with Bezenah too tired to score effectively and bleeding from the mouth. The no decision was seen in Nelson's favor. Referee Bun Foley had some difficult moments with both fighters. He couldn't get Bezenah to break from clinches, and he had to repeat warnings to Nelson about head butting. Bat was back to being Bat, and it looked and sounded good.

Meanwhile, Independence Day was shaping up to be a huge celebration for boxing fans. With two exciting fights on the docket, it was difficult to choose just where to turn your attention. Overshadowing the heavyweight championship battle between Jack Johnson and Fireman Jim Flynn, in Las Vegas, New Mexico, was the lightweight title match between Ad Wolgast and Joe Rivers in Vernon, California. The reason was simple, most fight fans believed: "The Johnson and Flynn contest is an even match in any sense. No one seriously regards Flynn as a fit opponent for the burly black. Neither in weight, in size, in reach, in strength, in skill— in fact, no requisites of a fighter—is the Colorado fireman to be classed with the champion; hence this uneven matching makes the Las Vegas affair seem like a farce."[52]

The Wolgast versus Rivers battle looked to be a far better pairing. The contest was viewed as being the first serious challenge Wolgast had faced since he took the title from Nelson on February 22, 1910.

> In the opinion of many ring experts, Wolgast is facing a crisis in his ring career. Rivers is recognized as one of the most dangerous boys in the lightweight brigade. He has fought his way honestly to a battle with the champion, and those who have seen him in action pronounce him in every department as formidable an opponent as his once great countryman, Aurelio Herrera.[53]

Johnson, a target for head butting and racial slurs, was awarded the fight because of his challenger's repeated fouling, while the lightweight confrontation proved to be boxing's most famous "double knockout." Late in the twelfth round, Joe Rivers went down, but in a delayed reaction, Wolgast fell atop Rivers. The referee, Jack Welch, clearly favoring champion Wolgast, helped him to his feet while counting out Rivers. The controversial ending stunned the boxing world, as eyewitnesses came forward to state that Wolgast had fouled Rivers.

Mickey McIntyre, "The Pride of Cape Breton," was scheduled next to meet Nelson in Winnipeg on July 12.[54] If you were going to travel all the way to Winnipeg, Nelson thought, then why not try to get the most out of the trip. However, McIntyre wasn't Bezenah, and he appeared to get the best of the Dane during the twelve-round "no decision." The *Edmonton Daily Bulletin* reporting that "Nelson was bleeding from the mouth, his left eye was closed, while his right lamp was badly discolored."[55]

Two days later, a rumor out of Chicago had Battling Nelson, former lightweight champion of the world, and Irma Kilgallen, the former Countess de Beaufort, as having been married in a Chicago suburb. A day later, it was denied by the Kilgallen family, who believed that the two reported lovebirds had not met in two years, and also by representatives of the Nelson family.

The report jarred Nelson, who was caught in Winnipeg as saying, "This marriage rumor is awful—honest, I haven't smiled in three days."[56] The former champion then displayed a picture in his watchcase. It was a profile of a smiling beautiful woman, "hair hung over her low forehead and a diamond lavalier around her shapely neck." The Battler then confirmed, "That's Miss Irma Kilgallen. I'm pretty much gone on her—have been for five years. I reckon she likes li'l old Bat some too. Time was when I thought I had a chance, but I took the count when she took The Count."[57]

"I'm free to admit that I am not married to Miss Kilgallen," the fighter stated reluctantly. "If I was do you think I'd be up here fighting a bunch of tin ears? I'd be down in Chicago honeymooning at the Annex."[58]

"Only seven weeks ago, I proposed that she and I start a honeymoon," Nelson surprised many by his admission. "'No, Bat, you and I had better just be good friends,' she was said to have replied. 'A burnt child dreads the fire I was friendly with that Count until I married him, and I've never liked him since.'"[59]

Nelson then went on to confess that Kilgallen had indeed turned him down and that the lavalier in the picture he had displayed was one he had given her. He believed she no longer had the piece of jewelry and questioned her interest in him. "What does a good looking

A panorama of the Vernon Arena during the Joe Rivers vs. Ad Wolgast fight on July 4, 1912. The fight would end in a controversial thirteenth-round victory for Wolgast (Library of Congress, Prints and Photograph Division, LC-USZ62–132446).

girl like Miss Kilgallen want of a banged up fighter for anyway?"[60] Then in a sad tone he added, "When I was a kid I was handsome, but that's a long time ago." He clearly didn't appreciate the publicity at this time, and stated half jokingly, "Irma's father will be watching me with a shotgun when I get back home."[61]

By the first week of the following month, however, a new name was being linked to the Battler, that of Denver cartoonist Fay King. It was said that the two had made the 14,147-foot journey up Pikes Peak, to be married on August 4. However, a priest that had been waiting for them there gave up and left. Both then decided to postpone the ceremony until a later date.[62] By late September, the *San Francisco Call*, one of the earliest dailies to link the two, had already noted that the couple was experiencing some rough spots in their relationship, no better exemplified then when the Battler, who never refused an interview, declined to discuss the topic.

Billed as a grudge match, the Battling Nelson versus Steve Ketchel clash held on September 2 in St. Joseph, Missouri, had an interesting twist.[63] The grudge was not Steve's but apparently that of Packey McFarland. "Packey and Nelson were great fighters in the old days," reported the *El Paso Herald*. "Packey failed to pay a bill that was past due and for which Bat had stood sponsor. This was the beginning of the break. Now that Nelson is fighting second raters Packey sees a chance to trim his lamps and he is ribbing Ketchel up to all of Bat's weak points which are legion just now."[64] This interesting twist proved to be the only thing interesting about the fifteen-round draw held that Monday afternoon.

When it comes to Danish fighters, much had been written about the Battler, and deservedly so. But it should also be noted that other Danes deserved notice during this period, boxers like Cyclone Johnny Thompson and "Fighting Dick" Nelson. Thompson, aka "Sycamore Kid," was a middleweight who fought from 1901 until 1914. He hailed from Sycamore, Illinois, and fought some familiar names like Dick Hyland, Rudy Unholz, and Packey McFarland. Nelson, alias Richard Christensen, was a New York City welterweight born in Frederiksberg, Denmark. He fought from 1905 until 1921 and took on some good challengers, including Dixie Kid, Young Corbett II, and George "Kid" Lavigne. Many outstanding Danish fighters were also approaching the horizon, including Anders Otto Petersen (December 16, 1902–April 28, 1966), a Danish flyweight who would win a silver medal in boxing at the 1920 Summer Olympics; Gotfred Svend Kristian Johansen (May 4, 1895–February 2, 1978), a Danish lightweight professional boxer who would compete in the 1920s; and Søren Peter Petersen (December 6, 1894–1945), a Danish heavyweight professional boxer who would later compete during the 1920s and 1930s.[65]

Back to his old stomping grounds of Hammond, Indiana, on November 14, Nelson was scheduled for a ten-rounder with local boy Art Stewart. Nelson did little to impress, however, even taking a nine count in the second round. Rallying back, one account said it best, "There was little steam to his punches."[66] Thankfully for the Dane, the fight entered the record books as a "ND10."[67]

On the same night, the idol of New York's East Side, Leach Cross, silenced One Round Hogan in the third round during their city clash. Both fighters fought over the lightweight limit. Afterward, Cross vented his views believing he was steps away from a lightweight title match; he was, in fact, days away from fighting a former champion.

For ten rounds, on November 28, Leach Cross exhibited just why he deserved a title shot.[68] Inflicting a great deal of punishment upon the Battler, Cross firmly outpointed Nelson.

"Cross weighed 138 pounds at the ringside and Nelson four ounces heavier. Cross started in with the left jabs to the face and right and left hooks to the head. The 'battler' was outclassed, but managed to land hard on the jaw with rights and lefts and had Cross crouching at the end of the initial round."[69]

Following the fight, Cross was ecstatic, even jumping out of the ring after shaking hands with Nelson. When the cheers at the end of the struggle subsided, Nelson held up his right glove for a hearing and shouted in a sign of pure sportsmanship: "Despite all that has been said of my poor condition, I am glad I got this opportunity of showing you all how feeble I am going up against one of the best men you've got here. I thank you."

"The Fighting Dentist," Louis Charles Wallach, aka Leach Cross, picked up a dental degree from New York University just in case his boxing career faltered (Library of Congress, Prints and Photograph Division, LC-DIG-ggbain-10655).

"Bat Still at It" was the article header in the *Tacoma Times* as Nelson took an early holiday gift, a six-round match against the light hitter Teddy Maloney on December 13.[70] Not much was expected from the Philadelphia fight, and not much was given during the six-round no decision. Not surprisingly, the partisan Philadelphia newspapers saw the fight as a draw for their hometown fighter. The same media had claimed that Maloney drew Ad Wolgast in six rounds back in October; though both fighters were covered with blood at the end of their struggle, fans who saw the fight believed the scrap belonged to Wolgast and "that the champion was stalling, fighting only when pushed."[71]

Heading northwest for a December 20 battle, it was on to the anthracite hills of Tamaqua, Pennsylvania, for Nelson. Having taken the ten-rounder against Jim Bonner, a graduate of the coal mines, The Battler was a bit surprised when his adversary overtipped the scales.[72] Bonner outweighed him by ten pounds and stood head and shoulders above the Dane. Nelson, true to the Battler's spirit, refused to take the weight forfeit. "I'm here for a test, not to take a man's forfeit," Nelson barked. "Let him keep his money. If he gives me the test tonight, I'm satisfied to let him keep the forfeit."[73] Nelson then gamely defeated Bonner, before heading home. With another ten-round no decision in his pocket, Nelson turned his attention to the holidays.

Having spent Christmas with his family in Hegewisch, Nelson was off to Columbus, Ohio, to meet Yankee Schwartz, a tough Philadelphia fighter on December 31.[74] As a seasoned veteran, Schwartz had fought many good fighters, including Joe Thiel, Tommy Devlin, Willie Ritchie, and Joe Mandot. "Nelson had the better of it in the second and seventh rounds, but in the others Schwartz was reportedly applauded for his rushing work." An eight-round no decision was how it appeared on Nelson's annual record.[75]

Following the Schwartz fight, Nelson repeated his desire for another title shot, claiming he would beat Willie Ritchie then retire. Ritchie took the lightweight crown (USA version), when after dropping the Michigan Wildcat twice in the sixteenth round a frustrated Wolgast fired two shots from the canvas at Willie's groin and was disqualified.

In 1912, at thirty years of age, Oscar "Battling" Matthew Nelson appeared in eleven fights, for a total of 114 rounds. His annual performance earns him one win, two draws and eight no decisions. His comeback, now in its second year, was stalled due to injury. The resurgence hasn't been pretty, but it has paid some bills and Nelson continues to endure.

On the social front, the Battler was accused of marrying Irma Kilgallen. Unfortunately, at least from Oscar's perspective, the hearsay proved to be fiction. However, the former Countess de Beaufort, and the alluring woman whose picture he carried in his watchcase, remained forever, so he claimed, in his heart. But Oscar had always been a master of contradicting his clarifications, and later dragged a different woman, cartoonist Fay King, to the top of Pikes Peak in an attempted marriage ceremony. Similar to many aspects of his comeback, his behavior outside of the ring was ambiguous and mercurial.

The year also records a few more notable clashes: Dropped twice and nearly out in the second round, Al Palzer knocked out the hard-punching Bombardier Billy Wells in the third of their June 28 New York battle; ex-feather champion Abe Attell fights to a bloody twenty-round draw against Harlem Tommy Murphy on August 3 in San Francisco; and Luther McCarthy knocked out onetime heavyweight contender Al Kaufmann in the second round on October 12 in San Francisco.

Twelve

1913

Fay and a Final Descent

> I have always felt that I would be the greatest fighter in my class. It is in the stars, and, although I am not superstitious, I can't help believing that I was ordained to be a successful fighter.
> —Oscar "Battling" Matthew Nelson[1]

Woodrow Wilson succeeded William Howard Taft as the twenty-eighth president of the United States, Pancho Villa returned to Mexico from his self-imposed exile in the United States to stir things up a bit south of the border, and the Sixteenth Amendment to the U.S. Constitution was ratified, authorizing the federal government to impose and collect income taxes. And, as unlikely as it may sound, all three events would play into the lives of many people, including Battling Nelson.

Over 500 days into his comeback, the Dane was still—and let's face it, perhaps the only person on earth who believed it was still feasible—trying to fight his way into contention for the lightweight title. Was it even realistic at this point? Of the three who had held the crown before him, none had done so. The Battler, who believed in the sui genris nature of skills, had now fought more post-title fights than the trio combined. If he was genuinely interested in a resurgence and not just picking up some easy money along a path that just happened to include some business and love interests, he needed to chart a more effective course. And he needed to do it quickly.

Only the Beginning

Before a large crowd at the Grunewald Theater in New Orleans, local boy Frankie Russell dominated Battling Nelson for ten rounds.[2] Having the best of not only a majority of rounds but of every round, Russell was awarded the decision by referee Wambsgans.

"Nelson protested against the decision, declaring that after his workout he was not feeling well and he and Russell had shaken hands in an agreement that no decision should be rendered that they did not wish to disappoint the crowd," stated the *Rice Belt Journal*. "At the end of the tenth round, however, Russell was declared the winner. Nelson had tried to shake hands at the opening of the tenth, but Russell refused."[3]

The one-sided affair saw a very slow Battling Nelson break his right hand in the last round while trying to deliver a right hook to the face of Russell. It was not the type of performance any prizefighter wants to begin a year with, and certainly not one trying to reestablish himself as a contender. Add to this an excess of unfavorable newspaper comments like, "He was nothing like his condition of one year ago" and "He never woke up," and you have a very unpleasant circumstance.[4]

The news just devastated Bat, in between his shouts for a March rematch against Russell, he just shook his head in disbelief.

Fay Barbara King

It takes a special person to enjoy the gifts and talents of a cartoonist, or a visual artist who creates a simple drawing showing the features of its subjects in a humorously exaggerated approach, especially a satirical one for a newspaper or magazine. And it takes a very special person to include such work inside a book, like an autobiography. But that was how much the art of cartooning meant to Battling Nelson.

Including the work of two of the foremost cartoonists in the world—T.A. Dorgan, known as TAD, the sporting cartoonist of the *New York Evening Journal*, and Robert Edgren, known as Bob Edgren, the sporting editor and cartoonist of the *New York Evening World*—in a book about your life in boxing, was as natural to Nelson as putting on gloves before a boxing match.

In the days before cost-effective photographic reproduction in newspapers, line drawings and cartoons offered a simple answer to illustrate articles. And not only were they solutions, but they were also entertaining, especially if you had the talent of a Dorgan or Edgren behind the pen. Nelson loved the caricatures of himself. Drawings depicting him with the moptop hairstyles or alongside a giant twice his size were as entertaining as a moving picture. He would pick up a newspaper and just begin laughing, motioning to others to share in a cartoon.

When we last left cartoonist Fay Barbara King, she and the Battler had just made their way to the top of Pikes Peak—sounds like the perfect cartoon scenario—to exchange marital vows. However, a priest of little patience and obviously not a boxing fan could wait no longer and left the summit for lower ground. This left the couple without a celebrant and, as it sounds,

The beautiful Mrs. Oscar Nelson, formerly Fay Barbara King, was a talented cartoonist (Library of Congress, Prints and Photograph Division, LC-DIG-ggbain-12341).

without an alternative plan. In January 1913, it appeared as if the couple had opted for a more conventional approach to matrimony, such as building a foundation through their families.

Three weeks into a new year, and as if the gong had been rung, Nelson began to fire off telegrams, in rapid succession, to Jack King of Portland, Oregon. During a thirty-six-hour period, he sent twenty telegrams from Denver pleading for his consent to marriage. Nelson was in Denver visiting with his twenty-three-year-old love interest, Fay King, who had been employed as a cartoonist for a local paper for over a year. It was believed that if Mr. King consented, the couple would then head to Hegewisch, where the marriage would take place on January 25.

Petite Miss King, who stood five feet five inches tall, weighed 123 pounds and had large engaging eyes, dark hair and a rounded chin, confirmed that for seven years—you can do the math—the courtship had gone on more smoothly. "I have kept company with many young men," said Miss King as she stood on the steps of an eastbound Rock Island train on the evening of January 21, 1912. "It seems like it had to be, but we only made up our minds today. I never could see anyone else than Mr. Nelson."[5] For the record, the couple met when she was sent to interview him.

Nelson had recently returned from Youngstown, Ohio, where he had sought the services of the "baseball surgeon," bonesetter Reese, who had been minding his mitts. The surgeon confirmed that the Battler would soon be back in the ring. Miss King also confirmed that the repair of his fighting mitts was no longer a prerequisite for marriage.

The Reverend W.E. Pearson, pastor of the Walker Station Lutheran Church in Moline, also received a telegram from the Battler: "Rev. W.E. Pearson, Moline: Will be married tomorrow. Can you perform the ceremony in Hegewisch? Battling Nelson."[6] Having officiated other services for the family—the reverend was once stationed in the Nelson's hometown—Mr. Pearson was more than happy to comply.

Nelson's manager Jack Robinson was said to have "chartered two trains to carry the bridal party to and from Hegewisch, hired a brass band to furnish music, obtained a marriage license, completed a holiday program for Bat's native city, arranged for a complete wedding party from preacher to ring bearers and ordered a wedding feast."[7]

Upon their arrival—for numerologists the future Mr. and Mrs. Nelson arrived at the LaSalle Station on track 13, occupying berth 13, and it was also the skidoo of January—the couple was met by a crowd of friends before speeding across Chicago on their special trains complete with band. After the wedding, the couple would return to Chicago. It would be a hasty honeymoon, however, as the Dane was scheduled for a clash in Racine, Wisconsin, on February 5.

"The ceremony was brief, but as the final words fell from the minister's lips the bride was overcome by the nervous strain, swayed, and toppled over into her husband's arms, sobbing violently. 'Bat' soothed his bride, and pretty soon she smiled and said, 'I feel much better after my cry.'"[8] Of the key players, Jack Robinson was best man and Miss Ida Nelson, sister of the groom, was maid of honor.

"I'm the happiest guy in the world," Nelson confirmed before commenting on the couple's future plans. "She'll probably devote her time to illustrating my map. But I'll stay in the ring. I've got to, as that's the only way I have of making a living."[9]

Following the ceremony the couple traveled to a wedding breakfast held in their honor at the Wellington Hotel. The event included a wedding program that featured a photograph of the couple taken back in August 1912, as they were leaving Pikes Peak, even noting that the trip ended in an engagement.

However, in less than a week the couple's relationship began to unravel. First the news that Mrs. Nelson decided upon a brisk exit to fill a contract as an artist on the *Denver Post*, thus postponing the couple's honeymoon. Then the disparaging headline that ran on January 28 in the *San Francisco Call* that read, "Mrs. Bat Nelson Calls Bat's Town a Disease." Unfortunately, this incident was followed by another article that implicated manager, Jack Robinson, as a supporter of her claim. Although the subtitle of the article read, "Fighter, Not Disheartened over Her Slam, Yearns to Get at Richie," those who knew the Dane knew better.

Thirty-six days after their wedding it was announced by friends of Mrs. Nelson that Battling Nelson would be greeted "with a summons in a suit for divorce when he arrives in Denver on March 5." That "she was kidnapped by Battling Nelson on the night of January 20 for her marriage three days later at the fighter's home will be the charge upon which the suit will be based."[10]

Feeling necessary to reiterate the facts as her legal team saw them, "Fay King remained three days as Nelson's wife. She left for Denver on Sunday night following the marriage and then went on to Portland, Oregon, to visit her parents before resuming her work at the *Post*."[11]

"Nelson heard of my reported engagement to a Denver man and he stopped his fighting engagements to come here for me," said Mrs. Nelson on February 28. "He took me by storm and after I was weak and a nervous wreck from resisting him and his proposals he forced me into a taxicab and rushed me off to the station."[12]

"I realized that I had made a mistake the day of the wedding and the first opportunity I got I hurried back to Denver," she confessed. "I will go right on working on the *Post* as though the affair had never happened. The marriage must not and will not stand."[13]

Everyone in Hegewisch was stunned by the news, especially those who took part in the event. Miss Ida Nelson, Bat's sister, even confirmed that she had received both a letter recently from her brother that gave no indication of any trouble, and one from her sister-in-law that in her words was "brimful of love."

Battling Nelson, who arrived in Savannah, Georgia, on this day, had no knowledge of any of his wife's intentions, stating that he planned to meet Mrs. Nelson either in Chicago or in Denver. The Battler reiterated, "We are on the best of Terms."[14]

"Wealth cannot compensate me for a loveless marriage," Fay King Nelson commented from Denver. "I will not ask a cent of alimony. I don't want money and beautiful houses without love."[15]

"As a friend Bat was everything in the world to me," she continued, "but friendship isn't marriage. I believe he will understand the unhappiness of my position sufficiently to assist rather than obstruct my efforts to obtain a divorce. I suppose everyone will wonder about it, but I was just trying to find happiness—that's all." She then stated her dissatisfaction with her ceremony in Hegewisch and ended her comments by stating, "I don't want to criticize Bat though. He is the best fellow in the world."[16]

On March 16, the *Times Dispatch* of Richmond, Virginia, ran likely the most creative literary approach to the Battler's dilemma that they titled, "Battling Nelson's Worst Knock Out! The Real Inside Story of the Little Lightweight Champion's Battle with Matrimony and Why He Got the Count So Soon." With a masthead depicting a cut and battered angel tearing up a postal card marital announcement of the couple, the article then details five rounds plus a post-mortem: Round one takes the reader back to Portland, Oregon, three years ago, just after Bat's visit to Yellowstone, and speaks to the Battler's infatuation, Miss King; round two takes place a year later with Bat armed with a $1,000 diamond engagement ring to lure Miss King to his corner; in round three the ring lands upon Miss King; round four is fought in Hegewisch on January 22 when the couple receives their marriage license; round five is fought at the Wellington Hotel in Chicago the next morning when Fay reads the following tribute to "My Friends," printed on the Wedding Breakfast menu card:

> Barrat O'Hara, Lieut.-Governor, Illinois, Joseph W. Latimer, My Attorney, Mark A. Foote, U.S. Commissioner, Johnny Coulon, World's Bantamweight Champion, Robert Clement, My Investor, William A. McGuire, Author of "The Divorce?" My Dramatist, John R. Robinson, My Manager, Fay King Nelson, My Bride, Kathryn Pearl Robinson, My Manager's Bride.[17]

This was followed by a quick exit and finally, The Post Mortem—two position statements by long-distance telegraph.

The first reads,

> Denver, Colo., March 12. Mrs. Fay King Nelson, wife of Battling Nelson, who has resumed her work as a cartoonist here, makes the following statement regarding their separation: "I don't want Battling Nelson nor any of the luxuries or money he can give me—I just want my freedom. And I intend to be freed from him, for I am going through with my plans for a divorce. His claim that there is another man in the case is absolutely false and he will have a hot time trying to prove this if he brings a counter suit.
>
> I won't have a thing to do with him, when he comes to Denver. I am going to get a divorce from him just as soon as it can be arranged. I won't even see him or have anything to do with him, except to have my attorney arrange for a settlement and the divorce.
>
> I realized that I had made a mistake the day of the wedding and the first opportunity I got I hurried back to Denver. I want to keep on working as a newspaper cartoonist and make my own living until I meet a man I can love, whether he is rich or poor.
>
> If Bat Nelson owned the whole of Chicago instead of most of Hegewisch, I wouldn't take a cent of his money. I have even refused to accept his wedding presents.
>
> I just want him to free me, for I never could be happy with him. I told him so repeatedly, but he rushed me off my feet when we were married. Until I meet a man I can love I want to work alone earning my own living. I never met such a man."[18]

The second telegraph reads,

> Atlanta, Ga., March 12. Battling Nelson's manager John R. Robinson, speaking for the pugilist about his domestic troubles, made this statement: "Battling Nelson is the cleanest minded and most honest man I have ever known, and I have been in the newspaper business, meeting all manner of men, for a lifetime. Mrs. Nelson and her folks are taking a foul advantage of him and I am not going to stand by and see him get the short end of the deal.
>
> I have read letters from Mrs. Nelson when she was plain Fay King that eulogizes the fighter to the sky. There are no words in the English language that she did not use in praising him and every word was the truth. These letters have continued for years. To use her own expression, he was a demi-god to her.
>
> Then she went back to Denver, under the hypnotic influence of the 'other man.' That's the entire answer. Nelson will never allow her to get a divorce. His hands are absolutely clean in this matter, but he is too game to show the pain he is suffering. After the time limit of two years for desertion, as provided by the laws of our state [Illinois] have passed, he will sue her for divorce. He will be the one to get the decree, not she. In the meantime, Attorney Latimer will look after the matter and see that no shyster lawyer, looking for a big fee from the Nelson bank roll, puts anything over on Bat. And if that 'other man' ever crosses Nelson's path, it's a job for the emergency hospital."[19]

To add insult to injury, and there was plenty of both, the cartoons used to illustrate the article were penned by Fay King.

Even Bat, likely to the displeasure of Attorney Latimer, put pen to paper to explain some of his views. On March 26, he wrote an article he titled "Bat Nelson in Philosophic Vein." In it he answered the question most had been asking him, "Am I matrimonially discouraged?"

> Emphatically no. Just because one attempt before the altar has been apparently unsuccessful I cannot see why I should sour on womankind and say the entire sex is forever cut from my calling list. I can still see the bright side of life, and I really believe no man can ultimately achieve all the happiness in life until he meets the right woman, and she looks upon him as the right man.[20]

Divorce has never been pretty, and having one play out before the public was painful for everyone involved. At a rate of 0.9 per thousand in 1913, it was still considered uncommon, and perhaps that added to the infatuation.[21] Some beat writers came to Bat's rescue and were quick to point to other boxers who had had their fair share of hard luck in tackling the matrimonial game. They included Young Corbett (William H. Rothwell), who had been recently separated; Kid McCoy, who had visited the altar no less than eight times; Richard K. Fox, who had just taken wife number three; Bob Fitzsimmons, who came to America with a wife and baby, later separated; and mention of Jack Johnson, who nobody knows how many times he has been married.

By April, it was reported that the couple had decided to try to stick it out for one year and then separate. The news came while the Nelsons were visiting the nation's capital, Washington, D.C. The following week, on April 12, Mrs. Battling Nelson made her visit to Manhattan and found it "Up to the Billing," even penning a short piece about her experiences for the *Evening World*.

On May 5, out of Chicago came the announcement that Mrs. Battling Nelson, Fay King, had requested that Labor Day would be the Dane's last fight—this because it would be the eighteenth anniversary of his fighting career. The newspapers were quick to jump on the news. "Eulogizing Nelson would mean nothing but a repetition of facts that have been printed thousands of times all over this continent. He is undoubtedly the most widely known and popular fighter that ever donned the gloves," stated the *Ogden Standard*, who went on to detail their claim:

> As an instance of his popularity we can recite what happened after Ad Wolgast wrenched the lightweight crown from Nelson. Wolgast paraded his honors for ten weeks and earned $10,000. Nelson went out before the public and within thirteen weeks gathered in $16,636. He leaves the ring with a fortune estimated at $300,00. His income is at the rate of $700 a month. He's entitled to every dollar, for he gave value for value received.[22]

In some related summer notes about the couple: the Reverend W.E. Pearson, pastor of Immanuel Lutheran Church in Moline, who married the Nelson's, had his resignation accepted and would be moving on to either Chicago or Willmar, Minnesota; Battling Nelson filed a $10,000 lawsuit against the Ridgway Construction Company of Boston, which operated the Nautical Gardens at Revere, for being ejected, along with his wife, from the property for improper dancing; and finally, in proof that anything related to Nelson during this period could make it into the press, Nelson's pet mule, Jinney, had disappeared from the former champ's home in Hegewisch.

After giving it an old-fashioned try, and having lived out much of her tumultuous relationship with the press, Fay King would slip away in November 1913. Battling Nelson would be granted a divorce in March 1916. In a world dominated by men, Fay King would become an extraordinarily gifted cartoonist, considered along with such names as Ethel Hays and

Nell Brinkley. She was also never hesitant to pass along some advice regarding relationships: "Funny wot a lotta faith some of these flapper brides have in the promises their new husbands make 'em, when history shows that this guy couldn't get along with the two or three wives he had before he married her!"[23]

Bearing in mind Nelson's marriage, and the distractions of his separation, we will return to the other ring.

Back on Track

The life of a boxer is short, a fighter even shorter; to be remembered for who you fought, even if it is shorter still, is better than not being recalled at all. Ray, or "Jack" Sorenson, whom the Battler would greet on February 5, just wanted to go the distance. "When Battling Nelson met Ray Sorenson at Racine the rounds were cut to two minutes by the club as it was feared the famous Battler might put the home boy away for the ten count and they did not want any of it," reported the *El Paso Herald*.[24] The fight would go the ten intervals to a "ND10."

For the Battler, the bout took a backseat to his new aspiration—or so he relayed to the press to ensure some free publicity—of becoming a racer. Having occasion to visit the Case automobile factory in Racine to view personally the creations of Louis Disbrow, along with a number of others, the fighter just couldn't resist the chance at getting behind the wheel. "Bat took the Case '30' racer out on the slippery pavements of Racine, and is credited with doing a mile at the rate of one hundred miles an hour. As he stepped from the car he remarked: 'I guess this automobile racing is just the thing that I am after. If I can get a driver's license from the Three A's, it's me for the track.' Incidentally, one of his wedding gifts to his bride was a Case '40' touring car."[25]

Setting his racing aspirations aside for the moment, it was back to the fight game on February 11. In a ten-rounder held at Tamaqua, Pennsylvania, Battling Nelson dropped Harry Dillon of New York four times before finally knocking him out in the tenth round.[26] The club physician wisely stopped the fight, fearing a fatality—taking four nine counts before a final blow can be a dangerous prelude. No doubt memorable to Dillion because of his opponent, the contest would also prove historic to Nelson, as he paid $132 for the privilege of fighting.

The promoter of the show was Bill Andrews, an old friend, one from the early days of Nelson's career. Late in the afternoon on the day of the fight, a large and intense snowstorm began brewing. As fight time neared, the drifts were reaching heights able to paralyze railroad traffic and therefore hinder attendance. As it neared the time to sound the opening bell, only a handful of fans were in the house. Andrews, noticeably upset, then confronted Nelson in his dressing room. "We've taken in just about enough to pay for the lights and hall rent and about half of Dillon's guarantee," spoke Andrews. "I haven't a dollar to pay you your guarantee."

"That's all right Bill," answered Nelson. "No use calling off the bout. Let it go on. I'll do without my divvy and make up the difference between what you've taken in and what Dillon's guarantee is." Coming up $132 short, Nelson then gave Andrews his check for the amount, stating, "I'm glad to do it, Bill, to show you that I appreciate your kindness of the other days."[27]

Boxing can cost you, and not just in the pocketbook. A recent heading in the *Evening*

Times read, "Cost of Success Heavy for Boxers, Many Masters of the Art of Fighting Pass from the Scene of Activity." The inspiration for the article was gleaned from a former lightweight contender named "Kid" Parker, of Denver, who had been institutionalized in an asylum. Suffering from hallucinations, he was one of many boxers who would likely spend his remaining days under near constant care, unable to cope with everyday living. Terry McGovern, who terrorized countless opponents in the ring, was sent to a sanitarium in Connecticut "because of apparently weakening mentality."[28] Off New York, at Blackwell's Island rested another famous lightweight, "Young" Griffo, considered by some as one of the cleverest of all boxers. Now down and out, he was "a victim of dissipation of years which has affected his mentality as well as his health."[29] Others victims mentioned in the article included Joe Gans, George Dixon and "Wilmington Jack" Daly. It was very clear, even at this time, the grave danger a boxer might face as a result of repeated concussive and sub-concussive blows.[30]

After such a fine show of sportsmanship in his previous bout, the last thing Nelson anticipated was an opponent turned wrestler biting him and drawing blood from his arm, but that is precisely what he got.[31] In return, Joe Burke from Wilkes Barre, Pennsylvania, got a ten-round pounding from the Battler that he wouldn't soon forget.[32] The scrap, held in Easton, Pennsylvania, on February 17, entered the record books as a ten-round no decision.

More of an exhibition than boxing, this match should never have been made. Burke—who weighed 150 pounds by the way—was not the type, or caliber of fighter, the Dane needed to face at this point in his career—the combined record of the five fighters Burke faced before Nelson was 9–4–0.[33]

In New Bedford, Massachusetts, on February 22, Battling Nelson fought twelve vicious rounds to a draw with Bay Wood of Fall River.[34] Wood decided to take it to the former champ through his rushing and aggressiveness. But Bat soon negated his opponent's efforts through vicious uppercuts.

The packed Saturday afternoon crowd was impressed with the Dane's one-armed defense—Nelson fought impaired, as his left was encased in an elastic bandage. Despite the fact that there were no knockdowns during the clash, Nelson managed to stagger a damaged Wood in the seventh round.

Cedar Rapids lightweight Frank C. Whitney was next to confront the Battler.[35] Managed by Billy Brown, Whitney was a dangerous boxer who had never been knocked out, or knocked down. The ten-round Atlanta engagement, held on March 5, was fought to an anti-climactic no decision.

Nelson again declared that he intended to keep on Willie Ritchie's trail until he received his title bout. Still scoffing at retirement, the Dane stated, "My stamina and punching powers are as good as they ever were. I am going much better than when I fought Leach Cross here. My hands are in grand shape. I am certainly going after Ritchie for a chance at the title. Ritchie figures me all in, and therefore ought to take the opportunity of getting some easy money. He looks like a papier mâché champion to me, and I think I can tear him into little pieces at about 30 pounds."[36]

"Another thing," Nelson couldn't resist spouting, "I am cleaning up at the rate of about $25,000 a year. I made $3,200 last week. Wouldn't a man capable of making $25,000 a year be foolish to retire from business at the age of 30? I am going to buy up that tenth part of Hegewisch which is owned by outsiders before I quit the game."[37]

During the next thirty-seven days, Battling Nelson would fight four times before entering the ring against his erstwhile nemesis Ad Wolgast. Although they could hardly be considered as adequate preparation for a fighter like the "Michigan Wildcat," they did fit the Battler's schedule and criteria.

It was Nelson versus Malone on March 27, 1913. Dancing ten rounds to a no decision against Denver fighter Mike Malone proved easy money for the Battler, who just happened to be in Pueblo, Colorado, on a vaudeville engagement, not to mention tending to some legal issues.[38] Malone, who had lost four of his past five previous decisions, was nothing more than a punching bag for Nelson.

It was back to New Bedford, Massachusetts, for another twelve-round draw with Bay Wood on April 19, followed by another local bout ten days later. "Battling Nelson lost the decision to Gilbert Gallant of Chelsea in a twelve round bout at the New Atlas A.A. here tonight," was the account out of Boston the following morning. "Gallant administered severe punishment to the former champion and had him wobbly in several rounds."[39] Gallant had the ability to fight when he wanted to, and since the fight was already in his hometown, he did so.

From Boston, it was back to the National Athletic Club in Philadelphia. There, hometown boy Pat Bradley bested Battling Nelson, the former lightweight champion, on May 3 in a six-rounder.[40] Bradley, took the affair—if you knew him you knew he hated to leave town—because it was in his backyard, and it was the former champion. Bradley was trying to match himself with quality fighters to ensure a better payday. Also, he felt that if he kept his distance, he could go the distance, which he did. Bradley's hometown partisan "ragsheets," I mean broadsheets, gave him the fight, but it entered the books as an "ND6."

On to Wolgast

"The idea of yanking the two old derelicts out of the Sargasso sea of pugilism seemed too amusing for anything," penned the irrepressible W.W. Naughton. "Where on all this wide earth is there a line of endeavor, apart from fisticuffs, wherein men are considered to have outlived their usefulness at either 25 or 35?" Wolgast represented the former age, while the Battler, only 31, the latter. "Nelson, after years of invincibility, suddenly faded away and lost his laurels at the age of 27," Naughton continues. "Wolgast was relieved of his championship at 24."[41]

Boston fighter Gilbert Gallant, a prolific boxer, headed west a couple of times hoping to capitalize on his ring abilities. He would fight from 1911 until 1927, with a majority of his victories east of the Mississippi River (Library of Congress, Prints and Photograph Division, LC-DIG-ggbain-10115).

When the dust settled around the aging jokes, it was back to boxing and the fact that the bout represented the unique opportunity to look back in time. "With both Nelson and Wolgast there is a little something on which to build a flimsy argument that, given the chance, things might be as they were," Naughton continued. "Neither of them was knocked out in the real sense when relieved of his title. Nelson was lurching across the ring at Richmond when referee Eddie Smith halted him and proclaimed Ad Wolgast the new king of 133 pounders. Wolgast lost his crown on a foul."[42] For those who weren't at the their battle in 1910, it would be the closest chance they would have to relive history.

"Battling" Nelson boxed Ad (Adolph Wolgust) Wolgast for ten rounds inside the Elite Arena in Milwaukee on October 13, in a contest that was one of the hardest and fastest ever seen. It was believed—the fight ending in the requisite no decision—that Wolgast defeated Nelson by taking eight of the ten rounds, with two seen as even.

> Nelson half blinded with the pain of punishment and shattered hands, left the ring grinning in ghostly fashion in response to the wild cheers of his friends. Wolgast, too fat and unfit to finish his ancient enemy, but rosy and rugged, was dog tired at the end—almost done in his efforts to land the knockout punch on his bruised and bleeding foe.[43]

The faces in the crowd were just mesmerized by the sheer presence of both of these gladiators in the ring. "Almost from the start of the scrap Wolgast was the master of the situation. He banged away with a left hook to the head and ribs, and sneaked in with a right now and then, that seemed like the Wolgast punches of old. But Nelson, his weary legs sagging under him, swayed this way and that, as lucky as a drunken man to get out of the danger of the knockout."[44]

As the final rounds approached, not a soul took their eye off the ring.

> Just before the ninth round closed Nelson got a punch full in the section just above the belt and would have collapsed completely but for the support of the ropes. The more humane in the crowd were shifting in their seats and uneasily murmuring that it should be stopped, but the appalling gameness of the Dane quieted the crowd. One rally by Bat, a tap landed on Wolgast, and the mob would break into a roar of approval. Nelson's gameness was appalling. More than one man asked his neighbor how it was possible, but never took his eye off the gory spectacle in the ring.[45]

And, just like that it was over. As the fighter's exited the ring, and their shadows passed over the cords one last time, the vibration shook droplets of blood from the ropes. In unison they sang, and wondered who would listen.

In what many believed—okay, hoped—was his last year as a professional fighter, Battling Nelson appeared in 11 fights, for a total of 112 rounds—an average of 10.1 rounds per battle. His annual performance earned him one win, one loss, two draws and seven no decisions to add to his career totals. For all intents and purposes the comeback trail appeared to be drawing to a close. But, if it had to come to an end, then it was best that it ended at the mitts of Wolgast, a fellow Hall of Famer.

There were other notable clashes in 1913: Luther McCarty picked up the "White Hope" heavyweight title by thrashing Al Palzer in an eighteen-round knockout on January 1 in Vernon, California; Frank Klaus captured the middle crown in a fifteen-round foul by Billy Papke on March 5 in Paris, France; after drawing Wolgast earlier in the year, Harlem Tommy Murphy took a twenty-round victory on April 19 in Daly City, California; on May 24, in Calgary, Alberta, Luther McCarty, after taking a low blow in a clinch from Arthur Pelkey, then died shortly after from a fractured neck; in his only heavyweight title defense against a black challenger, Jack Johnson, despite a broken left arm, retained his crown in a ten-round draw against Battling Jim Johnson on December 19.

A great image of Ad Wolgast boring in on "Harlem" Tommy Murphy during their February 22, 1913, battle at Daly City, California. This battle—taking place three fights prior to the final Wolgast vs. Nelson battle—ended in a draw (Library of Congress, Prints and Photograph Division, LC-DIG-ggbain-12574).

In a year filled with distractions, both in and around a ring, Nelson found himself in situations he would have never dreamed only five years ago. From being bitten by an opponent to being bitten by a three-day marriage, the bizarre and ridiculous became a reality. Nelson, as one might imagine, was on an emotional rollercoaster. He was not in a position to concentrate on the task at hand, and it showed.

While in Minneapolis, during the final weekend of the year, Oscar learned that the Reverend W.E. Pearson was now at Willmar—a distance just over 90 miles point-to-point—and decided to go see him. Pearson, as you recall, not only presided over the Battler's marriage to Fay King back in January, but was also a close friend of the Nelson family. From giving music lessons at the family home to conducting the funeral for the Battler's mother, he was someone Oscar could trust. And conviction, be it spiritual or otherwise, was what Nelson needed. He stayed through the service on Sunday and did not leave until Monday noon. He also saw fit to leave behind "a Christmas present of a roll of $100 as an expression of his kindly feelings for him."[46] But knowing Oscar, he left with much more.

Thirteen

1914–1917
At Long Last, Freddie Welsh

> I'm prouder of my clean record and honorable ring career than I am of all my lands, mines and money put together.
> —"Battling" Nelson[1]

The Progressive Era, a period from the 1890s until the 1920s, had passed into the hands of President Wilson, who continued to focus on eliminating corruption in government and providing enlightened legislative policies. Upon the outbreak of World War I in 1914, Wilson hoped to maintain a policy of neutrality, but any boxing referee could have told him that by ignoring the conflict between the powerful and the powerless, he was siding with the former.

1914

As common as weather reports, or so it seemed, were updates regarding Battling Nelson's financial condition. The protean nature of the accounts ranged from how little money Nelson actually had to large real estate transactions with the Dane as benefactor—some even noting, likely with the intent to amuse, the Battler chasing down an old debt. Granted, the Battler was a prodigious braggart about his ring earnings, and to some it may have been news, but the slant was getting as old as Bat himself.

For example, following the Wolgast bout, in which Nelson received in the neighborhood of $2,500, it was disclosed that he was cash poor. It had been no secret that his "white elephants" had come in the form of both real estate and mining propositions, but some simply found it difficult to believe. "Bat's money had been sunk in several doubtful mining schemes which had failed to materialize on anything but paper," claimed his old manager Billy Nolan. As one writer put it, "Seventeen years is a long time to stay in a game which is the toughest in the world to beat, clean up on every deal and then at the end find you have only been playing against the check-rack."[2] Also, in one of those instances you just couldn't make up, "Following his monologue at a Chicago vaudeville house, Abe Attell, former featherweight champion, was served with papers in a suit for $132.50 filed by Battling Nelson, former lightweight champion." The Battler claimed he loaned Attell $100 years ago and he would like it returned with interest.[3] Rounding up old debts, Nelson believed, was like calling on old favors—there if needed.

All things eventually surface in boxing, if of course you live long enough. One of the reasons Nelson didn't find the opportunities he had been looking for surfaced with regard to Ad Wolgast. "Wolgast's real reason for refusing to consider Nelson [in a rematch after he won the title] was that in the Port Richmond arrangements he [Ad] should be obliged to take the 'short end' in every detail, and Nelson continually taunted and insulted him."[4] A bit of a poor excuse, but nevertheless sometimes contract negotiations can turn around and haunt a fighter—okay, bite him in the ass. And Bat's insistence to his own set of terms and conditions—many times he would not budge an inch—contributed to the inefficiency of his comeback.

A photograph of Ad Wolgast (left) fighting against Willie Ritchie (right), the latter claiming the former one of the dirtiest fighters he ever fought. Wolgast lost his title on a foul in the sixteenth round against Ritchie on November 28, 1912 (Library of Congress, Prints and Photograph Division, LC-DIG-ggbain-11009).

Speaking of Wolgast, thanks to his manager Tom Jones, and some good scraps including a win over Joe Rivers up in Milwaukee on January 23, his return to form was garnering renewed attention. It was no secret Wolgast would like another shot at Ritchie, the man who took his title, but that could prove a difficult match. As one writer put it, "Ad was never what could be called popular with the rank and file of ring followers when champion, which was due to Ad's own vain ways and to Tom Jones' bombastic methods of securing publicity, but the run of hard luck experienced during the last year of Wolgast's reign helped turn sentiment in his favor."[5] As for the twenty-six-year-old Wolgast, he was just game to continue fighting.

In March, and proof that there is life after boxing, Battling Nelson was enlightened to learn that his former sparring partner, Dick Wheeler, had gone from a $10 pug to one of the highest salaried dancers in the world. Forsaking the gloves when the dance craze hit home, "he secured an engagement as a Texas Tommy dancer that took him to New York, where in a tournament held in the Winter Garden, he won the world's championship as a tango dancer."[6] He would now be touring the world for a couple of years with his dancing partner Gertrude Dolan. Additionally, another of Nelson's sparring partners, Charlie Edenberg of Milwaukee, had also forsaken the gloves for the stage. "Presenting a Difficult and Artistic Equilibristic Novelty," not as a dancer but as an entertainer, Edenberg had his show and perhaps a new calling. Bat himself enjoyed dancing—mentioning the avocation in his autobiography—and the stage had grown on him over time, so nobody would have been surprised if he too eventually turned to that option.[7]

Back to Bat's finances, even without regular bouts, The Dane was managing just fine according to *those* persistent and often contradictory news reports. Nelson had turned down an offer of $23,000 for two corner lots he owned in Hegewisch, stating he was not in need of money. Then, true to form, Bat also mentioned that he planned to keep the property and hold out for a better price.

The Progressive Party, formed in 1912 by former President Theodore Roosevelt, was known as the Bull Moose Party. In April, party headquarters in New York received a letter from a Bull Moose leader in Hegewisch which read, "Last election was my first vote and I traveled thousands of miles to cast it, putting myself out over $1,000 and had it not been for a good cause I would have passed it up, like I did all the other elections. BAT." A commonly held feeling by party members was that "anything that causes Bat Nelson to part with $1,000 must surely have a terrific grip on The Dane's innards."[8]

In May came news from England that Owen Moran had contracted tuberculosis and was feared as only having a short time to live. In his final fight appearance in the United States, on January 27, Moran was forced to stop boxing after seven rounds against Young Shugrue in New York—it was a sign to many that something was amiss. Moran had wisely stepped to the ropes at the end of the seventh rather than suffer a knockout. Known to most as the only boxer to make Battling Nelson take the full count, Moran recovered but quit boxing in 1916.

On July 7, Freddie Welsh, the pride of Pontypidd, Wales, defeated Willie Ritchie at the Olympia in London. The twenty-round "yawner" was a points victory for the Welsh Wizard who wisely chose not to punch it out against his hard-hitting antagonist. With the victory, the lightweight championship of the world returned to Great Britain after a lapse of eighteen years— England not owning a piece of the crown since Dick Burge lost to Kid Lavigne.

A much wiser Miss Irma Kilgallen had some free advice to give before she sailed on the *Aquitana* for Paris to continue her voice lessons: "The American father-in-law cannot understand the foreigner's viewpoint and a continual clash results," she says. "Any girl of this country who desires to marry a foreigner should spend at least two years abroad and any prospective bridegroom from Europe should live here that length of time."[9] It calls to mind the old Emerson quote, "Life is a succession of lessons which must be lived to be understood."

Having not fought since October 13, 1913, Oscar Nelson, still grappling with his life lessons, wasn't certain just where he stood with regard to the ring. Then, in what likely was a casual one-off affair, came word that Battling Nelson fought Cliff Ford to a six-round win at the Soo Opera House in Saulte Sainte Marie, Michigan, on August 19.[10] Testing the waters during a period of indecision, Nelson believed, was not always such a bad thing; besides it was "easy money," and that was precisely what he needed as the bills mounted.

On a lighter note, and likely a bit of a publicity stunt, a flash came across the wire in September: "Battling Nelson, former lightweight champion was knocked out by 'Professor' Griffin," a hypnotist, exhibiting at a local theater (Gary, Indiana).[11] Griffin, managing to do what few lightweights could, "made the fighter sing and dance until he was 'released.' Nelson had bet $300 he could not be hypnotized. He lost."[12] This was also the month Bat learned that his former manager, Billy Nolan, was going to reenter the fight game. Credited as being one of the shrewdest West Coast handlers ever, not only did he assist Nelson but he also took Willie Ritchie to new heights. From his large ranch near San Francisco, Billy was quick to point out that he'd had a few good fighters during his career and now intended to have a few more.

It seems every time Bat mentions he might want to fight again, the newspapers have a field day:

> Imagine old Methuselah with his beard down to his knees and his locks of snowy whiteness all a rippling in the breeze; his face all rough with wrinkles, such as garnish any sage, his eyes all red and rheumy from his exceeding age—imagine this description, and there you are, bing! bing! with a picture of Bat Nelson as he totters in the ring.[13]

Such was the fight game, and thankfully, Bat didn't take it to heart.[14] On December 18, the Battler was in South Bend, Indiana, fulfilling a stage obligation, along with visiting a few friends. Appearing at the Orpheum theater—a preliminary bout if you will, prior to his New York appearance next January at Hammersteins—Nelson was polishing a show called "The Hero of a Hundred Battles in a Knock-Out Monologue."

> Bat looks as good in the dress suit in which he appears at the Orpheum as in ring togs so many thousands have seen him wear. His monologue is pleasing although the majority would rather see him fight. But the one noticeable feature of his talk at the theater is the punch he puts into it, reminding one of the days when he cracked his opponents down in such short order.[15]

It was also noted that the Battler used good English, and appeared more the businessman than the fighter. Seems Methuselah still had options.

A tremendous amount of self-evaluation takes place prior to the retirement of a professional athlete. Not only do you want to be certain that it is the proper time, but also useful is an understanding of where you stand, if you do at all, in the history of the profession you are leaving. How will you be remembered? As if on cue, along came an article on December 19, a piece titled, "Fistiana's Roll of Honor, a Quintette of America's Most Prominent Sportsmen Select Twenty Greatest Fighters in the History of the Ring," that appeared in the *Ogden Standard*. Five prominent American sportsmen, Otto F. Stifel, Mike Whelan, Col. Sherwood Doyle, "Brooklyn Tommy" Sullivan and Harry S. Sharpe, were given the task of selecting the role of honor. There selections were: Jem Mace, John L. Sullivan, James J. Corbett, Robert Fitzsimmons, James J. Jeffries, Peter Jackson, Jack Johnson, Jack Dempsey, Tommy Ryan, Stanley Ketchel, Joe Walcott, Jack McAuliffe, George Lavigne, Joe Gans, Battling Nelson, Ad Wolgast, George Dixon, Terry McGovern, Abe Attell and Jimmy Barry.[16] This was fine company to keep. If there was any doubt in Nelson's mind where he stood, it had been answered.

Three days later, a photograph of Nelson appeared in the *Richmond Times* with the caption, "Battling Nelson, who met Andy Bezenah in Cincinnati a few days ago, is earnestly determined to regain the lightweight championship. He is working hard, and is seeking bouts with first raters. All who saw him in his match with Bezenah say he showed his old-time dash and aggressiveness."[17] Many believed Nelson had left the ring, so the account of his affair with Bezenah was a surprise. The Dane boxed four rounds in Cincinnati on the evening of December 16 against hometown boy Bezenah. According to the *Evening World* on December 17, "It was quite a comedy affair, amusing to the fans on that account, but presenting little to stir a crowd bent on enjoying some good milling."[18]

In other notable engagements of 1914: little-known Al McCoy flattened George Chip with a left uppercut at 1:55 in the first round in their April 6 clash in Brooklyn; Kid Williams knocked out little Johnny Coulon in the third round of their June 9 conflict in Vernon, California; Jack Johnson outpointed the hard-hitting Frank Moran during a twenty-round contest held on June 27 in Paris; and Sam Langford, nine inches shorter than his opponent Harry Wills, dropped the fighter in the fourteenth round of their November 26 campaign in Vernon.

For Nelson, the year was filled with mixed feelings regarding retirement. At times, he was certain that he had had an illustrious career and had nothing left to prove, yet seeing his name in columns such as "Today in Pugilistic Circles" or "Anniversaries of Ring Battles," marking anniversaries and not recent victories, wasn't easy to take, especially if you still believe you can fight.

Jack Johnson, pictured here, moved to Europe to escape a U.S. government indictment for violating the Mann Act (Library of Congress, Prints and Photograph Division, LC-DIG-ppmsca-31940).

1915

Battling Nelson knew it wasn't going to be easy to walk away from the fight game, and so, like so many other boxers, he looked for ways to find solace in or around the ring. Nelson was in New York on the third week of January, tending to some business—he had, as mentioned, a week's engagement at Hammerstein's Theater—and enjoying the destination for everything it had to offer. Being in the city gave him a chance to visit old friends and perhaps discover new opportunities. Manager Jimmy Johnston had arranged for the Battler to provide his expert opinion regarding the condition of Charley White and Freddie Welsh for their upcoming contest—hey, having a former champion like Nelson evaluating your fighters, Johnston understood, could create headlines. The Dane visited White's camp at Cooper's gymnasium first, followed by Welsh's encampment over at Ocean Park, sharing hints, striking poses, and dropping some subtle challenges. Maybe Bat contributed too much advice, as Charlie White called off the bout and was replaced by Willie Beecher. The ten-round Madison Square Garden affair would be seen as a victory for Freddie Welsh. And also a victory for Nelson, who again went public with a challenge for Welsh, this time to a finish fight and hopefully in Cuba—at, it was hoped, a new club being run by Billy Gibbons.

Nelson had little, or no intention—at least he didn't say so—to resume boxing in 1915. "But, the spark was fanned into a flame when he recently acted as chief second to Leach Cross in his tilt with Young Shugrue."[19] The Dane couldn't sit still and watch, or direct, when he would rather act. It was time again, he thought, to climb between the ropes.

Picking up a few (unregulated) side fights to line the pockets, or to scrap off a bit of ring rust, was often an option for a boxer, especially with a name like Nelson. With a limited audience, a fighter's performance on these occasions was seldom, unless done so on purpose, leaked to the press. Well, the press discovered one of Nelson's discreet four-round scraps. They then spoke of his performance, against an unnamed opponent, as "ludicrous" and "that the spectators were laughing."[20] Calling again for Bat's retirement and stating, "His last display of his former dash and vim was in his fight with Leach Cross in this city [New York] Thanksgiving afternoon two years ago. Adieu, Battling Nelson."[21]

In addition to assisting Leach Cross, Bat too needed assistance, only in legal form. Deciding to protect both his name and finances, it was time, he thought, to get aggressive. Frankly, he was sick and tired of others attaching the verb "Battling" onto themselves. No stranger to a law office, it was time to do something about it. Nelson believed,

> He has the exclusive right to it [Battling] and that the other ring men of more or less repute who have appropriated it should be enjoined and either prevented from using it or made to pay a royalty on the Nelson copyright. He threatens to bring his first action against "Battling" Levinsky.[22]

Nelson was also protecting his purse by again tracking down some more of his old debts—Tusser's sixteenth-century quote about a fool and his money certainly not applicable here—and bringing suit against those he felt had been negligent. Dancer Annette Kellermann, and her husband, James R. Sullivan, were at the end of Nelson's wrath in New York, as the Battler tried to recover $450. The prizefighter alleged "that December 27, 1910, he lent Annette Kellermann and her husband $1,000, which they promised to pay back. He has been able since then, he says, to collect $550, and he wants the remainder."[23]

Only days later, it came to light that Ad Wolgast had agreed to fight Battling Nelson on

Thirteen—1914–1917: At Long Last, Freddie Welsh

Annette Kellerman, the captivating Australian professional swimmer, vaudeville star, film actress, writer, and business owner, who borrowed money from the Battler (Library of Congress, Prints and Photograph Division, LC-DIG-ggbain-06126).

February 22, the fifth anniversary of their legendary forty-round clash at Port Richmond—the fight that gave Wolgast the title. The commemoration clash was hoped to be staged at Madison Square Garden if—and it wasn't a small if—a promoter could be found to take the fight. If not, there was life beyond our native shores.

After the Spanish-American War, Spain and the United States signed the Treaty of Paris (1898), by which Spain ceded Puerto Rico, the Philippines, and Guam to the United States for a considerable sum of money, $20 million. Cuba then gained formal independence from the United States on May 20, 1902, as the Republic of Cuba. The Battler found himself there on March 18, and back in the ring where he knocked out a fighter named Young Donnelly in the third round. Drawing equal attention was the attendance of both Jack Johnson and Jess Willard, who witnessed the Battler's Cuban debut. These two gladiators were on the island training for their scheduled battle in Havana on April 4—the date later moved to April 5.

Nelson next picked up a twenty-five-round victory over Jimmy Freyer in Havana on March 24.[24] The Battler, it was clear, was preparing himself for something, but just what wasn't certain. Two days later, it was announced that Freddie Welsh had signed articles while in Windsor, Ontario, for a ten-rounder against Battling Nelson on April 4 in Cuba—the lightweight champion had just completed an eight-round no decision against Patsey Druillard in Canada. But, also reported was that Welsh had signed for a ten-round match with Billy Wagner in Toledo on April 9. It seems like there just wasn't enough of the champion to go around. Welsh would end up taking the latter and scrapping the former, to the discontent of Nelson.

The Associated Press was also behind—they may not have been necessarily behind it, but certainly reported it—an interesting claim that the Welsh-Nelson bout would be a curtain raiser for the Johnson-Willard fight, and for only a Nelson take of $2,000; there were even reports that Nelson would referee the Johnson-Willard clash. Sounds like Bat was calling out favors and bending ears at a record rate.

Nelson really enjoyed Cuba, in particular the islanders' love for the sport of boxing. Although nobody ever expected Nelson to permanently leave Hegewisch, he did think twice about buying a home in Havana and perhaps opening a boxing club. This was confirmed candidly by a number of close friends.

Meanwhile, in between Bat's adventures, John R. Robinson was picking up pocket change by penning articles leading up to the Johnson versus Willard duel. (Maybe it was

"Robby" who was planting seeds with the Associated Press.) In one piece he discussed trademark punches and their effectiveness, comparing Johnson's uppercut to Nelson's hook to the liver, or Kid McCoy's famous corkscrew left. As might have been expected, he included Battling Nelson's prediction for the fight: "I believe Johnson will win, but there is so much about Willard to recommend him that I am not going to take a chance of betting against him."[25]

When the Welsh-versus-Nelson undercard to the Johnson-versus-Willard clash fell through, negotiations again began to match the fighters. By the first week in April, it was announced that "Battling Nelson and Freddie Welsh are going to inflict themselves on the poor Cubans in a 45 round 'battle' early in May. Nelson is to receive a meager $2,000 for his end, while Welsh is guaranteed $15,000."[26] As for Nelson in this instance, it was all about the title and not the purse. As for the fight, it was about finding a promoter and tackling the logistics. Nelson picked up one more fight in Havana, a virtually meaningless second-round knockout of Dale Gardner—more of a sparring session than an actual contest—before leaving Havana aboard the *Excelsior* and arriving in New Orleans, Louisiana, on May 17.

In a glimpse into the evolution of the fight game, some boxing clubs had been crying about the big losses they sustained in 1914:

> The Cream City A.C. of Milwaukee has had some bumpers the past year that would make others shudder. During that time the Cream City club had a loss of over $4,000 on the Willie Ritchie-Charlie White match; $50 on the second White and Welsh match and $1,000 on the Jack Dillon-Gunboat Smith contest. It was a case of playing the sucker act to the big demands of so-called stars, the same as many other clubs about the country have been doing.[27]

This was reality, and financial adjustments needed to be made at both ends of the fight game.

Uncertain about his ring future, but sure about some remodeling, Bat visited a Chicago beauty doctor—as they casually called it—to look first at reconstructing his left ear, followed by his right. One would think this action would confirm the end of Nelson's ring appearances, but in this case one would be wrong. Taking a few fights, Bat believed, could pay for his medical bills.

When Mrs. Ella Flagg, superintendent of schools in Chicago, went into her office she found a thick envelope resting prominently in her pile of mail. Inside it, she found a blue paperback book entitled *Ring Battles of Centuries*. She was a bit confused as to why she of all people would be interested in the art of self-defense until she read the inscription, "With kindest regards to the world's greatest woman, from Battling Nelson."[28]

A more detailed review of the book found that Nelson had contributed a chapter about his career. And, at the beginning of that chapter, was a remark about his education:

> I will never forget our first schoolhouse, because it was a dingy, one-room house, where all the children assembled for their studies, with one teacher. Now, we have several schools, with plenty of teachers. Ella Flagg Young, our Superintendent of schools gave me a lecture in 1890 which I never forgot, and helped to make me what I am today.[29]

After reading the chapter the superintendent penned a letter in appreciation, adding, "I have no doubt that you will continue in the same line of clean athletics that you have followed ever since you left the Henry Clay school at Hegewisch."[30]

Nelson, while packing for a journey to Mexico, was grateful for the superintendent's remarks. Hearing some exciting things about what was happening south of the border, Nelson headed to Juarez, Mexico. There the former lightweight champion decided to test the waters against

Texas fighter Bobby Waugh. The fight was scheduled for twenty rounds on September 7. Waugh, the lightweight state champion and undefeated in his last eleven bouts, agreed to meet at 133 pounds. "The fight was fast throughout, Nelson showing all his old time ability to assimilate punishment, but lacking both steam and cleverness to cope with his younger and more agile opponent."[31] The affair would enter the record books as a twenty-round loss and diminish Nelson's spirits. Nobody can blame Bat for taking the fight, as it was announced on August 27 by officials of the Villa government, "that if Battling Nelson defeats Bobby Waugh Labor Day, a purse of $25,000 will be raised to back Nelson against Freddie Welsh. The fight will be arranged for Christmas or New Year and will be for the world championship. Villa officials want to make Juarez a boxing center if they can."[32] Nelson was reported as saying, "If you give me a fight, Freddie, I'll guarantee to beat you over a 20, 25, 40 or 45-round route or I won't take a dollar for my work."[33] For Nelson, offers, not all good mind you, seemed to be falling from the sky. Out of the blue, a citizen's committee of El Paso, Texas, offered $5,000 for a match between Battling Nelson and Ad Wolgast. As expected, it was met by the press with the inevitable question, "What are they trying to do, rob the old men's home?"[34]

Forever determined—Bat wanted a swan song, and in his position, you certainly couldn't blame him—to be matched against Freddie Welsh for the lightweight championship of the world, Nelson turned to some good old-fashioned media tactics, in this case drawing a check on his bank for $10,000 made payable to Welsh immediately after fighting Nelson to a finish or a forty-five-round bout. The figure had been reduced from Nelson's June 24 offer of $20,000. A copy of the check was given to the media to print with their articles, then deposited with Promoter J.W. Coffroth with permission to secure telegraphic certificates of the check. "It is my guarantee that Welsh will be paid for his services if he agrees to meet me; if he accepts and a promoter is found, and I am sure quite a number of them will be only too anxious to handle the match."[35]

Later, Nelson again, no doubt prompted by Robinson, called out Welsh, "After the champion ran out on me in Havana, and a Denver club tried to match us, I made exactly the same offer that I am making now, but Welsh paid no attention to it. He's afraid of me. He is afraid to risk the title, preferring to trot over the 10-round no-decision rout."[36]

By October, Nelson who had been weighing his options for some time, announced his interest in becoming a fight manager. "Why fight yourself when you can have others fight for you?" he crooned. Undertaking management of Los Angeles bantamweight George Lammerson, Nelson was impressed with the youngster's speed and stamina and hoped to drive him toward a division title. But to do this would require not only his fighter's commitment to the task but also his own—Nelson still had the fight bug, having gone twenty rounds with Bobby Waugh only five weeks ago.

Proof of point: On November 5, in Kansas City, Missouri, fighter Jimmy Reagan took a points victory over Battling Nelson in ten rounds. It wasn't even close as Reagan outpointed, and outfought, the former champ. Nelson fought at catchweight, while Reagan was compelled to make 133 pounds. It wasn't pretty, but it was Nelson's last official fight of the year, last ten-round affair ever, and the last loss of his career—Jimmy Reagan now immortalized as the answer to a trivia question.[37]

The writer Jack Skelly penned an article about the aggregation of ring-worn, fought-out boxers who still refuse to retire. This new phenomenon of gladiators who refuse to throw up the sponge was not nostalgic in his view, but detrimental to the sport.

I mean such "has-beens" as Ad Wolgast, Battling Nelson, Tommy Murphy, Freddie Welsh and others, who were once a great credit to the ring, and in their heyday won many glorious victories. Why should these played-out ringsters keep going along trying to make a "come back" when they really know they are all in, and are only subjecting themselves to ridicule and humiliation by trying to fight against nature? Many of them go up against mere second and third-raters and have decisions rendered against them that will figure in their ring records just as prominently as their former great conquests.[38]

Using Ad Wolgast, twenty-seven, as an example, the writer criticized him for his haphazard barnstorming from town to town:

Sometimes winning, and more times losing cheap, unimportant bouts. If he is so wealthy, then why is he exposing himself to this humiliation was the point, as there are many other lucrative occupations Wolgast could engage in at present, instead of mixing up with a lot of boxing dubs here and there and everywhere, spoiling his good record and fistic fame.[39]

Then came Nelson:

Another one of those restless, former world's champions, who is not elevating himself in the eyes of the boxing public by his recent performances in the ring. He, like Wolgast, is rich in this world's goods, and can well afford to retire from the ring and take a more active interest in his real estate and other speculations. Why are they still so avaricious for the "filthy lucre" when their real fighting days are past and gone forever?[40]

The writer then used Billy Papke as an example of a man who retired with honor. "When Billy found his fistic prowess on the wane he was wise enough to step down and out at the proper time and not spoil his former splendid ring record."[41] There was no mention of Matty Baldwin, thirty-one, who was one of the oldest lightweights still in the ring.

Obviously the fighters questioned were not in the financial condition assumed, or they doubtful would have exposed themselves to such humiliation. It was a different time, and this meant new strategies and alternatives. Nelson was actually blazing new ground by trying to fight his way back into contention. And he was balancing that fine line between financial stability and mortification—not an easy task by any means. There were also alternative forms of income, most notably film. Generations that had never seen a fighter in their "heyday" could now witness them at their very best on celluloid, then perhaps meet these legends in person. The stage, plus film, equaled revenue. And there was also the question of ego: How do former fighter's feed their egos?

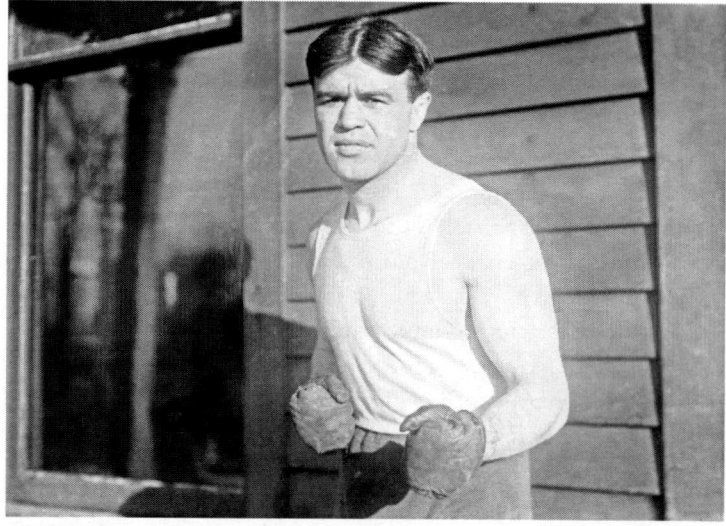

The prolific and ageless "Bunker Hill Bearcat," Matthew B. Baldwin, fought from 1902 until 1916 (Library of Congress, Prints and Photograph Division, LC-DIG-ggbain-10118).

Nelson loved the attention and the applause. Wolgast, who had held the title over 300 days longer than Nelson, was simply following in his footsteps.

Of the year's notable warfare: the Pottawatomie Giant, Jess Willard, knocked out Jack Johnson in the twenty-sixth round of their title match in Havana on April 5—Johnson later claiming to have taken a dive; Ted "Kid" Lewis took a close twelve-round decision over rival Jack Britton on August 31 in Boston; and in one of those "say it ain't low" battles, Johnny Ertle won on a fifth-round foul over Kid Williams. But because it was a dubious claim, Williams retained his bantam title.

In 1915, Nelson officially fought fifty-eight rounds against four prosaic opponents, winning two fights and losing two. To his credit, he came close to appearing on a decent card, and landing a worthy opponent, while living the old Edison adage: "Many of life's failures, are people who did not realize how close they were to success when they gave up."

1916

In 1916, the Mexican Revolution was in full swing, the Chicago Cubs played their first game at Weeghman Park (modern-day Wrigley Field), Norman Rockwell painted his first cover for the *Saturday Evening Post*, and the first forty-hour workweek officially began in the Endicott-Johnson shoe factories of western New York. Things looked, and felt, different for Oscar Nelson. Not since 1895 had he gone a calendar year—he was simply that prolific, that determined and that good—without participating in a single professional fight, but that would change in this annum, and not by choice.

Counsel for Battling Nelson, in his suit for annulment of his marriage to Mrs. Fay King Nelson, felt it tactically pertinent to release three letters to the public. Each was introduced as evidence in the case. They did so on January 31, 1916, and many newspapers, including the *Bismarck Daily Tribune*, decided to publish the letters in advance of the hearing. Nelson's counsel believed the release of the letters was proof that while Mrs. Nelson refused to live with her husband, she remained lavish in terms of endearment. One of the letters made public read:

Center section of panorama of Jess Willard versus Jack Johnson fight in Havana, Cuba, on April 5, 1915, or the longest heavyweight championship bout during the gloved era (Library of Congress, Prints and Photograph Division, LC-USZ62-121676).

Dear Boy Bat: All right, I'll not tell you to retire any more. I am very sorry wrote you so—but I thought I was doing right. From now on my song shall not be that of one who has fought well and needs rest, but one who is climbing from the bottom into the world of success anew. And here's luck to you, Bat, dear boy. May the laurels of success you are so bent on acquiring not smother all thought of your faithful "Lil" pal, Fay.[42]

While Nelson did not want to lose the case, which was clear, one could not be certain of what damage, if any, such a move might have on their future relationship.

In what would prove to be the first heartbreaking event of the year, the Wisconsin State Boxing Commission ruled on February 28 that Battling Nelson was "too far gone" to box Ad Wolgast—the two ring veterans had been matched for an April (12) battle in Wisconsin because it was one of the few states where decision fights were permitted. The humiliating news traveled like a lightning bolt across the country. For Oscar the news was gut wrenching—it's one thing for a fighter to read it in the press, but to be told you can no longer fight by a sanctioning body is embarrassing. For all intents and purposes, it was the first nail in his coffin.

Nelson finally completed the legal conditions for divorcing himself from his wife, Fay King, the Kansas City cartoonist, on March 1. Not appearing personally, or having anyone to present on her half, Mrs. Nelson defaulted. The official hearing the case, Judge Kersten, signed the formal decree.

Testimony in the Chicago courtroom was brief. Nelson's attorney, Emile V. Van Bever, announced, "Your honor, this is a charge of desertion. Service by copy of the bill. No contest by the defendant."[43] Nelson then took the stand and answered some very simple and direct questions from his attorney. Judge Kersten asked only one question, and it revolved around one of her departures. Also testifying was the plaintiff's father and his manager. Upon being notified that Mr. Nelson would be given a divorce, Fay King wished only to wait for confirmation before issuing a statement.

A few days after the decree was signed, Bat told his father, "Dad, you've got to come across with my property." Bat, as you recall, had deeded to his father $250,000 worth of real estate prior to his marriage. The father then barked, "Boy, you are foolish," and a feud erupted. Both father and son were soon speaking only through their attorneys. The father was quoted as saying, "Bat, is as foolish as a bat."[44] This was not what the Nelson family needed, not at this time and not under these conditions.

On March 10, it was reported that Nelson's father, sixty-nine years old, had disappeared Monday afternoon and could not be found. "At the time of his disappearance Mr. Nelson had about $500, which he had collected from tenants of the house owned by himself and his son."[45] Fortunately, the Dane's father was found and still in possession of the $500 roll.

Sensing that everything around him was falling apart, Oscar Nelson was feeling very alone, underappreciated, and in some cases, used. And just when he thought things couldn't get much worse, they did.

Irma Kilgallen Ends Life

On Tuesday, April 11, 1916, the final edition of the *Chicago Daily Tribune* ran the unbelievable bold headlines:

IRMA KILGALLEN ENDS LIFE

Thirteen—1914–1917: At Long Last, Freddie Welsh

The news came out of Omaha, Nebraska, that the daughter of Martin H. Kilgallen of 3230 South Michigan Avenue had shot herself to death inside her rooms at the Hotel Fontenelle.

Kilgallen had married the Chicago playwright, composer, actor and producer Joseph Edgar Howard only a month earlier in Los Angeles. But the Howards' relationship had been reported as volatile and with only limited contact—this incident believed to be only the second time they had seen each other since the marriage.

When Mrs. Howard arrived in Omaha, it was reported, she did not find her husband at the Fontenelle but another hotel. When she finally encountered Mr. Howard at the Rome Hotel, it was said to be in a situation that caused her concern and resulted in her immediate departure from the hotel. Mr. Howard later met up with his wife at the theater where he was appearing, and a contentious discussion took place. Before long, Mrs. Howard stated vehemently that she was returning to Chicago and left the building.

But Mrs. Howard changed her mind and did not go back to Chicago. Instead she returned to her rooms at the Hotel Fontenelle. She was joined in the evening by Mrs. Lamberti, the wife of a vaudeville actor playing on the bill at the Orpheum Theater where Mr. Howard was headlining. At about eight o'clock, the two ordered some refreshments; then Mrs. Howard stepped into the bathroom of the suite.

A moment later, Mrs. Lamberti heard a loud shot and became petrified. The bellboy, having just delivered room service, returned to the room, broke down the bathroom door and found Mrs. Howard on the floor. A .22 caliber revolver lay at her side as the blood flowed freely from the wound in her left temple.[46]

Located at 1806 Douglas Street in downtown Omaha, Nebraska, the Hotel Fontenelle was a newly built luxury hotel (1914) designed by the noted architect Thomas Rogers Kimball. In its rich history, this would be the first high-profile incident to occur inside its walls.[47]

At the Orpheum Theater, a grief-stricken Joseph Howard performed his turn in the show, claiming it was God's will that he do his work. The actor also informed a newsman that he was in the possession of a letter from his wife—it had been sent to her father. He did not disclose the contents of that letter, but it was presumed to hold some answers regarding her suicide. It was believed that Mr. Howard then went to another hotel and registered under an assumed name to avoid further annoyance.

Omaha, during this period, was one of eight other cities on vaudeville's well-known Orpheum Circuit. Shows were held each day at 2:15 and 8:15 p.m. and typically drew a large audience.[48] Ironically, it had also been in Omaha that Mr. Howard had learned that his second wife, Mabel Barrison, had died in Toronto; Mr. Howard, who was in the company of a Mabel McCane at that time, left two days later to attend his wife's funeral.

Irma's parents were reached via telephone in Chicago. But they were not provided details regarding their daughter's condition, only that she was seriously ill. As anticipated, they departed immediately for Omaha. They would take their daughter's body back to Chicago.

The Wedding

The wedding between Mr. Howard and Miss Kilgallen, which was held the second week in March, took everyone by surprise as their names had never been romantically linked. Said to have been an impromptu event, limited details were provided. However, it was noted that Mr. Howard and his new wife parted following the ceremony.

The Kilgallen family was as surprised as any. Their first indication of marital trouble was after the end of March, when Mrs. Howard telegraphed her father to meet her in Salt Lake City—the particulars of this meeting between father and daughter were not known. Mrs. Howard, who was not with her husband, then visited friends in Minneapolis before traveling on to Chicago.

It was at the time of Mrs. Howard's meeting with her father that she had just learned that Mr. Howard was found guilty of breach of promise to marry Miss Edith Witherspoon of Portland, Oregon; Mr. Howard was ordered to pay Miss Witherspoon $6,000. Unknown was what role this event had in the relationship between the newlyweds.

Back to Mrs. Howard's death: At the time of the incident there seemed to be a curious, yet substantial, interest in the belongings of the now deceased Mrs. Howard, in particular a pearl necklace. According to Mr. Howard, bequeathed to him was this necklace valued at $25,000; a $5,000 diamond ring had also been given to Mrs. Lamberti. And Mrs. Howard's furs, also highly valued, were ordered to be given away.

The Groom

"Joe" Howard's matrimonial adventures were well known to the public before Irma Kilgallen ever entered the picture. One might suppose that if Irma ever desired someone empathetic to tabloid gossip, Howard was it.

Joseph Edgar Howard was born on February 12, 1878, in New York City, New York. He ran away from home at the age of eight and landed in the Midwest, where he worked at a variety of jobs. From newsboy to bootblack, Howard worked hard, until he was found to have a good voice. At the young age of eleven, Howard appeared on vaudeville as a boy soprano and then toured in a stock company production, *Little Eva*. As his exposure grew, he met many well-known individuals including "Diamond Dolly" Emerson, a trendy Denver entertainer, and her daughter Ida. Turning heads on the stage as the "Emerson sisters," both mother and daughter were stunning, and suffice it to say that Howard noticed.

Joe and Ida hit it off immediately and eloped. The two then began appearing in burlesque shows before heading to New York. A syncopated novelty telephone number called "Hello, Ma Baby," published in 1899, soon brought the couple attention—it sold over a million copies of sheet music. Howard then branched out, away from his wife, and took a vaudeville role with a popular Canadian-born entertainer named Mabel Barrison, formerly Mrs. William Gaston.

Well, it wasn't long before Mrs. Howard was asking for, then receiving a divorce. While Ida Emerson would remain a burlesque "queen," Howard went on to be a very successful composer. Finding a home at the LaSalle Theater, Howard began penning a series of musical comedies. From 1905 until 1909, the little playhouse, along with Mr. Howard, gained national exposure.

Viewed as the ideal stage couple, Mabel Barrison, born Eva Maud Farrance on April 21, 1882, and Howard were married and enjoyed a several years of success together. But Mabel began suffering from a number of health issues that would cost the couple financially. Forced to give up the stage due to illness, Mabel went to live on a ranch in Texas.[49] In 1912, the couple was forced to entered bankruptcy. This happened just before Mabel died on November 1, at the youthful age of thirty. Many would remember her for starring in the Clyde Fitch play *The Blue Mouse* and singing "I Can't Do That Sum" in *Babes in Toyland*.

Thirteen—1914–1917: At Long Last, Freddie Welsh

Meanwhile, Mr. Howard had been appearing regularly with actress Mabel McCane in various productions. Ambitious and creative, Howard was relentless in his production; that he carried such an enormous financial burden surely played into the scenario. Often viewing Howard and McCane together, the public assumed they were married, as did the Howards' friends. Reported as engaged, the couple had even registered in a Chicago hotel as "Joe Howard and wife."

So it came as a bit of a surprise when Howard married Irma Kilgallen.

Word came on April 13 that Joseph Howard would take time off from his busy vaudeville tour to attend the funeral of his bride. "In an Omaha interview, Howard said his father-in-law, Martin Kilgallen, had expressed friendly sentiments toward him, and that his bride, formerly the Countess de Beaufort, had urged him to sell her $25,000 pearl necklace so he could pay a $6,000 judgment obtained against him in Portland, Oregon, in a breach of promise suit."[50]

Howard reportedly declined and stated, "You see, the lawyer from Portland had followed me to Minneapolis and offered to settle the judgement for $2,500. I told Irma about the offer and she handed me the necklace. I handed it back to her."[51]

While going over Irma's handbag with her father, Howard was again offered the necklace and declined. Mr. Kilgallen respected Howard's decision and assured him that if he ever needed anything, to just ask. The origin of the necklace was not noted; however some believe it was a gift from pugilist Battling Nelson.

> Howard kept secret of the train upon which he is coming to Chicago. He will remain in Chicago until Sunday morning, when he will go to Milwaukee. He says he probably will go to the Kilgallen residence upon arrival here [Chicago].[52]

An Enormous Tragedy

For five years, in an unfortunate relationship that played out before a captivated community, Irma Kilgallen had been harassed by the Chicago newspapers. "In the belief that the public would like to read of the doings of an erratic young lady with money and good looks, the papers played so heavily on her doings that the family house at 3230 South Michigan Avenue was constantly haunted by nervy newspaper reporters."[53]

Miss Kilgallen's adverse marriage to a count, which most anyone in her position would have foreseen as a storybook tale of love and adventure, turned into a complete travesty.

> He was rather a cheap specimen of Belgian nobility, and when Irma cast him off penniless he talked readily to the press of the city and her status with the feature-seeking papers was fixed. The divorce was replete with stories. How the Count Jacques von Mourik de Beaufort had thrown his heiress-wife over the banister of the Kilgallen home; how they tried to enter society here [Chicago]; how the count was whipped by the girl's father; all was sensationally told by the Chicago papers, this before traveling the world. The newspapers got stories in which she was pictured as calling him a money-seeker and he was accusing her of intimacies with Battling Nelson, the prizefighter.[54]

Once the count departed, the stories slowed and eventually ceased, and the dust settled. Then she married, of all people, a tabloid sensation himself, Joseph Howard.

> The suicide came just when the newspapers of Omaha scented a little scandal because Irma had slipped into the city unexpectedly and surprised her husband, Joe Howard, actor and song writer. The couple quarreled ... the name of the woman who was playing opposite Howard was mentioned and the bride of a few weeks left the theater sobbing.[55]

She lived the life of "disappointed womanhood" is how one of her close friends described her. With the soul of an artist, her creativity was exhibited through her painting, a craft nurtured by her parents.[56] The innocence of childhood—Irma was shielded from much of the adversities of the outside world—possessed her until her first marriage. The fiasco that erupted as a result, and what it created, tainted a "gentle heart that had been twisted and broken beyond all healing. She had been deceived with the cruelest of impositions. Every little dream that she had dreamed became the ugliest of nightmares."[57]

She met Joe Howard at a dancing party in the College Inn last fall, loved the attention, began to lift from depression and decided to remove herself to Los Angeles to spend the winter. The glow in her eyes was back. Her cheeks seemed to lift higher, and when she smiled—something she didn't do enough because she was self-conscious about the little space between her two front teeth—the beauty of her countenance would just melt your heart.

Going to Bat

On April 18, it was time to go to Bat:

> Prosecution of Joe Howard, actor husband of the late Irma Kilgallen Howard, on a charge of violating the Mann act, has been demanded by Oscar ["Battling"] Nelson, the pugilist. Nelson made the complaint to Hinton G. Clabaugh, divisional chief of the department of justice investigation bureau, and later said he had named a former sweetheart of Howard's as the woman in the case.[58] "I am out to get Howard's scalp because of his attitude and his comments since the suicide of Irma Kilgallen," said Nelson, "she cannot defend herself so it is up to her friends to do something. And she and I were kids together."[59]

Named after Congressman James Robert Mann of Illinois, the White-Slave Traffic Act, or Mann Act, in its original form made it a felony to engage in interstate or foreign commerce transport of "any woman or girl for the purpose of prostitution or debauchery, or for any other immoral purpose." Aimed to address prostitution, this was one of several acts of protective legislation aimed at moral reform during the Progressive Era.[60] Oscar was looking for a form of retaliation to ease his pain.

> When a man shows such disregard for the memory of a fine girl like Irma Kilgallen then it is only natural that those near to her should show a spirit of revenge," Nelson continued, "I remember the last time I saw Irma alive. It was just before she left for Omaha, where she committed suicide. Poor girl, she seemed to realize what her marriage to Howard meant. But she told me she had decided to try and make the best of it.[61]

Martin H. Kilgallen

Of Irish decent, Martin H. Kilgallen was born in Syracuse, New York, on September 9, 1858, to John and Catherine McCarthy Kilgallen. He would marry Anna Tracey (1863–1953), save, and sacrifice for his family, which would include his wife and two daughters, Tracey M. Kilgallen (1883–1906) and Irma. Success seemed to follow everything he touched, but it meant nothing if he could not provide happiness and opportunity for his family.

When he bought their magnificent mansion on Michigan Avenue, it was primarily for his daughter Irma, to shower her with the wonderful things in life he never had as a child. As he nurtured her in the fine arts, he hoped that her development would find her among society's most eligible ladies, which it did. Nonetheless, she attracted, or perhaps was simply blinded by, only false charm.

"I am an old man bereft of his daughter; let me alone," he said when he went from Chicago to get "his baby's body."[62] He had lived in the big house on Michigan Avenue since then, deprived of happiness, and with an illness for a year that did not worry him. He saw it simply as means to once again join hands with his little girl. Martin Kilgallen died at 11:25 p.m. on January 12, 1922, in his home.[63]

Joseph Edgar Howard

As a composer Joseph Edgar Howard would be celebrated for collaborating with songwriters such as Frank Adams, Will Hough and Harold Orlob, on such hits as "Hello, My Baby," "Goodbye, My Lady Love," "There's Nothing Like a Good Old Song," "Somewhere in France is the Lily," "On a Saturday Night," "Can't Get You Out of My Mind," "Love Me Little, Love Me Long," "Montana," "Silver in Your Hair," "Whistle a Song," "On the Boulevard," "San Francisco Frizz," "An Echo of Her Smile," "I Don't Like Your Family," "Blow the Smoke Away," "What's the Use of Dreaming?," "When You First Kiss the Last Girl You Love," "Honeymoon," "Be Sweet to Me, Kid," "I Wonder Who's Kissing Her Now," "Tonight Will Never Come Again" and "Cross Your Heart." He would also be acknowledged for his stage scores: *The Land of Nod*; *The Time, the Place and the Girl*; *The Girl Question*; *A Stubborn Cinderella*; *The Goddess of Liberty* and *The Prince of Tonight*.

In a periodically (1889–1915, 1939–1961) active career, Howard performed in night clubs, on radio (with Beatrice Kay), in recordings (Decca and Vocalion), on television (*The Gay Nineties Revue*, ABC, 1948–1949), in theaters and eventually even in motion pictures (*I Wonder Who's Kissing Her Now*). He published an autobiography entitled *Gay Nineties Troubadour: Autobiography of Joe Howard, American Composer of I Wonder Who's Kissing Her Now?* in 1956.

At the Chicago Opera House, Joseph Howard, reported as having been married at least nine times, dropped dead during a curtain call on May 19, 1961.

The Count de Beaufort

On March 3, 1915, a message given out by Charles T. Hass, of the Hass Detective Agency, claimed the Count de Beaufort died fighting with the army of France at Nieuport in February 1915. The message was signed "Princess of Luxemburg," the count's mother. Mr. Hass knew the count and had been employed by the Kilgallen family during the divorce proceedings. Miss Kilgallen at the time was not much affected by the news and hoped it was only a rumor, and it was.

The count went on to prove himself of tremendous benefit to the British admiralty in his intelligence work, particularly in mapping. He had posed in Germany, where he acquired much of his information, as a correspondent for Dutch newspapers. The *Bismarck Tribune* was so impressed with his actions that they ran a dapper photograph of the count beneath the March 30, 1917, headline, "Beaufort, Once Laughed at in America, Is Now British Hero."

On September 9, 1917, it was reported that the count had married Miss Helen F. Reiman of Terre Haute, Indiana. The couple, now Mr. and Mrs. Jack de Beaufort, had planned for an October wedding, but Captain de Beaufort's orders prompted them to get married much sooner. The couple had met at a military ball at Governor's Island, New York, the count having been one of thirty patriotic lecturers on the staff of the adjutant general of New York.

The count would later appear as a famous war correspondent in a photograph of him sitting aboard a Belgian gun carriage with his Corona typewriter in his lap. The image would appear in an advertisement for the Corona Typewriter Company, Incorporated, of Groton, New York.

It was Charles Dickens who said, "A man is lucky if he is the first love of a woman. A woman is lucky if she is the last love of a man." Irma Kilgallen was Nelson's first love, but not his last. She had everything he wanted in a woman, but a family who wanted him—there was simply no way Martin Kilgallen's daughter was going to marry a pugilist.

You remember everything about a first love, the way she walks, talks, smells and tastes when you kiss her. Just the thought of her sends shivers racing up and down your spine and gives you those fluttering butterflies deep in your stomach. You yearn, and oh how you yearn, for just another chance to make that first love into your last. To hold her again, to brush back the hair from her face and to once again melt with the sense of just being around her. That is how Bat had felt for the longest time. That is until Irma entered marriage with another man. It was then that he drifted from foreground to background, even as he left his heart in the former.

It was not just Bat's innocence that Irma loved, but also his accent, his funny laugh and his goofy rhetoric. It was these traits, she believed, that added much to his persona. Irma also found him fun to be with, and never dull. And, most of all, he was genuinely imperfect. Oscar Nelson never tried to be something he wasn't.

All Options Considered

Battling Nelson was stricken with appendicitis in Detroit, Michigan, on June 5, while conducting his monologue at a local theater. His hospital physicians pronounced his condition as "very serious" and stated that the Battler's condition would remain doubtful for several days. Thankfully Nelson recovered nicely, and it wasn't long before he was seeing a doctor about something other than his appendix.

With his ears, nose and lips now remodeled, Battling Nelson was a new man.

> Nelson, until a few days ago was the self-confessed homeliest man in the world. His ears were crushed out of shape and his nose knocked lop-sided. Recently he had his ears lanced and reshaped; his boomerang nose has been slit and reset in plaster of Paris so that it will be a perfect Grecian, and his lips molded to come to a cupid bow.[64]

And, not only is he trying to improve his personal appearance, but other things as well. "To accomplish all this he has engaged a staff consisting of: a beauty doctor, a social tutor, a mentor of deportment and a dancing instructor." The reason for the overhaul was simple: love. He did it for Fay King, the former Mrs. Nelson. "And when it's all done, if Fay can give him another 'turn down' she is a cartoonist without a soul for art, a humorist with no appreciation of the sweeter things in this existence."[65] Nelson's success at the plastic surgeon even prompted other pugilists to consider a resurfacing.

On October 26, Nelson was arrested for refusing to pay his streetcar fare after tendering a transfer, which the conductor refused to accept. Not objecting to the arrest, Nelson peacefully

Thirteen—1914–1917: At Long Last, Freddie Welsh

went along with the arresting officer, then posted a cash bond and left for his home in Hegewisch. It was likely, so Nelson thought, that the streetcar conductor didn't recognize the new and improved Battler.

More painful articles regarding the Battler's financial status hit in November. Some of the chatter Bat tried to head off by releasing some of his own statement:

> This is the way it all came about. Bat, as is well known, is the one big man Hegewisch, Illinois ever produced, and Bat always has been as proud of the old home as it has been of him. So most of the $200,000 which he accumulated in the heyday of his career went into Hegewisch real estate, then unimproved.[66]

When the Illinois Central Railroad chose not to build a station on property he owned, the Dane soon found himself swamped under city council ordinances. He was required to install sewers, pave streets and make numerous other improvements that slowly eroded his finances. The property gradually depreciated, leaving the Battler unable to recover even his initial investment.

In time for the holidays, Nelson joined the scrappers, Jess Willard, Packey McFarland, Charlie Cutler, Joe Welling and Johnny Coulon in the Ragen Athletic Club's annual benefit for the poor. All proceeds from the event went to those in need, offering a bit of well-needed Christmas cheer.

Nelson did not place an entry into his career totals in 1916, but he did enjoy reading about some outstanding conflicts: On February 7, in New Orleans, local teen sensation Pete Herman managed to go toe-to-toe with Kid Williams to a twenty-round draw; lightweight champion Jack Dillon managed to hold on to a ten-round no decision against a determined Frank Moran on June 29 in Brooklyn; and Jack Dempsey, who suffered two broken ribs in the second round, somehow managed to make distance in a ten-round no decision against John Lester Johnson on July 14 in New York.

1917

World War I (1914–1918), a war in which the Central Powers (Germany and Austria-Hungary, joined later by Turkey and Bulgaria) were defeated by an alliance of Britain and its dominions, France, Russia, and others, joined later by Italy and the United States, took center stage in 1917. President Wilson called for war on Germany, which the U.S. Congress declared on April 6. Although the United States had pursued a policy of non-intervention, avoiding conflict, especially following the sinking of the British liner RMS *Lusitania* on May 7, 1915, proved impossible. Suddenly, the art of self-defense took on a whole new meaning.

In a continued dissolution of his finances, Nelson sold his eighty-acre Hegewisch farm in January. Purchased by a car manufacturer, their intent was to build a plant and employ 1,500 to 2,000 men. The population of the most remote corner of Chicago would soon grow to 7,000 during the 1920s then remain stuck there for decades.

By February, Nelson was again talking about entering a boxing ring. He set up a twelve-round match against Pierce Mathews at the South Broadway Athletic club in St. Louis but kept postponing due to his plastic surgery. Finally, on March 17, Nelson met and knocked out Pierce Matthews in the eighth round. For Nelson, having not officially crawled between the ropes since November 1915, the bug was back.[67] Forever patriotic, The Battler let it be known that he was ready to join the U.S. Army or Navy if his country was "dragged into war." Naturally, this meant wiring Colonel Theodore Roosevelt. The message read,

> STILL IN THE RING AND WILLING TO ENTER ARENA IF MY COUNTRY TOSSES ITS HAT IN THE RING. IN CASE OF HOSTILITIES WOULD WANT TO JOIN YOUR REGIMENT. FOUGHT FOR MY COUNTRY ONCE IN THE FIRST SOUTH DAKOTA, COMPANY G. WILLING TO DO IT AGAIN. I AM NOT A MOLLYCODDLE. BATTLING NELSON.[68]

Knowing "TR," he was likely delighted by the note.

Like many other pugilists, Nelson was shocked to learn that Ad Wolgast had entered a Milwaukee sanatorium suffering from a mental disorder. Incompetent to manage his large estate, according to physicians, his wife filed a petition asking that she be appointed as guardian. The twenty-nine-year-old former lightweight champion's worth was estimated at $200,000. Wolgast, who never looked as if he fully recovered, did however reenter the ring. He would end his professional career in 1920.

In St. Louis, on April 17, Oscar "Battling" Matthew Nelson fought his last recorded professional fight, a twelve-round "no decision" against, you guessed it, lightweight champion Freddie Welsh. If it had to come to an end, and it did, then why not against the very best?

Welsh quickly proved why he was the champion, scoring cleverly from all angles and with power. His defensive prowess was superb, only being hit solidly less than half a dozen times. And Welsh's infighting dominated his opponent, who had mastered the craft.

> The contest was not all one sided, however. Nelson never failed to meet Welsh in the middle of the ring, and never during the fight did he back off an inch. In the eighth Nelson hit Welsh squarely, but the blow appeared low. The Briton backed up against the ropes, but the referee motion the boxers together again. Welsh, apparently angered, then began his only real attack. He slashed Nelson with right and left hooks and pummeled his body. Soon Nelson was bleeding, and at the end of round eleven both men were crimson from a cut in the Battler's lip. Nelson weighed 132; Welsh 135.[69]

Casting most of the criticism aside, three things have to be acknowledged: First, both fighters need to be recognized for their participation. The press had crucified the match prior to the first punch: "Any sensible follower of fisticuffs will agree that the match is a deplorable one. It ought to be canceled. It should never have been made. The fact that Welsh accepted it is a discredit to him; and the promoter who has to go to the old soldier's home for a boxer to pit against a champion is the poorest matchmaker imaginable."[70] Next, a tip of the hat to "The Welsh Wizard," Freddie Welsh, one

World lightweight champion Freddie Welsh, pictured here, defended his title successfully against Ad Wolgast and Charley White before losing it to Benny Leonard in 1917 (Library of Congress, Prints and Photograph Division, LC-DIG-ggbain-17113).

classy champion who really had no reason to take the fight. And, finally, a salute to Battling Nelson, who was able to leave the ring with the dignity and reverence he deserved.

It was a transformation that surprised some, but not those who knew him. Battling Nelson soon found himself once again under the big top. Circus owners typically spared no expense when it came to feature celebrities and thrilling acts. That's why Fred Buchanan, manager of the Yankee Robinson Three-Ring Wild Animal Circus, was proud to announce this season's greatest added feature attraction, Battling Nelson, the champion lightweight of the prize ring.

> The Great Dane has participated in over 300 ring battles during his twenty years as a professional fighter. Nelson is a wealthy man today and a genuine credit to the scientific doctrine of clean living, an object lesson to all men. Outside the largest cities this will be the first appearance of the champion of the fistic arena whose clean record, both in his profession and in private life, never in his entire career implicated or involved in any shady or dishonest transaction, classes him as a man among men. Battling Nelson the greatest of all champions, with his sparring partners and company of trainers, was the principal attraction at the big athletic show.[71]

Nelson would be appearing on the bill with Captain Irving's double group of performing lions; Alber's wonderful trained polar bears; Van Andrews' mixed group of leopards, jaguars and pumas; Ruth Le Nora and her performing mountain lions; and finally Colonel Hobb's educated horses led by Tango Chief, all blue-ribbon winners at the last Boston horse show.

Many who attended the show were disgusted by Nelson's showing. It was "a punk exhibition of the manly art of self-defense."[72] It wasn't pretty, and the reviews weren't good, but Oscar had always loved the circus. And it was proof that what goes around does actually come around.

Bat's patriotism got the best of him in November, so the Dane decided to wire President Wilson offering his services as an athletic instructor in the cantonments.

> ANY SUCKER WHO WON'T FIGHT FOR HIS COUNTRY SHOULD BE SENT TO GERMANY AND MADE TO FIGHT AGAINST IT.[73]

In breaking new ground, Battling Nelson followed his conscience in an endeavor to regain the lightweight championship. For this, he must be admired. In hindsight, or perfect vision, it is easy to question Nelson's decision to travel to the East Coast to begin his comeback, as well as his dedication to the training, choice of opponents, fight terms and conditions, fight frequency and even choice of management. All these factors played into the equation of a successful resurgence. When they are combined with the frustration of the no-decision era, inadequate personal finance, emotional upheaval, and injury, they present a complex scenario. Nelson's attempts at circumventing some of these factors, such as his decision to travel to Cuba and Mexico, must be acknowledged. In his failure to regain the crown, he created the perfect epilogue: a short-term, no-decision contest against the reigning lightweight champion.

Battling Nelson finished his official career with 131 total bouts. This breaks down as fifty-nine wins, nineteen losses, nineteen draws, thirty-three no decisions and one no contest. He was credited with thirty-eight wins by knockout.[74] Freddie Welsh, a member of the International Boxing Hall of Fame, was his last recorded fight.

Of the battles that took place this year, four additional come to mind, but to be honest with you, none had the emotional relevance of that of April 17, 1917, in St. Louis.[75]

Fourteen

1918–1954
The Final Rounds

> When I do retire people will say of me: "He was the most honest fighter that ever graced the ring, and if there were more like him it would be a boost to the game."
> —"Battling" Nelson[1]

In Abington, Massachusetts, on February 2, 1918, the "Boston Strongboy," crossed the great divide. "When I was a little boy, I tried to model my own career in the ring on his style of always fighting on the level," claimed Nelson having heard of the death of John Lawrence Sullivan while visiting Washington, D.C. "Now, I have laid aside the gloves, save for exercise or to teach some aspiring youngster. I can look backward with pride to the fact that I always did fight on the square."[2] The Dane then spoke to the indelible record left by the redoubtable Sullivan, his honesty and willingness to defend his championship. "While he was fighting, Sullivan hit it up pretty hard, but he finally saw the error of his ways and quit drinking," Nelson continued, "That was a great example for the young men of the country, and I am glad that he fought against liquor and the liquor habit. I am going to hear Billy Sunday today just because he is talking against drink, which is the curse of the country. Billy sure can hand it out in the right way, and you'll see me right up close to the platform, for I'm with Billy First, last and always."[3] When Nelson had finished his commentary about his mentor, it was as if ol' "Sully" died on cue.

Pen in hand and mind on opportunity, Nelson dashed off a February article for the *Washington Times* titled, "Bat Nelson Tells of Kaiser Dummy for All Soldiers." The Battler claimed, "I can't teach individually every one of the 1,500,000 American boys who are going over to lick the Kaiser, but the Battling Nelson Kaiser dummy can work for me. That's why I am trying to have the dummy used in both the army and navy."[4] It was the Dane's hope that the armed services would have it installed everywhere, even reminding the navy that if you cut the leg straps the dummy turns into a life buoy capable of keeping five men afloat indefinitely. Thus the advent of the Battling Nelson Boxing Dummy Company, which gave birth to punching bags graphically designed to look like the Kaiser himself—Wilhelm II or William II, the last German emperor (Kaiser) and king of Prussia.[5] You certainly can't blame Bat for bottling his patriotism—or is it bagging?—into something useful for the war effort.

As a former boxing champion, financial opportunities just didn't drop out of the sky, not during this period. Nelson knew he would have to make more opportunities than he found. The Battling Nelson Boxing Dummy Company, he believed, just made sense. Strong enough to sell the product, Nelson needed to find a way to make it profitable—his business prowess had been open to question, and he had a tendency to throw good money after bad.

"Terrible" Terry McGovern died, of pneumonia and kidney ailment, in Brooklyn, New York, in the charity ward of King's County Hospital on February 26. Born in Johnstown, Pennsylvania, on March 9, 1880, he was quick to garner amateur accolades and by 1899 claimed the bantam title with the retirement of Jim Barry. On September 12, 1899, McGovern stopped English champion Pedlar Palmer in the first round to undeniably capture the world's bantam crown—the first world championship bout under Queensberry Rules to end by a one-round knockout. It would be a crown he would never defend, as he moved up in weight. Then, on June 23, 1900, he stopped George Dixon in eight rounds to win the world featherweight title. McGovern defended the feather crown six times, all knockouts, before losing to Young Corbett in the second round of their November 28, 1901, clash in Hartford, Connecticut. For Battling Nelson, his record gate for a six-round indoor fight against McGovern was a highlight he cherished. Fighting to a no decision at the National Athletic Club on March 14, 1906, the gate receipts totaled an astounding $23,000. McGovern's amassed ring earnings were said to have amounted to more than $200,000. Yet, one of the greatest fighters of all time died penniless.

If you thought a fool and his money were soon parted, you haven't met a boxer. Overconfidence seems to always be transposed onto anybody and any anything a pugilist comes in contact with. Self-assurance may build a champion, but a sound balance sheet builds a successful businessman.

On March 16, 1918, at the Billy Sunday tabernacle, Bat and "Kid" Murphy, former featherweight champion of the U.S. army, offered to put on an exhibition bout at a big athletic carnival held for soldiers and sailors. Both fighters wanted to do something to help the boys in khaki, and this appeared to be the perfect opportunity. It was quite by accident that the former fighters bumped into each other in Washington, D.C. Both were followers of Billy Sunday and attended as many services as they could at the tabernacle.

A popular outfielder in baseball's National League during the 1880s, William Ashley "Billy" Sunday (November 19, 1862–November 6, 1935) would become the most celebrated and influential American evangelist during the first two decades of the twentieth century. He made his Major League debut on May 22, 1883, for the Chicago White Stockings and slowly developed into a proficient fielder and terror along the base paths. It was these skills that caught the attention of the Pittsburgh Alleghenys in 1888, where he played for three seasons. Sunday ended his career with the Philadelphia Phillies on October 4, 1890.

Murphy was quick to add, "Bat and I thought we might do something to help it [the war effort] along. Of course, we're both out of training, but neither of us have ever smoked, chewed, or drank, and we're in fair condition. I'll bet the soldiers will all want to see Battling Nelson, knowing he was the greatest lightweight champion the class ever had."[6]

What finer way to promote the Kaiser Dummy, Nelson thought, than with another stint as part of "The Original Yankee Robinson Annual Tour," this the 77th annual event. Nelson traveled from spring until early summer with the circus. Having toured earlier in the year with his "Walloping the Kaiser" show, Nelson was confident the event would play well and that he would once again get the best of the mustached mannequin—the Battler was even captured for posterity in an army training film. With mounting legal bills, not to mention the cost of launching a new company, it was Nelson's hope that he would soon be seeing dollar signs over dummies.

Entering the U.S. Exemption Board Office, Division No. 20 of Chicago, on September 12, 1918, Battling Nelson and filed his Registration Card. On Serial Number 5287, he stated his permanent home address as 13446 Burley Avenue, Hegewisch, Cook County, Illinois—nobody in the office had the nerve to challenge the Battler regarding his city entry. His present occupation was as an athletic instructor and his nearest relative was listed as Neils Nelson, his father, who could be found at the same address. Nelson describing himself as of medium height and build, with blue eyes and light hair, and signed his name as Battling Nelson. He was at the country's service if needed.

Suffering from a serious bout against the Spanish influenza in October, Nelson had to be hospitalized at St. Luke's in Chicago. Reported penniless as a result of legal technicalities and now medical bills, the former champion appealed to his friends for assistance, and they responded—an organization that he had aided in the past, Boy's Brotherhood Republic, sent a check for $203 to cover his immediate needs. The Battler's recovery was a bit slow, but thankfully he did regain his health. Worth noting is that fighter Charlie White at one point wanted to hold a benefit for the Battler, but the Dane nixed it, stating, "I'm no beggar. All I want is for some of those guys I once loaned money to come across and pay me back."[7] By the end of the month, the Battler felt compelled to return most, if not all, the money he had received.

In a sign of just how deep Nelson's generosity—often claimed to be inexhaustible to those in need and partially accountable for his financial standing—had been in the past, on October 12, a man named E.S. Fitch dropped by a Chicago newspaper with a $5 bill and the accompanying explanatory note: "Sporting Editor: Battling Nelson does not know me, but fourteen years ago my friends gave a benefit for me while I was in the hospital undergoing an operation. Nelson volunteered his services, as I presume he has done for scores of others. Herewith is $5, which, I hope will or can be used as a nucleus of a fund to aid him in his hour of need. Possibly it will shame a few others whom he has financially aided to do likewise. Will try to do more later. E.S. Fitch, Telegraph operator, Western union, main office."[8]

One might believe that in the sport of boxing, it was a small enough world that everyone knew everyone else. Nevertheless, such was not always true. In the world of fund-raisers and exhibitions, the improbable becomes probable, and often to the delight of the fans. Standing in the ring of Howard's Arcade Gym was the imposing figure of Sam Langford, and a mere twenty feet away stood the Battler.

"Who's the colored person?" spoke Nelson to some friends.

"Why, that's Sam Langford," spoke a friend.

"It is, hey?" an astonished and surprised Nelson spoke.

Then Langford approached the group and was asked if he knew the man in front of him—Nelson. "No, chief, I don't know this here person. Who is he?"

He was then told, "that's Battling Nelson." Langford then smiled and said, "Well, well, Bat, I'm glad to meet you," and they shook hands warmly.[9]

Langford was forced to scrap against other black opponents while white boxers hid behind the color line—refusing to fight the greatest non-champion in boxing history. As a result, he found himself in circumstances such as fighting seventy-five bouts against only five opponents: Jim Barry, Jeff Clarke, Joe Jeanette, Sam McVey, and Harry Wills. Brawling in an era where not all fights were recorded, Langford was as versatile as he was prolific—performing in all classes. From lightweight to heavyweight, he recorded 117 knockouts in an estimated 350 total bouts.

Since we're mentioning legends, boxing belonged to William Harrison "Jack" Dempsey in 1918, who went an impressive 20–1 on the year with seventeen kayoed. Appearing unbeatable, his victims included Bill Brennan, Jim Flynn, Fred Fulton, Battling Levinsky, Carl Morris, Arthur Pelkey, and Gunboat Smith. "The Manassa Mauler" would capture the world heavyweight championship in 1919 and keep it until 1926—for seven years and two months, Dempsey, with his movie-star looks, was the perfect champion for the recalcitrant and raucous 1920s.

Nelson respected Dempsey, and vice versa—even if Jack considered Bat a bit quirky. They would often toss remarks at each other, like opening-round jabs, always in jest, always with civility. Dempsey had heard plenty of stories about Nelson—not surprisingly, many from the Dane himself—and admired his resilience, but could also see that the ring had taken a toll on the brawler. Nelson's thought process had slowed, and his behaviors were occasionally misunderstood.

Most thought that if the month of January was an indication of how the rest of the year was going to progress, then it was going to be one heck of a ride. From Edsel Ford succeeding

French lightweight boxer Louis de Ponthieu (left), American heavyweight Carl Morris (center) and American lightweight boxer Leach Cross (right). Battling Nelson believed Morris could take the heavyweight title from Jack Johnson (Library of Congress, Prints and Photograph Division, LC-DIG-ggbain-09912).

his father at the helm of the Ford Motor Company to the Eighteenth Amendment to the U.S. Constitution, authorizing Prohibition, change proved inescapable. As for bad news, as if Prohibition wasn't enough to some, that too was plentiful. For example, Theodore Roosevelt, the twenty-sixth president of the United States, died in his sleep on January 6, 1919. The man who was responsible for initiating many anti-trust laws, successfully engineering the U.S. bid to build the Panama Canal (1904–14) and negotiating the end of the Russo-Japanese War in 1905, never found a challenge, or a challenger, too big to handle. Nelson, like many in the fight game, loved "TR," because he was one of them. Roosevelt was a "man's man," bigger than life and the leading force of the Progressive Era. And Nelson was his fighter, a relentless, durable, indefatigable machine, incapable of defeat, just like himself. Roosevelt was a father figure to Nelson, and his death put an end to an epochal era, a period that formed Nelson into who and what he was. There was now a sense of insecurity—Nelson felt it, as did others—that just wouldn't go away.

By the end of May, the Battler began a sixteen-week engagement in the Middle West that kept him busy throughout the summer. The stage, a far safer confine than the ring, provided him both a creative and financial outlet for his boundless energy. And, speaking of safer, Nelson was fully aware of the sacrifice being made by his fellow countrymen. Members of the Boxers Loyalty League had been tireless in entertaining wounded soldiers at hospital bases and were fittingly remembered by the Red Cross as World War I was concluding. Each of the many boxers, including Nelson, received a gold medal suitably inscribed. The presentations were made by Major Gillette, chief of the Atlantic division of the Red Cross, and Dan Morgan, president of the league. It was a proud moment for many, and for the sport of boxing.

Jack Dempsey landing a right punch to the jaw of giant Jess Willard on July 4, 1919, in Toledo, Ohio, inside the Bay View Park Arena (Library of Congress, Prints and Photograph Division, LC-USZ62-41454).

The Dempsey-Willard fight, on July 4, ushered in boxing's "Golden Age," and it belonged to Jack Dempsey—his annual performances now accumulating into an impressive

Fourteen—1918–1954: The Final Rounds

career. Down an exhaustible seven times in round one, jaw and ribs shattered and his cheekbone split, Jess Willard somehow managed to survive until the third round when his corner wisely threw in the towel. Dempsey's kingdom had been defined. Believe what you want to believe, and state what you may, but just try arguing that Dempsey was not the most colorful, dynamic, exciting and savage fighter of his time, and perhaps all time. It can't be done.

Nelson, familiar with Dempsey's skills, had wired Rickard offering his services as referee for the contest back on May 12. The telegram also stated,

> PRICE OPTIONAL. WOULD DO IT FOR YOU FOR NOTHING. PUT IT UP TO WILLARD AND DEMPSEY.[10]

While Nelson would not referee the clash, he would witness it as a fight reporter for the *Chicago News*. In pragmatic Nelson style, when he found hotel accommodations at a premium, he simply "decided to pitch a tent on the shores of Maumee Bay on which to live."[11] The blue tent, located within the bounds of the arena and adorned in white paint with "Bat Nelson," stayed in its location for a few days before it had to be moved.

Nelson, who would gain a level of notoriety by taking a bath—which, by the way, wasn't frequent regardless of the liquid—in a barrel of lemonade as part of the festivities, was somewhat taken aback when a salesman at a local sporting goods store had no idea who he was. Nelson thought it would be great publicity to have a pair of boxing gloves at the venue with a sign stating, "These gloves are from Messrs. _____, and are used by Battling Nelson." The salesman agreed and wrapped up the gloves for the Dane. While heading for the door, Nelson was questioned regarding payment. A bit stunned, Nelson said, "Say, Mister, you get the ad and I get the gloves; that ought to be a square deal; what more do you want from a man of

Harry Houdini, restrained by Benny Leonard, jokes with heavyweight champion Jack Dempsey (Library of Congress, Prints and Photograph Division, LC-DIG-ggbain-50392).

my reputation? I am Battling Nelson, the greatest lightweight champion that ever lived." The clerk then responded, "Well, I don't care who you are, and I never heard of you in my life. You can't work that game, so come across with the coin."[12] With that, Bat left the parcel with the salesman and headed to another store.

Okay, now back to the lemonade story. Seems like Bat was wondering around Toledo, and like many of those attending the first big fight after the First World War, he was doing everything possible to stay cool. The weather was beastly hot—a few degrees below hell by consensus opinion—and cool drinks, if you could find them, was at a premium. Most of the concessions, as fate might have it, were in the hands of Dr. Jack Kearns, Dempsey's manager. And when Jack and his associates, never far from a buck, saw a chance to sell one of the franchises for a nice sum, they did so. A party from Chicago decided to take their chances on a lemonade stand, so they rushed their supplies—lemon juice, tub, cups, etc.—from their hometown to Toledo. Setting up a small shack close to the arena—after all proximity is everything when it comes to lemonade—they began mixing their concoction in preparation for the following day's event. Once accomplished, it was off to set up an ice delivery.

As we have learned, Nelson was having trouble finding a permanent address for his tent, so he was looking for a cool place to nod off around dusk, and the shack was it. In addition to finding the facility, he was also impressed that someone was nice enough to draw him a bath, so he stripped to his undergarments and nodded off in the tub. Well, nobody remembers who found him, but the next day word had spread that the lemonade was "Ordained," "Nelsonized," "Battleized," or just plain not worth drinking. When sales of lemonade quickly went in the tank, Kearns was forced to quickly assist the vendor in changing his premier offering to ice water.

With so many people at, or covering, the fight, it was easy to pick up conversations between ring fans. Grantland Rice was there, as was Ring Lardner, even another Bat, that being Bat Masterson, who was writing for the *New York Morning Telegraph*. James J. Corbett was also wandering about and noting tidbits for an article he was writing. "Joe Gans was the greatest lightweight that ever lived and don't let anyone tell you otherwise," was the word from Nelson, who was quick to draw a crowd.

> Terry McGovern was a better all-around fighter than Young Corbett, but Corbett knocked Terry kicking both times. Jim Coffey was an infinitely better man than Frank Moran, yet Moran whipped him each start. Ring history records a hundred cases where great fighters went down to defeat before poorer men who somehow or other had their number.[13]

"Gans could whip every man I whipped about ten times faster than I did," Nelson admitted. "He could have gone against some who gave me awful beatings and knocked them kicking in a round or two with one hand tied behind his back."[14] Nelson, who could remain humble for only a certain length of time, then went on to set the record straight on his behalf regarding his notorious 1906 low blow. Frankly, as many times as he had stated his case, few believed him, and at this point it really didn't matter. Gans was tired of rolling over.

"Gans knew more about the science of fighting better than all the men I met put together. He was a master ringman, skilled in every department of the game," Nelson proclaimed. "His footwork was marvelous, his speed bewildering, his stock of tricks inexhaustible and he was game to the core."[15] These were not the words of an intolerant person, but a man proud of his association with the handsome, ebony-skinned Joe Gans, one of the all-time greats. If

Nelson had had a dollar for every time his name appeared anywhere in conjunction with Gans, he never would have encountered financial difficulties.

Hanging up the gloves gave Nelson an opportunity, and there were many, to read how others saw his career, ring assessments, or obituaries if you will. More and more he was being acknowledged for the tremendous ring attributes he possessed. "Battling Nelson Was Example of What Courage Will Do to Advance Pugilist in Ring Career," was an article picked up by a few newspapers. "The Durable Dane's rise to eminence in fistiana wasn't all due to the dogged, irresistible attack and his famous 'left half scissors' punch. It was his Viking courage and persistence—the unshakable belief in his own talents even in the hour of defeat—which made 'a place in the sun' for him in the Queensbury realm," the article read. "Every blow directed at the Nelson physiognomy brought the Dane's adversary that much nearer defeat. In his prime he was impervious to punishment. He invited blows—any number of them—for he had no fear of them. Bat used to explain his indifference to wallops by saying that he wasn't human. And he believed it."[16] Bat appreciated the accolades, hoping it would squelch some of the contemporary accounts of his financial misgivings.

Niels Nelson, aged seventy-three, died on November 12, following a week's illness with pneumonia. In addition to the Battler, he left behind five sons and one daughter. Oscar's relationship with his father, which had faltered in the beginning owing to his desire to box, gradually improved—the pinnacle likely that of Oscar's championship reign. Despite some very modest financial investments made by both, they remained fairly close until the fallout over Oscar's property and subsequent lawsuit. Since it is often the last memory that is called to mind first when a person you love perishes, the Nelsons legal battles would quietly haunt Oscar for the rest of his life.

The Roaring Twenties

According to the 1920 U.S. Census, Battling Nelson, along with his brother Henry, an invalid whom he had cared for since the days in New Mexico, were still residing at 13446 Burley Avenue in Chicago. His neighbors—many of whom knew the Battler but seldom saw him due to his extensive travel schedule—had a diverse selection of surnames, including Argadine, Boran, Carlson, Cebera, Cebula, Davey, Faulk, Giemzik, Hazel, Hefron, Kivialkowski, Kolodziej, Korting, Obare, Pietrucha, Popovich, and Tomicheski, and represented the melting pot that made up Chicago's Eighth Ward. They were proud of the Nelson family and grateful for Bat's efforts to keep Hegewisch fresh in the memory of every resident.

Bat was named as chief beneficiary in his father's will—which was filed for probate on February 20. The testament left $225,000 of the $250,000 estate to the boxer, while the difference was divided among his siblings. While it was always hoped that this circumstance would not cause problems for the family, it became difficult to avoid.

In New York, at the Pennsylvania Hotel over on 425 Seventh Avenue, and having been employed by the *Kansas City Post* and *Denver Post*, was Fay King, cartoonist and feature writer for the *New York Evening Journal*. As evidence of her success and notoriety, she appeared as herself in the Goldwyn film *The Great White Way* in 1924. By 1925, her strip *Girls Will Be Girls* had gathered considerable attention, as did the charming young cartoonist. But Fay loved her privacy and preferred long walks from her Manhattan residence—by 1930, she was living at the Commodore Hotel at 109 East Forty-Second Street—over a midtown social gathering. As time passed, she viewed Oscar as the honest and honorable man he was, and in many ways took pity on him.

In the spring, it was claimed that Nelson had severed all connection with boxing to turn his full attention to the real estate business—a commercial enterprise he had long been associated with. Home building in the Chicago suburbs would now occupy the Dane's time, enhanced by being the beneficiary of his father's estate. Newspaper reports, more filler than fact, noted the dispute but failed to mention any sympathy for the Nelson family. They also failed to note whose earnings had created the bulk of that estate. Also, the Battler had not turned his back on boxing; in fact he was one of sixteen old-time ring champions invited as guests at a reunion dinner given by Major A.J. Drexel-Biddle, president of the International Sporting Club, held in New York on May 2, 1920. The Dane may not have been in a ring, but his passion remained.

Quickly learning that more conflicts could be settled outside the ropes than in, Nelson brought suit for $225,000 against the Nemours Trading Corporation in the U.S. District Court on July 13, 1920, as damages for his arrest last month on a charge of petty larceny. According to two private detectives employed by the company, "he had in his possession three pairs of shoes, two worth $4 a pair, for which he had receipts, and another, worth $6, for which he had nothing to show. He was arraigned before Magistrate[17] McQuade in the Night Court, on East Fifty-seventh Street, in New York, where he was discharged upon his explanation. According to his attorney, Robert K. Kuzmier of 52 Wall Street, the former champion didn't wait for the receipt for the third pair of shoes, as he was in a hurry."[18]

Nelson's charges against his accuser broke down to $75,000 for threats made against him, $75,000 for being taken to the police station without a warrant and $75,000 for wrongfully being charged with petty larceny. As for why Nelson was in New York, he was appearing with his company at some of F.F. Proctor's New York Theaters, like the one on Twenty-Third Street, near Sixth Avenue.

Back on the road in the fall, with his own company, Nelson was pushing a one-act sketch that played various major markets, such as Philadelphia. If he could sustain himself in these selected cities, he felt, he could get over some of his financial hurdles. It was becoming a redundant pattern of the next great opportunity paying for the financial mistakes of its predecessor.

Meanwhile, interest in boxing had grown in New York under the new Walker boxing bill. This was confirmed by the first six bouts conducted in Madison Square Garden by Tex Rickard—Tex had secured the rights to promote live events from Madison Square Garden in New York in 1920.[19] Passed in 1920, the Walker Law reestablished legal boxing in the state following the three-year ban created by the repeal of the Frawley Law.[20]

> The gross receipts for six shows have amounted to $225,300 of which the State has been enriched by $11,265 in taxes. Considering the fact that no champions had appeared in any of the fights made the information far more impressive. Willie Jackson and Eddie Fitzsimmons, two lightweights far away from the championship timber, drew $62,000 at their meeting last week, This is just a little less than Joe Gans and Battling Nelson got for their championship in Goldfield in 1900.[21]

"Battling Nelson filed a petition for an injunction in the Superior court asking that his four brothers and one sister—they all live in the West—be restrained from interfering with his management of his Hegewisch property valued at $150,000. He requested a similar injunction against Robert E.L. Woods, who became administrator of the property when Nelson's father, Neils Neilsen of Hegewisch died last year."[22] Bat's contention was simple. The property was not his father's, and hence the other sons and daughter had no legal claim — the property deeded over to his father years before his death to conserve it for the fighter. The father's will, which supports the claim, bequeaths the estate back to the fighter. But, Woods and Nelson's siblings were seeking to break the will according to Battling Nelson. This was certainly not the way the Nelson family had hoped to spend the holidays.

On the final day of the year, Battling Nelson was granted a referee's license by the New York state boxing commission. Nonetheless, his career as a referee never took off, as Bat was more interested in allowing the fighters to fight it out than breaking them up as the Commissioner's Office requested. It was just Bat being Bat.

On the road in 1921, with "Battling Nelson, King of All Champions and His Boxing Dummy," his "Big Burlesque Show," which carried fourteen entertainers and nearly forty girls, performed twice daily and appeared at places like the National Winter Garden, on Second Avenue at Houston Street in New York. Most certainly work, even if the Dane seemed to enjoy every minute of it, he built some lasting friendships, joked, laughed and even managed to sell a few dummies along the way.

Forever an advocate of the sweet science, Nelson wasn't going to let anyone tear down his game without giving his opinion. On March 25, in Chicago, "Thomas R. Quayle, speaking for the Lake County [Illinois] Law Enforcement league and for the Federated Churches of Chicago, told the legislative boxing sub-committee today that any form of professional boxing 'is vicious,' denounced professional boxers as 'poor citizens.'"[23] Taking in the tale, which also included the remarks of the late Theodore Roosevelt, were pugilists Charlie White, Harry Forbes and Battling Nelson. There was no word as to whether or not Mr. Quayle lived to make it to another speaking engagement.

With the founding and publishing of *The Ring* in 1922 by Nat Fleisher, boxing now had a publication for the ages. Covering the fight game as no publication had done before, it became the conscience of "the sweet science" and "the Bible of Boxing." "Non-participants," or those around the sport, were no longer shoved into the background, unknown fighters became famous worldwide, and forgotten fighters were dusted off and placed into the proper historical context. In February 1931, Nat Fleisher himself penned "Battling Nelson, the Durable Dane," recounting the Dane's "courage, perseverance, endurance, power and physical fitness," and examining his marathon bouts. Another notable article was George Barton's "Durable Dane Greatest Marathon Fight." For boxers like Nelson, *The Ring* became the scrapbook of their life, a storehouse for events they could no longer remember.

When Jack Dempsey took center stage in the fight game, Bat couldn't resist adding his commentary — whether asked, or not.

"Dempsey does with two or three punches what it took others hours to do," Nelson stated while beginning his homily, "I can see things in Jack's fighting that could be improved, though. In the first place Jack boxes with his feet in the wrong position, like he's punching a bag. He should have the right foot back a bit in case he's hit. He should also cover up a bit more when he steps in to trade punches. You know he's careless that way."[24] Bat then added, "Someday, you know a fellow like the late Jim Barry, with a terrible punch (you know Barry had it) will hit Jack on the button and he won't remember any more. An ounce of prevention — you know — that's my dope."[25]

Dempsey, Babe Ruth, Bill Tilden and Bobby Jones defined the "Golden Age of Sports" and quickly reduced their predecessors, and many of their competitors for that matter, to the fine print buried pages deep in the sports section. This as a new breed of sportswriter also emerged—Haywood Broun, Paul Gallico, Ring Lardner, W.O. McGeehan, Grantland Rice and Damon Runyon—and exalted their heroes in ways never before imaginable. The symbiotic relationship between the sportsman and scribe could now be fine-tuned to a pinnacle, as the manly art of modified murder, or the cauliflower industry, was soon romanticized into belletristic monuments for the ages.

Never turning a blind eye to opportunity—even if many times he should have—Nelson seemed always there to assist those in need. Best known for being a member of the 1920 American Olympic Team, Joie Ray was being investigated for filing excessive expense accounts and could be suspended by the AAU. If the organization took action, Ray stated he would take up professional boxing. Well, that was all Bat needed to reach out, stating he would be interested in being his manager, teacher and trainer. Nelson's assistance was not necessary, however, as Ray overcame his adversity and represented the United States in three Olympic Games held in the 1920s, earning a bronze medal for the 3000-meter team race in 1924.[26]

And in more proof of Nelson's willingness to lend a hand, passing by a house in Chicago early in 1922, Nelson heard a baby crying and a woman screaming.[27] Taking it upon himself to enter the residence, the Battler found a man striking a woman, along with another man. The Battler then warned both men about their behavior and a fight erupted. A police patrol arrived on the scene and took the entire party to the station. Nelson landed in a cell where he was detained for several hours until he was identified and released. The authorities warned the Battler that if he wasn't careful, his chivalrous proclivities might someday find him back within the same confines.

Bruises healed, it was off to Indianapolis to salute a friend in May. A testimonial show, which included boxing bouts and exhibitions, was being held for the "Hoosier Bearcat," Jack Dillon—this type of event almost routine to retired boxers. Among those giving exhibitions were Nelson, Jack Britton, Ray Bronson, Johnny Buff, Mike and Tommy Gibbons, Harry Greb and Johnny Wilson. Three real bouts were also held, one of which included former bantam champion Johnny Ertle. For most it was worth the train fares just to see Greb. Known as "The Pittsburgh Windmill," Greb would be named the seventh-greatest fighter of the past eighty years by *The Ring*.

Was it how quickly they remember, or how quickly they forget? At Boyle's Thirty Acres in Jersey City on July 27, 1922, while watching champion Benny Leonard slug it out with contender Lew Tendler, the Battler sought a better view and decided to head to the press stand. Seeing plenty of seats available, the Dane bored in but was thrown out.

With his ego now in check, as if it ever was, Nelson traveled to Washington, D.C., in November 1922, for two reasons. The first was to close a deal with the William P. Armstrong Company to manufacture Battling Nelson boxing dummies. The Dane still certain that the mannequins belonged in every gym across the country, he had been peddling them nearly everywhere, from vaudeville houses to army bases. The second, to continue developing a quartet of fighters he had in his stable. Those working with the former champion: Sergeant Ray Smith, a light heavyweight; Ray O'Malley, a featherweight; Frankie Kenard, a junior lightweight; and George Lamerson, a lightweight. The Battler was convinced he had a couple of champions in his midst; having been looking for fighters in and around the Philadelphia area since August, Nelson finally felt he had found a worthy group. The Dane and his group of hopefuls then headed to the West Coast in December to match with area fighters.

In one of those "say it ain't so," or "ordained," moments, Oscar Nelson announced on March 9, 1923, that he intended to marry a schoolgirl from London named Dora Klein. That's correct, within the next three months he was headed to the altar again, this time with his twenty-three-year-old bride whom he hadn't seen since she was six years old. The Dane noted that they had been corresponding regularly through the mail and decided it was time to get engaged.

There was a time when a story like this made headlines; fortunately for Oscar that time had come and gone. Thankfully for the pair, they were never hitched. Embarrassing as the incident was, it drew attention to Oscar's frail mind-set at the time.

Boxing fans from all over the area gathered at the armory over at Sixteenth Street and Michigan to pay tribute to Harry Gilmore, Sr., a gladiator from the bare-knuckle days and beloved gymnasium owner. Professor Harry Gilmore, as he was called, owned the Boxing and Health Institute at No. 24 E. Adams Street, near State, in Chicago. Suffering from poor health, Gilmore was compelled to move to California, and thus it was only appropriate to send him off with a testimonial event on Tuesday, September 9, 1924, at 8:00 p.m. Although the festivities included four amateur boxing bouts and numerous wrestling contests, the highlight of the evening was Harry himself, who although past the age of seventy sparred a couple of rounds with the Durable Dane. Oscar loved the attention, and the fans loved him—events

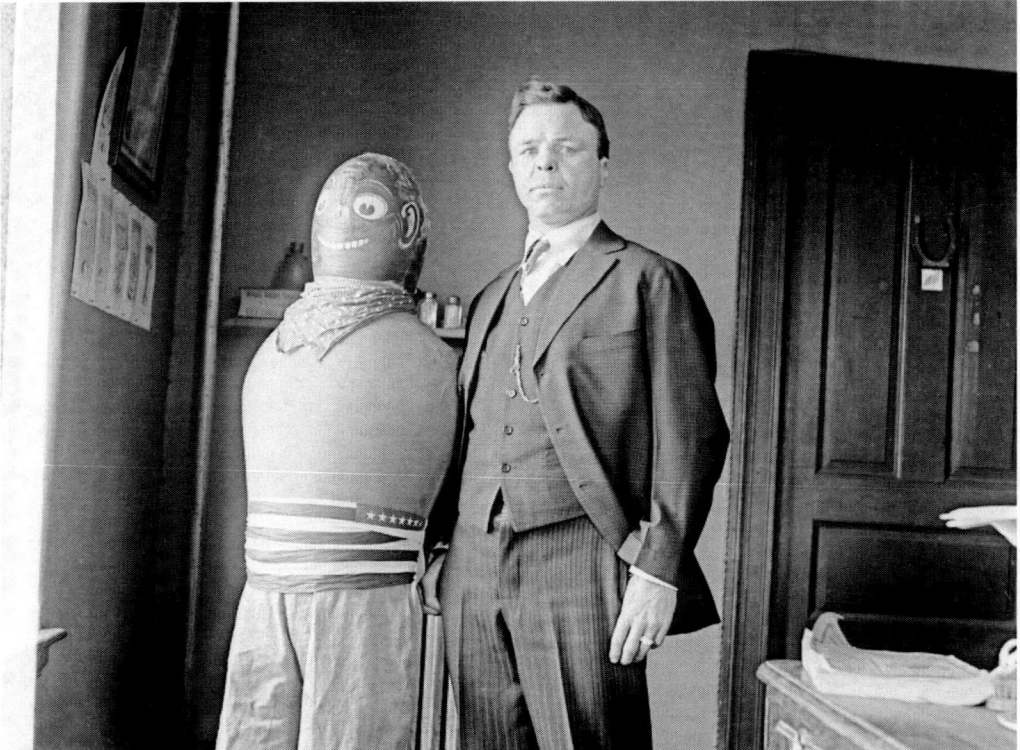

"Battling" Nelson alongside one of his manufactured punching bags, or dummies (Library of Congress, Prints and Photograph Division, LC-DIG-npcc-00260).

like this create lasting memories for generations that never had an opportunity to witness these boxing treasures in their prime.

By early 1927, and in another sign that something just wasn't right, Oscar Nelson was arrested on a charge of disorderly conduct. This after he refused to surrender peacefully to authorities who had been called to his home. The police had a warrant—a charge had been lodged, and then dismissed, in a western state that went unnamed—to recover stolen motion-picture films of the fight seventeen years ago between Ad Wolgast and the Battler. As a consequence of the incident, Nelson was then ordered to undergo an examination at the psychopathic hospital. When his condition was deemed not such to warrant holding him, he was discharged upon arraignment in Municipal Court on March 3. It was another humiliating event, and one more episode he did not understand.

Oscar Nelson was finding himself forgetful, more and more displaced by time. He would leave the house and forget where he was going, or even why. People would greet him on the street and he simply had no idea who many of them were. And, while that happens to many individuals as they get older, it was the frequency of occurrence that concerned those around him.

The death of three—why does bad news always seem to come in the form of a trilogy?—former opponents struck a note with the Battler. The first, William H. Rothwell, aka Young Corbett II, dropped dead on the street in front of a theater in Denver, Colorado, on April 10, 1927. According to physicians, his death was due to heart trouble. Corbett had returned to Denver two years prior, and it had been several years since he fought in the ring.[28] His mastery of the art of humiliation, no better exemplified than with his confrontation with McGovern, gained the featherweight champion a bit of notoriety, but the name of Nelson was often called to mind with his own. Although he dropped back-to-back contests to Nelson (KO by ten, KO by nine) in 1904 and 1905, the confrontations were memorable—if only for the haunting 1909 images of the bloodied face of Corbett—for their sheer brutality.

Aurelio Herrera died in a San Francisco hospital on April 12, 1927, following a long illness. Ironically, his death would follow Young Corbett by hours, a boxer he met often in the ring. His name is typically recalled for not only his fight with Nelson, but also for his loss to Abe Attell in Chicago on March 28, 1904, and for his impressive five-round knockout of Young Corbett on January 12, 1906.

Then "The Pride of Pontypridd," Freddie Welsh, died on July 29, 1927, in New York. Having picked up the lightweight title from Ritchie in 1914, he defended it twice before losing to Benny Leonard in a ninth-round knockout. Welsh then joined the U.S. Army during World War I. Commissioned a captain, Welsh was assigned to rehabilitation of wounded veterans at Walter Reed Hospital in Washington, D.C. He fought six more times before retiring, and always found a smile when someone mentioned he was the only fighter whose last name was also his nationality. Death may end a life, Nelson thought, but not an association.

Many quality fighters emerged during the twenties: Tiger Flowers, Harry Greb, Frankie Genaro, Gene Tunney, Tommy Loughran, Young Stribling and Jack Sharkey, to name only a few. Oscar watched them come and go, mingled with a few at dinners or fights, and even felt worthy, if asked, to comment on their style. However, it had now been a decade since the Dane last battled, and the images were fading.

Nelson was ringside at Soldier Field on September 23, 1927, for the rematch between world heavyweight champion Gene Tunney and former champion Jack Dempsey. Watching from the working press area with stopwatch in hand, Nelson was stunned when he saw Tunney drop to the canvas, but still managed to start his clock. As pandemonium erupted in the amphitheater, Dempsey stood foolishly over Tunney, disobeying the referee's instructions to move to the far corner. Everyone was screaming, "Go back, Jack, go back!" When a member of the working press, who was dictating the fight blow-by-blow over the wire, saw Oscar with his watch, he asked him about the time: "How much time? How much time has passed? When Tunney hit the deck, how much time?" Nelson's response was swifter than Dempsey's retreat, "Sixteen seconds, he's been down for sixteen-seconds."

Forever known as the "Long Count Fight" because a referee apparently took longer than usual to count to ten while Tunney was down, thus unfairly giving him extra time to recover and go on to win the fight, the battle was fought under new rules regarding knockdowns. The fallen fighter, in this case Tunney, would have ten seconds to rise to his feet under his own power after his opponent moved to a neutral corner (one with no trainers). And it was Dempsey's camp that insisted on the rule's implementation for the fight. Tunney went on to retain the world title by a unanimous decision. In a fight that continues to be debated today, many contend that the champion was on the canvas for thirteen seconds, while Oscar insisted it was sixteen. For months, and even years after the bout, Oscar would spin a slight variation of the story to those who would listen. It always hit a crescendo when Oscar shouted, "Sixteen seconds, he's been down for sixteen seconds."

Taking into consideration the full extent and duration of its fallout, the stock market crash of '29 was the most devastating stock market crash in the history of the United States. Beginning on Black Tuesday, October 24, 1929, it flattened the economy. The crash signaled the beginning of the ten-year Great Depression that affected all Western industrialized countries. Many, like Oscar Nelson, who could not afford to lose anything, lost nearly everything. And the economic recovery from the disaster was slow and painful. By 1932, stocks were worth only about 20 percent of their value back in the summer of 1929, and by the following year, nearly half of America's banks had failed, and unemployment was approaching fifteen million people, or 30 percent of the workforce. For many pugilists, their world was reduced from finding their next fight to locating their next meal.

Turn the Page, 1930–1954

It was the great orator Benjamin Franklin, a heavyweight from many perspectives, who quipped, "I wake up every morning at nine and grab for the morning paper. Then I look at the obituary page. If my name is not on it, I get up." As Oscar Nelson grew older, the frequency with which he turned to such pages increased, as did his familiarity with the names that appeared. Another person from the past surfaced on November 29, 1931, with the passing of John D. "Bonesetter" Reese. The popular healer and natural master of orthopedic surgery, born in Wales, died of heart disease in a Youngstown, Ohio, hospital. Among Reese's other famous patients were Ty Cobb, Will Rogers, Gene Tunney and Honus Wagner.

Times were tough, and the little things in life now meant more. Promising to be a historic event, and it was, the first annual CYO intercity boxing meet, between New York and Chicago, was held at Wrigley Field on July 31, 1935. A crowd of 40,000 had a once-in-a-lifetime chance to view a special group of individuals, and it began with the referees: Jack Dempsey, Gene

Tunney, Jimmy Braddock, Max Baer, Benny Leonard, Jimmy McLarnin, Barney Ross, Tony Canzoneri and Teddy Yarosz.

When Nelson's invitation arrived for the event, he was thrilled to accept. It came at one of those times—we all have them, the fewer the better—when he was feeling forgotten, something he dreaded. Standing alongside him would be Johnny Coulon, Harry Forbes, George Gardner, Jimmy Barry, Sammy Mandell, Benny Yanger and Jack McAuliffe. These ring legends would interact with the young scrappers, giving them fighting hints or just providing overall inspiration. And, if that were not enough, two former great lightweights, Packey McFarland and Jack Britton, who were coaches of the Chicago CYO and New York CBC team respectively, would also be there directing the festivities. How ironic to see both McFarland and Britton, once one of boxing's fierce rivalries, now sending pupils into the ring on their behalf.

James Edward Britt died of a heart attack in his San Francisco home on January 21, 1940, and was interred at Holy Cross Cemetery (Colma, California). Following his bout with Nelson, it would be Britt who would battle the undefeated Packey McFarland, losing in a six-round knockout. Britt's loss to McFarland was one of three he would endure in his last four fights, ending his career with three consecutive fights against Johnny Summers in London. With a record of thirteen wins, seven losses, one draw and two no decisions, he will be borne in mind most for his quartet of battles with Nelson. He also fought five other Hall of Famers: George "Kid" Lavigne, Young Corbett II, Joe Gans (twice), Terry McGovern, and Packey McFarland. In the short span of twenty-three professional fights, he spent over 40 percent of the time battling the very best the sport had to offer. The son of a former San Francisco supervisor, Jimmy emerged from the tough "South 'o Market" district of the city to become a contender for the lightweight championship. A benefactor of wise real estate investments, Britt had retired comfortably in his hometown. Because of his association with the Britt family, this death hit Oscar particularly hard. When a smile came across his face at one point, it was in regard to Willus and some of the hysterical moments they shared together—Willus had an answer for everything even if you didn't have a problem.

Folks who knew the Dane knew of his enthusiasm for the sport he loved, along with his ability to spin a line or two; Nelson was one of many who learned the art of intimidation through the antics of John L. Sullivan. But they also knew him for his sarcasm and his ability to laugh. Slapstick, be it at the circus, the cinema, or through cartoons, always put a smile on his face. As bad as things got in the final years, he tried to maintain a smile.

In contrast to his ring reputation was Nelson's appreciation of poetry, especially if it had something to do with himself. Examining his 1908 autobiography, the first poem included, titled "Battling Nelson," appears on page 151; he then jumped from a biographical sonnet to "How a Woman Sees a Fight and Fighters," by Miss Etta Foster, a tale of a Nelson v. Britt fight, thirty-three pages later. Then, on page 197, it was poet Fred Eldridge's five verses about Nelson's training camp—the first poem many had ever read that was inspired by a boxer's preparation for a fight. Then, two pages after that, he published a verse titled "The Battler at Los Angeles Assisting San Francisco's Destitute," by English Jack. A mere four lines short of a villanelle, with little attempt to mirror one, it was doubtful that W.H. Auden felt threatened by lines such as:

> *Who is that little sun-burned man,*
> *Who takes in so much dough?*
> *It's Battling Nelson, he replied.*
> *At least they told me so.*[29]

Ya see, Nelson was selling newspapers on the street... you remember. Finally, near the end of his work, it was time for a sonnet to acknowledge Nelson's defeat of Gans, at the hands of the fighting Dane, with "That Little Battling, Fighting Dane," by Mr. R.H. Guelich. While it is not known just how much Oscar's interest in poetry grew, if at all, one has to give him credit for crossing into the genre and including it in his autobiography. As he got older, he kept a clipping of one of the poems in his wallet and was quick at the draw if needed.

James Wood "Sunny Jim" Coffroth passed away at the age of seventy on February 6, 1943. Since suffering a heart attack on January 29, he had been struggling with his health and required an oxygen tent to breath. Recognized as boxing's first large-scale promoter, Coffroth's promotions had become legendary: Corbett-Jeffries, Bob Fitzsimmons–George Gardner, Battling Nelson–Joe Gans and Stanley Ketchel–Jack Johnson. The political climate, along with competition, drove him into other directions, like horse racing. In 1916, he opened a horse-racing track in Tijuana, Mexico, and established the first $1 million stake. His patriotism led Coffroth and associates to raise $7.5 million for World War I relief funds primarily through boxing exhibitions featuring Jack Dempsey and Benny Leonard. For Oscar, Coffroth's death was a loss of another piece of his past, in a puzzle he was often struggling to keep together.

Battling Nelson, following a five-day bout with pneumonia, walked out of Cook County Hospital on July 12, 1948, one very thankful man. He had been pronounced serious last Tuesday when he entered the hospital and now felt well enough to return to his clerk's job at the main Chicago post office. At the time of his illness Bat was living in a small hotel on the south fringe of Chicago's Loop. Age wasn't all that exciting; anyone can get old, Nelson thought, all you have to do is live long enough.

Only a few newspapers picked up on it, the fiftieth anniversary of Battling Nelson's first professional fight on September 3, 1946. Others wondered, who was left to remember the Durable Dane? Still nimble at age sixty-four, Bat impressed newsmen with his recollection of his very first professional fight against Wallace's Unknown—told as if he had just stepped out of the big top. However, many of the people, places and things associated with that era had slipped into darkness—names like Joe Gans and Terry McGovern rolled off his tongue, even when details of later fights could not be recalled. He admitted being a bit cocky, and always willing to fight anybody at the drop of a hat, or purse—the swagger, jibes and racial slurs just a part of the fight game. Old, bored, and less mobile, Nelson was now fighting daily just to survive.

Another puzzle piece was lost on March 17, 1949, with the death of Owen Moran. His greatest moment had come at Nelson's expense on November 26, 1910. The Durable Dane, with his iron chin, dropped like a rock when out of nowhere came a hammer-wielding right in the eleventh round. "The Fearless" applied his trade until 1916, when he finally hung up the gloves.

From 1942 until March 1950, Oscar Nelson took a temporary job in the Chicago post office. The wartime job couldn't have come at a better time as Nelson was broke and living in squalid hotels with his second wife Edna. He learned at one point that if he proved himself a veteran of the Spanish-American War he could earn a pension, but his attempt failed when he learned he had lost his discharge papers. Still recognizable, if of course you followed boxing, the bespectacled Nelson remained lean, with a full head of brownish-gray hair and trademark "trimmed" cauliflower ears. At the drop of a hat, he would strike a pose or recite his ring highlights, and did so whenever asked by a co-worker or member of the media.

On March 15, 1950, friends of the Battler went to work to try to assist their sixty-seven-year-old friend who had tried, but failed, to obtain a pension from the Veterans Administration. Led by Douglas Anderson, Chicago secretary for Senator Paul Douglas of Illinois, they hoped to introduce a private bill, if necessary, to get Nelson his pension. The Battler, who insisted that he served in the army from May to September 1898, was told by a VA spokesperson that they could not find records to verify his claim. He would later assert—having faced serious financial problems—that when he lost his last home in Hegewisch, he also misplaced many of his newspaper clippings and papers, one of which was believed to be his discharge papers.

With no official records to support the application, Nelson needed to submit affidavits from men with whom he served to verify his claim. Which of course wouldn't be easy, but the Battler intended to do whatever it took for the agency to reconsider his application. Oscar Nelson was facing a crisis he never thought possible. Having been released from his job as a provisional postal worker only last week, this left him with a pension of only $22 per month, so he desperately needed the additional $90 a month the war veteran's pension would provide. Anderson, who remained confident, affirmed that his office had supplied two affidavits and even a photograph of Nelson in uniform to support the claim. Everyone involved tried to remain optimistic, even if the outlook was uncertain.

When Nelson picked up the newspaper on the morning of April 9, 1950, he learned that his ex-manager, John R. Robinson, had died the previous day. Born on Prince Edward Island, Robinson came to the United States in 1893. A war veteran—Spanish-American, Boer Wars, Nicaraguan Revolution and World War I—and an extremely talented athlete, Robinson lettered in a variety of sports at the University of North Carolina. A gifted journalist, he left his mark at the *Boston Traveler* and the *Fort Worth Record* before eventually extending his business prowess into the paper industry, at companies such as the Butler Paper Company, Rex Paper Company and the Import Paper Company. His work at the *Chicago Herald-Examiner*, from 1934 until 1939, served only to solidify his reputation as an outstanding journalist. Robinson then moved on to positions at the Northeast Mississippi Council, from 1941 until 1943.

Returning to his beloved Chicago, Robinson served as publicity chairman of the Chicago Newspaper Publishers Association and assisted in a variety of wartime efforts before operating his own public relations firm. A recipient of numerous war honors, Robinson was also commander of the United Spanish-American War Veterans. He was survived by his widow, Lucille, and a brother Wallace.

On the morning of November 13, 1951, two Chicago thugs were waiting patiently for their next target. When they spotted what looked to be a frail sixty-nine-year-old man coming their way, they decided he was it. They rushed and assaulted him on Chicago's State Street, between Eighth and Ninth, in an attempted robbery. Having wrestled him to the ground, the two hoodlums managed to badly cut the lower lip of their victim before he somehow rose to his feet. It was then that their target, Battling Nelson, was able to fire an uppercut that dropped one of the ruffians before both managed to flee. The police arrived shortly thereafter. The former champion's instinctive physical powers were still there, even if his mental faculties were not. Under protest, as one might have guessed, Nelson was taken to the county hospital for repairs. Following five stitches, the Battler returned to his residence at 620 State Street.

After the loss of his job at the post office, Oscar Nelson's health, not to mention that of his wife, quickly deteriorated. Often too proud to ask or unwilling to accept assistance, they appeared to get by on a shoestring. The couple maintained a private and transient lifestyle—many observed and yet were oblivious to the Nelsons' state of penury in which a daily triumph could be as simple as a meal, be it hot or cold.

Forever Adversaries

Although Nelson's name was far more recalled with regard to Joe Gans, the media loved to reminisce about, then embellish upon, the rivalry between the "Durable Dane" and the "Michigan Wildcat," Ad Wolgast. And it worked, because the fighters detested each other.

Beginning with the basics: Denmark-born Nelson was five years, eight months and three days older than Wolgast, who was born in Cadillac, Michigan. Both then settled in the Midwest and came from large families. Nelson's professional debut was prior to 1900, or nine years, nine months and seven days ahead of Wolgast's first pro fight. Both gladiators used the fight city of Milwaukee—training out of Paddy Dorrell's Beanery in the Bowery—to help launch their careers. Both were lightweights, Nelson three inches taller with a two-inch reach advantage.

Taking into consideration the various sources for professional boxing records, suffice it to say that both men have equal records. One could argue the details, such as Nelson having a few more defeats or hundreds of more rounds fought, but essentially, wins, losses, draws and other statistics do not heavily favor either boxer.

Wolgast held the lightweight title for 1,010 days, Nelson for 623 days, with a difference of 387 days. Nelson fought forty-seven recorded times after his title loss, Wolgast forty-six. When both warriors finally lost their title, they did so to a Hall of Fame caliber boxer.

Both pugilists met and married independent women, Mildred Wolgast and Fay King, who met each other and respected one another. In fact, on September 13, 1913, while in Portland, Oregon, both announced that their husbands would no longer fight each other for as long as they both shall live. A month later, both fighters—don't let me fail to mention that both were stubborn pugilists with selective hearing—fought to a ten-round no decision in Milwaukee. So much for who wears the pants in the family, and who ended up with them—both women eventually sued for divorce.

To Nelson, Wolgast was a "cheese champion," "cheap," and simply a "dirty fighter." To Wolgast, Nelson was a "snake," "hypocrite," and clearly a "dirty fighter." Both men-at-arms were indefatigable, confident, courageous combatants, who would do anything not to lose. The punishment each could endure was proof of their indestructibility. Both mercenaries broke bones, damaged limbs and suffered some of the same illnesses, like appendicitis. And both even sought plastic surgery in a bout with resurfacing.

Their forty-round battle on February 22, 1910—a rematch of their July 13, 1909, clash—was one of the most unscrupulous title fights on record. Agreeing ahead of time to a no-holds-barred battle, they pushed, pulled, and punched one another in a foul-ridden clash that saw both even bite one another. When it was over, only Wolgast had his vision, and you can take that any way you would like.

There has long been a story of the rivalry between Thomas Jefferson and John Adams, both the last surviving members of the original American revolutionaries. Although they both agreed on the fundamentals—democracy, mixed with life, liberty and the pursuit of happiness—their opinions on how to get there gradually differed. The competitiveness between the two was intense, both stubborn beyond remorse. When the end came for both, on July 4, 1826, Adams's last words were, "Thomas Jefferson still survives." He was mistaken. Jefferson had died five hours earlier at Monticello.

Battling Nelson and Ad Wolgast were the last surviving members of the marathon prizefighters. They were old-fashioned pugilists, who bored in and fought out. Their disdain for each other fueled their competitiveness and their irrepressible quest to reach the pinnacle of their profession. And sadly, in January 1954, both men were alone, insolvent and institutionalized. Stories were told how Wolgast, who would be under medical care for more than half of his life, spent hours in a makeshift sanatarium gym training for his next battle with Nelson. And how Nelson would strike a pose and babble incessantly about how he was being fouled by Wolgast. On February 7, 1954, Wolgast would have drawn pleasure in knowing that he had outlasted the "Durable Dane," if of course he could comprehend it. He could not.

Not to Be Forgotten

He would sit, head down, looking at the floor, head twitching slightly and elbows touching his thighs. A leg would occasionally twitch or bob, and when it did, he would drive the corresponding elbow harder into his thigh. Both hands would come together, slightly shaking and rise to form a circle before his index fingers pushed into his forehead to begin the backward motion that pushed his brownish-gray hair back from his widow's peak, his thumbs gradually disappearing behind his rebuilt tin ears. The look on his face had no depth, and the man who once could never stop talking said nothing. The art of the sweet science was now the horror of the sweet silence.

A sad, feeble, eighty-pound human being, who once could have his way with any man inside a ring, was ordered committed to the Chicago State Hospital on January 4, 1954. Judge Walter J. Stevens of Sterling, Illinois, acting county judge in the Psychopathic Court in Chicago, issued the commitment order. It was the melancholy voice of Dr. Clarence B. Geary that broke the news that Mr. Nelson was suffering from "an incurable senile dementia."

Characterized by a decrease in cognitive abilities, senility erodes a person through memory loss, making them unable to concentrate or to make a sound judgment. With a stooped posture, wrinkled skin, decrease in muscle strength and some vision issues, Nelson exhibited some, but not all, symptoms of senility. His mental deterioration, or the loss of his intellectual ability, is what concerned his doctors and led to their diagnosis.

Protesting their brother's commitment were Charles F. Nielsen, superintendent of schools at Paradise, California, and Arthur Nelson of Chicago, a railroad employee. An empathetic Judge Stevens told them that they could remove Mr. Nelson from the hospital if they could provide him with private institutional care. That is when Charles stated that he would happily take him to California but had nobody to care for him. It was heart wrenching for both of them to witness the degradation of their brother and to accept that there was so little they could do for him.

Contrasting this against the knowledge that somehow Oscar Nelson managed to bury his wife Edna, aged sixty, just last week on December 26 made the situation even more difficult to accept. Somehow this very proud and extraordinary man was able to call on what few faculties remained to accomplish the task.

Oscar had no idea that from this day forward, the day of his commitment to the state hospital, his count had begun. In 816 hours, or 34 days, Oscar "Battling" Matthew Nelson would die of lung cancer at the macabre institution also known as Dunning State Hospital.

Conditions at the overcrowded institution would be considered reprehensible by today's standards. Long poorly ventilated, narrow and congested hallways were lined with mattresses placed on hardwood floors. Patients roamed the halls or sat motionless in wooden chairs across from their temporary berths. Those between the barren walls were victims of alcohol, abortion, domestic violence, mental abuse, narcotics and many other illnesses difficult to diagnose and even more difficult to treat. As deplorable as it sounds from a patient's perspective, to slip away under such circumstances had to be even more painful for the families to accept, yet this was the state of mental health in this country.

The Veteran Boxing Association put up $300 for a funeral of one of their own; the remainder was paid for by cartoonist Fay King. Inside Egan's Southside Mortuary, Alderman Egan, the undertaker, did a marvelous job placing the former champion, in a pinstriped suit complete with shirt, tie and silk handkerchief. Noticeably fragile, he was set inside a large gray metal casket, adorned on the outside with a floral-type pattern. The open casket was draped from behind with large ferns, and flowers—beautiful arrangements from his surviving brothers and his ex-wife, Fay King—adorned both sides.

Small groups of people gathered—naturally an outpouring of older individuals from Hegewisch was clearly evident—to pay their final respects to the Battler. Friends, neighbors, boxers, trainers, managers, seconds, everyone had a terrific tale to tell of the Dane. You could wallpaper the room with adjectives to describe Oscar, "proud," "tough," "indestructible," "honest"—they seemed endless. A funeral service was held on February 10, conducted by the Reverend Arthur Mohns of the Chicago Lawn Methodist Church. As large limousines bearing the Battler's body passed through the streets of Chicago and then out to Eden Gardens (Eden Memorial Gardens) for burial, some noticed, but most simply went about their day. Pallbearers Tony Zale and Tommy Kluth were at the head of the casket, followed by others including Johnny Coulon, Sammy Mandell and Earl Mastro.[30]

A simple gray grave marker, adorned on both sides by a graphic of a pair of boxing gloves, reads, "OSCAR NELSON, JUNE 5, 1882–FEB. 7, 1954, 'BATTLING NELSON,' MEMBER OF VETERAN BOXER'S ASSOCIATION." It rests beside that of his wife, also a simple gray grave marker, adorned on both sides by a graphic of what looks to be a bow, that reads: "Mrs. Oscar (EDNA) Nelson, 1893 (then a graphic of a pair of boxing gloves) 1953, VETERAN BOXER'S ASSN."

The Joe Gans versus Battling Nelson trilogy is still considered by most historians as one of the greatest trilogies in boxing, and one of the most memorable in all of sports. And rightfully so as it captured our imagination, placed two of the greatest warriors of not only their time, but of all time, into a coliseum for a triad of historic battles.

> He will wipe away every tear from their eyes, and death shall be no more, neither shall there be mourning, nor crying, nor pain anymore, for the former things have passed away.—Revelation 21:4

Appendix: Records

Abbreviations: KO=Knocked out opponent; KO by=Knocked out by opponent; W=Won by Decision; L=Lost by decision; WF=Won on foul; LF=Lost on foul; D=Draw; ND=No Decision; NC=No Contest; *EX*=Exhibition. The number of rounds completed follows the abbreviation.

Official Record

Battling Nelson
(The Battler, Durable Dane) Born: June 5, 1882, Copenhagen, Denmark
Died: February 7, 1954, Chicago, Illinois
Right-handed; 5'7½"; 133 pounds
Managers: Teddy Murphy (1903–1904), Billy Nolan (1905–1907), Willus Britt (1908–1909), John Robinson (1910–end)

Notes: The period from 1896 until 1908, references Nelson's account of fights, rounds and money received, followed by additional particulars. Reference: Oscar "Battling" Matthew Nelson, *Life, Battles and Career of Battling Nelson, Lightweight Champion of the World* (Hegewisch: self-published, 1908), p. 16; selected exhibitions appear in italics. Because of a number of factors, boxing records during Nelson's era often differ, or are incomplete. Anomalies will be noted where applicable.

1896

Sep 3	Wallace's Unknown	Hammond, IN	KO1

Notes: Number of fights—1, Rounds—1, Money Rec'd—None.

1897

June 5	Ole Olson	Hegewisch, IL	W3

Notes: Number of fights—1, Rounds—3, Money Rec'd—$3.00.

1898

May 10	Freddie Green	Sioux Falls, SD	W7
May 11	Soldier Williams	Sioux Falls, SD	KO8

Notes: Number of fights—2, Rounds—15, Money Rec'd—$20.00; Green was carried from the ring unconscious; some sources claim only three rounds for Williams fight.

1899

Jan 1	Eddie Herman	Hegewisch, IL	D6
Apr 6	Eddie Penny	Chicago, IL	KO1
May 3	Bull Winters	Chicago, IL	KO1
June 1	Unknown John Smith	Chicago, IL	KO2

Notes: Number of fights—4, Rounds—10, Money Rec'd—$15.00; Nelson, as he saw it, began his professional career on January 1, 1899, with the Herman fight.

1900

Jul 4	Feathers Vernon	West Pullman, IL	ND6
Aug 30	Charles Dougherty	Chicago, IL	KO1
Sep 14	Joe Hedmark	Chicago, IL	L6
Sep 21	Harry Griffin	Chicago, IL	W6
Oct 8	Young Bay	Chicago, IL	W6
Nov 2	Clarence Class	Chicago, IL	D6
Nov 12	*Jack Readle*	*Chicago, IL*	*EX3*
Nov 12	*Joe Curtin*	*Chicago, IL*	*EX3*
Nov 15	Black Griffo	Chicago, IL	KO3
Nov 22	Ed Burley	Chicago, IL	KO5
Dec	Pete Boyle	Chicago, IL	LF4
Dec 1	Danny McMahon	Chicago, IL	D4
Dec 7	Joe Percente	Chicago, IL	WF2
Dec 8	Jack Martin	Chicago, IL	W6

Notes: Number of fights—14, Rounds—61, Money Rec'd—$179.00 (includes exhibitions in total); Joe Hedmark was Nelson's first loss; the November 12 bouts were held the same date as part of Eddie Santry's benefit; Nelson fought in two Chicago bouts on December 1.

1901

Mar 17	Black Griffo	Chicago, IL	KO3
Apr 19	Mickey Riley	Milwaukee, WI	L6
May 3	Charles Berry	Milwaukee, WI	D6
May 18	Harry Fails	Omro, WI	ND6
May 24	Harry Fails	Rhinelander, WI	D10
Nov 10	Billy Heck	West Pullman, IL	ND4
Nov 15	Joe Percente	Milwaukee, WI	L6
Nov 29	Eddie Santry	Chicago, IL	NC6
Dec 2	Joe Percente	Milwaukee, WI	D6
Dec 16	Mike Walsh	Chicago, IL	KO6
Dec 17	Charles Berry	Milwaukee, WI	L6

Notes: Number of fights—11, Rounds—65, Money Rec'd—$606.73; the result of the Santry bout was predetermined and likely viewed as a no contest. Nelson recorded the fight as "L6."

1902

Jan 13	Frank Colifer	West Pullman, IL	KO5
Jan 21	Charles Berry	Fond du Lac, WI	L8
Mar 13	Joe Percente	Oshkosh, WI	W8

Mar 17	Kid Ryan	Chicago, IL	KO5
Mar 21	"Cyclone" Johnny Thompson	Chicago, IL	W6
Apr 5	William Rosser	Harvey, IL	KO1
Apr 12	Danny McMahon	West Pullman, IL	D6
May 17	Pudden Burns	Hegewisch, IL	W6
Jun 14	"Battling" Billy Hurley	Hammond, IN	D6
Dec 2	Elmer Mayfield	Hot Springs, AR	W10
Dec 26	Christy Williams	Hot Springs, AR	KO17

Notes: Number of fights—11, Rounds—78, Money Rec'd—$724.50; Rosser fight was shortest of Nelson's career.

1903

Jan 3	George Brownfield	Hot Springs, AR	ND4
Jan 6	Sammy Maxwell	Hot Springs, AR	KO11
Mar 17	Adam Ryan	Little Rock, AR	D15
Apr 5	Jack Robinson	Hot Springs, AR	ND6
Apr 24	"Cyclone" Johnny Thompson	Milwaukee, WI	W6
May 22	Stockings Kelly	Milwaukee, WI	KO4
Jun 16	Young Scotty	Fond du Lac, WI	W8
Jun 19	Mickey Riley	Milwaukee, WI	D6
Jun 20	Larry McDonald	Harvey, IL	KO4
Jun 27	Clarence English	Kansas City, MO	D15
Jul 15	Mickey Riley	Ashland, WI	NC11
Jul 24	Mickey Riley	Hurley, WI	D15
Aug 26	Eddie Sterns	Michigan City, IN	NC9
Sep 3	"Dare Devil" Tildon	Chicago, IL	ND2
Oct 16	Charles Neary	Milwaukee, WI	L6
Nov 10	George Memsic	Milwaukee, WI	W6
Dec 28	Clarence English	St. Joseph, MO	W15

Notes: Number of fights—17, Rounds—142, Money Rec'd—$2,307.50; Nelson lists Maxwell fight as "KO11," while other sources list it as "KO10"; Nelson lists Ryan fight as "D15," while other sources list it as "D20"; the Robinson fight had the parameter that "nobody must be knocked out"; police intervened during July 15 bout with Riley; Riley fight on July 24 is incorrectly listed as July 23 on page 17 of Nelson's autobiography; Sterns fight likely a "NC9"; police intervened during September 3 bout with Tilden. Nelson acknowledged payment for Tilden fight. Not all sources recognize Tilden bout; Young Scotty had conditions altered; Nelson subbed for Eddie Santry on 8/26 in controversial loss; Club Neary parameters on 10/16 amount to a controversial loss.

1904

Jan 16	Art Simms	Milwaukee, WI	KO3
Feb 5	Jack O'Neil	Milwaukee, WI	W6
Apr 6	Joe "Spider" Welsh	Salt Lake City, UT	KO16
Apr 12	*Tommy Markham*	*Eureka, UT*	*EX3*
May 20	Martin Canole	San Francisco, CA	KO18
Jul 29	Eddie Hanlon	San Francisco, CA	KO19
Sep 5	Aurelio Herrera	Butte, MT	W20
Nov 29	Young Corbett II (HOF)	San Francisco, CA	KO10
Dec 20	Jimmy Britt	San Francisco, CA	L20

Notes: Number of fights—9, Rounds—115, Money Rec'd—$13,303.00 (includes exhibitions in total); some reports have Simms saved by the bell in the third round; police intervened in bout with Welsh.

1905

Feb 28	Young Corbett II (HOF)	San Francisco, CA	KO9
May 22	Abe Attell (HOF)	Philadelphia, PA	ND6
Jun 2	Kid Sullivan	Baltimore, MD	D6
Jun 6	Jack O'Neil	Philadelphia, PA	ND6
Sep 9	**Jimmy Britt**	**Colma, CA**	**KO18**
	—White Lightweight Championship of the World		

Notes: Number of fights–5, Rounds–45, Money Rec'd–$25,591.00.

1906

Mar 14	Terry McGovern (HOF)	Philadelphia, PA	ND6
Aug 13	*Willard Bean*	*Salt Lake City, UT*	*EX3-paid*
Sep 3	**Joe Gans (HOF)**	**Goldfield, NV**	**LF42**
	—Lightweight Championship of the World		

Notes: Number of fights—3, Rounds—51, Money Rec'd—$35,271.50 (includes exhibitions in total); exhibitions where Nelson was paid are recognized as such.

1907

Jul 31	Jimmy Britt	San Francisco, CA	L20
Oct 19	*Tom Freebury*	*Red Lodge, MT*	*EX4-paid*
Oct 23	*Charles Berry*	*Billings, MT*	*EX4-paid*
Oct 26	*Mark Nelson*	*Minot, ND*	*EX4-paid*

Notes: Number of fights—4, Rounds—32, Money Rec'd—$10,500.00 (includes exhibitions in total).

1908

Jan 13	Jack Clifford	Ogden, UT	KO5
Feb 4	Rudolph Unholz	Los Angeles, CA	ND10
Mar 3	Jimmy Britt	Los Angeles, CA	ND10
Mar 31	Abe Attell (HOF)	San Francisco, CA	D15
May	*Jack Grace*	*Seattle, Portland, WA*	*EX3*
Jul 4	**Joe Gans (HOF)**	**Colma, CA**	**KO17**
	—Lightweight Championship of the World		
Jul 5	*Red Cornett*	*Livermore, CA*	*EX4-paid*
Sept 1	*Jeff Perry*	*San Francisco Bay*	*EX3*
Sep 9	**Joe Gans (HOF)**	**Colma, CA**	**KO21**
	—Lightweight Championship of the World		
Sep 27	*Joe Galligan*	*Chicago, IL*	*EX3*

Notes: Number of fights—10 (includes exhibitions in total), Rounds—91, Money Rec'd—$32,965.57; Total to this point: Number of fights—92, Rounds—710, Money Rec'd—$121,486.80; Grace exhibition replaced a canceled fight with Kid Scaler in Seattle; Perry exhibition aboard the USS *Ohio*.

1909

May 29	**Dick Hyland**	**Colma, CA**	**KO23**
	—Lightweight Championship of the World		

Jun 22	Jack Clifford	Oklahoma City, OK	KO5
	—Some sources question this fight as a title defense.		
Jul 13	Ad Wolgast (HOF)	Los Angeles, CA	ND10

Notes: Referee confirmed that Clifford fight was stopped by deputy in charge.

1910

Jan 21	Eddie Lang	Memphis, TN	KO8
	—Some sources question this fight as a title defense.		
Feb 22	**Ad Wolgast (HOF)**	**Port Richmond, CA**	**KO by 40**
	—Lightweight Championship of the World		
Oct 10	Monte Dale	Kansas City, MO	KO3
Oct 31	Anton LaGrave	San Francisco, CA	D15
Nov 26	Owen Moran (HOF)	San Francisco, CA	KO by 11

Notes: Lang as a title defense could be questioned.

1911

Jul 3	*Ned Whitman*	*North Bend, WA*	*EX6*
Jul 4	*Percy Cove*	*Bellingham, WA*	*EX6*
Aug 4	Tommy Gaffney	Medford, OR	KO5
Sep 19	Billy Nixon	Boston, MA	KO10
Oct 3	Milburn "Young" Saylor	Boston, MA	L12
Oct 11	Willie Beecher	New York, NY	ND10
Oct 17	"Philadelphia" Pal Moore	Boston, MA	L12
Oct 19	George Alger	Augusta, ME	ND6
Oct 25	Monte Dale	Manchester, NH	W15
Nov 6	Frank Loughrey	Watervliet, NY	ND10
Nov 10	Tommy Moore	Buffalo, NY	KO9
Nov 25	Louis de Ponthieu	Buffalo, NY	ND10
Nov 30	Joseph Spero	Toronto, Ont., Can	KO6
Dec 4	Andy Bezenah	Jeffersonville, IN	ND10
Dec 15	Bobby Wilson	Utica, NY	ND10
Dec 18	Willie Howard	Brooklyn, NY	ND10
Dec 22	George "One-Round" Hogan	Brooklyn, NY	ND10
Dec 31	Jack Redmond	New Orleans, LA	W20

1912

Jan 9	Tommy O'Rourke	Springfield, MO	ND10
Feb 26	Young Togo	Fort Smith, AR	W6
Mar 1	Sammy Trott	Dayton, OH	D15
Jul 1	Andy Bezenah	Winnipeg, Man., Can	ND12
Jul 12	Mickey McIntyre	Winnipeg, Man., Can	ND12
Sep 2	Steve Ketchel	St. Joseph, MO	D15
Nov 14	Art Stewart	Hammond, IN	ND10
Nov 28	Leach Cross	New York, NY	ND10
Dec 13	Teddy Maloney	Philadelphia, PA	ND6
Dec 20	Jimmy Bonner	Tamaqua, PA	ND10
Dec 31	Yankee Schwartz	Columbus, OH	ND8

Notes: Nelson broke both his hands in the fight against Trott.

1913

Jan 3	Frankie Russell	New Orleans, LA	L10
Feb 5	Ray (Jack) Sorenson	Racine, WI	ND10
Feb 11	Harry Dillon	Tamaqua, PA	KO10
Feb 17	Joe Burke	Easton, PA	ND10
Feb 22	Bay Wood	New Bedford, MA	D12
Mar 5	Frank Whitney	Atlanta, GA	ND10
Mar 27	Mike Malone	Pueblo, CO	ND10
Apr 19	Bay Wood	New Bedford, MA	D12
Apr 29	Gilbert Gallant	Boston, MA	L12
May 3	Pat Bradley	Philadelphia, PA	ND6
Oct 13	Ad Wolgast (HOF)	Milwaukee, WI	ND10

Notes: Russell was awarded the decision by the referee, L10. Nelson broke his right hand in the Russell fight; The rounds were cut to two minutes for Nelson's fight with Ray Sorenson; Nelson did not anticipate paying for opportunity to fight Dillon. Some sources misspell Bay Wood's name as Ray Woods; Whitney fight believed to be a no decision rendered by prior agreement.

1914

Aug 19	Cliff Ford	Sault Sainte Marie, MI	W6
Dec 16	Andy Bezenah	Cincinnati	ND4

Notes: The Ford fight, listed in a number of record books, could not be verified by multiple reliable sources; Nelson's December 16 four-round bout—terms and conditions unavailable—with Andy Bezenah in Cincinnati is not included in many sources.

1915

Mar 18	Stewart "Young" Donnelly	Havana, Cuba	KO3
Mar 24	Jimmy Fryer	Havana, Cuba	W25
Apr 24	Dale Gardner	Havana, Cuba	KO2
Sep 6	Bobby Waugh	Juarez, Mexico	L20
Nov 5	"Fighting" Jimmy Reagan	Kansas City, MO	L10

Notes: Gardner fight not listed in many sources; while in both Mexico and Cuba, Nelson may have participated in other selected "one-off" battles; Philadelphia fighter Jimmy Fryer has also had his last name spelled Freyer and Freer; Reagan's name also spelled Regan.

1917

Mar 17	Pierce Matthews	St. Louis, MO	KO8
Apr 17	Freddie Welsh (HOF)	St. Louis, MO	ND12

Notes: The Matthews fight appears in some, but not all records; although a no-decision bout, Welsh's title was said to be at risk if he lost inside the scheduled twelve rounds.

1923

Jan 23	Dick Hyland	Fresno, CA	EX3
Jun 10	Phil Salvatore	Los Angeles, CA	EX3

Ring Totals

W	L	D	ND	NC	TB	—	KO	W	WF	KO'd	L	LF
60	18	19	36	3	136		39	20	1	2	14	2

The record below is that accepted by the International Boxing Hall of Fame in Canastota, New York.

W	L	D	ND	NC	TB	—	KO	W	WF	KO'd	L	LF
59	19	19	33	1	131		38	20	1	3	14	2

Oscar "Battling" Matthew Nelson was inducted into the International Boxing Hall of Fame in Canastota, New York on Sunday, June 7, 1992. The IBHOF inducted twenty-nine members on this date. He was one of eight; the others are Lou Ambers, Panama Al Brown, Jack Dempsey "Non Pareil," Mike Gibbons, Ted "Kid" Lewis, Packey McFarland and Harry Wills—to be included in the "Old Timer" category.

Chapter Notes

Preface

1. Bert Randolph Sugar, *Boxing's Greatest Fighters* (Guilford: Lyons Press, 2006), p. 175.

Chapter One

1. Oscar "Battling" Matthew Nelson, *Life, Battles and Career of Battling Nelson, Lightweight Champion of the World* (Hegewisch, IL: self-published, 1908), p. 11.
2. *Ibid.*, p. 7.
3. *Ibid.*
4. The use of the Danish language was now banned in schools.
5. "Deciding to Leave," Museum of Danish America, accessed January 15, 2016, http://www.danishmuseum.org/ explore/danish-american-culture/immigration.
6. *Ibid.*; immigration reached its peak in 1881–90 when 88,000 Danes entered the United States.
7. Only Danish Mormons can be said to have emigrated for religious reasons, and theirs was not a flight from persecution so much as a gathering.
8. See the Library of Congress Local History & Genealogy Reference Services and Danish Immigration to America: Danes in America for additional information.
9. During the 1860s and 1870s, full-rigged ships and barks, or sailing ships, typically with three masts, in which the foremast and mainmast are square-rigged and the mizzenmast is rigged fore-and-aft.
10. This act, which halted all legal immigration of Chinese laborers, is considered by many to be the first major exclusionary immigration restriction on an entire nationality enacted by the United States. Both the Page Act of 1875 and the Chinese Exclusion Act of 1882 resulted from public fear of the Chinese influence in the labor market and the economy. They were also derived from deplorable prejudice and the public misconception that these immigrants could not assimilate into American culture.
11. Roger Daniels and Otis L. Graham, *Debating American Immigration, 1882–Present* (Lanham, MD: Rowman & Littlefield, 2001), p. 94.
12. In 1898 the company was bought by DFDS [Det Forenede Dampskibs-Selskab (literally The United Steamship Company)], another Danish shipping company, and the name was changed to Scandinavian America Line.
13. "Chester Alan Arthur," The Presidents, Overview, Public Broadcasting System, accessed January 15, 2016, http://www.pbs.org/wgbh/americanexperience/features/biography/presidents-arthur.
14. Wikipedia article on the Panic of 1873 quotes bank reserves falling, during September and October 1873, from $50 million to $17 million. See en.wikipedia.org/wiki/Panic_of_1873.
15. Oscar "Battling" Matthew Nelson, *Life, Battles and Career of Battling Nelson, Lightweight Champion of the World* (Hegewisch, IL: self-published, 1908), p. 7.
16. "Oshkosh, Wisconsin," Wikipedia, Historical Population, United States Census Bureau, accessed January 15, 2016, https://en.wikipedia.org/wiki/Oshkosh,_Wisconsin.
17. Many Danish settlers found work in the dairy and farming communities in the northern states of the USA, mainly in Wisconsin, Minnesota, the Dakotas, Illinois, Michigan and Iowa.
18. Nelson, *Life, Battles and Career of Battling Nelson, Lightweight Champion of the World* (Hegewisch, IL: self-published, 1908), pp. 7–8.
19. *Ibid.*, p. 8.
20. On April 11, 1873, the city was incorporated at the State House and named Hammond, Indiana, after George H. Hammond.
21. Nelson, *Life, Battles and Career of Battling Nelson, Lightweight Champion of the World* (Hegewisch, IL: self-published, 1908), p. 9.
22. *Ibid.*
23. *Ibid.*
24. *Ibid.*, p. 10.
25. *Ibid.*.
26. *Ibid.*, p. 11.
27. *Ibid.*
28. *Ibid.*, pp. 11–12.
29. *Ibid.*, p. 21.
30. *Ibid.*, p. 20.
31. *Ibid.*; the infamous "no mas" quote referencing boxer Roberto Duran's response (if he actually said it) to referee Octavio Meyran in his rematch with Sugar Ray Leonard on November 25, 1980.
32. *Ibid.*
33. *Ibid.*; in 1908, Oscar Nelson recalled that his

mother still had the letter and that she was a witness to the fact that he made good to his childish brag.

34. William Frederick Cody (1846–1917) was a U.S. showman who gained his nickname for killing 4,280 buffalo in a short period of time to feed railroad workers. He subsequently devoted his life to his traveling Wild West Show.

35. The distance from Huron, South Dakota, to Miller, was a northwestern trek of forty miles.

36. Nelson, *Life, Battles and Career of Battling Nelson, Lightweight Champion of the World* (Hegewisch, IL: self-published, 1908), p. 22.

37. "Sioux Falls, South Dakota," Wikipedia, Historical Population, United States Census Bureau, accessed January 15, 2016, https://en.wikipedia.org/wiki/Sioux_Falls,_South_Dakota.

38. *Ibid.*

39. Nelson, *Life, Battles and Career of Battling Nelson, Lightweight Champion of the World* (Hegewisch, IL: self-published, 1908), p. 22.

40. *Ibid.*

41. *Ibid.*, p. 26.

42. *Ibid.*, p. 27.

43. *Ibid.*, p. 28; taking Nelson at his word, it is worth noting that both the amateur and professional records of Solider Williams cannot be verified.

44. A photograph of Oscar Nelson in uniform with Company G, First South Dakota, exists. It was even used in a promotional flyer for the Famous Pennsylvania Whale Shaker Knit Sweater manufactured by the Pennsylvania Knitting Mills. Notes and information found appear to indicate that the volunteer company was never fully recognized.

45. Oscar "Battling" Matthew Nelson, *Life, Battles and Career of Battling Nelson, Lightweight Champion of the World* (Hegewisch, IL: self-published, 1908), p. 29.

46. Nearly a decade later, on page 31 of his autobiography, Nelson would state, "He [Herman] was fast on his feet, shifty on the order of Abe Attell," at least for the first three rounds. A compliment indeed as Attell was world featherweight champion from 1906 to 1912.

47. Nelson would occasionally claim the fight as a victory for himself, such as in the *Salt Lake Herald* on September 17, 1905, where his complete record was printed inside the newspaper. The fight was, however, a draw.

48. Oscar "Battling" Matthew Nelson, *Life, Battles and Career of Battling Nelson, Lightweight Champion of the World* (Hegewisch, IL: self-published, 1908), p. 34; it was not unusual for those collecting a purse, like club bartenders, to skim off a bit from the hat without a fighter's knowledge. Needless to say, a ring upset over a club favorite seldom enriches a take.

49. By 1970, almost 360,000 Danes had settled in the USA, with the five most common Danish surnames in the northern part of America being Jensen, Nielsen, Hansen, Pedersen and Andersen.

50. Oscar "Battling" Matthew Nelson is the name proclaimed on the very first line of his autobiography.

51. Nelson, *Life, Battles and Career of Battling Nelson, Lightweight Champion of the World* (Hegewisch, IL: self-published, 1908), pp. 30–31.

52. Nelson, *Life, Battles and Career of Battling Nelson, Lightweight Champion of the World* (Hegewisch, IL: self-published, 1908), p. 12.

Chapter Two

1. Oscar "Battling" Matthew Nelson, *Life, Battles and Career of Battling Nelson, Lightweight Champion of the World* (Hegewisch, IL: self-published, 1908), p. 21.

2. And that this growth would be sustained in the decade that followed was equally impressive.

3. Nelson, *Life, Battles and Career of Battling Nelson, Lightweight Champion of the World* (Hegewisch, IL: self-published, 1908), p. 35.

4. Nelson would manage to hold on to only a dollar and a half of the purse. The dollar, torn during the brawl, was saved as a keepsake, or "memento of my first mixup with a 'culled person,'" he would state in his autobiography.

5. Nelson, *Life, Battles and Career of Battling Nelson, Lightweight Champion of the World* (Hegewisch, IL: self-published, 1908), p. 35.

6. *Ibid.*, p. 35; to have Nelson compare anyone to Terry McGovern was a compliment.

7. The Internet site boxrec.com supports the Young Griffin claim stating Harry Griffin at another venue.

8. Nelson, *Life, Battles and Career of Battling Nelson, Lightweight Champion of the World* (Hegewisch, IL: self-published, 1908), p. 38.

9. Eddie Santry (1876–1919) was a Chicago resident whose death was attributed to a "nervous breakdown," although his friends said his heart was broken over his defeat for the state legislature. According to sources, including BoxRec.com, Santry ended his career with an impressive record, having fought some very good fighters, including Aurelio Herrera, Tommy Sullivan, Young Corbett II, Oscar Gardner, Terry McGovern and George Dixon.

10. Nelson, *Life, Battles and Career of Battling Nelson, Lightweight Champion of the World* (Hegewisch, IL: self-published, 1908), p. 39.

11. The bodies depicted, in order, are Christy Williams, Ed Burley, Feathers Vernon, Black Griffo and Joe Gans.

12. Nat Fleischer, *Ring* magazine founder, ranked Dixon as the number one featherweight of all time.

13. Nelson, *Life, Battles and Career of Battling Nelson, Lightweight Champion of the World* (Hegewisch, IL: self-published, 1908), p. 40.

14. *Ibid.*

15. Siler was also filing a story about the contest as chief correspondent for the *Chicago Tribune*; other notable fights Siler officiated were matchups between Fitzsimmons and Jim Jeffries, Fitzsimmons and Peter Maher, and Terry McGovern and Pedlar Palmer.

16. Nelson, *Life, Battles and Career of Battling Nelson, Lightweight Champion of the World* (Hegewisch, IL: self-published, 1908), p. 40.

17. *Ibid.*, p. 45.

18. *Ibid.*, p. 47.

19. *Ibid.*, p. 48.
20. *Ibid.*
21. *Ibid.*, p. 52.
22. *Ibid.*
23. *Ibid.*
24. *Ibid.*, p. 53.
25. *Ibid.*, p. 55.
26. *Ibid.*, p. 59.
27. *Ibid.*, p. 60.
28. *Ibid.*, p. 117.
29. San Francisco's Joe Choynski (1868–1943), "The California Terror," "Little Joe," engaged with boxing's elite fighters, including Jim Corbett, Bob Fitzsimmons, Kid McCoy, Joe Walcott, Tom Sharkey and Jack Johnson; he fought from about 1888 until 1904.
30. Nelson, *Life, Battles and Career of Battling Nelson, Lightweight Champion of the World* (Hegewisch, IL: self-published, 1908), p. 68.
31. Malachy Hogan refereed the famous Martin Flaherty v. Dal Hawkins fight held on March 17, 1897, in Carson City, Nevada. Sounds a little too coincidental for the likes of most boxing historians.
32. Nelson, *Life, Battles and Career of Battling Nelson, Lightweight Champion of the World* (Hegewisch, IL: self-published, 1908), p. 71.
33. *Ibid.*
34. Nelson, *Life, Battles and Career of Battling Nelson, Lightweight Champion of the World* (Hegewisch, IL: self-published, 1908), p. 72.
35. Nelson would later state that he believed it was that very moment that his quest for championship began.
36. This railroad line operated from 1847 until 1980.
37. Nelson, *Life, Battles and Career of Battling Nelson, Lightweight Champion of the World* (Hegewisch, IL: self-published, 1908), p. 80.
38. *Ibid.*, p. 82.
39. *Ibid.*, p. 94.
40. *Ibid.*, p. 96.
41. *Ibid.*
42. *Ibid.*, p. 98.
43. *Ibid.*, p. 100.
44. *Ibid.*, p. 101.
45. *Ibid.*; a fireman in this case is a person who tends a furnace or the fire of a steam engine aboard a train.
46. While the rules of the house stated that such an event was for mornings only, Oscar felt he could wait no longer. Later, Nelson would claim that his first manager accompanied him on his trip to Milwaukee.
47. He did not elaborate how he met Murphy, or how his new manager happened to be in town.
48. Nelson, *Life, Battles and Career of Battling Nelson, Lightweight Champion of the World* (Hegewisch, IL: self-published, 1908), p. 102.
49. *Ibid.*, p. 104.
50. *Ibid.*
51. Pneumonia, the only thing that could, finally took Mickey Riley down for good on September 21, 1936.
52. Nelson, *Life, Battles and Career of Battling Nelson, Lightweight Champion of the World* (Hegewisch, IL: self-published, 1908), p. 113.
53. *Ibid.*
54. *Ibid.*
55. Fight not recognized in *The Ring Record Book and Boxing Encyclopedia*.
56. Nelson, *Life, Battles and Career of Battling Nelson, Lightweight Champion of the World* (Hegewisch, IL: self-published, 1908), p. 116.

Chapter Three

1. Nelson, *Life, Battles and Career of Battling Nelson, Lightweight Champion of the World* (Hegewisch, IL: self-published, 1908), p. 30.
2. Akron Art Simms (1878–1923), holds victories over Ole Olsen, Loudon Campbell, and Eddie Gardner; fought from about 1895 until 1918; first fighter Nelson fought with over thirty victories; Simms had sparred with Nelson at Gilmore's training quarters.
3. Nelson, *Life, Battles and Career of Battling Nelson, Lightweight Champion of the World* (Hegewisch, IL: self-published, 1908), p. 125.
4. Brooklyn-born Jack O'Neil holds victories over Young Erne, Kid Herrick and Harry Scroggs; fought from about 1900 until 1916; prolific boxer with over 100 recorded bouts; O'Neil was also spelled O'Neill on occasion.
5. San Francisco resident Joe "Spider" Welsh holds victories over Frank McConnell, Louie Long and George Fuller; fought from about 1899 until 1907; never beat a fighter with over nine recorded victories.
6. Nelson, *Life, Battles and Career of Battling Nelson, Lightweight Champion of the World* (Hegewisch, IL: self-published, 1908), pp. 127–129.
7. *Ibid.*, p. 129.
8. Ireland-born Martin Canole (1882–1965) holds victories over Danny Duane, Arthur Cote and Fred Bryson; fought from about 1901 until 1912; fought out of Fall River, Massachusetts.
9. Nelson, *Life, Battles and Career of Battling Nelson, Lightweight Champion of the World* (Hegewisch, IL: self-published, 1908), p. 133.
10. *Ibid.*
11. *Ibid.*, p. 134.
12. San Francisco's Eddie Hanlon (1885–1942), "Cute Eddie" holds victories over Kid Broad, Tim Callahan and Young Corbett II; fought from about 1901 until 1914; fought many of the most competitive fighters in the division including Owen Moran, Kid Herman, and Aurelio Herrera.
13. "Contest between Eddie Hanlon and 'Battling' Nelson," *Roswell Daily Record*, July 28, 1904, p. 3.
14. "Eddie Hanlon Is Put Out of the Way," *Rock Island Argus*, July 30, 1904, p. 1.
15. It was the fighter's first purse over $1,000.
16. Waldemar Young (July 1, 1878–August 30, 1938) was an American screenwriter. He wrote for eighty-one films between 1917 and 1938 and was the grandson of Brigham Young.
17. The father of Hollywood directors Leo and Ray McCary, some believe he was given his nickname, "Uncle Tom," because of his personal relations with many black fighters.

18. San Jose, California (Bakersfield is also claimed)—born Aurelio Herrera (1876–1927), hard puncher who holds victories over Eddie Santry, Kid Broad and Kid Goodman; fought from about 1895 until 1909; knockout artist.

19. Nelson, *Life, Battles and Career of Battling Nelson, Lightweight Champion of the World* (Hegewisch, IL: self-published, 1908), p. 138.

20. *Ibid.*
21. *Ibid.*, p. 141.
22. *Ibid.*
23. *Ibid.*, p. 142.

24. "Corbett-Nelson Bout Nov. 29" *Rock Island Argus*, Last Edition, October 22, 1904, p. 2.

25. Denver's Young Corbett II (1880–1927), William H. Rothwell holds victories over George Dixon, Terry McGovern, and Young Erne; fought from about 1896 until 1910; world featherweight champion (1901).

26. And we have been silly enough all these years to believe that the GOAT, the "Greatest of All Time," Muhammad Ali was the first to perfect such jabber.

27. Nelson, *Life, Battles and Career of Battling Nelson, Lightweight Champion of the World* (Hegewisch, IL: self-published, 1908), p. 145.

28. *Ibid.*
29. *Ibid.*
30. *Ibid.*
31. *Ibid.*, p. 153.
32. *Ibid.*

33. San Francisco's Jimmy Britt (1879–1940), James Edward Britt, holds victories over Frank Erne, Young Corbett II, and Johnny Summers; fought from about 1902 until 1909; fought Battling Nelson four times.

34. Fighting Britt, Nelson would have a two-inch height and reach advantage.

35. Nelson, *Life, Battles and Career of Battling Nelson, Lightweight Champion of the World* (Hegewisch, IL: self-published, 1908), p. 153.

36. "Britt's Cleverness Offsets Many Rushes, Victor Is in Distress Several Times but Finishes Strongly," *San Francisco Call*, December 21, 1904, p. 10.

37. *Ibid.*

38. Having shaken the hand of Eddie Graney on the way to the ring, Corbett wanted to bury old scores. Graney was the referee in the Corbett v. Jimmy Britt battle.

39. "Britt's Cleverness Offsets Many Rushes, Victor Is in Distress Several Times but Finishes Strongly," *San Francisco Call*, December 21, 1904, p. 10.

40. *Ibid.*
41. *Ibid.*

42. Nelson, *Life, Battles and Career of Battling Nelson, Lightweight Champion of the World* (Hegewisch, IL: self-published, 1908), p. 154.

43. "Britt's Cleverness Offsets Many Rushes, Victor Is in Distress Several Times but Finishes Strongly," *San Francisco Call*, December 21, 1904, p. 10.

44. *Ibid.*
45. *Ibid.*

46. Nelson, *Life, Battles and Career of Battling Nelson, Lightweight Champion of the World* (Hegewisch, IL: self-published, 1908), p. 150.

47. "Terry Stills Holds the Feather Title, Veteran Billy Edwards Discourses on Modern Weight Classes," *St. Paul Globe*, December 27, 1904, p. 5.

48. *Ibid.*
49. *Ibid.*
50. *Ibid.*
51. *Ibid.*
52. *Ibid.*

53. The idol of the more contemporary boxer "Jersey" Joe Walcott, who chose to use his idol's name as his own ring name in his honor.

54. Walcott, who will return to the ring in 1906 (losing his welterweight title in the process), will never regain his old form as a prizefighter.

55. Afterward, Gans vacates the title, which was awarded to Britt. And, two years later, he will claim that the fight had been fixed by his and Britt's managers.

56. "Battling Nelson and His Record," *Salt Lake Tribune*, December 11, 1904, p. 2.

57. "Battling No Nickname," *Havre Herald*, December 15, 1904, p. 6.

58. *Ibid.*

Chapter Four

1. Nelson, *Life, Battles and Career of Battling Nelson, Lightweight Champion of the World* (Hegewisch, IL: self-published, 1908), p. 30; the origin of Nelson's name could vary depending upon the point he was trying to make.

2. "Battling Nelson Stops Corbett in Ninth Round," *San Francisco Call*, March 1, 1905, p. 10.

3. *Ibid.*
4. *Ibid.*

5. Feinting was the act of delivering a deceptive or pretended blow, thrust, or other movement, and can be viewed as a mock attack. It is made in order to distract or deceive an opponent.

6. "Battling Nelson Stops Corbett in Ninth Round," *San Francisco Call*, March 1, 1905, p. 10.

7. Oscar Nelson would never again battle Young Corbett II. However, Corbett would battle until 1910, against the likes of Kid Sullivan, Young Erne, Eddie Hanlon, Aurelio Herrera, and Terry McGovern. His recognized ring record would stand at Bouts: 112, Won: 68, Lost: 22, Drew: 16, NC: 6, KOs: 47.

8. "No Dissipation for B.A.T.," *Desert Evening News*, April 1, 1905, p. 28.

9. *Ibid.*
10. *Ibid.*
11. *Ibid.*

12. San Francisco's Abe Attell (1880–1970), Abraham Washington Attell, "The Little Hebrew," or "The Little Champ," holds victories over George Dixon, Harry Forbes, and Young Erne; fought from about 1900 until 1917; world featherweight champion (1906–1912).

13. "Lewis Unable to Weigh In," *San Francisco Call*, May 20, 1905, p. 7.

14. "Lewis Matched to Box Nelson," *Evening World*, May 6, 1905, p. 2.

15. Nelson believed that even if Lewis made weight, any damage that he might inflict would be limited. When Lewis failed weight, Nelson had few options—already in Philadelphia, Nelson had incurred the associated expenses—thus Attell.
16. "Nelson Meets Boxer Attell," *San Francisco Call*, May 22, 1905, p. 3.
17. "Battling Nelson Worsted," *New York Times*, May 22, 1905, p. 8.
18. "Dane Makes Poor Showing in Philadelphia," *San Francisco Call*, May 23, 1905, p. 7.
19. Nelson, *Life, Battles and Career of Battling Nelson, Lightweight Champion of the World* (Hegewisch, IL: self-published, 1908), p. 157–158.
20. Washington, D.C.'s Kid Sullivan (1879–1949), Harry Sheehy, holds victories over Young Corbett II, Kid Goodman, and Joe Tipman; fought from about 1900 until 1913.
21. "Nelson and Sullivan Go Six Rounds to a Draw," *San Francisco Call*, June 3, 1905, p. 7.
22. Nelson, *Life, Battles and Career of Battling Nelson, Lightweight Champion of the World* (Hegewisch, IL: self-published, 1908), p. 164.
23. Belladonna, or deadly nightshade, was a drug prepared from the leaves and root of this plant, containing atropine.
24.. Nelson, *Life, Battles and Career of Battling Nelson, Lightweight Champion of the World* (Hegewisch, IL: self-published, 1908), p. 165.
25. *Ibid.*, p. 168.
26. "Britt and Sullivan Will Fight in July," *San Francisco Call*, June 15, 1905, p. 7; obviously a stipulation to the deal was that Sullivan not lose to Nelson.
27. Brooklyn-born Jack O'Neil holds victories over Harry Scroggs, Kid Herrick and Young Erne; fought from about 1900 until 1916; fought over 100 recorded bouts.
28. O'Neil, many believed, took only the second round.
29. Nelson, *Life, Battles and Career of Battling Nelson, Lightweight Champion of the World* (Hegewisch, IL: self-published, 1908), p. 168.
30. *Ibid.*, p. 169.
31. "Coffroth's Bid the Highest," *San Francisco Call*, August 9, 1905, p. 10.
32. Nelson, *Life, Battles and Career of Battling Nelson, Lightweight Champion of the World* (Hegewisch, IL: self-published, 1908), p. 169.
33. *Ibid.*
34. Nelson, *Life, Battles and Career of Battling Nelson, Lightweight Champion of the World* (Hegewisch, IL: self-published, 1908), p. 170.
35. *Ibid.*
36. "Each Wants Eddie Graney but Refuses to Name Him," *San Francisco Call*, August 27, 1905, p. 37.
37. *Ibid.*
38. *Ibid.*
39. Nelson, *Life, Battles and Career of Battling Nelson, Lightweight Champion of the World* (Hegewisch, IL: self-published, 1908), p. 173.
40. "Thrilling Story of the Great Battle between the Dane and the Californian," *San Francisco Call*, September 10, 1905, p. 41.
41. *Ibid.*; the text is selected from a comprehensive list printed in the newspaper.
42. *Ibid.*
43. *Ibid.*
44. *Ibid.*
45. *Ibid.*
46. *Ibid.*
47. *Ibid.*
48. *Ibid.*
49. Naturally, the fight footage was framed as to not include the entire corner where the incident occurred, so you only see Britt's head and shoulders drop to the canvas.
50. Nelson, *Life, Battles and Career of Battling Nelson, Lightweight Champion of the World* (Hegewisch, IL: self-published, 1908), p. 178–183; Jack London, "How Different People View Fighters, Brain Beaten by Brute Force," *San Francisco Examiner*, September 10, 1905.
51. Jack London, "How Different People View Fighters, Brain Beaten by Brute Force," *San Francisco Examiner*, September 10, 1905.
52. *Ibid.*
53. A berserker is an ancient Norse warrior who fought in a wild frenzy.
54. Nelson, *Life, Battles and Career of Battling Nelson, Lightweight Champion of the World* (Hegewisch, IL: self-published, 1908), p. 178–183; Jack London, "How Different People View Fighters, Brain Beaten by Brute Force," *San Francisco Examiner*, September 10, 1905.
55. Jack London, "How Different People View Fighters, Brain Beaten by Brute Force," *San Francisco Examiner*, September 10, 1905.
56. *Ibid.*
57. *Ibid.*
58. Nelson, *Life, Battles and Career of Battling Nelson, Lightweight Champion of the World* (Hegewisch, IL: self-published, 1908), p. 186.
59. *Ibid.*, p. 187.
60. *Ibid.*, p. 185–190; "Tragedy is Mirrored in Face of Britt's Father," *San Francisco Examiner*, September 10, 1905.
61. "Tragedy is Mirrored in Face of Britt's Father," *San Francisco Examiner*, September 10, 1905.
62. *Ibid.*
63. *Ibid.*
64. "Thrilling Story of the Great Battle between the Dane and the Californian," *San Francisco Call*, September 10, 1905, p. 41.
65. *Ibid.*
66. *Ibid.*
67. *Ibid.*
68. *Ibid.*
69. *Ibid.*
70. *Ibid.*
71. "Not Invincible," *Minneapolis Journal*, September 20, 1905, p. 12.
72. "Battling Nelson at Football Game," *Hawaiian Star*, October 30, 1905, p. 7.
73. *Ibid.*
74. "Battling Nelson," *Paducah Sun*, September 21, 1905, p. 2.

75. "Battling Nelson to Marry," *Topeka State Journal*, November 10, 1905, p. 1.
76. "Battling Nelson Bows to Dan Cupid's Wiles, " *San Francisco Call*, November 10, 1905, p. 10.
77. "Actress Lands Fighting Man," *San Francisco Call*, December 18, 1905, p. 11.
78. Nelson, *Life, Battles and Career of Battling Nelson, Lightweight Champion of the World* (Hegewisch, IL: self-published, 1908), p. 171.

Chapter Five

1. Nelson, *Life, Battles and Career of Battling Nelson, Lightweight Champion of the World* (Hegewisch, IL: self-published, 1908), p. 51.
2. "Bat Nelson Has Angered an Actress," *Minneapolis Journal*, January 5, 1906, p. 9.
3. "Bat Nelson Is Tooting a Horn," *Minneapolis Journal*, January 5, 1906, p. 9; and, yes, this was the spelling in the subtitle.
4. "Would Prefer to Fight on Coast," *Minneapolis Journal*, January 5, 1906, p. 9.
5. The *Evening Star* (Washington, D.C.) ran an article, on February 7, 1906, titled "Battling Nelson a Thrifty Lad," stating that since the Britt fight he had given his father and mother $14,000 with no strings attached.
6. "Nelson Deeds Away Property," *San Francisco Call*, January 26, 1906, p. 10.
7. Battling Nelson, "Prize Ring Stories for Fight Fans," *Spokane Press*, February 2, 1906, p. 4.
8. *Ibid.*
9. *Ibid.*
10. *Ibid.*
11. *Ibid.*
12. *Ibid.*
13. *Ibid.*
14. *Ibid.*
15. *Ibid.*
16. *Ibid.*
17. *Ibid.*
18. Robert Edgren, "All About Battling Nelson, Told by His Sparring Partner," *The World*, February 16, 1906, p. 14.
19. *Ibid.*
20. *Ibid.*
21. *Ibid.*
22. *Ibid.*
23. *Ibid.*
24. *Ibid.*
25. For additional details, refer to "Famous Athlete Visits Nelson and Is Surprised," *Evening World*, March 10, 1906, p. 6.
26. "Straight Queensberry Rules—Fight All the Time—That Suits Nelson and McGovern Too," *The World*, March 12, 1906, p. 10. This is a synopsis of a Robert Edgren column.
27. Brooklyn's Terry McGovern (1880–1918), Joseph Terrence McGovern, "Terrible," holds victories over Pedlar Palmer, George Dixon and Joe Gans; fought from about 1897 until 1908; world bantamweight champion, world featherweight champion.
28. McGovern would enter the ring with a record of 59–5–4, while "Battling" Nelson will stand at 40–10–3; bear in mind, however, that complete and accurate fight records were not a hallmark of the sport.
29. Exact measurements can be found in "Expert View of the Chances of Both McGovern and Nelson," *The World*, March 14, 1906, p. 10.
30. John J. McGuigan was the manager of the National Athletic Club.
31. Nelson would quote $23,543 house, with his guarantee $5,000, and a privilege of 50 percent, or $11,771.50.
32. "Expert View of the Chances of Both McGovern and Nelson," *The World*, March 14, 1906, p. 7.
33. *Ibid.*
34. *Ibid.*
35. "Battling Nelson Beat the 'Terror' in Oddest Fight," *The World*, March 15, 1906, p. 12.
36. Brooklyn's Terry McGovern scored eighteen consecutive knockouts, 1899–1900, including eleven within three rounds.
37. "Battling Nelson Beat the 'Terror' in Oddest Fight," *The World*, March 15, 1906, p. 12.
38. Nelson, *Life, Battles and Career of Battling Nelson, Lightweight Champion of the World* (Hegewisch, IL: self-published, 1908), p. 193.
39. *Ibid.*
40. *Ibid.* See insert "Victory Came Easy—Nelson."
41. *Ibid.* See insert "I Earned a Draw—McGovern."
42. *Ibid.* See insert "McGuigan on the Fight."
43. "Terry's Mother Weeps as Returns Are Read, " *The World*, March 15, 1906, p. 12.
44. *Ibid.*
45. "Mrs. McGovern after Terry, " *Topeka State Journal*, March 20, 1906, p. 10.
46. *Ibid.*
47. "Teasing His Old Dad," *Bisbee Daily Review*, April 1, 1906, p. 14.
48. "San Francisco Earthquake, 1906," Center for Legislative Archives, National Archives; www.archives.gov.
49. "Pugilist Sells Papers," *Minneapolis Journal*, April 21, 1906, p. 3.
50. "Ladies Admire Battling Nelson," *Bisbee Daily Review*, May 18, 1906, p. 1.
51. The Nelson team was actively training for the Herrera fight; however, Billy Nolan had heard rumors days in advance of the weigh-in that a hustle was in the works.
52. "Pugilists Tell Fishing Yarns," *Los Angeles Herald*, August 7, 1906, p. 6.
53. "Nelson Takes a Vacation," *San Francisco Call*, July 24, 1906, p. 7.
54. A yellowtail is a marine fish that has yellow coloration on the fins. There are several species, including the large sport fish yellowtail of Southern California, the yellowtail flounder of the Atlantic coast from Labrador to Virginia, and the yellowtail snapper of Bermuda and the West Indies.
55. "Pugilists Tell Fishing Yarns," *Los Angeles Herald*, August 7, 1906, p. 6.
56. Nelson, *Life, Battles and Career of Battling Nelson,*

Lightweight Champion of the World (Hegewisch, IL: self-published, 1908), p. 200.

57. "Nolan Will Stand by Word to Nevada Promoters," *San Francisco Call*, August 6, 1906; the telegram was pictured on the front of the sports page.

58. "Sacramento Sports Make a Bold Bid for the Championship Fight," *San Francisco Call*, August 6, 1906, p. 1.

59. According to Nelson, he first received a telegram asking him his terms to fight Jack Clifford in Goldfield. Nelson wired back his terms. He then received a telegram from Rickard accepting his $5,000 guarantee and $5,000 side bet, but would prefer a meeting with Gans and offered $15,000. Nelson then returned, "Raise the bid to $30,000 for Gans and match accepted." Rickard then accepted.

60. "Promoter Praises the Work of Nolan," *San Francisco Call*, August 13, 1906, p. 6.

61. Baltimore's Joe Gans (1874–1910), Joseph Gant, "Old Master," holds victories over Kid Herman, Mike Twin Sullivan, and Jack Blackburn; fought from about 1891 until 1909; world lightweight champion; rated the greatest lightweight boxer of all time by boxing historian and *Ring* magazine founder, Nat Fleischer.

62. "Gans Wins in His Fight with Nelson," *Evening Star*, September 3, 1906, p. 1.

63. *Ibid.*

64. "Gans Retains Title and Gives World Its Greatest Fight," *Salt Lake Herald*, September 4, 1906, p. 1.

65. *Ibid.*

66. *Ibid.*

67. Nelson, *Life, Battles and Career of Battling Nelson, Lightweight Champion of the World* (Hegewisch, IL: self-published, 1908), p. 205.

68. "Gans Retains Title and Gives World Its Greatest Fight," *Salt Lake Herald*, September 4, 1906.

69. *Ibid.*

70. "Battler Not Dead, as Reported in Salt Lake," *Salt Lake Tribune*, September 7, 1906, p. 9.

71. "Mr. Nolan, Who Was," *Minneapolis Journal*, September 9, 1906, p. 3.

72. "Gans-Nelson Fight Leads to Two Killings," *Fairmount West Virginian*, September 21, 1906, p. 6.

73. "Prize Ring," *Evening Times*, October 10, 1906, p. 2.

74. *Ibid.*

75. "Battling Nelson to Marry," *Evening Star*, October 17, 1906, p. 15.

76. Advertisement for the Ridgeway Theater, Monday Evening, November 19, 1906, *Colfax Gazette*, November 16, 1906, p. 2.

77. "Battling Nelson Wants to Take a Hand in Presidential Contest," *Evening Times*, December 3, 1906, p. 6.

78. *Ibid.*

Chapter Six

1. Nelson, *Life, Battles and Career of Battling Nelson, Lightweight Champion of the World* (Hegewisch, IL: self-published, 1908), p. 45.

2. *Ibid.*, p. 210.

3. The hotel was requisitioned for the war effort in 1917, and the very first headquarters of the newly formed RAF took up part of the hotel from 1918 to 1919.

4. Nelson, *Life, Battles and Career of Battling Nelson, Lightweight Champion of the World* (Hegewisch, IL: self-published, 1908), p. 212.

5. "Nelson on a Strike," *Topeka State Journal*, January 29, 1907, p. 6.

6. "Battling Nelson Likes England," *Topeka State Journal*, March 8, 1907, p. 2.

7. "Hegewisch Wiped Off the Map: Battling Nelson on the Warpath," *Rock Island Argus*, March 15, 1907, p. 1.

8. *Ibid.*

9. "Bat Nelson as a Banker," *Spokane Press*, March 28, 1907, p. 3.

10. "Battling Dane's Lack of Showy Style in the Gymnasium Makes It Easy to Get Price against Him in the Ring," *San Francisco Call*, July 25, 1907, p. 10.

11. "Britt Wins from Dane on Decision," *Los Angeles Herald*, August 1, 1907, p. 8.

12. *Ibid.*

13. *Ibid.*

14. *Ibid.*

15. Nelson, *Life, Battles and Career of Battling Nelson, Lightweight Champion of the World* (Hegewisch, IL: self-published, 1908), p. 221.

16. *Ibid.*

17. "Failed to Get Revenge," *Salt Lake Herald*, September 21, 1907, p. 10.

18. "Nelson Leaves His Manager," *Pacific Commercial Advertiser*, October 30, 1907, p. 5.

19. Grass Valley, California's Jack Clifford (1884–1924), Jack Clifford Trenberth, holds victories over Rufe Turner, Kid Fredericks, and Jack Wade; fought from about 1901 until 1914; Clifford died in Jerome, Arizona, from injuries as a result of an accident in a blacksmith shop.

20. "Boy from Hegewisch Displays His Old Time Stamina in Ring," *San Francisco Call*, January 14, 1908, p. 8.

21. German-born Rudy Unholz (1881–1916), Rudolf Unholz, "Boer" holds old victories over Jack Redmond, Jack Clifford, and George Memsic; fought from about 1902 until 1914; Unholz died of tuberculosis in Glendale, California; the Pacific Athletic Club Pavilion/Naud Junction held the fight that saw ticket prices as follows: General Admission, $2; Reserved Seats, $3, $5, and $10.

22. Finding a bit of solace in Australia where he picked up the Australian welterweight title in 1909, Unholz returned to the United States two years later. He would close his career in 1914, having fought a couple of good fighters in his later years including Ad Wolgast.

23. "Dane Forces Fighting from Start, but Fails to Score Knockout," *San Francisco Call*, March 4, 1908, p. 6.

24. *Ibid.*

25. "Battler Not 'All In,'" *San Francisco Call*, March 4, 1908, p. 6.

26. *Ibid.*
27. "Eddie Smith Will Referee Bout in Place of Eddie Graney," *San Francisco Call*, March 31, 1908, p. 8.
28. *Ibid.*
29. *Ibid.*
30. *Ibid.*

Chapter Seven

1. Nelson, *Life, Battles and Career of Battling Nelson, Lightweight Champion of the World* (Hegewisch, IL: self-published, 1908), p. 86.
2. William M. Mendenhall established a health spa, with limited accommodations, there in the 1870s from springs that had been diverted through tunnels originally bored for gold prospecting.
3. Nelson, *Life, Battles and Career of Battling Nelson, Lightweight Champion of the World* (Hegewisch, IL: self-published, 1908), p. 226.
4. "Prize Fighter Entertained on Battleship," *Daily Capital Journal*, June 24, 1908, p. 1.
5. "Oh, See Willis' Eye! He Boxed Bat," *San Francisco Call*, June 28, 1908, p. 33.
6. *Ibid.*
7. *Ibid.*
8. *Ibid.*
9. *Ibid.*
10. "Sympathy for Beaten Champion Is Expressed in Wife's Kiss," *San Francisco Call*, July 5, 1908, p. 33.
11. "Nelson Shows His Superiority in Early Stages of the Fight, Punishing Gans Severely," *San Francisco Call*, July 5, 1908, p. 34.
12. "Fight for World's Title Is Spectacular from First Round to Last," *San Francisco Call*, July 5, 1908, p. 34.
13. *Ibid.*
14. "Thousands Cheer for King of Ring," *San Francisco Call*, July 5, 1908, p. 35.
15. *Ibid.*
16. *Ibid.*
17. *Ibid.*
18. "Old Master Knows End Has Come," *San Francisco Call*, July 5, 1908, p. 35.
19. *Ibid.*
20. "Fight for World's Title Is Spectacular from First Round to Last," *San Francisco Call*, July 5, 1908, p. 34.
21. *Ibid.*
22. *Ibid.* Referee Jack Welsh did not retire; in fact he went on to arbitrate many title fights, including Abe Attell versus Moran, Monte Attell versus Danny Webster, and Jack Johnson versus Jess Willard.
23. "Dixon Says Coffroth Knifed Him," *San Francisco Call*, July 5, 1908, p. 34.
24. *Ibid.*
25. Nelson, *Life, Battles and Career of Battling Nelson, Lightweight Champion of the World* (Hegewisch, IL: self-published, 1908), p. 231.
26. *Ibid.*
27. *Ibid.*

Chapter Eight

1. Nelson, *Life, Battles and Career of Battling Nelson, Lightweight Champion of the World* (Hegewisch, IL: self-published, 1908), p. 86.
2. Also an option for Nelson, though unlikely for numerous reasons, was a battle with undefeated Packey McFarland.
3. "Bat Nelson Knocks Out Veteran Joe Gans," *Evening Star*, September 10, 1908, p. 14.
4. *Ibid.*
5. *Ibid.*
6. *Ibid.*
7. *Ibid.*
8. "Nelson Is Lightweight Champion—Defeats Gans in Twenty-One Rounds," *Evening Times*, September 10, 1908, p. 2.
9. *Ibid.*
10. Nelson, *Life, Battles and Career of Battling Nelson, Lightweight Champion of the World* (Hegewisch, IL: self-published, 1908), p. 158.
11. *Ibid.*, p. 159.
12. For the record, Jack Powell played sixteen seasons and fell fifty-five games short of winning 300 games as a pitcher. But he also fell forty-six games short of losing 300 games with a winning percentage of .491.
13. Nelson, *Life, Battles and Career of Battling Nelson, Lightweight Champion of the World* (Hegewisch, IL: self-published, 1908), pp. 160–161.
14. *Ibid.*
15. George Dixon died, penniless, three years after retiring.
16. "Lightweight Champion of World Signs for Setto before the Footlights," *San Francisco Call*, September 13, 1908, p. 34; a review and a listing of the "Cast of Characters" can be found in the September 15, 1908, issue of the *San Francisco Call* on page 7.
17. Admission to the Union for New Mexico did not occur until 1912.
18. "Nelson Scores Two Knockouts," *Pacific Commercial Advertiser*, October 4, 1908, p. 7; incident happened on September 23, 1908.
19. *Ibid.*
20. "Father Proud of Battler," *Salt Lake Herald*, September 25, 1908, p. 12.
21. "Battling Nelson's Father Stops Over," *Salt Lake Tribune*, September 25, 1908, p. 11.
22. "Prays Battling Nelson to Join the Church," *Evening World*, September 30, 1908, p. 16.
23. "Nelson Contributes to Testimonial Fund," *San Francisco Call*, October 11, 1908, p. 34.
24. *Ibid.*
25. The 1908 World Series was held from October 10 through October 14, with Games 1 (10/10), 4 (10/13) and 5 (10/15) held at Bennett Park in Detroit, Michigan.
26. "Bat Nelson says Chicago Cubs Spell Class," *San Francisco Call*, October 14, 1908, p. 8.
27. *Ibid.*
28. "Do a Press Agent Act That Takes The Cake...," *Evening Star*, November 15, 1908, p. 4.
29. "Arrest Bat Nelson in Dog Fight Raid," *Los Angeles*

Herald, November 24, 1908, p. 10; Nelson was arraigned at Burnham and his case was dismissed.
  30. "Bat Will Run For City Council," *Hawaiian Star,* December 9, 1908, p. 6.
  31. Nelson, *Life, Battles and Career of Battling Nelson, Lightweight Champion of the World* (Hegewisch, IL: self-published, 1908), p. 32.
  32. *Ibid.,* pp. 73–79.
  33. *Ibid.,* pp. 248–250.
  34. *Ibid.,* p. 39.
  35. *Ibid.,* pp. 23–25.
  36. *Ibid.,* p. 216.

Chapter Nine

  1. Nelson, *Life, Battles and Career of Battling Nelson, Lightweight Champion of the World* (Hegewisch, IL: self-published, 1908), p. 39.
  2. Donald F. Anderson, *William Howard Taft: A Conservative's Conception of the Presidency* (Ithaca, NY: Cornell University Press, 1973), p. 57.
  3. White House visits are typically scheduled well in advance, so Nelson may have known the date and just placed the short notation inside. Judging by the typeface, it looks as if it was added during a later production stage.
  4. Nelson, *Life, Battles and Career of Battling Nelson, Lightweight Champion of the World* (Hegewisch, IL: self-published, 1908), Introductory, p. ii.
  5. Miss Fay Barbara King, noted Denver cartoonist, will soon be linked to Oscar "Battling" Nelson; Hegewisch, one of the seventy-seven community areas of Chicago, Illinois, is located on the city's far south side.
  6. The treatise—not only a mirror into pugilism at this time, but also into our nation's history—is worth a read, if only for the views expressed by one temporarily at boxing's summit.
  7. *Theodore Roosevelt,* 1913, autobiography (New York: Macmillan), section 2, "The Vigor of Life," paragraph 3, Great Books Online, bartleby.com.
  8. At the age of twenty-eight, Ralph Waldo Rose died of typhoid fever in San Francisco.
  9. *Theodore Roosevelt,* 1913, autobiography (New York: Macmillan), section 2, "The Vigor of Life," paragraph 26, Great Books Online, bartleby.com.
  10. "Bat and President Both Profit by Meeting," *San Francisco Call,* January 17, 1909, p. 33.
  11. "Bat Nelson Will Rest," *Newport Miner,* February 4, 1909, p. 6.
  12. His recovery was a mystery to the press—likely a purposeful move by the Battler—who thought he had simply vanished and noting that matchmaker Baron Long was the last to hear from the fighter by letter back on February 15.
  13. "Nelson Willing to Take on Five Britons," *San Francisco Call,* March 2, 1909, p. 10.
  14. "Latest News about Battling Nelson," *Pacific Commercial Advertiser,* March 15, 1909, p. 3.
  15. "Battling Nelson's Book Causes Trouble," *Daily Missoulian,* March 26, 1909, p. 6.
  16. "Battling Nelson's Agent?" *Topeka State Journal,* April 10, 1909, p. 2.
  17. The Miles Brothers, Coffroth's filmmakers of choice, had made well over $100,000 on previous Nelson battles. As Dan Streible writes in *Fight Pictures: A History of Boxing and Early Cinema,* theater owners broke gender barriers by welcoming women in to see the film.
  18. This stated clearly on a souvenir envelope created by an unknown area printer. San Francisco's Dick Hyland (1885–1965), William Uren, holds victories over Aurelio Herrera, Maurice Thompson, and Leach Cross; fought from about 1906 until 1920; in a career that saw many managers, including Jack Kearns, Dick Hyland's career was not properly supervised.
  19. BoxRec, Dick Hyland Biography, boxrec.com.
  20. *Ibid.*
  21. Boxing beat writers often recalled his knockout by the hands of local favorite Frankie Neil as a turning point in his career.
  22. The building is now registered as a California Historical Landmark and is listed on the National Register of Historic Places (NPS-82000960). It was located at the corner of Webster Street and Central Avenue.
  23. International Boxing Hall of Fame, Inductees Biography, www.ibhof.com.
  24. He was the son of James Coffroth, one of California's first legislators.
  25. The Olympic Club was an athletic club and private social club in San Francisco, California. Its main "City Clubhouse" was located in San Francisco's Union Square district. Membership to the prestigious club was revered by many.
  26. "James C. Kennedy Dead: Well-Known Sporting Man Expires Suddenly on Brighton Beach Train," *New York Times,* April 21, 1904.
  27. International Boxing Hall of Fame, Inductee Biography, www.ibhof.com.
  28. Bay Area meaning the region around San Francisco Bay, in north central California. Oakland is the hub of the East Bay, San Jose of the South Bay.
  29. With its dozen cemeteries, Colma had previously been known as the "city of the dead," but Coffroth put it on the map. He opened an arena on Sickles Street, just fifty feet south of the San Francisco City limits, a block from the present-day County Line Cleaners.
  30. "Fatally Pounded in Ring. Tenny's Death May Stop Prizefighting in San Francisco," *New York Times,* March 2, 1906, p. 4; worth noting is that Willus Britt, along with Coffroth, Eddie Graney, Morris Levy and Mark Shaughnessy, surrendered themselves to authorities. All were charged with manslaughter.
  31. Among the scams Ruef masterminded was the "fight trust," in which a handful of promoters was given permits to hold fights within the city limits. One of the alleged members of the fight trust was Coffroth.
  32. "Big Fight Awaits the Fans This Afternoon," *San Francisco Call,* May 29, 1909, p. 14.
  33. *Ibid.*
  34. "About the Andrews Hotel," accessed January 15, 2016, http://andrewshotel.com/about.html; rumor has it that, at one time, the establishment had a rather unsavory reputation.

35. "Big Fight Awaits the Fans This Afternoon," *San Francisco Call*, Saturday, May 29, 1909, p. 14.

36. This was not an unusual ring tactic by an underdog. And it was also guaranteed that any tomfoolery that had taken place with a fighter's most precious ring armaments would now be to your advantage.

37. "Big Fight Awaits the Fans This Afternoon," *San Francisco Call*, Saturday, May 29, 1909, p. 14.

38. BoxRec, Eddie Smith biography, boxrec.com.

39. A great example being his August 20, 1901, service inside the Reliance Athletic Center, Oakland, California.

40. "Battler Fights, and Guides Moving Picture Men," *San Francisco Call*, May 30, 1909, p. 34.

41. Ibid.

42. Ibid.

43. "Great Crowd Sees Nelson Knock Hyland Out in Twenty-Third Round," *San Francisco Call*, May 30, 1909, p. 33.

44. Ibid.

45. Ibid.

46. Derivations of the phrase date back to the twelfth century, and Chaucer even used one circa 1395; however the Gans version remains the most widely used.

47. "Nelson Blossoms Out as a Real Hog Rancher," *San Francisco Call*, June 7, 1909, p. 13.

48. "Nelson Arrives on Flying Trip," *Los Angeles Herald*, June 10, 1909, p. 4.

49. "Five Rounds with Nelson Ends Clifford," *San Francisco Call*, June 23, 1909, p. 8.

50. "Nelson Knocks Out Clifford in Fifth," *Los Angeles Herald*, June 23, 1909, p. 4.

51. "Bat Nelson Pushes Sale of His Book," *San Francisco Call*, June 24, 1909, p. 8.

52. "Kid Cupid Arrives," *Desert Evening News*, June 26, 1909, p. 8.

53. Learning his lesson, Oscar was quietly conducting a relationship with a woman, whose name will be revealed later, on the QT. The depth of their relationship will slowly be revealed.

54. Cadillac, Michigan's Ad Wolgast (1888–1955), Adolphus Wolgast, holds victories over George Memsic, Frankie Burns and Owen Moran; fought from about 1906 until 1920; world lightweight champion, defended title successfully six times.

55. BoxRec, Ad Wolgast, boxrec.com.

56. Ibid.

57. Out-of-state fights were commonly out of a fighter's control, thus making him an underdog and possible decision victim.

58. Wolgast was 3 1/4 inches smaller in height than Nelson.

59. Because the kidney lies directly below the area being hit, known as the costovertebral angle, tapping disturbs the inflamed tissue, causing pain.

60. "Fight by Rounds," *Los Angeles Herald*, July 14, 1909, p. 4.

61. "Goes to Swell Hotel and Occupies Room Engaged by Friend—Defies Notice to Vacate Apartments," *Wenatchee Daily World*, August 5, 1909, p. 2.

62. Henry William "Harry" Vardon (1870–1937) was a professional golfer from the bailiwick of Jersey and a member of the fabled Great Triumvirate (Vardon, Taylor and Braid) of the sport in his day. He won the Open Championship a record six times and also won the 1900 U.S. Open.

63. "Ten Thousand Fails to Tempt Bat Nelson," *San Francisco Call*, Wednesday, October 13, 1909, p. 10.

64. Willus was the mastermind behind the Ketchel v. Johnson fight held at Colma, California, on October 16, 1909. From dressing Ketchel to look larger and staging sparring knockouts for the press, to making "a deal" with Johnson then double-crossing him, Britt was either one of the most deceitful managers in the business or a man of unmitigated brilliance.

65. This was the historic fight that was eventually held on July 4, 1910, in Reno, Nevada. The story of Nelson's offer hit the wire out of Boston and was picked up by many papers including the *Evening Times* out of Grand Forks, North Dakota.

66. "Battler's Theatrical Tour Gets the Coin," *San Francisco Call*, November 23, 1909, p. 10.

67. Ibid.

68. "Bat Nelson Agrees to Meeting with Wolgast over 45-Round Route," *Los Angeles Herald*, December 24, 1909, p. 12.

Chapter Ten

1. Nelson, *Life, Battles and Career of Battling Nelson, Lightweight Champion of the World* (Hegewisch, IL: self-published, 1908), p. 14.

2. "Bat Nelson Plans a Tour of World," *San Francisco Call*, Sunday, January 9, 1910, p. 37.

3. Redwood, New York, born Tommy Ryan (1870–1948), Joseph Youngs, holds victories over Mysterious Billy Smith, Nonpareil Jack Dempsey, and Charley Johnson; fought from about 1887 until 1911; world welterweight champion and world middleweight champion.

4. An American boxing promoter who would become known for his onetime part ownership of Max Schmeling, Billy McCarney also managed a stable of boxers including heavyweights Luther "Lute" McCarty and Natie Brown. Born in 1872 in Philadelphia, McCarney enjoyed promoting boxing, that is until his twenty-one-year-old fighter "Lute" McCarty died tragically in the ring. McCarney, then living in Springfield, had seen a bright future for his fighter, even lining up a fight for him against Jack Johnson, it had been reported. Billy McCarney died in 1948 in New York City.

5. BoxRec, Eddie Lang, boxrec.com; Chicago's Eddie Lang; holds victories over only one fighter with over two professional fights; fought from about 1907 until 1916; his brother was boxer Young Sweeney (Ira Lang).

6. Ibid.

7. "Durable Dane Shows He Still Has Wallop," *San Francisco Call*, Saturday, January 22, 1910, p. 21.

8. "Bat Nelson Growing Deaf," *Tacoma Times*, January 28, 1910, p. 2.

9. "Bat Nelson Plans a Tour of World," *San Francisco Call*, Sunday, January 9, 1910, p. 37.

10. Ranked number nineteen greatest title fight of all time by *Ring* magazine in 1996.

11. "Battling Nelson Pounded to Pulp," *Marion Daily Mirror*, February 23, 1910, p. 6.
12. *Ibid.*
13. "Nelson Wants Another Chance," *Tacoma Times*, January 28, 1910, p. 2.
14. "The Fight by Rounds," *Los Angeles Herald*, February 23, 1910, p. 10.
15. *Ibid.*
16. *Ibid.*
17. *Ibid.*
18. "Bat's Father Says It Was Bad Mistake," *Salt Lake Herald-Republican*, March 1, 1910, p. 7.
19. *Ibid.*
20. Taken from notes that appeared in the *Seattle Republican*, March 11, 1910, p. 1.
21. Two days before the fight the club was having trouble dealing with Jones concerning the images. Jack Robinson shrewdly suggested that the club buy out Jones, or Wolgast if you will—he was promised $500 if Nelson won and $1,500 if the Battler lost, half of which Nelson was to pay.
22. Comparison appeared in the *Spokane Press*, March 3, 1910, p. 9.
23. "Nelson Again Working Rival Fight Promoters," *Spokane Press*, March 3, 1910, p. 9.
24. "Nelson Has Won a Good Fortune," *Daily Standard*, March 23, 1910, p. 4.
25. "Won't Shave Battling Nelson," *Bridgeport Evening Farmer*, April 5, 1910, p. 7.
26. Called the "Grand Dame of Broad Street," the hotel has hosted numerous U.S. presidents.
27. These Philadelphia architects also designed the Boldts' famous landmark residence, Boldt Castle, in the Thousand Islands. Some believe that Chicken à la King was created there in the 1890s by hotel cook William "Bill" King. "The Bellevue-Stratford Hotel," Wikipedia, accessed January 15, 2016, https://en.wikipedia.org/wiki/The_Bellevue-Stratford_Hotel.
28. "Judge Knocks Out Battling Nelson," *Salt Lake Tribune*, April 8, 1910, p. 13.
29. *Ibid.*
30. "Battling Nelson Tells Speaker Cannon He Missed His Calling," *Salt Lake Herald-Republican*, May 18, 1910, p. 12.
31. *Ibid.*
32. Al Herford, a well-known Baltimore politician, "signed Gans to iron-clad contract, which made him practically a slave for many years," this according to the *San Francisco Call*. The McGovern encounter, "one of the most barefaced fakes in the history of boxing," according to *The Call*, nearly destroyed the Chicago fight game.
33. Gans had Benny Selig, his new manager, to thank for the turnabout in his career.
34. "The Passing of Joe Gans," *Tacoma Times*, August 10, 1910, p. 2.
35. *Ibid.*
36. "Battling Nelson and Abdul the Turk Now Involved in Literary Pursuits," *Salt Lake Tribune*, September 1, 1910, p. 10.
37. "Battling Nelson Says He'll Return," *Evening Times*, September 7, 1910, p. 3.

38. "'Bat' Nelson Here," *Topeka State Journal*, September 14, 1910, p. 6.
39. The Smith Automobile Company, of Topeka, Kansas, was an early U.S. automobile manufacturing company. The company produced the Veracity, Smith, and Great Smith lines of automobiles from 1902 to 1912. They were the first automobiles made west of the Mississippi River and the first to make it to the top of Pikes Peak.
40. Denver's Monte Dale; holds victories over Jack Redmond, Freddie Weeks and Muggsy Schoel; fought from about 1908 until 1919.
41. "Nelson and Hogan to Don Gauntlets," *San Francisco Call*, October 12, 1910, p. 11.
42. "La Grave to Meet Battling Nelson," *San Francisco Call*, October 18, 1910, p. 2.
43. "La Grave Backers Bet Confidently," *San Francisco Call*, October 26, 1910, p. 11; San Francisco's Anton La Grave (1887–1920), Antoine La Grave, before meeting Nelson had defeated only one fighter with over twenty wins, Joe Reilly; he fought from about 1907 until 1918.
44. "Anton La Grave Holds Battling Nelson to a Draw at 15 Rounds," *Los Angeles Herald*, November 1, 1910, p. 12; the subtitle of the article was a bit of a contradiction, for if the former champion's punches lacked steam, then how could La Grave have endured a terrific pounding?
45. By 1877 all eighteen of the city's slaughterhouses had relocated to the Bayview sector of San Francisco, thus the name.
46. "Nelson Arouses Slumbering Fans," *San Francisco Call*, November 2, 1910, p. 11.
47. "Congratulations from Battling Nelson," *Topeka State Journal*, November 3, 1910, p. 1.
48. United Kingdom's Owen Moran (1884–1949), "The Fearless," holds victories over Abe Attell, Jim Driscoll, and George Dixon; fought from 1900 until 1916; recognized by some historians as a world bantamweight champion.
49. "Gamest of the Game Finally Takes Count," *San Francisco Call*, November 27, 1910, p. 47; the subtitle read, "For First Time in Ring Career of 14 Years Bat Hears the Fatal 'Out,' Britisher Outfights the Former Champion throughout Eleven Rounds."
50. *Ibid.*
51. *Ibid.*
52. *Ibid.*
53. *Ibid.*
54. *Ibid.*
55. *Ibid.*
56. "Nelson Reported Not to Be Wealthy," *Evening Times*, December 9, 1910, p. 3.
57. The *Almanach de Gotha* is a directory of Europe's royalty and higher nobility, from a German perspective.
58. "Couldn't Work the Count de Beaufort," *Bismarck Daily Tribune*, February 24, 1910, p. 4.
59. "Father in Law and Creditors Beat Beaufort," *San Francisco Call*, December 3, 1910, p. 1.
60. *Ibid.*
61. *Ibid.*
62. *Ibid.*; the *San Francisco Call* reports incorrectly

October 21; her chauffeur, who had been caught speeding then arrested, explained to the Municipal Court that he was taking physicians to St. Luke's.

63. Ibid.
64. Ibid.
65. "Countess Beaufort Will Sue Husband," *Washington Times*, November 13, 1910, p. 11.
66. Ibid.
67. Ibid.
68. "Was Engaged to Battling Nelson," *Winchester News*, November 17, 1910, p. 2.
69. Claimed in an interview with Fay King, of all people. A couple of articles claim the later date of 1908.
70. "Was Engaged to Battling Nelson," *Winchester News*, November 17, 1910, p. 2.
71. Ibid.
72. "Why I Am Making a Fool of Myself," *Spokane Press*, December 19, 1910, p. 4.
73. On November 17, the count was sued for an overdrawn account at a bank. He was also facing issues with other creditors.
74. "Count Is Hit on Vaudeville Stage: Creditors Cheer," *San Francisco Call*, November 21, 1910, p. 1.
75. Ibid.
76. "Swears Out Warrant," *Topeka State Journal*, December 3, 1910, p. 6.
77. "Why I Am Making a Fool of Myself," *Spokane Press*, December 19, 1910, p. 4.

Chapter Eleven

1. Nelson, *Life, Battles and Career of Battling Nelson, Lightweight Champion of the World* (Hegewisch, IL: self-published, 1908), p. 88.
2. For those historians who have had to confirm a fighter's official record, this has proven to be a nightmare in subjectivity.
3. "Country Real Estate," *San Francisco Call*, March 9, 1911; these ads ran in numerous issues in the classified ads section.
4. "Battling Nelson Now Is Political Orator," *Salt Lake Tribune*, April 5, 1911, p. 12.
5. "Passing a forged check for $100 upon the Commercial National Bank," was the charge made in an indictment returned on May 11 by the district grand jury against Robinson, now reported as formerly press agent for Battling Nelson. The *Washington Times* reported that "Robinson had not been arrested, as his whereabouts were unknown, but Nelson made good on the bank's loss." The *Times* also stated on May 11, "Cashing of the check, signed 'B. Nelson,' and drawn upon a Kansas City bank, was made through an introduction of Robinson by Ralph P. Pratt, secretary to Commissioner Johnston. Pratt says he took Robinson to the bank April 4, when he introduced himself as Nelson's press agent. Pratt says he is acquainted with Nelson. The check was returned marked 'No funds.' Nelson made restitution to the bank on April 21." Robinson was later arrested while in Chicago at the request of Washington police. The unintentional incident proved an embarrassment to everyone involved.
6. "Count Beaufort Again Victim of Thrashing," *Washington Times*, February 27, 1911, p. 2.
7. "Angry Husband Whips Count de Beaufort," *Washington Herald*, April 22, 1911, p. 6.
8. "Alas, the Poor Count!" *Twice-a-Week Plain Dealer*, May 9, 1911, p. 2.
9. "Count Forgiven by Kilgallen," *Tacoma Times*, April 7, 1911, p. 7.
10. Spokane's Tommy Gaffney, Fred McKay; holds victories over Frankie Edwards and Battling Dane—just one of the many capitalizing on the name of Battling Nelson; fought from about 1911 until 1913; not too much is known about Gaffney other than he spent time wanted by the law.
11. "Garvin's Corner," *Seattle Star*, June 24, 1911, p. 4.
12. Boston's Billy Nixon; holds victories over George Alger, Tommy Rawson, Sr., and Frank Carsey; fought from about 1908 until 1917.
13. "Nelson Stops Billy Nixon by Low Blow in Hub," *Evening World*, September 20, 1911, p. 12.
14. Indiana's Milburn Saylor (1889–1921), James Milburn Saylor, "Young Saylor and Kangaroo Kid," holds victories over Jack Redmond, Matty Baldwin and Ray Bronson; fought from about 1908 to 1921; a prolific fighter of over 100 bouts.
15. "'Bat' about All In," *Evening Times*, October 7, 1911, p. 3.
16. New York's Willie Beecher (1893–1957) holds victories over Young Corbett II, One Round Hogan and Lockport Jimmy Duffy; fought from about 1908 until 1921; a prolific fighter of over 100 bouts; fought some great fighters (Ted "Kid" Lewis, Freddie Welsh, Abe Attell, Jack Britton) thanks to being managed by Dan Morgan.
17. "Bat Nelson Takes Punishment to Win," *Salt Lake Tribune*, October 12, 1911, p. 12.
18. German-born Philadelphia Pal Moore (1891–1943), Paul Walter Von Franzke, holds victories over Al Delmont, Jim Driscoll, and Dick Hyland; fought from about 1907 until 1922; a prolific fighter of over 100 bouts and one of five pugilist brothers; not to be confused with "Memphis" Pal Moore.
19. Driscoll had been ill for some time and returned to Wales two weeks later to recuperate.
20. Cambridge's George Alger; holds victories over Charles Neary, Bay Wood and Eddie Flynn; fought from about 1908 until 1920; a prolific fighter of over 100 bouts.
21. "Nelson Loses to a Second Rater," *Rock Island Argus*, October 20, 1911, p. 3.
22. "Pink Tea Boxing Matches," *Omaha Daily Bee*, October 29, 1911, p. 40.
23. Ibid.
24. BoxRec.com.
25. Philadelphia's Frank Loughrey, Frank Loughlin, holds victories over Battling Hurley, Johnny Dohan, and Johnny "Kid" Alberts; fought from about 1909 until 1920; a prolific fighter of over 100 bouts.
26. "Frank Loughrey Gives Nelson Another Setback," *Evening World*, November 7, 1911, p. 12.
27. Chicago's Tommy Moore, who had only one impressive victory, that of Rudy Unholz (1911); fought from about 1898 until 1915.

28. French fighter Louis de Ponthieu (1892–1953), Theophile Regnier, holds victories over Tommy O'Keefe, Harry Condon, and Paul Til; fought from about 1908 until 1919; held French featherweight title.
29. De Ponthieu suffered a career-ending injury during a Christmas Day battle in 1919 that would require his right arm to be amputated on January 27, 1920.
30. Buffalo's Joseph Spero, known more for whom he lost to, including Sammy Baker, Fighting Zunner and Battling Nelson, rather than those he defeated; fought from about 1911 until 1916.
31. Cincinnati's Andy Bezenah (c. 1880–1943), holds victories over Sig Hart, Maurice Sayers, and Young "Kid" Farmer; fought from about 1901 until 1915.
32. Utica's Bobby Wilson (1885–1920), Robert Sequino, holds victories over Paddy Sullivan, Matt Wells, and Matty Baldwin; fought from about 1908 until 1916.
33. Brooklyn punching bag Willie Howard, "Ridgewood Terror," known for having fought and lost to Jack Redmond, Battling Nelson, and Philadelphia Pal Moore; fought from about 1908 until 1914.
34. San Francisco's One Round Hogan (1889–1959), George F. Hogan, holds victories over Knockout Brown, Johnny Frayne, and Tommy McFarland; fought from about 1910 until 1926; popular during the city's four-round era of the early 1910s.
35. "Hogan Hammers Battling Nelson," *Washington Herald*, December 23, 1911, p. 10.
36. Milwaukee's Jack Redmond (1883–1968), Henry Fred Hoppe, holds victories over Ray Bronson, Ad Wolgast, and Rudy Unholz; fought from 1904 until 1921; regarded as one of the better lightweight contenders of the early twentieth century.
37. Nelson, *Life, Battles and Career of Battling Nelson, Lightweight Champion of the World* (Hegewisch, IL: self-published, 1908), p. 58.
38. All this before even considering his balance sheet.
39. Missouri's ring sacrifice Tommy O'Rourke had a short career, the highlight of which was his fight against Battling Nelson.
40. "Tommy O'Rourke to Meet Smith Monday," *Tulsa Daily World*, April 6, 1912.
41. Japanese-born Young Togo, "The Yellow Peril," or "Jap Togo," fought from about 1907 until 1915.
42. "Battling Nelson to Try Once More," *Evening Standard*, March 11, 1912, p. 2.
43. *Ibid*.
44. "Battling Nelson, Big Financier," *Evening Times*, March 26, 1912, p. 3.
45. Columbus, Ohio-born Sammy Trott, holds victories over Andy Bezenah, Grover Hayes and Steve Ketchel; fought from about 1910 until 1915.
46. "Battling Nelson to Try Once More," *Evening Standard*, March 11, 1912, p. 2.
47. *Ibid*.
48. Louis Roehm acted as matchmaker for the Dayton Gymnastic Club, and his cousin George Roehm was entrusted with the refereeing. George had been a respected amateur fighter and knew the importance of giving a fighter a square decision—something Nelson appreciated.
49. "The Latest in Sports," *Maui News*, March 23, 1912, p. 1.
50. "Battling Nelson Tells How He Was Bunged Up in Ring Career," *Albuquerque Evening Herald*, April 19, 1912, p. 7.
51. *Ibid*.
52. "Wolgast and Rivers Place Shadow on Las Vegas Bout," *Evening Times*, July 3, 1912, p. 3.
53. *Ibid*.
54. Nova Scotia's Mickey MacIntyre (1890–1922), Michael MacIntyre, "Pride of Cape Breton," holds victories over Leo Kossick, Billy Griffith and Bay Wood; fought from about 1911 until 1916; Canadian welterweight champion.
55. boxrec.com/boxer/8998, see footnote.
56. "Nelson Jarred by Cupid's Uppercuts," *San Francisco Call*, July 20, 1912, p. 25.
57. *Ibid*.
58. *Ibid*.
59. *Ibid*.
60. *Ibid*.
61. *Ibid*.
62. "Nelson Sidesteps Undertaker as His Life's Matchmaker," *San Francisco Call*, August 5, 1912, p. 1; *The Call* was one of the earliest to substantiate the relationship between the two.
63. Chicago's Steve Ketchel, Lester Oakes, holds victories over Maurice Thompson, Stanley Yoakum and Charlie "Kid" Dalton; fought from 1910 until 1915; managed by Willie Ritchie.
64. "White Sox Are Slated for Game in El Paso on Training Trip," *El Paso Herald*, September 2, 1912, p. 7.
65. By the end of the twentieth century, many Danes will emerge, including Jimmi Bredahl, Johnny Bredahl, Gert Bo Jacobsen, Brian Nielsen and Mads Larsen. Later, you will have the likes of Thomas Damgaard and Mikkel Kessler to solidify the tremendous reputation of Danish fighters.
66. "Bat Nelson Had a Shade on Art Stewart," *The Day Book*, November 15, 1912, p. 29.
67. In the short career of West Hammond, Illinois' Art Stewart, his only boxing claim to fame will be fighting the Battler to this ten-round no decision.
68. New York's Leach Cross (1886–1957), Louis Charles Wallach, "The Fighting Dentist," holds victories over Dick Hyland, Willie Fitzgerald, and Young Erne; fought from about 1905 until 1921; defeated Ad Wolgast twice; one of the seven fighting Cross brothers.
69. "Cross Outpoints Battling Nelson," *Omaha Daily Bee*, November 29, 1912, p. 10.
70. Philadelphia's Teddy Maloney, Henry Maloney, holds victories over Battling Singer, Hughey McGovern, and Yankee Schwartz; fought from about 1906 until 1913.
71. "Wolgast to Be in Good Shape," *Evening Times*, October 22, 1912, p. 3.
72. Summit Hill, Pennsylvania's Jim Bonner, James J. Bonner, holds victories over Tommy Lowe, Tim Callahan, and Johnny Marto; fought from about 1904 until 1917.

73. "Battling Nelson Decides to Try Again for Championship," *Evening Times*, December 31, 1912, p. 3.

74. Philadelphia's Yankee Schwartz, Julius Schwartz, holds victories over Biz Mackey, Patsy Kline, and Joe Mandot; fought from about 1905 until 1915; a prolific fighter of over 100 bouts.

75. The fight was also reported by multiple sources, including *The Call*, as a ten-round battle.

Chapter Twelve

1. Nelson, *Life, Battles and Career of Battling Nelson, Lightweight Champion of the World* (Hegewisch, IL: self-published, 1908), p. 88.

2. Louisiana's Frankie Russell (1891–1922), Frank Merenda, holds victories over Jack White, Steve Ketchel, and Knockout Brown; fought from about 1911 until 1920; later career victories included Rocky Kansas and Ad Wolgast.

3. "Russell Beats Nelson," *Rice Belt Journal*, January 4, 1913, p. 3.

4. Ibid.

5. "Battling Nelson Will Wed Denver Newspaper Artist," *Salt Lake Tribune*, January 22, 1913, p. 10.

6. "Moline Minister to Tie 'Bat' Nelson," *Rock Island Argus*, January 22, 1913, p. 5.

7. "Bat Nelson Signs for Life Battle Today," *San Francisco Call*, January 23, 1913, p. 7.

8. "Nelson Succumbs to God of Love," *San Francisco Call*, January 24, 1913, p. 8.

9. Ibid.

10. "Former Lightweight Champion Will Be Met at Denver by Summons in Divorce Suit," *San Francisco Call*, February 28, 1913, p. 3.

11. Ibid.

12. Ibid.

13. Ibid.

14. "Nelson and Hegewisch Both Are Staggered," *San Francisco Call*, March 1, 1913, p. 8.

15. "Fay King Nelson Is Tired of Love," *East Oregonian*, March 1, 1913, p. 10.

16. Ibid.

17. "Battling Nelson's Worst Knock Out!" *Times-Dispatch*, March 16, 1913, p. 56.

18. Ibid.

19. Ibid.

20. "Bat Nelson in Philosophic Vein," *Honolulu Star-Bulletin*, March 26, 1913, p. 9.

21. The divorce rate peaked at 4.6 in 1993.

22. "Battling Nelson Out of Game," *Ogden Standard*, May 17, 1913, p. 8.

23. "Judge Men by Their Past Wives, Fay King Advises Flappers," *Syracuse Evening Telegram*, February 18, 1921, page number unavailable.

24. "Shortened Rounds Hurt Boxing Bouts," *El Paso Herald*, February 20, 1913, p. 8; the obscure figure of Ray (Jack) Sorenson, aka Neil Allison, who according to numerous sources never defeated a fighter with over one career victory; fought from about 1911 until 1921, but nobody can be certain.

25. "Battling Nelson Aspires to Be Racer," *Washington Times*, May 3, 1913, p. 14.

26. Philadelphia's Harry Dillion holds victories over Frankie Smith and Kid Butler; fought from about 1903 until 1915; a tomato can whose claim to fame was climbing into the ring with Battling Nelson and Fred Halsband.

27. "Story of Nelson Hard to Believe," *Grand Forks Daily Herald*, February 19, 1915, p. 10.

28. "Cost of Success Heavy for Boxers," *Evening Times*, February 10, 1913, p. 6.

29. Ibid.

30. In 1928 a forensic pathologist, Dr. Harrison Stanford Martland, who was the chief medical examiner of Essex County in Newark, New Jersey, wrote in a *Journal of the American Medical Association* an article in which he noted the tremors, slowed movement, confusion, and speech problems typical of the condition known as dementia pugilistica.

31. "Bat Nelson Walloped Joe Burke," *The Day Book*, February 8, 1913, p. 10.

32. Pennsylvania's Joe Burke holds victories over Handsome Charlie Smith, Kid Henry, and Jim Bonner; fought from about 1907 until 1914; fought his entire career in Pennsylvania and New York.

33. See boxrec.com.

34. Fall River's Bay Wood, James Baywood or Jim Baywood, holds victories over Johnny Gallant, Peter Sullivan and George Alger; fought from about 1910 until 1921; name often misspelled as Ray Wood or Ray Woods.

35. Cedar Rapids' Frank Whitney (1887–1933), Fighting Carpenter, holds victories over Grover Hayes, Frankie White and Jack Redmond; fought from about 1908 until 1919; a later career victory over Ad Wolgast managed to get him fights with Freddie Welsh (L), Frankie Callahan (D) and Lockport Jimmy Duffy (L).

36. "Battler Is After New Title-holder," *Evening Standard*, March 6, 1913, p. 2.

37. Ibid.

38. Colorado's Mike Malone holds victories over Tommy Houck, Phil Knight and Harry Schafer, none of whom had ten victories at the time they fought Malone; fought from about 1904 until 1915.

39. Boston's Gilbert Gallant (1891–1939), holds victories over One Round Hogan, Eddie Murphy, and Leach Cross; fought from about 1911 until 1927; fought many of his opponents multiple times; had impressive back-to-back victories over Leach Cross.

40. Philadelphia's Pat Bradley, holds victories over Willie Moody, Handsome Charlie Smith, and Knockout Brown; fought from about 1911 until 1924; never liked leaving Philadelphia, which often left him to take whatever fights he could get to pay the bills.

41. "Nelson-Wolgast Go Should Be Classy," *Salt Lake Tribune*, October 12, 1913, p. 3.

42. Ibid.

43. "Bat, Game to Last, Takes Walloping," *San Francisco Call*, October 14, 1913, p. 7.

44. Ibid.

45. Ibid.

46. "Church Notes," *Willmar Tribune*, December 31, 1913, p. 4.

Chapter Thirteen

1. Nelson, *Life, Battles and Career of Battling Nelson, Lightweight Champion of the World* (Hegewisch, IL: self-published, 1908), p. 216.
2. "Is Bat Nelson In Need Of Mazuma?" *Evening Times*, January 23, 1914, p. 8.
3. "Nelson Sues Attell," *Evening Times*, January 31, 1914, p. 6.
4. "Defeated Champs Deserve a Chance," *Evening Times*, February 6, 1914, p. 6.
5. *Ibid.*
6. "Footwork as Boxer Convinced Him He Could Dance—Now He's Champion," *The Day Book*, March 23, 1914, p. 16.
7. Nelson, *Life, Battles and Career of Battling Nelson, Lightweight Champion of the World* (Hegewisch, IL: self-published, 1908), p. 91, "Next to fighting, I'd rather dance than do anything else."
8. "Bat Nelson Is Regular Moose," *Bridgeport Evening Farmer*, April 11, 1914, p. 8.
9. "Don't Hurry to Wed, Advice of Irma," *Tacoma Times*, July 14, 1914, p. 8.
10. Giving historians the benefit of the doubt—which can be dangerous with the fight game—this bout will be acknowledged through record books and not multiple contemporaneous newspaper accounts. The fight appears in a few sources, including *The Ring Record Book and Boxing Encyclopedia*.
11. "Hypnotize Battling Nelson," *Clovis News*, September 11, 1914, p. 2.
12. *Ibid.*
13. "Personal Touches in Sport," *Evening Public Ledger*, September 26, 1914, p. 14.
14. Thankfully, because his career would have ended in the record books with Cliff Ford (1914), instead of the elite fighter Freddie Welsh (1917).
15. "Battling Nelson Visits Friends in South Bend," *South Bend News-Times*, December 18, 1914, p. 8.
16. "Fistiana's Roll Of Honor," *Ogden Standard*, December 19, 1914, p. 21.
17. "Former World's Champion Lightweight Boxer Battling Nelson Attempts to Come Back," *Richmond Times-Dispatch*, December 22, 1914, p. 4.
18. "Bat Nelson's Attempt to Fight Again Amuses Cincinnati Fandom," *Evening World*, December 17, 1914, p. 18.
19. "Johnson-Willard in Spot," *Omaha Daily Bee*, January 24, 1915, p. 4-S.
20. "Coulon May Again Be Champion; Bantam Title May Revert to Him," *El Paso Herald*, January 11, 1915, p. 6.
21. *Ibid.*
22. "Bat Nelson Going to Law to Protect Name," *Rock Island Argus*, January 12, 1915, p. 10.
23. "Battling Nelson Sues Annette Kellermann," *Bridgeport Evening Farmer*, February 11, 1915, p. 8.
24. Nelson claimed he gave up $7,500 in theater engagements to fight in Havana to prove he could whip Welsh. He also stated that he knocked out a fighter named Dale Gardner in the second round as sourced from the *El Paso Herald*, May 13, 1915.
25. "Favorite Uppercut of Negro Too Short," *Tacoma Times*, April 2, 1915, p. 2.
26. Funny how that $2,000 figure happened to match the AP report.
27. "Nelson Anxious to Fight Welsh," *El Paso Herald*, June 24, 1915, p. 7.
28. "Battling Nelson, Author," *Bennington Evening Banner*, August 9, 1915, p. 4.
29. *Ibid.*
30. *Ibid.*
31. "Waugh Beats Battling Nelson," *Topeka State Journal*, September 7, 1915, p. 3.
32. "Nelson May Meet Welsh," *Evening Star*, August 27, 1915, p. 15.
33. "Boy! Page Freddie Welsh," *Washington-Herald*, August 22, 1915, p. 8.
34. "Wagner's Watch Tower," *Bridgeport Evening Farmer*, September 3, 1915, p. 8.
35. "Battling Nelson Isn't Kidding He Wants Bout with Welsh," *Tacoma Times*, October 5, 1915, p. 2.
36. *Ibid.*
37. Reagan, who hailed from San Francisco, had tremendous respect for Nelson. Before he retired he had also fought Jimmy Hanlon, Benny Leonard, and Monte Attell. His surname has been incorrectly spelled Regan in many sources.
38. "Wornout Boxers Injure the Game," *Grand Forks Daily Herald*, December 7, 1915, p. 8.
39. *Ibid.*
40. *Ibid.*
41. *Ibid.*
42. "Spicy Letters in Nelson Divorce Case," *Bismarck Daily Tribune*, February 1, 1916, p. 6.
43. "Spouse Platonic, Bat Wins Divorce," *Rock Island Argus*, March 2, 1916, p. 3.
44. "Bat in More Trouble," *Topeka State Journal*, March 10, 1916, p. 10.
45. "Nelson's Father Disappears," *Topeka State Journal*, April 13, 1916, p. 12.
46. The coroner's jury in the inquest over the body of Mrs. Joseph E. Howard, formerly Irma Kilgallen of Chicago and divorced wife of the Count de Beaufort, at Omaha returned a verdict of suicide.
47. Senator John F. Kennedy and his wife Jacqueline stayed there during his campaign for the 1960 presidential election, and it was headquarters for Senator Robert F. Kennedy's 1968 Democratic Nebraska primary campaign. The hotel was demolished in 1983.
48. Just as a point of information, admission ranged from ten cents for children or gallery seats to fifty cents for adult main floor seats in the evening.
49. She was said to have been diagnosed with tuberculosis.
50. "Howard Attends Bride's Funeral," *Rock Island Argus*, April 13, 1916, p. 3.
51. *Ibid.*
52. *Ibid.*
53. "Was Chicago Girl Hounded to Death by Newspapers?" *The Day Book*, April 11, 1916, p. 28.
54. *Ibid.*
55. *Ibid.*
56. "Countess' Life a Tragedy," *Chicago Tribune*, April 11, 1916, p. 3.

57. Ibid.

58. Clabaugh received charges against Howard from Nelson and also from the Illinois Vigilance Association, but was not disposed to act right then because of the absence of the commercial feature. This according to *The Day Book*, April 19, 1916.

59. "Battling Nelson Invokes Mann Act," *Ogden Standard*, April 18, 1916, p. 5.

60. The act's ambiguous language of "immorality" meant it could be used to criminalize consensual sexual behavior between adults.

61. "Battling Nelson Invokes Mann Act," *Ogden Standard*, April 18, 1916, p. 5.

62. "M.H. Kilgallen, Chicago Heights Builder Is Dead," *Chicago Tribune*, January 13, 1922, p. 3.

63. Ibid.; obituary in *Chicago Tribune* contradicts other sources with regard to number of children.

64. "Nelson to Be Beau Brummel of Ring," *Evening Times Republican*, October 14, 1916, p. 1.

65. "Homely Bat Nelson Takes 'Beauty Cure' to Win Back Wife," *Grand Forks Daily Herald*, October 17, 1916, p. 8.

66. "Little Scraps about the Scrappers," *El Paso Herald*, November 25, 1916, p. 16.

67. "Poor Old 'Bat,'" *Free Trader-Journal*, April 17, 1917, p. 6; the story also appeared in other newspapers including the *Honolulu Star-Bulletin*, the *El Paso Herald*, and the *Daily Missoulian*; the Nelson versus Mathews fight has not been recognized by some sources.

68. "Battling Nelson to Shoulder Gun," *Harrisburg Telegraph*, March 19, 1917, p. 12.

69. "Welsh Outclasses Battling Nelson in Twelve Rounds," *Bisbee Daily Review*, April 18, 1917, p. 5.

70. "Welsh-Nelson Bout Is Boxing Farce," *Free-Trader Journal*, April 6, 1917, p. 6.

71. "Battling Nelson, a Big Feature with the Yankee Robinson Show," *Glasgow Courier*, June 22, 1917, p. 12.

72. "The Weeks Doings," *Alliance Herald*, August 16, 1917, p. 4.

73. "Bat Nelson Would Help," *Tacoma Times*, November 24, 1917, p. 6.

74. International Boxing Hall of Fame, Inductees Biography, www.ibhof.com.

75. In 1917, Benny Leonard picked up the lightweight title with a ninth-round kayo of Freddie Welsh in New York on May 29; Leonard then knocked out featherweight champ Johnny Kilbane in the third round of their July 25 battle in Philadelphia.

Chapter Fourteen

1. Nelson, *Life, Battles and Career of Battling Nelson, Lightweight Champion of the World* (Hegewisch, IL: self-published, 1908), p. 93.

2. "Nelson Pays Tribute to John L.'s Ring Honesty," *Washington Times*, February 3, 1918, p. 14; Sullivan's egocentric style, particular with regard to his financial earnings in the ring, influenced Nelson.

3. Ibid.

4. "Bat Nelson Tells of Kaiser Dummy for All Soldiers," *Washington Times*, February 3, 1918, p. 14.

5. The Battling Nelson Boxing Dummy Company was located at 505 Jennifer Building in Washington, D.C. The Kaiser ruled the German Empire and the Kingdom of Prussia from June 15, 1888, to November 9, 1918.

6. "Battling Nelson and Kid Murphy Offer Services," *Washington Times*, March 5, 1918, p. 15.

7. "Looking 'Em Over," *Washington Times*, October 25, 1918, p. 18.

8. "Returns His Coin to Nelson," *Washington Times*, October 12, 1918, p. 10.

9. "Bat Meets Sam for the First Time," *Washington Herald*, January 1, 1918, p. 10.

10. "Battling Nelson Offers to Referee World's Championship Bout," *Bisbee Daily Review*, May 13, 1919, p. 2.

11. "Willard at Toledo; Will Start Work," *Grand Forks Daily Herald*, June 2, 1919, p. 12; people often forget that Toledo, a rather liberal town at the time, was then served by more than ten railroad companies, making it easy for those living in the northeastern United States to travel to the fight.

12. "Willard Soon Forgotten," *Richmond Times-Dispatch*, August 10, 1919, p. 13.

13. "Battling Nelson Pays Great Tribute to Gans," *Richmond Times-Dispatch*, July 6, 1919, p. 18.

14. Ibid.

15. Ibid.

16. "Battling Nelson Was Example of What Courage Will Do to Advance Pugilist in Ring Career," *Bridgeport Times and Evening Farmer*, September 27, 1919, p. 4.

17. The Battler declared that only a few minutes before he entered the store, he had had a conference with Governor Smith at the Biltmore Hotel, as the Dane was being considered for appointment as a member of the State Boxing Commission.

18. "Battling Nelson Sues for $225,000," *The Sun and the New York Herald*, July 14, 1920, p. 20.

19. By 1924, Rickard began putting together the financing to construct a new Garden, which he completed the following year.

20. The law instituted rules that better ensured the safety of combatants while reducing the roughness of the sport. The law limited matches to fifteen rounds, no more marathon bouts like Nelson so favored. It also required a physician in attendance, restricted certain aggressive acts such as head butting, and created a regulatory commission, the New York State Athletic Commission; the Frawley Law was repealed and went out of existence on November 15, 1917; the Walker Law went into effect on May 24, 1920.

21. "Interest in Boxing Grows in New York," *Washington Herald*, November 5, 1920, p. 13.

22. "Battling Nelson at It Again," *North Platte Semi-Weekly Tribune*, December 24, 1920, p. 11.

23. "All Professional Boxing Vicious, Declares Quayle," *Bisbee Daily Review*, March 26, 1921, p. 5.

24. "Dempsey Boxes with Feet Wrong, Says Bat Nelson," *Washington Times*, July 12, 1921, p. 13.

25. Ibid.

26. Ray was elected to the U.S. National Track and Field Hall of Fame in 1976. He died on May 13, 1978,

in Berrien Springs—a Michigan boxing town, so they say—after a short illness.

27. The incident took place on February 5, 1922.

28. Young Corbett II was inducted into the International Boxing Hall of Fame in 2010. He was the first member of this elite of boxing to fight against Battling Nelson.

29. Nelson, *Life, Battles and Career of Battling Nelson, Lightweight Champion of the World* (Hegewisch, IL: self-published, 1908), p. 199.

30. The *Ring* was one of the few publications that thought enough to cover "The Wake of Battling Nelson," in a wonderful and very sensitive piece written by Francis Donegal in May 1954.

Bibliography

Books

Anderson, Donald F. *William Howard Taft: A Conservative's Conception of the Presidency.* Ithaca, NY: Cornell University Press, 1973.
Andre, Sam, and Nat Fleischer. *A Pictorial History of Boxing.* New York: Bonanza Books, 1981.
Baker, Mark Allen. *Title Town USA, Boxing in Upstate New York.* Charleston, SC: History Press, 2010.
Cavanaugh, Jack. *Tunney, Boxing's Brainiest Champ and His Upset of the Great Jack Dempsey.* New York: Ballantine Books, 2006.
Daniels, Roger, and Otis L. Graham. *Debating American Immigration, 1882–present.* Lanham, MD: Rowman & Littlefield, 2001.
Dempsey, Jack, with Barbara Piattelli Dempsey. *Dempsey.* New York: Harper & Row, 1977.
Goldman, Herbert G., ed. *The Ring Record Book and Boxing Encyclopedia.* New York: Ring Publishing Corporation, 1985.
Kahn, Roger. *A Flame of Pure Fire.* New York: Harcourt Brace, 1999.
Lynn, Kenneth S. *Hemingway.* New York: Simon & Schuster, 1987.
Nelson, Oscar "Battling" Matthew. *Life, Battles and Career of Battling Nelson, Lightweight Champion of the World.* Hegewisch, IL: self-published, 1908.
Oates, Joyce Carol. *On Boxing.* Garden City, NY: Dolphin/Doubleday, 1987.
Roberts, James B., and Alexander G. Skutt. *The Boxing Register.* Ithaca, NY: McBooks, 2002.
Roberts, Randy. *Jack Dempsey: The Manassa Mauler.* Baton Rouge: Louisiana State University Press, 1979.
Roosevelt, Theodore. *Theodore Roosevelt: An Autobiography.* New York: Macmillan, 1913.
Sugar, Bert Randolph. *The Ultimate Book of Boxing Lists.* Philadelphia: Running Press, 2010.
_____. *Boxing's Greatest Fighters.* Guilford, CT: Lyons Press, 2006.
Ward, Geoffrey C. *Unforgettable Blackness: The Rise and Fall of Jack Johnson.* New York: Knopf, 2004.

Archival Sources

The Center for Legislative Archives, National Archives
International Boxing Hall of Fame, Canastota, New York
The Library of Congress
The Library of Congress Local History & Genealogy Reference Services and Danish Immigration to America: Danes in America.
Museum of Danish America

Articles and Blog Entries

Barton, George. "Durable Dane Greatest Marathon Fighter." *The Ring,* May 1954, pp. 26–27.
Donegal, Francis. "The Wake of Battling Nelson." *The Ring,* May 1954, pp. 40, 53.
Fleischer, Nat. "Battling Nelson, the Durable Dane." *The Ring,* February 1931, pp. 38, 43.
Holtz, Allan. "Ink-Slingers Profiles: Fay King." *Stripper's Guide,* January 23, 2013, http://strippersguide.blogspot.com/2013_04_21_archive.html.

"James W. Coffroth, sportsman: The Champion Fight Promoter of the World, a Leading Light in the Boxing World and His Rise to Prominence." *Baseball Magazine* 8, no. 6 (1912): p. 53.
Levanetz, Joel. "James Wood Coffroth (1872–1943), Promoter of Boxing, Horse Racing and Tourism." *Journal of San Diego History* 55 (2009): pp. 217–230.
Nicolaisen, Steve, and the editors of *Boxing Illustrated*. "Boxing's Centennial:100 Years of Great Fights and Fighters." *Boxing Illustrated*, November 1992, pp. 22–51, 86–113.
"Obituary. Hon. James W. Coffroth." *New York Times*, October 18, 1872.
Slater, Marilyn. "Who Was Fay King?" *Looking for Mabel Normand*, November 8, 2008.

Internet Sources

The Andres Hotel, andrewshotel.com/about.html
BoxRec, www.boxrec.com
The Cyber Boxing Zone, www.cycberboxingzone.com
Heritage Auctions, www.ha.com
International Boxing Hall of Fame, www.ibhof.com
JO Sports, Incorporated, josportsinc.com/main.php
Norway Heritage, www.norwayheritage.com

Magazines

Boxing Illustrated
The Journal of San Diego History
The Ring
Sports Illustrated

Newspapers

Albuquerque Evening Herald
Alliance Herald
Bennington Evening Banner
Bisbee Daily Review
Bismarck Daily Tribune
Bridgeport Evening Farmer
Bridgeport Times and Evening Farmer
Chicago Tribune
Clovis News
Colfax Gazette
Daily Capital Journal
Daily Missoulian
Daily Standard
Day Book
Desert Evening News
El Paso Herald
Evening Public Ledger
Evening Standard
Evening Star (Washington, D.C.)
Evening Times (Grand Forks, ND)
Evening Times Republican
Evening World
Fairmount West Virginian
Free-Trader Journal
Glasgow Courier
Grand Forks Daily Herald
Harrisburg Telegraph
Havre Herald
Hawaiian Star
Honolulu Star-Bulletin
Los Angeles Herald
Marion Daily Mirror
Maui News
Minneapolis Journal
Newport Miner
New York Sun Special
New York Times
North Platte Semi-Weekly Tribune
Ogden Standard
Omaha Daily Bee
Pacific Commercial Advertiser
Rice Belt Journal
Richmond Times-Dispatch
Rock Island Argus
Salt Lake Herald
Salt Lake Herald-Republican
Salt Lake Tribune
San Francisco Call
San Francisco Examiner
Seattle Republican
Seattle Star
South Bend News-Times
Spokane Press
St. Paul Globe
The Sun and the New York Herald
Syracuse Evening Telegram
Tacoma Times
Times-Dispatch
Topeka State Journal
Tulsa Daily World
Twice-a-Week Plain Dealer
Washington Herald
Washington Times
Wenatchee Daily World
Willmar Tribune
Winchester News
The World

Index

Numbers in ***bold italics*** indicate pages with photographs.

Abdul the Turk 166, 174–175
Alger, George 192
Andrews, Bill 208
Arthur, Chester 8
Ashton, Bill 32
Attell, Abe 45, **53**, **57**, 58, **59**–61, 74–75, 100, 103, 113, ***114***–115, 117, 121, 130, 136, 141, 147, 151, 156, 201, 213, 217, 246
Attell, Monte 148, 186

Baker, Harry 165
Baldwin, Matty 80, 172, 192, ***222***
Bardell, Jimmy 27
Barrison, Mabel 225–226
Bay, Young 22
Bean, Willard 88
Beecher, Willie 192, 218
Bellangero, Marguerite 73
Berger, Sam 63, 65, 105, 112
Berry, Charles 25, 28–29, 109, 140
Bezenah, Andy 194, 197–198, 217
Bonner, Jimmy 200
Boston Strong Boy *see* Sullivan, John L.
Bowker, Joe 54, 74, 103
Bowser, Paul 162
boxing as a reflection of society 131–134
Boyle, Peter 23, 140
Bradley, Pat 210
Brand, CAD 144
Britt, James, Sr. 169
Britt, Jimmy, Jr. 42, 44–45, 47–51, 53–55, 57–58, 61–64, **65**–73, 75, 78–79, 83–84, 89, 93, 98, 104, 105–109, 112–113, 121, 134, 136, 140–141, 144, 159, 191, 248
Britt, Willus 63, 65–66, 71. 93, 104, 117–121, 124, 141, 150, 159, 159n64, 169, 248

Britton, Jack 223, 244, 248
Brock, Phil 113, 192
Broun, Haywood 244
Brownfield, George 34
Bryan, William Jennings 143
Buff, Johnny 244
Burke, Joe 209
Burley, Ed 22, 132
Burns, Pudden 31
Burns, Tommy 87, 100, 109, 140

Cannon, Joseph G. 172
Canole, Martin 41–42, 54, 58
Chambers, Arthur 52
Chicago State Hospital 252
Choynski, Joe ***30***
Class, Clarence 22
Clifford, Jack 43, 92–93, 110–111, 152–155
Clinton, Dr. Charles A. 60
Cobb, Ty 137, 247
Coffroth, James W. 62–66, **72**, 79, 87, 117, 121, **125**, 126, 128–129, 136, 147–150, 166, 177, 180–181, 191, 221, 249; classic promotions 149
Colifer, Frank 28–29
Collins, Tim 52
Collyer, Sam 51–52
Conley, Frankie 186, 195
Copenhagen, Denmark 3–5, **6**–8, 87, 100, 133
Corbett, James J. 23, 58, 78, 80, 147–149, 217, 240, 249
Corbett, Young, II 38–39, 42, 44–48, 50–51, **53**–58, 60, 75, 77, 79, 82, 148, 199, 207, 235, 240, 246, 248
Cornett, Red 118, 121
Cortelyou, George B. 145
Coulon, Johnny 195–196, 206, 217, 231, 248, 253
Cove, Percy 190
Croll's Gardens 148

Cross, Leach 113, 148, 161, 199, **200**, 209, 218, ***237***
Curtin, Joe 22

Dale, Monty 175–176, 193
Daline, John 11–12
Dalton, Charlie 111, 153
Daniels, Frank 38
Danish fighters 199, 199n65
Davidson, Jay 144
de Beaufort, Count Jacques Alexander Albert von Mourik 183–184, ***185***–186, 189–190, 227, 229–230
de Milt, Gertrude 73–74, 76
Demont, Al 192
Dempsey, Jack 133, 217, 231, 237–***239***, 243–244, 246–247, 249
Dennis, S.A. 135
Densham, Jack 146
de Ponthieu, Louis 193, ***237***
Dillon, Harry 208
Dillon, Jack 220, 231, 244
Disbrow, Louis 208
Dixon, Charlie 93, 125–126, 134
Dixon, George 22, 44–45, 51, 79, 82, ***132***, 134, 173, 209, 217, 235
Donnelly, Stewart "Young" 219
Donohue, Young 80–81
Donovan, Prof. Mike 50–51
Dorgan, T.A. 144, 203
Dorrell, Paddy 29
Dougherty, Charles 21
Driscoll, Jem 146, 186, 192

Earp, Virgil 92
Earp, Waytt 90, 92
Edenberg, Charlie 215
Edgren, Robert W. 79–81, 84, 144, 203
Edison, Thomas 24, 223
Edwards, Billy 51–52

Emerson, Dolly 226
Emerson, Ida 226
English, Clarence 37, 39
Erne, Frank 47, 82, 142, 149, 154, 173–174, 193
Ertle, Johnny 223, 244
Excelsior 220
Eyton, Charles 156

Fails, Harry 26
Fay, Celia 73
Finley, Nick 36
Finnegan, J. Ignatius 146
Fitzgerald, Willie 66, 72
Fitzpatrick, Sam 176
Fitzsimmons, Bob 23, 52, 58, 71, 74, 80, 87, 116, 207, 217, 249
Flagg, Ella 220
Fleisher, Nat 243
Flynn, Fireman Jim 109, 121, 151, 197, 237
Flynn, Will 38
Forbes, Harry **41**, 53, 60, 243, 248
Ford, Cliff 216
Ford, Henry 40–**41**, 137
Freebury, Tom 109
Frisby, Jack 33
Fryer, Jimmy 219

Gaffney, Tommy 190
Gallant, Gilbert **210**
Gallico, Paul 244
Gans, Joe 15, 47–48, 53–55, 58, 60, 82, 89, 91, 102, 104–105, 107, 110, 112, 116, **120**, 133–135, 140–143, 148–153, 159, 162, 165, 175, 178, 187, 209, 217, 240–242, 248–249, 251, 253; bring the bacon home 124; death 173–174; fights Nelson I 91n59, 92–101; fights Nelson II 117–127; fights Nelson III 128–131
Gardner, Dale 105, 220
Gardner, George 66, 92, 248–249
Gardner, Jimmy 48, 66, 121
Gardner, Oscar 44
Garfield, James 8
Garvin, Rev. Joseph L. 190
Gibbons, Billy 218
Gibbons, Mike 244
Gibbons, Tommy 244
Gibson, Charles Dana **182**–183
Gilmore, Harry, Sr. 245
Gleason, John J. 117, 166
Goldfield, Nevada 15, 89–90, **91**–**97**, 98–100, 104, 125, 134, 162–163, 174, 242
Goodman, Kid 148
Grace, Jack 118, 121, 124, 150, 153–154, 156, 164, 176

Graney, Eddie 63–64, 66–68, 70–72, 93, 114, 128, 166
The Great Wallace Shows (circus) 12, *13*
Greb, Harry 244, 246
Green, Freddie 16–17
Greggains, Alex 41, 104
Griffin, Harry 22
Griffin, Jim 170, 176
Griffin, Young 22
Griffo, Black 22–23, 132
Griffo, Young 22, 209

Hall, Edna 99
Hanlon, Eddie 42, 54, 56, 58, 60, 66, 93, 148
Harry Corbett's 47, 50, 58, 62, 93
Hart, Marvin 47, 74, 87, 100
Hart, Sig 27, 172
Harvey, Charley 125
Hawkins, Dal 22
Heck, Billy 26
Hedmark, Joe 21–23, 140
Heenan, John C. 145, 193
Hegewisch, Illinois 20, 28–29, 31, 36, 39, 42–43, 51, 111, 127, 135, 139, 159, 164, 171, 184, 189, 190, 200, 204–207, 209, 215, 219–220, 231, 236, 241–243, 250, 253; as Burnham 104; family settlement 3–19; founding 10
Herford, Al 60–61, 174n32
Herman, Eddie 18
Herman, Kid 60, 77, 88, 104
Herrera, Aurelio 43–44, 54, 66, 77, 79, 82, 87–88, 92, 100, 108, 197, 246
Hertz, Johnny 28
Hester, Sid 162–163
Hogan, George "One-round" 176, 194, 199
Hogan, Malachy 30
Holly, Dave 53
Hot Springs, Arkansas 31, **33**, 34, 77, 132
Howard, Joseph Edgar 225–229
Howard, Willie 194
Howe, Lizette 76
Howell, Ernest E. 134
Hurley, Billy 31–**32**
Huron, South Dakota 15–16
Hyland, Dick 145, 147, **148**–153, 159, 161, 192, 199

Jackson, Young Peter 53, 60, 121, 173, 217
Jeanette, Joe 161, 236
Jeffries, Jim 22, 51–52, 58, 64–66, 71, **74**, 78, 87, 116, 133, 136, 141, 148–149, 160, 172–174, 175, 180, 186, 217, 249

Johnson, Battling Jim 211
Johnson, Jack 27, 74, 109, **133**, 140–**141**, 145, 148, 160–161, 164, 172–175, 180, 186–187, 197–198, 207, 211, **217**, 219–220, **223**, 237, 249
Johnson, Gov. John A. 99
Johnson, John Lester 231
Jones, Robert T. 244
Jones, Tom 156, 162, 168, 215
Jordan, Billy 48, 55, 66–67, 105–106, 121

Kearns, Jack 240
Keefe, Willie 130
Kellermann, Annette 218–**219**
Kelley, S.J. 40–41
Kelly, Eddie 111, 114, 121
Kelly, Spider 42, 47, 55, 65, 105
Kelly, Stockings 36, 47
Kennedy, James C. 149
Ketchel, Stanley 109, 116, 140, 159–**160**, 161, 164, 187, 217, 249
Ketchel, Steve 199
Kid, Dixie 53, 199
Kilgallen, Irma 154, 182–186, 189–190, 198–199, 201, 216; suicide 224–230
Kilgallen, Martin H. 183–186, 227
Kilgallen, Mrs. Martin H. 183–186, 228
King, Fay 199, 201, **203**–208, 212, 223–224, 230, 241–242, 251, 253
Klaus, Frank 211
Klein, Dora 245
Kluth, Tommy 253

La (le) Grave, Anton 176–178
Lang, Eddie 162–163, 191
Langford, Sam 53, 151, 180, 217, 236–237
LaPage, Poley 37
Lardner, Ring 240, 244
Lavigne, George "Kid" 47, 142, 199, 215, 217, 248
Lendl, Bobby 153
Leonard, Benny 232, **239**, 244, 246, 248–249
Levinsky, Battling 218, 237
Levinson, Sol 150
Levy, Morris 61–62
Lewis, Nate 77
Lewis, Ted "Kid" 223
Lewis, Willie 58–59
Little, George 172
Livingston, Cora 162
Loeb, William, Jr. **143**, 145
London, Jack 68, **69**–70, 144
Long, John 145
Loughrey, Frank 193

Lucania 103
Lusitania 231
Lynch, William 41

Madison Square Garden 104, 149, 192, 218–219, 242
Maher, Peter 116
Majestic 99, **100**, 102, 192
Malone, Mike 210
Maloney, Teddy 200
Mandell, Sammy 248, 253
Markham, Tommy 41
Martin, Jack 23
Masterson, Bat 240
Mastro, Earl 253
Matthews, Pierce 231
Maurice, Billy 33
Maxwell, Sammy 34
May, Jim 121, 126
Mayfield, Elmer 33
McAuliffe, Jack 142, 217, 248
McCarey, Tom 43, 43n17, 87–88, 111
McCarney, Billy 163, 163n4
McCarty, Luther 211
McCoy, Al 217
McCoy, Kid 58, 207, 220
McDonald, Duncan 44
McDonald, Frank 45, 55, 92–93
McDonald, Larry 37
McFarland, Packey 110, 112–113, 121, 136–137, 148, 175, 199, 231, 248
McGeehan, W.O. 244
McGovern, Terry 22, 43–46, 51–52, 58, 75, **79**–81, **82**–87, 89, 100, 104, 116, 174, 191, 209, 217, 235, 240, 246, 248–249
McGuigan, Jack 61, 83, 85
McIntyre, Mickey 198
McKee, John B. 194, 197
McKinley, William 23, 26
McLatchey, Billy 30
McMahon, Danny 23, 30
McVey, Sam 161, 236
Mellody, Billy "Honey" 100
Memsic, George 38–39, 111
Merkle, Fred 42
Miles Brothers 151
Miller, South Dakota 16
Millett's Training Quarters 64, 118, 124, 163, 176
Mitchell, Charlie 52
Monroe, Jack 52
Moore, "Philadelphia" Pal 192
Moore, Tommy 193
Moran, Frank 217, 231, 240
Moran, Owen 130, 146, 155, 177–182, 184, 186, 192, 195, 215, 249
Moran, Tommy 21, 42
Morgan, Dan 238

Morrissey, John 193
Mourik de Beaufort *see* de Beaufort
Moynihan, Patrick H. 139
Mulligan, Col. Andy 33
Murphy, Harlem Tommy 60, 75, 82, **112**–113, 192, 201, 211, **212**, 222
Murphy, Teddy 37–38, 43–45, 47–50, 54, 73

Naughton, W.W. 192, 210–211
Neary, Charles 38, 140
Neil, Frankie 54, 58, 93, 121, 148–149
Nelson, Vice Adm. Horatio 4, 16
Nelson, Mark 109
Nelson, Mary (mother) 3, 5, 19, 28, 42, 54, 169; death 190–191
Nelson, N(i)els (father) 3, 5, 19, 28–29, 31, 54, 77–78, 83, 87, 100, 101, 124, 135, 169, 224; death 241, 242–243
Nelson, Oscar "Battling" Matthew **62**, **65**, **106**, **118**, **129**, **165**, **170**, **245**; artifacts **126**; attempted robbery 250; autobiography (1908) 2, 18, 22, 37, 50, 70, 131, 137, 139, **143**–146, 152, 161, 195, 203, 215, 248–249; automobile accidents 172, 175; automobile racing 208; Bellevue-Stratford Hotel incident **158**–159, 171–172; birth 3; brain injury 209; buggy incident 81; champion's physique 139–140; child 7–12; Christmas 195; Cuba 219–220; CYO boxing meet 247–248; death 253; death rumor 98; deeding property 77–78; disorderly conduct/film 246; duck hunting 109; earthquake relief 87; extortion letters 110; family name 19; father's approval 31; father's beneficiary 241; fiftieth fight anniversary 249; fight preparation 81; fighting style 178; financial downfall 171, 189, 213, 231; first loss 21; fishing 88–89; Fleet Week 1908 118; football 73; Great Smith automobile 175, 175n39; greatest fighters 216–217; hearing loss 164; Kaiser dummy 234–236, 244; left half scissors hook 22, 29–30, 39, 44, 47, 132, 144, **148**, 152, 241; lemonade incident 239–240; Mexico 220–221; money obsession 78, 134; moniker 43, 54; Murphy conflict 50; notoriety 78; plastic surgery 230; pneumonia 249; poetry 248; post office 249; rail travel 31, 35; religion 190; retirement 118, 154, 196; ring earnings (1896–1908) 140; ring tricks 60–61; ROKO 81, 118; siblings 19; sparring with Willus Britt 119–120; stable 244; stage 61–62, 77, 134, 136–137, 160, 171, 175, 216, 238, 242–243; teenager 19–20; turning point 34; vices 58, 78; visiting Europe 1907 102–103; White House visit 143n3, 144–145
Newhouse, Frank 42, 44
Nixon, Billy 191–192
Nolan, Billy 43, 55, 61, 63–64, 66–67, 71–73, 79–81, 84, 88–89, 91–93, 98–99, 103–105, 107, 109, 172, 174, 213, 216

O'Brien, Philadelphia Jack 52, 58, 74, 137–138, 160
Olson, Ole 15, 36
O'Neil, Harry 108–109
O'Neil, Jack 40, 61
O'Rourke, Tommy 195
Oshkosh, Wisconsin 9
O'Toole, Mike 36

Palmer, Pedlar 51, 79, 82, 116, 235
Palzer, Al 201, 211
Papke, Billy 116, 130, 140, 161, 187, 211, 222
Pearson, Rev. W.E. 204, 207, 212
Pelkey, Arthur 211, 237
Penny, Eddie 18
Percente, Joe 26–29, 140
Perry, Jeff 118–119, 147, 150, 163
Pope, Alexander 34
Porteous, Dave 154
Powell, Jack 37, 132

Quayle, Thomas R. 243

Rawlings, George 164
Ray, Joie 244
Readle, Jack 22
Reagan, Jimmy "Fighting" 221
Redmond, Jack 192, 194
Reed, Johnny 118
Reese, John D. "Bonesetter" 196, 204, 247
Reiger, Frank 30
Reilly, Jimmy 38
Rice, Grantland 240, 244
Rickard, George Lewis "Tex" 89, **90**–93, 97, 99, 121, 126, 128, 166, 239, 242
Riley, Mickey 24, 36–37, 39, 61, 140
The Ring (magazine) 243–244

284 Index

Rishel, W.D. 97–98
Ritchie, Willie 148, 200–201, 209, **214**–216, 220, 246
Rivers, Joe 197–**198**, 215
Robinson, Jack 35
Robinson, John R. 163–166, 169–170, 189, 189n5, 204–206, 219, 221, 250
Rocap, Billy 61
Roche, Billy 44–45, 48–50, 73
Rockwell, Norman 223
Roosevelt, Teddy, Jr. **24**
Roosevelt, Theodore 23, **25**–26, 76–**77**, 104, **143**–145, 177, 215, 232, 238, 243
Root, Jack 52, 74
Rose, Ralph 145
Ross(l)er, William 30, 134
Ruef, Abe 149
Ruhlin, Gus 87, 149
Runyon, Damon 173, 244
Russell, Frankie 202–203
Ruth, Babe 244
Ryan, Adam 26, 34
Ryan, Kid 29
Ryan, Paddy 9, 37
Ryan, Tom 29
Ryan, Tommy 34–35, **52**, 58, 74, 100, 162, 217

Santry, Eddie 22, 27–28, 34, 37, 44, 47, 50, 140
Saylor, Milburn "Young" 191–192
Scaler, Kid 110, 118
Schmitz, Eugene 149
Schwartz, Yankee 200
Scotty, Young 36
Selig, Ben 99, 117, 121, 124, 126, 180–181
Sharkey, Jack 246
Sharkey, Tom 58, 73
Siler, George 23, 50–51, 66, 92–96, 115–116, 146
Simms, Art 40
Sinclair, Upton 76
Sioux Falls, South Dakota 16

Smith, Eddie 114–115, 128, 130, 151–153, 164, 166–171, 211
Smyth, R.A. 92, 112–113, 119, 136
Sorenson, (Ray) Jack 208
Spanish-American War 17–18, 18n44, 249–250
Spero, Joseph 193
Squires, Bill 109
Star Theatre, Chicago 20
Sterns, Eddie 37–38, 140
Stevens, Ashton 70
Stewart, Art 199
Sullivan, Dave 53
Sullivan, James R. 218
Sullivan, John L. 9, **10**, 37, 52, 78, 84, 93, 217, 234, 248
Sullivan, Kid 60–62
Sullivan, Larry 92
Sullivan, Mike Twin 109, 140
Sullivan, Tommy 53, 217
Sullivan, Yankee 145
Summers, Johnny 146
Sunday, Billy 234–235

Taft, William Howard 143, 195, 202
Taylor, Kid 163
Tendler, Lew 244
Tenny, Harry 149
Thompson, Johnny 30, 35–36, 153, 170, 172, 175, 199
Tilden, Bill 244
Tilden, "Dare Devil" 38–39
Titanic 195
Togo, Young 195–196
Trott, Sammy 196
Tunney, Gene 246–248
Tuthill, Harry 45

Unholz, Rudolph 110, **111**–112, 121, 199
Unknown John Smith 18–19

Van Buren, E.L. 89
Vernon, Feathers 20, 131–132
Veteran Boxing Association 253
Villa, Pancho 202, 221

Walcott, Barbados Joe 52–53, 58, 74, 174, 217
Wallace's Terrible Unknown 12, 14, 17, 19, 249
Walsh, Jimmy 54, 74, 100, 121, 141
Walsh, Mike 28
Waugh, Bobby 221
Weinig, Al 149
Wells, Bombardier Billy 201
Welsh, Freddie 113, **135**–136, 144, 146, 186, 192, 215, 218–222, **232**–233, 246
Welsh, Jack 121, 123, 125–126, 128
Welsh, Joe "Spider" 41–42, 54–55, 97
Wheeler, Dick 215
White, Charley 218, 220, 232, 236, 243
White, Jabez 48, 146, 174
Whitman, Ned 190
Whitney, Frank 163, 209
Willard, Jess 219–220, **223**, 231, **238**–239
Williams, Christy 34, 132
Williams, Soldier 17
Wills, Harry 133, 217, 236
Wilson, Bobby 194
Wilson, Woodrow 195, 202, 213, 231, 233
Winters, Bull 18
Wolgast, Ad 152, 154, **155**–160, 162–172, 175–176, 180–181, 186, 192, 194–195, 197–**198**, 200–201, 207, 210–211, **212**, 213, **214**–215, 217–219, 221–224, 232, 246; rivalry with Nelson 251–252
Wood, Bay 209–210

Yanger, Benny 43–44, 248
Yankee Robinson Three-Ring Wild Animal Circus 233, 235

Zale, Tony 253